# The Scientist Within You:™

## Experiments and Biographies
## of Distinguished
## Women in Science

*Instructor's Guide*
*for use with students ages 8-13*

By

Rebecca Lowe Warren
and
Mary H. Thompson

Second edition, completely revised

**ACI** ***Publishing***
P.O. Box 40398
Eugene, OR 97404-0064

## The Scientist Within You:™

### Experiments and Biographies of Distinguished Women in Science

By Rebecca Lowe Warren and Mary H. Thompson

The activities in this book have been tested and are safe when carried out as suggested. The authors and publishers can accept no responsibility for any damage caused or sustained by use or misuse of ideas or materials mentioned in the activities.



First Printing 1994

Second Printing 1996, completely revised



**Publisher's Cataloging in Publication Data**

Warren, Rebecca Lowe.

The Scientist Within You: Experiments and Biographies of Distinguished Women in Science/by Rebecca Lowe Warren and Mary H. Thompson. — 2nd ed., rev.

p. cm. (The Scientist Within You; 1)

Includes bibliographies and index.

An instructor's guide for use with ages 8 through 13 includes 25 Discovery units with hands-on experiments and activities based on the work of 23 women scientists and mathematicians:

1. Women in science - Juvenile literature. 2. Science - Experiments - Juvenile literature. 3. Women scientists - Biographies - Juvenile literature. [1. Women in science. 2. Science - Experiments. 3. Women scientists - Biographies]

I. Thompson, Mary H. II. Title. III. Series

Q130.W255 1996 920.72 W [B] 95-79962

ISBN 1-884414-16-8: $21.95 Softcover

The Scientist Within You™ series is available at special discounts for bulk purchases for sales promotions, premiums, fundraising, or educational use. For details, contact the publisher.

Published by

**ACI *Publishing***

Post Office Box 40398

Eugene, OR 97404-0064 U.S.A.

(541)689-2154 Fax: (541)689-1369

Printed in the United States of America

***In memory of our mothers***

*Helen Myers Lowe*

*Eunice Lewis Haworth*

## Photo Credits

Florence Bascom — Bryn Mawr College Archives, p.76
Marie Sklodowska Curie — The Schlesinger Library, Radcliffe College, p.86
Emmy Noether — Bryn Mawr College Archives, p.98
Winifred Goldring — Courtesy of John N. Krumdieck, New York State Museum, p.106
Barbara McClintock — Cold Spring Harbor Laboratory, New York, p.112
Chien-Shiung Wu — American Institute of Physics, Emilio Segre Visual Archives, p.128
Jewel Plummer Cobb — Courtesy of Dr. Jewel Plummer Cobb, p.136
Reatha Clark King — Courtesy of Dr. Reatha Clark King, p.142
Elma Gonzalez — Courtesy of Dr. Elma Gonzalez, p.148
Mae C. Jemison — Courtesy of Dr. Mae C. Jemison, p.158
Nancy Wallace — Courtesy of Nancy Wallace, p.164

Authors' photographs:
Rebecca Lowe Warren — Thomas Berkemeier
Mary H. Thompson — Jack Liu

Cover Design — Mark Smith

Miriam the Alchemist (p.6), Hypatia (p.12), Trotula (p.20), Hildegard of Bingen (p.26), Martine de Beausoleil (p.32), Maria Merian (p.38), Caroline Herschel (p.44), Mary Anning (p.50), Ynes Mexia (p.92), and Dorothy Crowfoot Hodgkin (p.120) were drawn by artist Helen Carroll.

# Table of Contents

## Preface

**The Scientist Within You** highlights women's achievements in science and mathematics from the first century A.D. to the present. Included are paleontologists, geologists, astronomers, mathematicians, chemists, physicians, an entomologist, and atomic physicists. Their noteworthy accomplishments are "translated" to students through hands-on experiments and activities. Both information and activities are appropriate to ages 8 through 13.

**The Scientist Within You** provides 25 discovery units.

- 23 units spotlight women scientists, their work, and its importance. (The biographical information may be read to the students or summarized by the teacher. Units include photographs or drawings of the scientists.)
- All units feature a hands-on experiment/activity duplicating the scientist's work or demonstrating a scientific principle relevant to her work. (An instructor's guide is provided for each unit.)
- Each unit lists a bibliography.
- Each unit offers a newsletter that can be duplicated and shared with students, parents, and teachers.
- These units help develop learning skills and common curriculum goals including evaluation of information, oral and written expression, reasoning skills, fundamental concepts in science, and mathematical relationships.

Although we encourage you to begin with Discovery Unit 1 since it introduces "Ten Steps for Conducting Experiments" and to conclude with "A Celebration!" in Discovery Unit 25, **The Scientist Within You** is a flexible curriculum. You know best what works with your students. Please feature as many of these women as your time, energy, and lesson plans allow. "Where do we go from here?" offers suggestions and additional resources for enhancing students' learning experiences in science and mathematics.

This book covers almost 2,000 years of history. Since the concept of time is a confusing one for children, a time-line helps. Following each unit, add the scientist's name and a memento of her work to the time-line, e.g., a dinosaur for Mary Anning, a chocolate box for Miriam the Alchemist. Such mementos not only add relief to the time-line, but jog the memory — "Oh, yeah . . . the snowflake woman studied mathematics."

The classroom can be a positive "agent of change." By highlighting the achievements of women scientists, girls and boys will learn that women have been problem-solvers in mathematics and science. Stereotypes of a scientist as the "man in the white coat" will be replaced with inclusive images. These new images will positively impact girls' expectations of themselves, their performance in math and science, and their employment in the higher paid scientific fields.

**The Scientist Within You** is intended to inspire not only girls but every young person's interest in science and mathematics. We hope this interest, inspired in the elementary and middle school years, will be sustained throughout their educational experience. And to you, the teachers and leaders who have chosen to guide young minds in their pursuit of knowledge, we say a heartfelt "thank you!"

*"The more one learns about that which one knows nothing of, the more one gains in wisdom. One has, therefore, through science, eyes with which it behooves us to pay attention."*

—Hildegard of Bingen, 12th century natural scientist

## The Authors

Rebecca Lowe Warren is an author and college instructor living in Portland, Oregon. Her science class at Marylhurst College spotlights the contributions of women in science and mathematics. She is co-author of **The Scientist Within You, volume 2**, and of **CELEBRATE THE WONDER: A Family Christmas Treasury** published by Ballantine/Epiphany in 1988. Her interests include long-distance running, hiking, and working with Habitat for Humanity. Husband Roger is a salesman and daughter Holly, a student at Occidental College, Los Angeles.

Mary H. Thompson is a publisher, teacher, and journalist. An advocate for excellence in education, she conducts workshops and writes reports on educational equity issues. She is co-author of **The Scientist Within You, volume 2**. She lives with her husband Jarvis in Eugene, Oregon. They have three sons and a daughter. She has lived in Greece and enjoys foreign travel. Her favorite pastimes are reading mysteries and playing an occasional game of Mah-Jongg.

Rebecca and Mary became acquainted through the American Association of University Women (AAUW) when both were serving on the Oregon State Board of Directors. Inspiration for **The Scientist Within You** originated following AAUW's release of the report entitled "Shortchanging Girls, Shortchanging America." Sharing a commitment to gender equity, Rebecca and Mary pooled their talents to create a book that highlights the contributions of women in science and inspires girls and boys to discover the scientist within themselves.

**The Scientist Within You: Experiments and Biographies of Distinguished Women in Science** is the first in a series. The second volume is **The Scientist Within You: Women Scientists from Seven Continents.**

## Acknowledgments

From finding craters on the moon to confirming Ostrogradsky's formula, the authors humbly acknowledge this work as a collaborative effort.

Teachers Jackie Barthel-Hines of La Grande and Deborah Totten of West Linn reviewed the materials and shared their helpful evaluations.

Frances Caldwell, Equity Resource Center Coordinator, generously shared resources and enthusiasm.

Betsy Weaver, Tom Berkemeier, and David Weaver provided information, Katie Bulger loaned her chemistry kit, and the students in the "Women Scientists Through the Ages" class at Marylhurst College applauded the project.

Roger and Holly Warren lent encouragement, patience, and creative suggestions.

Jarvis Thompson provided puzzles and the clues to elusive items, James Thompson helped computers speak to each other, and Jana Triskova Thompson introduced the authors to electronic research.

Helen Carroll translated ideas into drawings and helped bring images of many of the scientists to the readers.

Mark Smith created an "audacious" cover for an "audacious" book.

Dan Poynter and Mindy Bingham shared their publishing models and expertise, and Penelope C. Paine helped us move into the marketplace.

Rosemarie Atencio alerted us to many publishing and marketing opportunities, and Yolanda Bombardier found our niche in the card catalog.

Finally, we acknowledge the following people who mailed, faxed, and phoned resource suggestions to share with us and our readers:

Margaret Tunstall, American Association for the Advancement of Science; Betty Jones and Lola Rogers, National Science Foundation; Gaelyn Davidson, National Research Council; Ann Benbow, American Chemical Society; Jesús Martínez, Sandia National Laboratories; Gail Whitney, Saturday Academy; Heidi Lynch, Women's Educational Equity Act Publishing Center;

Mary Ruthsdotter, National Women's History Project; Judith Scollon, Society for the Advancement of Chicanos and Native Americans in Science; Helen Raymond, Family Math/EQUALS; Marsha Matyas, American Physiological Society; Melanie Dewberry, Math/Science Resource Center;

Catherine Jay Didion, Association for Women in Science; Libby Palmer, Operation SMART; and Kaitlin Schneider, National Black Child Development Institute.

# Our Photo Page

*"Our most important task is the guidance and inspiration we can give to young people through the process of education."*

**— Dr. Jewel Plummer Cobb**

Affix photograph of your student scientists.

# Discovery Unit No. 1

## Who Are Scientists?
## An Introduction

### MAGICAL EGG Experiment

**Time-line:**

- 1 A.D. - Today — Scientists featured in **The Scientist Within You**

**Key points:**

☛ Scientists ask questions about the natural world. To learn the answers to these questions, scientists conduct experiments.

☛ When students conduct experiments to discover answers to questions, they become like scientists.

☛ "Ten Steps for Conducting Experiments" is a logical series of steps to help students plan, conduct, and evaluate experiments.

**Supplies:**

✔ A sheet of newsprint listing the "Ten Steps for Conducting Experiments" (See page 2, "In Advance.")

✔ A balloon

✔ A half-gallon glass juice bottle into whose neck a peeled hard-boiled egg will rest but not fall through

✔ One hard-boiled egg, peeled (When preparing egg for this experiment, boil for 15 minutes. Peel egg prior to class.)

✔ One paper napkin torn in half

✔ Matches

✔ A "My Notes" sheet for each student (See page 4.)

✔ Pencil for each student

✔ ***The Scientific Gazette*** for each student

✔ The time-line in place (no names yet)

**Steps:**

1. Distribute "My Notes" sheet.
2. Conduct the MAGICAL EGG Experiment. (See instructor's guide, page 2.)
3. Complete "My Notes."
4. Review the experiment using "Ten Steps for Conducting Experiments."
5. Assist students in clean-up.
6. Introduce the time-line.
7. Distribute ***The Scientific Gazette.***

**For next time:**

- Announce the next scientist.

**Bibliography:**

Wyler, Rose. **The First Book of Science Experiments.**

## Instructor's Guide:

### MAGICAL EGG Experiment

### Background Information:

Scientists ask questions, form hypotheses, conduct experiments, form new hypotheses, ask more questions, etc. The MAGICAL EGG Experiment is designed to show students how scientists use a logical series of steps to find answers to their questions.

### Instructions:

#### In Advance

Copy the following "Ten Steps for Conducting Experiments" onto newsprint:

1. Ask a question.
2. Collect information.
3. Create a hypothesis.

   [Note: This is an "educated guess," an "If . . ., then . . ." statement that can be tested.]

4. Plan an experiment that will test your hypothesis.

   [Note: An experiment usually has two groups: an experimental group and a control group. One condition is changed in the experimental group. This change is the independent variable. There are no changes made in the control group.]

5. Decide what equipment is needed to conduct the experiment. Obtain the equipment.
6. Conduct the experiment.
7. Make and record observations.
8. Evaluate results.

   [You must be able to show how the independent variable caused the change in the experiment's results. This change is called the dependent variable. If common sense tells you that something went wrong in the experiment, check the equipment and repeat the experiment.]

9. Repeat the experiment. Compare results.
10. Decide if the experiment answered your question.

#### Today

1. Blow up the balloon and tie it closed.

**Ask . . .**

*What is in the balloon?* [Air]

**Ask . . .**

*What does this inflated balloon teach us about air?*

[Air takes up space and exerts pressure. When we blow up a balloon, we increase the density of the air and air pressure inside the balloon. The air pressure inside the balloon is greater than the atmospheric pressure — or air — outside the balloon.]

### Conduct first half of experiment:

1. Rest the peeled egg on the bottle neck so students can see that the egg is too large to fall into the bottle. (Rest with the pointed end downward.)
2. Lay the egg aside.
3. Crumple the paper napkin, light it, and quickly drop the burning napkin into the bottle.
4. Quickly place the egg with the pointed end downward on the bottle neck.
5. After a few seconds, the egg will enter the bottle!

> **Ask . . .**
>
> *What do you think caused the egg to go into the bottle?*
>
> [The egg went into the bottle because of atmospheric pressure. The burning napkin heated the air inside the bottle and some of it escaped. Air pressure in the bottle dropped making the atmospheric pressure greater than the air pressure under the egg. The atmospheric air pushed the egg into the bottle. The egg was not sucked into the bottle; **the egg was pushed into the bottle.**]
>
> **Ask . . .**
>
> *How can I get the whole egg out of the bottle?*

6. Instruct students to jot down their ideas to question #1 on their "My Notes" sheets.

> **Ask . . .**
>
> *Who would like to share their ideas?*

7. Listen to responses and try some of the suggestions.
8. Instruct students to jot down their ideas to question #2 on their "My Notes" sheets.

> **Ask . . .**
>
> *Who would like to share any new ideas?*

9. If a student suggests blowing air into the bottle, conduct the second half of MAGICAL EGG Experiment If not . . .

> **Ask . . .**
>
> *What do you think would happen if I blew air into the bottle?*

## Conduct second half of experiment:

1. Rinse the burnt paper out of the bottle.
2. Tilt the bottle so the pointed end of the egg rests in the neck.
3. Press the mouth of the bottle firmly against your lips; blow hard into the bottle; move your mouth away; and voilá, the egg "shoots" out. The outcome (no pun intended) is spectacular.
4. Instruct the students to complete step #3 of "My Notes."

## Review what happened:

1. As a class, discuss how the "Ten Steps for Conducting Experiments" was used in the MAGICAL EGG Experiment.

> Step 1: We asked the question: How do we get the whole egg out of the bottle?
>
> Step 2: We learned why the egg went into the bottle.
>
> Step 3: We created a hypothesis: If air pressure forced the whole egg **into** the bottle, then air pressure can force the whole egg **out** of the bottle.
>
> Step 4: We planned to blow air inside the bottle.
>
> Step 5: To conduct this experiment, we used a bottle with the egg in it and our lungs as the source of air.
>
> Step 6: We conducted the experiment.
>
> Step 7: We made observations and recorded them on our "My Notes" sheets.
>
> Step 8: We evaluated whether or not the whole egg came out of the bottle.
>
> Step 9: We repeated the experiment.
>
> Step 10: We decided if the experiment answered our question in Step 1.

2. Assist students in cleaning up.

# My Notes

by ______________________________, Scientist

**MAGICAL EGG Experiment**

**Answer Questions #1 and #2 when the egg is in the bottle.**

1. How can I get the whole egg out of the bottle? ______________________

______________________________________________

______________________________________________

______________________________________________

______________________________________________

2. How can I use air to get the whole egg out of the bottle? ______________

______________________________________________

______________________________________________

______________________________________________

______________________________________________

**Do Step #3 after experiment is completed.**

3. This is what happened: ______________________________

______________________________________________

______________________________________________

______________________________________________

______________________________________________

______________________________________________

# The Scientific Gazette

**Who Are Scientists?** **An Introduction**

## Science looks like magic!

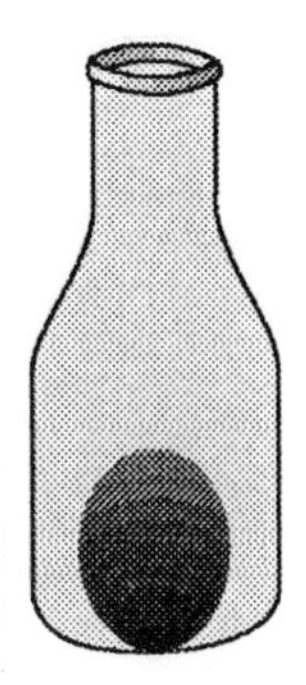

One moment the peeled hard-boiled egg was too large to go through the bottle neck into the bottle. The next moment, the egg easily slipped through the bottle neck. No one even pushed it!

Was our instructor a magician? Were our eyes deceiving us? Did the cafeteria workers serve magic eggs for breakfast?

The magic didn't seem to stop there. The instructor blew into the bottle and the egg shot out of there like the Enterprise in warp drive.

We think the magic began with the fire in the bottle. This fire heated the air in the bottle. Since warm air rises, some of this warm air escaped between the egg and the rim of the bottle. Now the amount of air inside the bottle was less than the atmospheric pressure or air outside the bottle.

That's when the atmospheric pressure pushed the egg into the bottle. Later, when the instructor blew into the bottle, the egg was pushed out of the bottle.

Science looks like magic!

## The Scientist Within You

Today was the beginning of an exploration into science. In the weeks ahead our class will learn about women scientists who made important contributions in science and mathematics.

Some of these women lived in the twentieth century while others lived hundreds of years ago. One of them, Miriam the Alchemist, lived almost 2,000 years ago in northern Africa.

Some of these women scientists worked in laboratories while others traveled thousands of miles to collect rare plants, study fossils, or conduct experiments in space.

## Are you like a scientist?

Do you like to ask questions?

If you answer "yes," then you may be like a scientist. Scientists ask questions like "What causes hurricanes?" or "Why do bears hibernate?" After they ask a question, scientists try to find the answer by conducting one or more experiments.

Are you like a scientist?

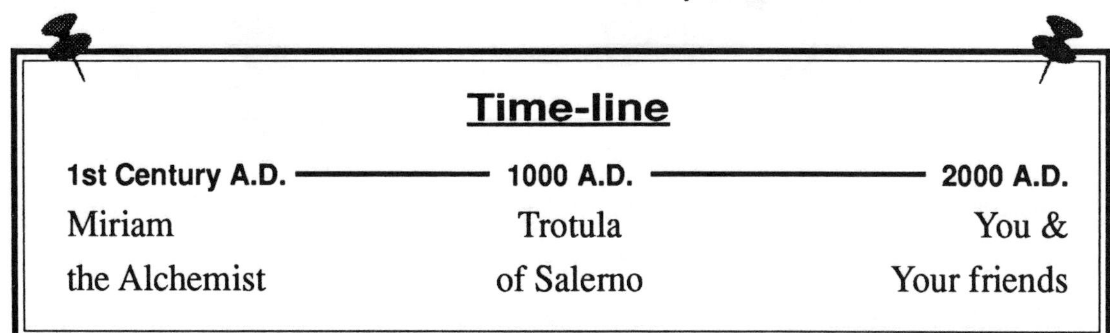

Miriam the Alchemist as she might have appeared in her laboratory 1900 years ago.

# Discovery Unit No. 2

## Miriam the Alchemist

### CHOCOLATE ICING Experiment

---

**Time-line:**

- **0 - 100 A.D. Miriam the Alchemist**
- Around 50 A.D. - Romans learn to use soap
- 1st Century A.D. - Chinese make paper from rags and tree bark

**Pronunciation guide:**

- Alchemist [AL-kah-mist]

**Key points:**

☛ Miriam the Alchemist lived over 1,900 years ago in Alexandria, Egypt.

☛ As an alchemist, Miriam tried to understand what substances like metals were made of and how heat changed them.

☛ Miriam worked in a laboratory with equipment that even today's scientists would recognize. She invented some of this equipment including the water bath which is still used in laboratories as well as in kitchens where we call it a double boiler.

☛ In the CHOCOLATE ICING Experiment, students will discover how Miriam's invention uses water to supply heat more slowly and more evenly.

**Supplies:**

✔ A double boiler

✔ A small saucepan

✔ Small heating element

✔ Mixing spoon

✔ One 1-oz. square semi-sweet baking chocolate (This is in addition to the chocolate squares listed under Chocolate Icing Recipe.)

✔ A box of graham crackers

✔ Knives for spreading the chocolate icing

✔ Chocolate Icing Recipe
- two 1-oz. squares semi-sweet baking chocolate
- one 14-oz. can sweetened condensed milk

✔ A "My Notes" sheet for each student

✔ ***The Scientific Gazette*** for each student

**Steps:**

1. Point out Alexandria, Egypt, on a map or globe. (See page 8.)
2. Share highlights of Miriam the Alchemist's life.
3. Distribute the "My Notes" sheet.
4. Conduct the CHOCOLATE ICING Experiment. (See instructor's guide, page 9.)
5. Assist students in clean-up.
6. Distribute ***The Scientific Gazette.***
7. Add Miriam the Alchemist's name and a memento to the time-line.

**For next time:**

- Announce the next scientist.

---

**Bibliography:**


Alic, Margaret. **Hypatia's Heritage.**

Kelly, Marguerite, and Elia Parsons. **The Mother's Almanac.**

## Biography of MIRIAM the ALCHEMIST First Century A.D.

Miriam the Alchemist lived in a time when people did not use last names like we do today. Your name might include: the name of the city in which you lived like the woman philosopher Arete of Cyrene*; a title you earned or inherited such as Queen Cleopatra; your ethnic background like Miriam the Jewess; a relationship in your family — Pliny the Elder and Pliny the Younger; or, like Miriam the Alchemist, your name might include your profession.

### Early Chemists

Alchemists tried to understand the secret of life. To Miriam the Alchemist everything, including people, plants, animals, and even rocks, were alive. The metals in rocks were living organisms and metals, like people and animals (and even plants, if you think about it), change over a period of time. Miriam believed that as metals got older, they became more valuable until they became the oldest and most valuable of metals — GOLD!

### Making Gold

Alchemists thought that if they heated metals, they could speed up the aging process and create gold in their laboratories. Some alchemists wanted to make gold so they could be rich. Others, like Miriam, thought that making gold would reveal the secret of how all living things change over time.

To learn this secret, Miriam spent hours conducting experiments using equipment that a present-day scientist would recognize. Miriam the Alchemist invented some of this equipment including a **water bath**, a special device that allowed her to heat a substance or mixture slowly. Today's scientists still use the **water bath** in their laboratories. Many cooks also use this invention of Miriam the Alchemist's, but they call it a **double boiler** instead.

* Arete of Cyrene was a well-known scholar in the late 5th century B.C. She taught for 35 years in Greece but apparently came from Cyrene, a city in northern Africa.

**Alexandria, Egypt**

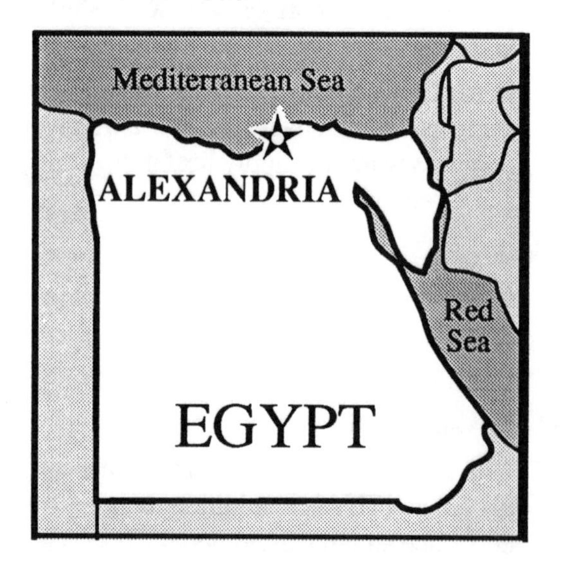

## Instructor's Guide:

### The CHOCOLATE ICING Experiment

## Background Information:

In setting up the experiment, all equipment (same material and size), temperature settings, length of time, etc., must be the same for the chocolate in the saucepan as for the chocolate in the double boiler. Aim for an independent variable so there is little doubt that the water has heated the chocolate more slowly and more evenly (the dependent variable) than the saucepan placed directly on the burner.

Two suggestions: (1) You may wish to select students to conduct portions of the experiment, and (2) If your school prohibits the preparation and consumption of food in the classroom, use 2 squares semi-sweet baking chocolate and only do Parts A and B of the CHOCOLATE ICING Experiment.

## Instructions:

1. On the chalkboard (or newsprint) write the directions for Parts A and B. Point out how the experiments are alike except for one condition. This difference is called an **independent variable**. Stress the importance of having one independent variable in an experiment.

Part A
- Turn burner onto medium high heat.
- When burner has warmed up, place saucepan on burner.
- Add a square of semi-sweet baking chocolate and wait 45 seconds.

Part B
- Fill lower half of double boiler with 1 or 2 inches of hot water.
- Turn burner onto medium high heat.
- When burner has warmed up, put double boiler on burner and bring water to a boil. Set upper half in place.
- Add a square of semi-sweet baking chocolate and wait 45 seconds.

2. Allow time for each student to write down on the "My Notes" sheet a hypothesis for Part A.
3. Conduct Part A.
4. Give students time to record what happened and to write their hypothesis for the results of Part B.
5. Conduct Part B.
6. Give students time to record what happened and to complete "My Notes."
7. Add the second square and the can of condensed milk to the double boiler. Stir over low heat until the chocolate has melted. Refrigerate to thicken. Several hours later, spread the experiment on graham crackers and enjoy.
8. Assist students in cleaning up.

# My Notes

by ______________________________, Scientist

The CHOCOLATE ICING Experiment

**Part A — The square of chocolate in the saucepan will:**

This is my hypothesis: ______________________________

______________________________

This is what happened: ______________________________

______________________________

**Part B — The square of chocolate in the double boiler will:**

This is my hypothesis: ______________________________

______________________________

This is what happened: ______________________________

______________________________

The independent variable in this experiment is ______________________________

______________________________

The dependent variable is ______________________________

______________________________

What questions does this experiment answer? ______________________________

______________________________

______________________________

______________________________

## Miriam the Alchemist Invents Scientific Equipment

Miriam the Alchemist, a scientist who lived in Alexandria, Egypt, in the first century A.D., invented some of the equipment that she used in her laboratory. One of these inventions was a water bath.

A water bath is not only found in laboratories but also in kitchens where it is called a double boiler.

We conducted an experiment to compare how well a square of chocolate melts in a saucepan compared to a square of chocolate that melts in a double boiler. The double boiler worked so well that we ate the experiment.

## My Invention

Miriam the Alchemist invented equipment that helped her do her work. This is a drawing of an invention I want to make:

## Scrolls Served as Books

Alexandria, Egypt, was famous for its excellent schools and universities. Students came from many countries to study and to visit the city's famous library with its 700,000 books.

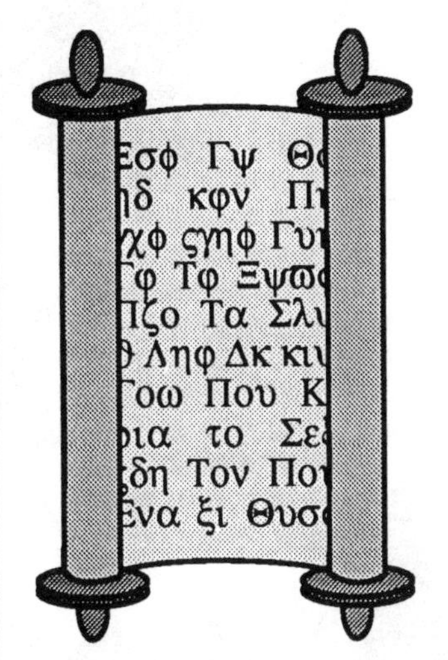

In the first century A.D. (about 1900 years ago), books were written by hand and were really roll books — long sheets of paper (papyrus) rolled around rods.

## Just Imagine . . .

What would Miriam the Alchemist have thought of our microwave ovens? Imagine how she might have used this source of heat in her experiments.

How would you set up an experiment that compares heating a substance with a double boiler to heating that same substance with a microwave?

**Experiments you can eat?** Some science experiments can be eaten. Others cannot. **More Science Experiments You Can Eat** by Vicki Cobb is a book filled with edible experiments. Your library may have a copy.

Hypatia, a 4th century mathematician, lectured at a 700-year-old university in Alexandria, Egypt.

# Discovery Unit No. 3

## Hypatia
## Mathematics

### CURVE EXPLORATION

**Time-line:**

- **370 - 415 A.D. Hypatia**
- 300s - In India, mathematicians create the concept of zero

**Pronunciation guide:**

- Hypatia [Hi-PAY-shaw]
- Theon [THEE-on]
- conic [CAWN-ick]

**Key points:**

- ☛ Hypatia was a famous mathematician who lived in Alexandria, Egypt, and taught at a university that was almost 700 years old.
- ☛ Hypatia studied conic sections, the curves that result when a plane (or flat surface) passes through a cone.
- ☛ A cone party hat will show how curves result from conic sections.
- ☛ Through the CURVE EXPLORATION, students will discover that these curves are everywhere.

**Supplies:**

- ✔ A cone hat pattern for each student (Duplicate page 16.) For best results, mount pattern onto heavier paper before assembling hats.
- ✔ A pair of scissors for each student
- ✔ Tape, glue, or staples
- ✔ "My Notes" sheet for each student
- ✔ ***The Scientific Gazette*** for each student

**Steps:**

1. Point out Alexandria, Egypt, on a map.
2. Share highlights of Hypatia's life.
3. Distribute hat patterns (and sheets of heavier paper) and supplies.
4. Create two conic sections from a cone party hat. (See instructor's guide, page 15.)
5. Distribute "My Notes."
6. Conduct the CURVE EXPLORATION.

   Give students adequate time to explore the classroom (or outdoors — or both) and to record their list of discoveries on their "My Notes" sheets.
7. Distribute ***The Scientific Gazette***.
8. Add Hypatia's name and a memento to the time-line.

**For next time:**

- Announce the next scientist.

**Bibliography:**


Alic, Margaret. **Hypatia's Heritage**.

Perl, Teri. **Math Equals**.

## Biography of HYPATIA 370 - 415 A.D.

Hypatia's father, Theon, was a famous mathematician who wanted his daughter to be a perfect human being. He not only decided what subjects Hypatia should study but how she should exercise. They lived in Alexandria, Egypt, during the waning years of the Roman Empire.

### Greek Mathematics

Like her father, Hypatia became a famous mathematician and teacher at a university that was almost 700 years old. Hypatia was very interested in Greek mathematics, an unpopular subject with the Romans who were not very creative mathematicians.

Like the German mathematician Dr. Emmy Noether, the ancient Greeks loved to discover the "Big Ideas" in mathematics. Some people look at a circle and just see a circle, but these Greeks looked at a circle and saw it as the most perfect shape in the universe. From shapes and curves (the circle is a curve whose points are the same distance from a fixed point), these ancient Greeks discovered "Big Ideas" or universal truths.

### Conic Sections

Hypatia loved Greek mathematics. One shape that interested her was a right angle cone. When you cut a single cone with a flat plane (like a knife), you end up with several pieces. These pieces and their curves are called **conic sections** (sections of a cone).

### The Death of Greek Mathematics

Hypatia's interest in mathematics, conic sections, and astronomy made her one of the most famous teachers in the world and the university at Alexandria one of the few that offered courses in Greek mathematics. When Hypatia died, the Western World's interest in Greek mathematics died too.

**Add your notes about Hypatia here:**

## Instructor's Guide:

### CREATING CONIC SECTIONS FROM A PARTY HAT

### Background Information:

To a Greek mathematician like Hypatia, the cone was a very significant shape. If you cut this cone with a flat plane (such as a knife), you create pieces or conic sections. These sections have one of four kinds of curves — circle, ellipse, parabola, or hyperbola. The kind of curve depends upon the angle at which the plane intersects the cone. We are going to concentrate only on the circle and ellipse. To Hypatia's way of thinking, if a circle (the most perfect curve/shape in the universe) "lodges" in a cone, then the cone becomes significant.

Circles are curves. From **Webster's Ninth New Collegiate Dictionary** comes this definition of circle: "a closed plane curve every point of which is equidistant from a fixed point within the curve."

Ellipses are also curves with two fixed points instead of the circle's one.

### Instructions:

1. Distribute hat patterns and supplies. Explain how to assemble hats. (The solid lines of the hat should meet at the seam). Have tape, paste, and/or staples available for assembly. Assemble hats.
2. Use your hat as an example.

> **Explain . . .**
>
> *Like Hypatia, we are going to see what curves we get if we divide a cone into pieces. Instead of using a knife to cut through the cone, we will use scissors and cut around the cone. The results will be the same.*

☛ **Point out the solid line on the hat.**

> **Explain . . .**
>
> *This line is parallel to the base (or bottom) of the party hat. Let's cut this line and see what curve we get.*

✂ **Cut along this solid line.**

> **Ask . . .**
>
> *What is the shape or curve you have cut?*
>
> **Explain . . .**
>
> *In mathematics a circle is considered a curve.*

☛ **Point out the dotted line on the hat.**

> **Explain:**
>
> *This line is not parallel to the base but is at a slant. Let's cut this line and see what curve we get.*

✂ **Cut along this dotted line.**

> **Ask:**
>
> *What is the shape or curve you have cut?*
>
> [In mathematics an ellipse is considered a curve. (Some students may identify their curve as an "oval." Informally speaking, an oval is a "broad ellipse.")]

4. Assist students in cleaning up.
5. Distribute "My Notes."
6. Conduct the CURVE EXPLORATION (described under "Order of Events," page 13).

## Cone Hat Pattern

**Cut on outer lines**
**Fold on dashed line A - B**
**Roll A-C edge to fit in crease made by A - B fold**
**Tape the flap**

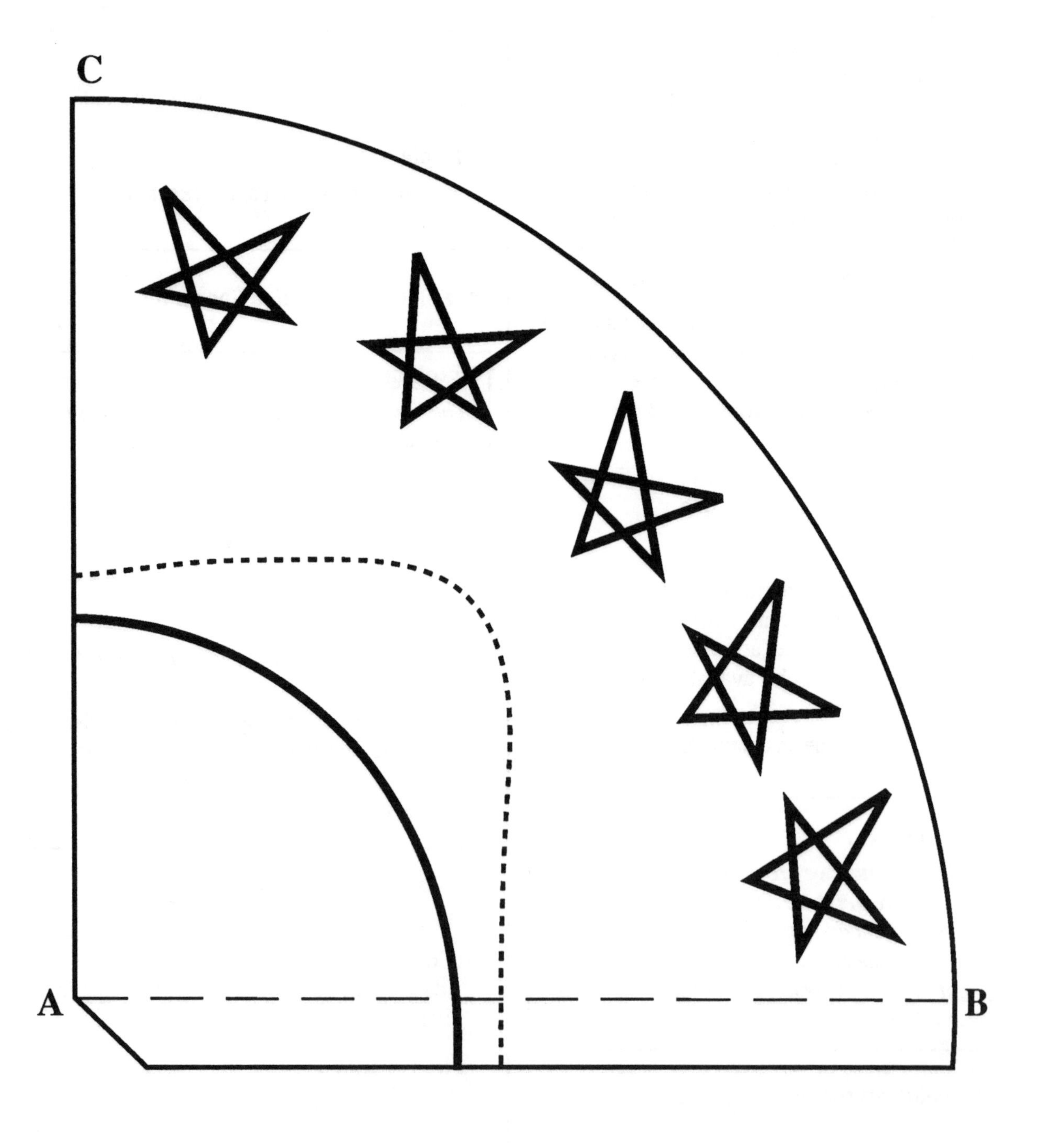

# My Notes

by ______________________________, Scientist

CURVE EXPLORATION, Page 1

**Conic sections from right angle cones have one of four kinds of curves.**

Cut number 1 along the solid line gave me a ____________ .

I found this curve in these places:

________________________________________

________________________________________

________________________________________

________________________________________

________________________________________

________________________________________

________________________________________

________________________________________

________________________________________

________________________________________

________________________________________

________________________________________

________________________________________

________________________________________

________________________________________

________________________________________

# My Notes

by ______________________________, Scientist

**CURVE EXPLORATION, Page 2**

Cut number 2 along the dotted line gave me an ____________ .

I found this curve in these places:

_____________________________________

_____________________________________

_____________________________________

_____________________________________

_____________________________________

_____________________________________

_____________________________________

_____________________________________

Conic sections also include the parabola which looks like an arch that widens at the base, like a deep bowl. Examples include a batter's fly ball or a satellite dish. Look for parabolas in your classroom and outdoors. List your discoveries.

_____________________________________

_____________________________________

_____________________________________

_____________________________________

_____________________________________

_____________________________________

_____________________________________

# The Scientific Gazette

**Mathematics** — **Hypatia**

## Party Hats and Ice Cream Cones

The party hats meant business — math business. Hundreds of years ago a woman mathematician named Hypatia studied the shape of party hats or right angle cones. When you cut this cone into pieces, you get **conic sections** and **curves**. Two of the curves are circles and ellipses.

To the Greeks, the circle was the most perfect shape (or curve) in the universe. If you got a circle from cutting a cone, that made the cone very important too. Greek mathematics was Hypatia's favorite subject, and she spent years studying, teaching, and writing about conic sections.

Hypatia lived from 370 to 415 A.D. and taught at a 700 year-old university in Alexandria, Egypt.

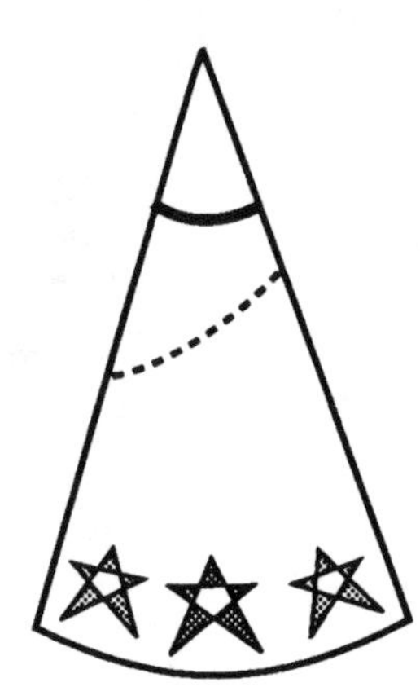

If you cut a cone (the party hat) along the solid top line, you get a curve called a

_______________

If you cut the cone along the dotted line, you get a curve called an

_______________

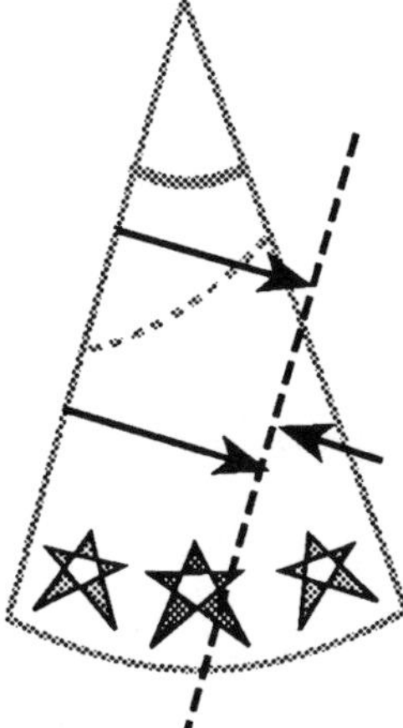

If you cut the cone along the line which is parallel to the opposite side of the cone, you get a curve called a parabola.

### Discovering Curves

We did a "Curve Exploration" in our group. I discovered that curves can be found everywhere. I found the curve called a circle in these places:

_______________

_______________

The curve called an ellipse was more difficult to find. Examples we discovered were:

_______________

_______________

An example of a parabola is:

_______________

**At Home:** With an adult's help, create conic sections in the kitchen, e.g., slice a banana, hot dog, carrot . . .

Trotula of Salerna, Italy, was an 11th century physician, a medical school instructor, and the writer of medical texts.

# Discovery Unit No. 4

Trotula of Salerno
Medicine

## CLEAN HANDS - DIRTY HANDS Experiment

### Time-line:

- **11th century - Trotula of Salerno**
- 1066 - Halley's Comet reappears
- 1090s - Gondolas recorded in Venice, Italy

### Pronunciation guide:

- Trotula [Trow-TWO-la]

### Key points:

- Trotula was an 11th century physician who taught in Salerno, Italy, at one of the few universities in Europe open to women.
- Trotula advised her patients to eat balanced diets, get plenty of exercise, avoid stress, and wash their hands!
- To demonstrate the importance of cleanliness, class members will conduct the CLEAN HANDS - DIRTY HANDS Experiment.

### Supplies — Today:

- ✔ A petri dish for each sample (or a plastic bug box with a magnifying lid)
- ✔ Agar culture medium (Agar can be purchased at science supply stores and health centers specializing in herbal remedies. The cost is approximately $5.75/ounce. This yields 1 1/2 quarts of culture — sufficient medium for 25 petri dishes.)

  Prepare in advance: Bring 2 quarts of water to a boil in the top portion of a double boiler. Add 2 boullion cubes and 1 ounce agar. Stir gently to mix. Boil 10 minutes. Pour enough culture into the sterilized petri dishes to cover the bottom; add lids; and store upside-down to prevent condensation from contaminating the culture. Keep refrigerated until it is time to conduct the experiment. Remember to keep all equipment as germ-free as possible, e.g., don't use an unsterilized measuring cup to pour the culture into the petri dish.
- ✔ Sources of bacteria
- ✔ Sterile cotton swabs
- ✔ Adhesive tape to seal petri dishes
- ✔ Labels to identify source of bacteria
- ✔ Part A of "My Notes"

### Steps — Today:

1. Point out Salerno, Italy, on a map (page 22).
2. Share highlights of Trotula of Salerno's life.
3. Conduct CLEAN HANDS - DIRTY HANDS Experiment. (See instructor's guide, page 23.)
4. Complete Part A of "My Notes."
5. Store petri dishes upside-down in a warm place.
6. Assist students in clean-up.

### Supplies — 4 to 6 days later:

- ✔ Petri dishes with bacteria
- ✔ Magnifying glasses
- ✔ Bucket
- ✔ Chlorine bleach
- ✔ Part B of "My Notes"
- ✔ *The Scientific Gazette* for each student

**Continued next page**

**Steps — 4 to 6 days later:**

1. Examine bacteria but DO NOT UNSEAL PETRI DISHES.
2. Complete Part B of "My Notes."
3. Instructor destroys bacteria. (See disposal instructions, p. 23.)
4. Assist students in clean-up.
5. Distribute ***The Scientific Gazette.***
6. Add Trotula's name and a memento to the time-line.

**For next time:**

- Announce the next scientist.

**Bibliography:**


Alic, Margaret. **Hypatia's Heritage.**

Gardner, Robert. **More Ideas for Science Projects.**

Ogilvie, Marilyn Bailey. **Women in Science.**

Tocci, Salvatore. **Biology Projects for Young Scientists.**

Vare, Ethlie Ann, and Greg Ptacek. **Mothers of Invention.**

## Biography of TROTULA OF SALERNO 11th century

Trotula of Salerno was a physician over 900 years ago in southern Italy. She graduated from and taught at the medical school at the university in Salerno, the first university in Europe. For hundreds of years this university was one of a few in Europe that admitted women.

Not much is known about Trotula's personal life. She was a member of a noble family, a university student and, later, a teacher at the medical school in Salerno. Her husband was Johannes Platearius, physician, and their two sons, Matthias and Johannes the Younger, were medical writers.

Although Trotula's medical specialty was the diseases of women, she treated a variety of illnesses including toothaches, lice, eye disease, cancer, and deafness. Instead of recommending cures based on astrology or superstition, this famous physician used medicines, massage, and surgery. Trotula gave common sense advice. She told her patients to eat balanced diets, get plenty of exercise, avoid stress, and wash their hands!

For 400 years her medical books were copied by hand and remained in print for another 300 years. These texts were used in medical schools for 500 years. The most famous of these books was Trotula's **The Diseases of Women**. "No book so good of its kind had ever been written, and none followed it for centuries." (Dr. Kate Hurd-Mead, **History of Women in Medicine From Earliest Times to the Early 19th Century**)

Unfortunately, the credit for writing Trotula of Salerno's books was often given to other physicians and writers. By the 1900s, the idea that a woman of Trotula's intelligence and medical accomplishments had lived in the 11th century seemed so unlikely that historians omitted her from the history of medicine.

This decision helps explain why so few people have ever heard of this woman physician whose medical skill and knowledge made her famous in 11th century Italy.

## Instructor's Guide:

### CLEAN HANDS - DIRTY HANDS
### Experiment

## Background Information:

Please read and carefully follow the Background Information before proceeding with this experiment.

This experiment requires more equipment and special safety precautions since some of the bacteria collected may be pathogenic (disease-causing). The health of the instructor and students requires care in the collection and storage of samples, and extreme caution in the observation and disposal of bacterial growth. **Adult supervision of this experiment is essential.**

**Collect** samples from a variety of places: nostril and tongue are a must, sink drain, drinking fountain, floor, textbook, desktop (instructor's and student's), sponge, telephone mouthpiece, sidewalk, etc. **Be sure to have a petri dish with a sample from a hand washed with soap and water. Also leave one petri dish sealed and free of any samples.** When touching the cotton swab to the agar, do not break the agar's surface. Wash hands after collecting samples.

**Store** dishes upside down so condensation does not contaminate sample.

**Observe** but do not open petri dishes since some of the bacteria collected could be pathogenic. Use a magnifying glass to distinguish bacteria from fungi. Bacteria (one-celled organisms of the kingdom Monera) grow in spherical colonies while fungi (organisms in the kingdom Fungi) appear as fine strands.

**To dispose** of samples, follow this procedure: Wear plastic gloves! In a bucket create a bleach-and-water solution that is 10 to 20% chlorine bleach. Open petri dishes and submerge samples and containers in the chlorine solution. Soak for several hours before lifting out petri dishes. Pour solution down the drain and discard sample residue in the garbage.

Confirm disposal suggestion with your local public health department to learn if the above procedure meets public health requirements for your region.

## Instructions:

### Today

1. Discuss experiment.
2. Select locations from which students will collect samples.
3. Divide students into collection groups.
4. Assign samples to collect.
5. Explain procedure for collecting samples and distribute supplies.
6. Collect samples and discard cotton swabs.
7. Seal, label, and store petri dishes.
8. Direct students to wash hands.
9. Distribute "My Notes." Students complete Part A. Collect "My Notes."

### 4 to 6 days later

1. Distribute magnifying glasses.
2. Display sealed petri dishes.
3. Allow time for students to examine bacterial samples.
4. Share observations.
5. Distribute "My Notes" and complete Part B.
6. Destroy samples.
7. Assist students in clean-up.

## Enrichment Activity:

➡ Check your school library for books on bacteria. Perhaps the class can identify the cultures grown in their "petri dishes."

# My Notes

**by ________________________________, Scientist**

**Part A:**

What is the question you want this experiment to answer?

____________________________________________________________

____________________________________________________________

List the places (the sources) from which you and others collected samples. Circle the one that you think will show the most bacterial growth.

____________________________________________________________

____________________________________________________________

**Part B: — 4 to 6 days later**

Draw what you observe in the petri dish containing no sample.

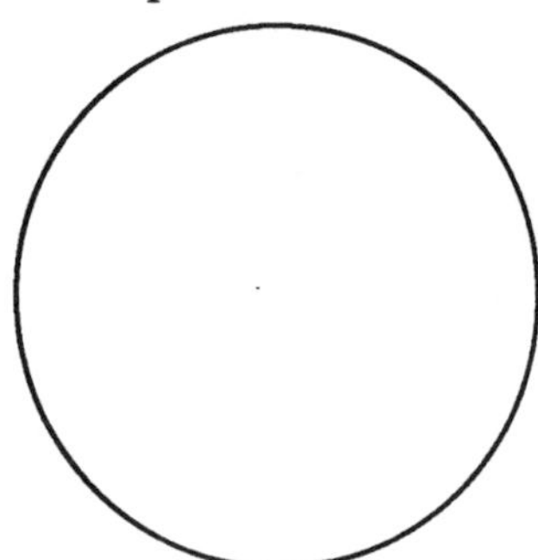

Draw what you observe in the sample from the hand washed in soap and water.

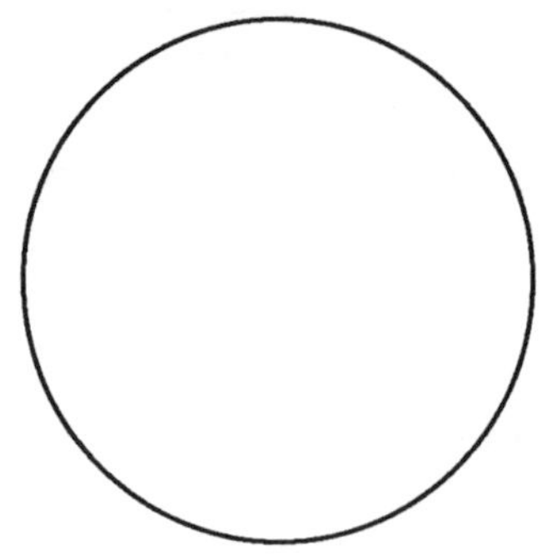

Draw what you observe in the sample containing the most bacterial growth.

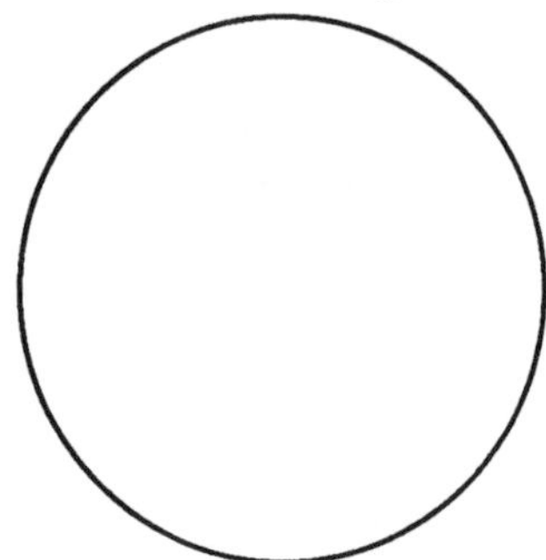

Identify the source ____________________

Is this the sample you circled in Part A?

Yes ☐ No ☐

Did the CLEAN HANDS-DIRTY HANDS Experiment answer the question you wrote down in Part A? __________

Explain: ____________________________

____________________________________

____________________________________

____________________________________

____________________________________

____________________________________

# The Scientific Gazette

**Medicine** **Trotula of Salerno**

## One of the "Ladies of Salerno"

In the 11th century, Trotula was a physician who taught at the university in Salerno, Italy. Universities in Italy were open to women, but universities in other European countries were not. So many women attended or taught at this university in southern Italy that they were called the "Ladies of Salerno."

Not only did Trotula teach at the medical school, but she also practiced medicine. She treated a variety of ailments including deafness, lice, cancer, and toothaches. Instead of trying to cure patients through superstition or magic, Trotula of Salerno used ointments, massage, warm baths, surgery, and common sense.

To stay healthy, Trotula advised her patients to eat a balanced diet, practice cleanliness, get plenty of exercise, and avoid stress. This remains good advice.

### Bacteria has "can-do" attitude

Bacteria, although very small, are able to do many things. Some bacteria cause disease, spoil food, and pollute water. Other bacteria fight disease, help digest food, and decompose leaves, grass clippings, and kitchen compost.

Bacteria are very simple organisms that are neither plants nor animals. Called "lower organisms," bacteria live and grow wherever they can find a food source.

## A Hot Dog is a "Seldom" Food

In the Healthy Eating Pyramid developed by the Center for Science in the Public Interest (CSPI), each of the major food groups is divided into "Anytime," "Sometimes," and "Seldom" categories. For example, fresh fruit is an "anytime" food; potato chips are a "sometimes" treat; and a bologna sandwich, hot dog on a bun, and taco salad fall into the "seldom" category.

To request a sample newsletter and the Center's catalogue of publications (including copies of the Healthy Eating Pyramid), write CSPI Pyramid, 1875 Connecticut Avenue, N.W., Suite 300, Washinton, D.C. 20009, or call (202) 332-9110. "A Kids Against Junk Food" curriculum is available for teachers.

Persons who exercise at least 30 minutes per session, three times a week, are not only strengthening muscles, hearts, and lungs, but are also reducing stress. Discover which friends and family members get plenty of exercise; learn what forms of exercise are their favorite activities, e.g., jogging, ballet, basketball, soccer . . .; and create a graph or table to show your findings.

### Clean Hands - Dirty Hands Experiment

In the petri dish containing a sample I collected from ______________________, I observed:

Hildegard of Bingen, a 12th century writer, composer, poet, abbess, and scientist, wrote a nine-volume encyclopedia of natural history.

# Discovery Unit No. 5

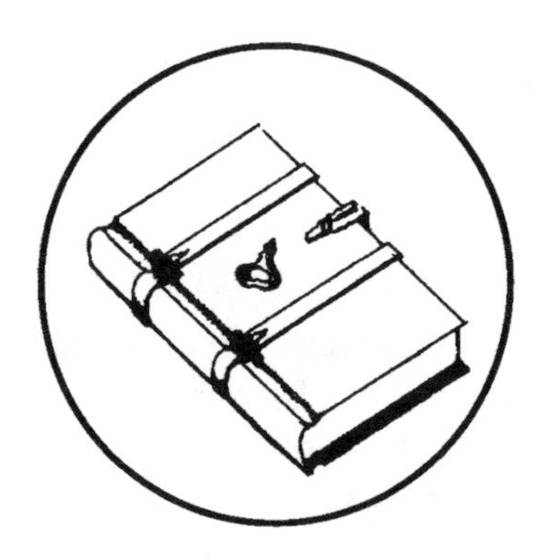

## Hildegard of Bingen
## Natural Science

### A Universe of Questions and Answers

**Time-line:**

- **1098 - 1179 Hildegard of Bingen**
- 1100s - Chinese are raising silkworms to make silk cloth

**Pronunciation guide:**

- Bingen [BING-jun], Germany

**Key points:**

☛ Hildegard of Bingen was a natural scientist who lived in Germany almost 900 years ago.

☛ A natural scientist explores the physical universe.

☛ Hildegard's nine-volume encyclopedia of natural history features plants, animals, stones, and metals.

☛ Like Hildegard, students in a UNIVERSE of QUESTIONS and ANSWERS will ask many questions about nature, and, like Hildegard, students will discover the answers to their questions.

**Supplies:**

✔ Several sheets of newsprint
✔ Felt pens
✔ "Dot" stickers — five stickers for each student
✔ "My Notes" sheet for each student
✔ Supplies to make a UNIVERSE OF ANSWERS Scrapbook
✔ ***The Scientific Gazette*** for each student

**Steps:**

1. Point out Bingen (on-the-Rhine), Germany. (See map, page 28.)
2. Share highlights of Hildegard's life.
3. Compose A UNIVERSE OF QUESTIONS Collage.
4. "Dot" vote. (See instructor's guide, page 29.)
5. Brainstorm resources.
6. Divide into discovery groups.
7. Distribute "My Notes" sheet. Groups discuss questions, make assignments, and set deadlines.
8. (Next 4-5 days) Create A UNIVERSE OF ANSWERS Scrapbook.
9. Distribute ***The Scientific Gazette***.
10. Add Hildegard of Bingen's name and a memento to the time-line.

**For next time:**

- Announce the next scientist.

**Bibliography:**


Achterberg, Jeanne. **Woman as Healer**.

Alic, Margaret. **Hypatia's Heritage**.

Kass-Simon, G., and Patricia Farnes. **Women of Science: Righting the Record**.

Ogilvie, Marilyn Bailey. **Women in Science**.

Stein, Sara. **The Science Book**.

Strehlow, Dr. Wighard, and Dr. Gottfried Hertzka. **Hildegard of Bingen's Medicine**.

## Biography of HILDEGARD OF BINGEN 1098 - 1179

Hildegard of Bingen was a writer, composer, poet, abbess, and scientist. As abbess, Hildegard supervised the convent's property and fellow workers, traveled on horseback through Germany and France to teach theology and medicine, and corresponded with the Pope and the Emperor of the Holy Roman Empire. Hildegard of Bingen was one of the most influential and powerful women of the twelfth century.

### The Tenth of Ten

Born in 1098, Hildegard was the tenth of 10 children. At the age of 8, she was sent to live with her Aunt Jutta, an abbess of a small convent in Germany. Aunt Jutta supervised Hildegard's education. Thirty years after her arrival at the convent, Hildegard succeeded her Aunt Jutta as abbess.

### Begins Writing

When Hildegard was 42 years old, she began writing. From 1140 to 1179, Hildegard wrote 14 books (some were more than one volume) including two biographies, 70 songs, and a play. She became Germany's first naturalist — or natural scientist.

### Nine-Volume Encyclopedia

A natural scientist explores nature. Hildegard's nine-volume encyclopedia of nature described 230 plants, 60 trees, more than 30 local fish, birds, reptiles, mammals, stones, and metals. Her 72-chapter book on birds included flying insects like wasps, bees, mosquitoes, and locusts.

Her volume on mammals began with fictional stories about elephants, camels, bears, and unicorns and moved on to nonfictional accounts of weasels, badgers, and otters.

### Germany's First Medical Writer

Hildegard was also Germany's first medical writer. She knew the medicinal benefits of over 400 plants. Some of the names she gave to plants remain in use today. Like Trotula of Salerno (who died shortly before Hildegard's birth), Hildegard advised cleanliness, exercise, and proper diet. A balanced diet avoided too much cold or raw food, and too much meat or fat, but included seafood, vegetables, and grains.

### Her Curiosity

Nothing escaped Hildegard's curiosity. From the down-to-earth ant to the far-flung universe, this abbess of medieval Germany was not afraid to ask questions nor hesitant to discover the answers. Her enthusiasm is contagious. Like Hildegard, we can ask questions about our world and universe, and, like Hildegard, we can set out to discover and record the answers.

◆ ◆ ◆

## Instructor's Guide:

### A UNIVERSE OF QUESTIONS
### Collage

## Background Information:

The purpose of A UNIVERSE OF QUESTIONS is to allow students the luxury of asking questions and then to provide time for discovering the answers. The supreme rule in brainstorming is not to criticize, denounce, ridicule, or dismiss a question. This rule applies to instructor and students.

## Instructions:

### Today

After sharing highlights of Hildegard's life:

1. Brainstorm questions.
2. Record students' questions on the sheets of newsprint entitled "A UNIVERSE OF QUESTIONS" Collage.
3. Distribute 5 "dot" stickers to each student.
4. Explain "dot" voting. (Each student places 5 stickers on the collage. All 5 stickers may go toward one favorite question or 1 sticker for five great questions; 3 on one terrific question and 2 on another, etc.)
5. "Dot" vote.
6. Check voting results.
7. Pick the top 10 questions.
8. Brainstorm resources for each of the 10 questions.
9. Divide class into 10 discovery groups.
10. Give each group a question. (Assign question according to a group's interest or use the "pick-question-out-of-the-hat approach" — your choice.)
11. Distribute "My Notes."
12. Determine a deadline date for this project.
13. Allow time for groups to discuss their question, decide resources, make assignments, set deadlines, and complete today's section of "My Notes." (Scheduling library time may be necessary.)
14. Circulate to answer questions.
15. Collect "My Notes."

### A UNIVERSE OF ANSWERS
### Scrapbook

16. Give each group a page (make this simple or elaborate — your choice) from A UNIVERSE OF ANSWERS Scrapbook. They write their group's question at the top of this page and return the page to you.
17. Add Hildegard's name and memento to the time-line.

(Between today and the deadline date, discovery groups may need to meet to share information, make new assignments, etc.)

### Several days later

The discovery groups meet and write their answers on the pages of A UNIVERSE OF ANSWERS Scrapbook. Groups may share their answers and pages.

1. Collect the pages.
2. Assemble scrapbook.
3. Redistribute and complete "My Notes."
4. Distribute ***The Scientific Gazette***.

# My Notes

by ______________________________, Scientist

**A UNIVERSE OF QUESTIONS AND ANSWERS**

*"There is no creation that does not have a radiance."*

Hildegard of Bingen

## — TODAY —

1. This is our discovery group's question: ______________________________

______________________________

______________________________

2. Our resources are: ______________________________

______________________________

______________________________

______________________________

______________________________

3. My assignment is: ______________________________

______________________________

______________________________

4. My deadline is: ______________________________

## — SEVERAL DAYS LATER —

**The answer to our question is:** ______________________________

______________________________

______________________________

# The Scientific Gazette

**Natural Science** | **Hildegard of Bingen**

## The Abbess who Loved Curiosity

Hildegard of Bingen, Germany, was one of the most powerful and influential women of the 12th century. She was a writer, a composer, an abbess, and a natural scientist. One of her 14 books was **Physica** (FIZZ-ee-cah), a nine-volume encyclopedia describing hundreds of plants, animals, and minerals. Hildegard was Germany's first naturalist. Nothing escaped her curiosity.

To celebrate Hildegard's curiosity, our class created A UNIVERSE OF ANSWERS Scrapbook. We brainstormed questions, "dot" voted to pick the "top 10," and searched for the answers to these questions. Each page in the scrapbook features a question and its answer.

*The more one learns about that which one knows nothing of, the more one gains in wisdom. One has, therefore, through science, eyes with which it behooves us to pay attention.*

Hildegard of Bingen
1098 - 1179 AD

Some other questions I have thought of are:

______________________________

______________________________

______________________________

______________________________

______________________________

______________________________

## Music Endures Through Ages

The beautiful music composed by Abbess Hildegard of Bingen can be found on England's Hyperíon label. One release entitled "A Feather on the Breath of God" is available both on CD and tape. Your classical music store may have it in stock or can order it.

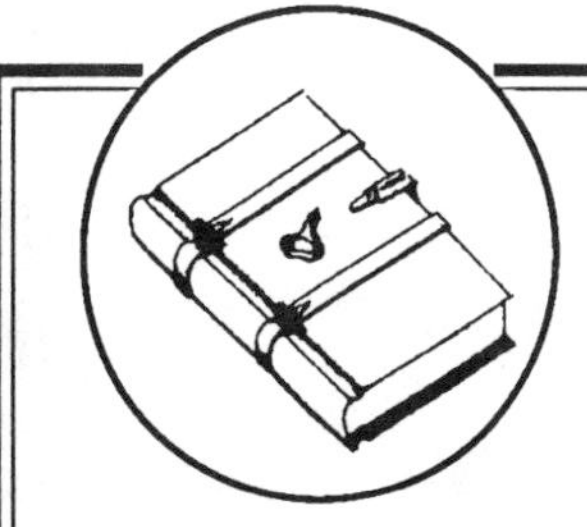

### At Home

Locate **The Science Book** by Sara Stein. This 263-page book provides information on animals, plants, bugs, senses, and thoughts. Suggestions and experiments astound and engross parent and child. From making a homemade hot-air balloon to looking at blood vessels, this book encourages scientific thinking and exploration, and is meant "to last for years."

Baroness Martine de Beausoleil, a 17th century geologist, studies a rock sample at her worktable.

# Discovery Unit No. 6

## Martine de Beausoleil
## Geology

### WATER IN - WATER OUT Experiment

---

**Time-line:**

- **17th century - Baroness Martine de Beausoleil**
- 1630 - Shah Jahan builds the Taj Mahal
- 1665-1667 - Isaac Newton explains gravity, develops calculus, and suggests a theory of color

**Pronunciation guide:**

- Beausoleil [Bow-so-LAY]
- hydraulics [high-DRAW-licks]

**Key points:**

☛ Baroness Martine de Beausoleil was a geologist in France in the 1600s.

☛ For 30 years this scientist studied geology, mathematics, chemistry, physics, and hydraulics. Hydraulics is the study of how water moves under pressure.

☛ The WATER IN - WATER OUT Experiment will demonstrate how water pressure is greater at the bottom of a container.

**Supplies:**

✔ A permanent marker
✔ An empty one-gallon plastic milk or juice carton prepared in advance (See instructor's guide, page 35.)
✔ A hammer
✔ One large nail
✔ A basin or sink into which the carton can be dipped and filled
✔ A great location (a sink, the outdoors, etc.) for conducting this experiment
✔ A "My Notes" sheet for each student
✔ ***The Scientific Gazette*** for each student

**Option:**

If you want every student to conduct this experiment, use one large can per student. Collect several hammers, nails, and plastic basins so individuals can prepare their containers and conduct their experiments.

**Steps:**

1. Point out Paris, France, on a map.
2. Share highlights of Martine de Beausoleil's life.
3. Distribute "My Notes" sheet.
4. Conduct the WATER IN - WATER OUT Experiment.
5. Distribute ***The Scientific Gazette.***
6. Add Baroness Martine de Beausoleil's name and a memento to the time-line.

**For next time:**

- Announce the next scientist.

---

**Bibliography:**


Alic, Margaret. **Hypatia's Heritage.**

Lewis, James. **Rub-a Dub-Dub Science in the Tub.**

## Biography of BARONESS MARTINE DE BEAUSOLEIL 17th century

Baroness Martine de Beausoleil was a geologist, a scientist that studies rocks in order to learn the history of the earth.

Not much is known about the baroness except that she spent 30 years studying geology, mathematics, chemistry, physics, and hydraulics.

### Making the King Rich

In the 1630s Martine de Beausoleil wrote about the discovery of valuable rocks. All rocks are made up of minerals and some minerals (like gold, copper, silver, and iron) are more valuable than others.

Baroness Martine de Beausoleil explained which minerals were valuable, reported that such minerals existed in France, and urged the king of France to extract these valuable mineral and ore deposits so he could become the richest ruler in Europe.

### Studies Hydraulics

Geology was not the baroness's only interest. Hydraulics was another. Hydraulics is the study of how water moves under pressure. Think about squeezing a washcloth or letting the water from the hose run downhill. Studying how water moves under these conditions is hydraulics. With the washcloth you are forcing the water to move out of the cloth by squeezing; with the water from the hose, gravity is making the water run downhill.

### 350 Years Ago

Baroness Martine de Beausoleil lived about 350 years ago in France. In history books there is not another woman geologist mentioned in Europe or the United States for almost 200 years. Baroness de Beausoleil was a pioneer in her field.

Add other information here:

## Instructor's Guide:

### The WATER IN - WATER OUT Experiment

### Background Information:

The WATER IN - WATER OUT Experiment demonstrates how water pressure is greater at the bottom of a container since the water above it is pushing down. The greater the pressure, the stronger the stream. More depth creates more pressure because more water is pushing down on the water below.

### Instructions:

1. Prepare plastic carton in advance.

   Use the hammer and nail to make four holes in a stair-step pattern on the same side of the carton. (It's important that the holes be the same size!) Beginning from the top, label these holes A, B, C, and D.

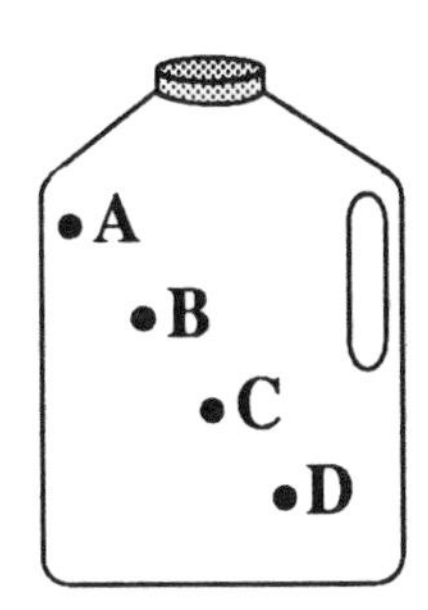


   To make scooping water into the carton easier, cut off the top portion of the carton:

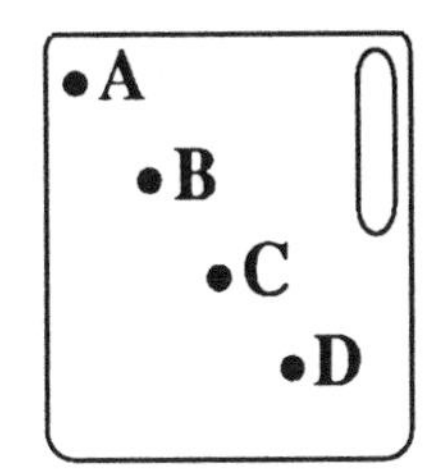


2. Distribute "My Notes."

**Explain the Experiment . . .**

*Let's explore the field of hydraulics and see how water moves under pressure.*

*There are four holes on one side of this plastic milk carton. I am going to fill the carton with water and then we will watch how the water pours out of the four holes.*

3. Point out the holes and how they are at different heights from the bottom of the container. Point out that the holes are labeled A, B, C, and D.
4. Allow students time to complete Question #1 in "My Notes."
5. Discuss their answers to Question #1.
6. Conduct the WATER IN - WATER OUT Experiment.
7. Allow students time to complete Question #2 in "My Notes."
8. Discuss their answers to Question #2.

**Ask . . .**

*Why did the stream from Hole "D" squirt out the farthest?*

[Water pressure is greater at the bottom of a container.

Think of a swimming pool and how the pressure on your eardrums increases when you dive into the deep end. The deeper you dive, the greater the pressure. What's true for the milk carton is true for the swimming pool.]

9. Distribute ***The Scientific Gazette*** allowing time to complete fill-ins.
10. Assist students in clean-up.

# My Notes

by ______________________________, Scientist

**WATER IN - WATER OUT Experiment**

This is an experiment in hydraulics, the study of how water moves under pressure.

**Answer Question # 1 before the experiment.**

1. Which stream of water will be strongest: A, B, C, or D? ______ (This guess is your hypothesis.)

   Why? ______________________________

   ______________________________

   ______________________________

**Answer Question # 2 after the experiment.**

2. Which stream was strongest? ______

   Which was weakest? ______

   Show how the water poured out of the holes.

   How did the results of the experiment compare with your hypothesis?

   ______________________________

   ______________________________

   What have you learned about water pressure from this experiment?

   ______________________________

   ______________________________

## Baroness Martine de Beausoleil, Woman Geologist from the 17th Century

Baroness Martine de Beausoleil lived about 350 years ago in France. She was a geologist, a scientist that studies rocks to learn about the history of the earth.

The baroness also studied mathematics, chemistry, physics, and hydraulics. **Complete this sentence:** Hydraulics is ______________

______________________________________

______________________________________

Our experiment with the milk carton showed us how water pressure is greater at the bottom of a container. That's why the water from Hole "D" squirted the farthest. The deeper the water-filled container is, the greater the water pressure is. Water pressure at the bottom of a 6' swimming pool is greater than the water pressure in the milk carton. How about the water pressure at the base of a 200' dam? Or 4470' below sea level on the floor of the ocean 1000 miles west of Seattle, Washington?

**Water is the only substance on earth that "comes" in three different forms:**

- **LIQUID**
- **SOLID**
- **GAS**

**When have you seen water as a solid?**

**When have you seen water as a gas?**

## HOW STRONG ARE YOU?

List some ways you can "force" water to move:

1. ______________________________

______________________________

2. ______________________________

______________________________

3. ______________________________

______________________________

One way to force water to move is called displacement. If you fill a bathtub with water and the water flows over the rim when you climb in, then you have caused water displacement. Since your weight is heavier than the water, you stay in the tub and the water leaves.

Instead of using a bathtub to show displacement, use a glassful of water and a handful of rocks or marbles.

## At Home

Explore books that feature experiments with water. In **175 Science Experiments To Amuse and Amaze Your Friends** (1988), author Brenda Walpole devotes 38 pages to experiments, tricks, and things to make highlighting the "amazing characteristics of liquid water."

Entomologist Maria Sibylle Merian traveled to South America in 1699 to collect exotic specimens that included a crocodile, snakes, an iguana, and 20 jars of butterflies.

# Discovery Unit No. 7

## Maria Sibylle Merian
## Entomology

### ART FOR BUGS' SAKE Project

**Time-line:**

- **1647 - 1717 Maria Sibylle Merian**
- 1680 - The dodo bird becomes extinct
- 1706 - Benjamin Franklin is born in Massachusetts

**Pronunciation guide:**

- Merian [MURR-ee-un]
- metamorphosis [met-ah-MORE-fa-sis], a change of physical form
- entomologist [ent-tah-MALL-oh-just]

**Key points:**

☛ As a young girl, Maria learned art so she could draw insects better.

☛ Maria Merian became an entomologist, a natural scientist who studies insects.

☛ To study and collect insects and flowers, this 18th century woman scientist traveled to Surinam in South America.

☛ In the ART FOR BUGS' SAKE Project, students will combine art and science to create detailed and accurate pictures of insects.

**Supplies:**

✔ Insects. . . (Two days before, collect insects as a class activity or ask students to bring insects in well-sealed, ventilated, see-through containers the day before the ART FOR BUGS' SAKE Project.)

✔ A magnifier ("Bug Boxes" are ideal. These are small plastic boxes with magnifiers in the lids. If not available, use magnifying glasses.)

✔ A "My Notes" sheet for each student

✔ Colored pencils, felt pens, crayons, etc.

✔ ***The Scientific Gazette*** for each student

**Steps:**

1. Point out Frankfurt, Germany, on a map.
2. Share highlights of Maria Sibylle Merian's life. During the narrative, point out Holland and Surinam on a map.
3. Distribute "My Notes" sheet.
4. Enjoy the ART FOR BUGS' SAKE Project. (See instructor's guide, p. 41.)
5. Share and display completed "My Notes" sheets.
6. Release insects.
7. Distribute ***The Scientific Gazette***.
8. Add Maria Merian's name and a memento to the time-line.

**For next time:**

- Announce the next scientist.

**Bibliography:**


Alic, Margaret. **Hypatia's Heritage.**

Kass-Simon, G., and Patricia Farnes. **Women of Science: Righting the Record.**

Ogilvie, Marilyn Bailey. **Women in Science.**

Schiebinger, Londa. **The Mind Has No Sex?**

## Biography of MARIA SIBYLLE MERIAN 1647 - 1717

Maria Merian was born in Frankfurt, Germany. From her artist stepfather, she learned to draw and mix paints. She sketched and painted flowers, fruit, birds, worms, flies, mosquitoes, and spiders. Maria's fascination with wildlife, particularly insects, motivated her to become a better artist.

### Her Own Business

When Maria was 18, she married Johann Graff, also an artist. They moved to Nuremberg, Germany, where Maria opened her own business selling fabrics handpainted with her floral designs. Maria developed a water-color paint that withstood washings.

One of the fabrics she sold was silk which is made from silkworm caterpillars. Silk was expensive so Maria studied caterpillars hoping to find another type of caterpillar that produced a thread as fine as silk. In the five years she looked, she found none.

### The First Book

Her search for a silkworm substitute may have been unsuccessful, but it led to Merian's first book of information and illustrations; **Wonderful Metamorphosis and Special Nourishment of Caterpillars** was published in 1679. Merian had become an entomologist, a natural scientist who studies insects.

### Divorce

In the 1680s Maria divorced Johann Graff, took back her maiden name, and moved to Amsterdam, Holland, with her two daughters. She studied Latin and was introduced to the flora (plants and flowers) and fauna (animals) of Surinam, a country on the northeast coast of South America. In 1699, at the age of 52, Merian and daughter Dorothea sailed for Surinam.

### Surinam

For two years they collected, studied, and drew insects and plants. Of special interest to them were the moths and butterflies. They gathered caterpillars, fed them, and observed their metamorphosis (a change of appearance or structure) into moths or butterflies.

Forced by malaria to return to Holland in 1701, Merian and Dorothea arrived with a crocodile, snakes, 20 jars of butterflies and an iguana. These and other exotic specimens were displayed in Amsterdam's town hall.

### Worms, Larvae, Moths, and Bees

Over the next four years, Merian wrote a two-volume book describing the life cycles of worms, larvae, moths, bees, and butterflies found in Surinam. A third volume was completed by Dorothea after Merian's death in 1717.

### Contributions

In a time when few women were working outside their homes, Maria Merian owned her own business, traveled thousands of miles to collect exotic specimens, and combined her powers of observation and creativity to produce books that even impressed Czar Peter I of Russia who hung her portrait in his study. Like the caterpillars she studied, Merian created her own metamorphosis. She began as a craftswoman and became an entomologist.

## Instructor's Guide

### ART FOR BUGS' SAKE Project

#### Background Information:

Maria Sibylle Merian lived before photography was invented. In a time without 8" x 10" magnified glossies, artists' drawings of flora and fauna provided visual accounts of nature to persons who could not see these wonders firsthand.

And there were wonders! In the 1600s the newly-developed microscope magnified the world at one's fingertips while the New World expanded the treasure trove of exotic flora and fauna. Maria Merian's art and her scientific discoveries in Surinam combined magnification and novelty. Her books did not disappoint a public appreciative of art and hungry for information.

#### Instructions:

**Two days before**

1. Collect insects as a class or assign this task to students. Specify "well-sealed, ventilated, see-through containers."
2. If necessary, review characteristics of insects: 6 legs and a body divided into 3 sections — head, thorax, and abdomen.
3. Decide format most suitable for your class e.g., one insect center to which students take turns coming, 4 to 5 centers with students divided into groups, or a "bug box" for each student.

   Include magnifying glasses and art supplies at the center(s).

**The day of the project**

1. Distribute "My Notes."
2. Organize class into the format of your choice.

**Explain . . .**

*When Maria Merian was drawing insects, photography had not been invented. Instead of looking at a photograph to learn what a butterfly from South America looked like, a person studied an artist's picture of the butterfly.*

*Pretend you are Maria Merian. And pretend your picture is the only way some people will have of knowing what your insect looks like. Your picture must be "larger than life" to show the details.*

3. Encourage students to take their time.
4. Allow adequate time for the ART FOR BUGS' SAKE Project.
5. Share and discuss pictures.
6. Display pictures.
7. Assist students in clean-up.

#### Enrichment Activity (Optional):

This project might be the beginning of a unit on insects. The next step could be identifying the insects and collecting information about them.

# My Notes

by ______________________________, Scientist

ART for BUGS' SAKE Project

<u>This is my larger-than-life-size detailed drawing of a bug.</u>

# The Scientific Gazette

**Entomology** | **Maria Sibylle Merian**

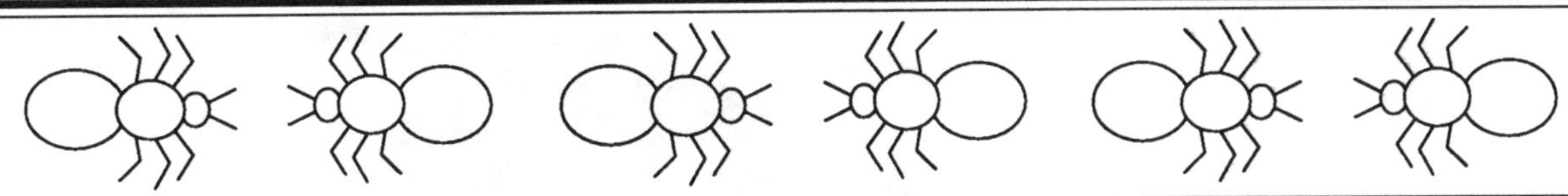

## Entomologist Maria Merian Learns Art for Bugs' Sake

In the 1660s Maria Merian learned how to mix paints and sketch so she could draw insects more accurately. A decade later Maria spent five years studying caterpillars. She owned a hand-painted fabric business and wanted to find a substitute for the silkworm's expensive thread. She found no substitute but wrote **Wonderful Metamorphosis and Special Nourishment of Caterpillars** which was published in 1679.

Maria Merian became an entomologist, a natural scientist who studies insects. She learned Latin, traveled to India, and lived in Surinam for two years. Returning to Holland in 1701, Merian and daughter Dorothea arrived with a crocodile, snakes, 20 jars of butterflies and an iguana.

For the next 16 years, Merian wrote and illustrated books about the plants and animals (the flora and fauna) of Surinam. Worms, larvae, moths, and bees were featured. Merian's work so impressed Czar Peter I of Russia that he hung her portrait in his study. She died in 1717 and her daughter Dorothea finished the third volume of the **Metamorphosis of Insects of Surinam.**

### INSECTS ARE INTERESTING

- Mosquitoes live in the Arctic Circle and in the tropics.
- The brine-fly lives in salt.
- The European stag beetle measures 2 1/4" long.
- Grasshoppers have 900 distinct muscles.
- The Atlas moth of India has a wing span of 12".
- The dragonfly cruises at 25 mph.

—from **"The Insects"** by Peter Farb & the Editors of **LIFE**

Over 700,000 different insects have been identified. Entomologists believe 1 to 10 million insects have yet to be discovered!

Despite their differences, adult insects have these traits in common:

- 6 legs.
- A body divided into three sections: head, thorax and abdomen. The six legs are attached to the insect's thorax.

**Metamorphosis** means a change of appearance or structure. Three insects that go through *metamorphosis* are:

______________________

______________________

______________________

Astronomer Caroline Herschel discovered eight comets and saw Halley's Comet twice in her lifetime.

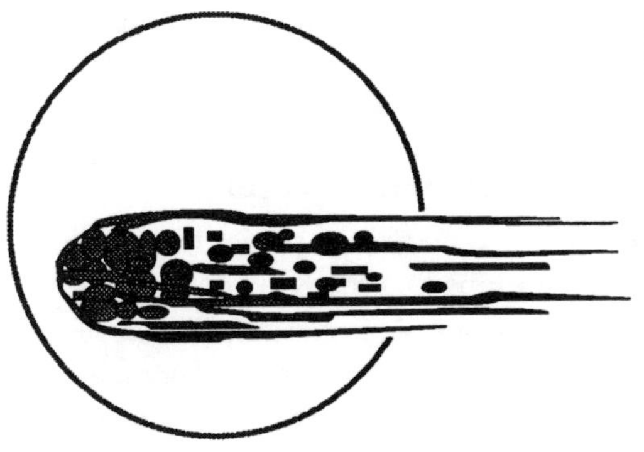

# Discovery Unit No. 8

## Caroline Lucretia Herschel
## Astronomy

### COMET IN A BAG Demonstration

**Time-line:**
- **1750 - 1848 Caroline Lucretia Herschel**
- 1758 and 1835 - Halley's Comet
- 1816 - Stethoscope invented

**Pronunciation guide:**
- Herschel [HER-schull]

**Key points:**
- ☛ Caroline Herschel was 4' 3" tall.
- ☛ Herschel worked with her brother William. During their lifetimes, they were the only sister-brother astronomer team in the world.
- ☛ Among her many achievements in astronomy was the discovery of 8 comets.
- ☛ The COMET IN A BAG will demonstrate how rock fragments, moisture, elements such as carbon and iron, and sub-zero temperatures combine in space to create a comet.

**Supplies:**
- ✔ A two-quart plastic freezer bag
- ✔ 3/4 cup regular sand
- ✔ 1 1/2 cups water
- ✔ One charcoal square broken up to make 2 Tablespoons (This is the carbon ingredient.)
- ✔ One rusty nail
- ✔ A metal file for shaving the nail
- ✔ Heavy-duty work gloves
- ✔ An ice chest or cooler
- ✔ Dry ice (a piece about 9" square)
- ✔ A "My Notes" sheet for each student
- ✔ Sheets of newsprint for the collage
- ✔ *The Scientific Gazette* for each student

**Steps:**
1. Draw a line 51" from the floor. Ask students to walk by the line (without telling them why). Jot down the names of students who come up to or beyond this height. Share that these students are as tall or taller than Caroline Herschel was **as an adult**.
2. Point out Hanover, Germany, and England on a map.
3. Share highlights from Caroline Herschel's life.
4. Make a COMET IN A BAG. (See instructor's guide, page 47)
5. Distribute "My Notes," complete questions, and collect "My Notes."
6. Begin the collage. When the collage is finished (days or a week from now), distribute "My Notes" and give students time to complete "Fun Facts About Comets."
7. Distribute ***The Scientific Gazette.***
8. Add Caroline Herschel's name and a memento to the time-line.

**For next time:**
- Announce the next scientist.

**Bibliography:**

Alic, Margaret. **Hypatia's Heritage.**

Higgins, Frances Lowry. **Sweeper of the Skies: A Story of the Life of Caroline Herschel, Astronomer.** (Juvenile)

Ogilvie, Marilyn Bailey. **Women in Science.**

Osen, Lynn M. **Women in Mathematics.**

## Biography of CAROLINE LUCRETIA HERSCHEL 1750 - 1848

Born in Germany on March 16, 1750, Caroline was the fifth of six children. The four oldest were boys with brother William, twelve years older than Caroline, being her favorite. When Caroline was nine, William left home to study music in England.

### Halley's Comet

Also at age nine, Caroline saw Halley's Comet on one of its regular 76-year visits. Her father's interest in astronomy was contagious. Halley's Comet was the topic of many family discussions and Herr Herschel wondered aloud if his 9-year-old daughter would be alive three-quarters of a century later to see the comet again. Not only would Caroline Herschel be alive, she would be a famous astronomer credited with discovering 8 comets!

### Cinderella

Meanwhile, Caroline was the Cinderella of the household. Since her father was away from home much of the time, Caroline's mother decided how her daughter should be raised. Frau Herschel could not read or write, and she believed it was not important to educate her daughter. Caroline's job was to clean and to knit. She enrolled Caroline in knitting school and allowed her to take dressmaking classes. Caroline wanted to take singing lessons, but her mother refused.

### William Returns

After Herr Herschel died, William returned to Germany and rescued Caroline from her Cinderella life. He was an organist and composer, and wanted to train Caroline to become a professional singer. William not only taught her how to copy music and sing, but also gave her classes in accounting, algebra, geometry and trigonometry. Like his father, William enjoyed astronomy, and Caroline was willing to assist her brother. She never became a professional singer.

### For Half a Century

William discovered the planet Uranus and became so famous that the King of England made him the Court Astronomer. For the next 50 years, this sister-brother astronomer team studied the stars. They "swept the heavens" which meant they "divided" the sky into sections and then used their homemade telescopes to survey and identify every star, every ray of light, and every bit of matter in that section. They studied the rings around Saturn, the polar ice caps on Mars, and the mountains on the moon.

### Their Telescopes

One of their homemade telescopes was called the Great Telescope, "the eighth wonder of the world for a span of fifty years." The tube was so large that a person taller than Caroline could walk through its length. Through their telescopes they discovered two satellites of Uranus, two more satellites of Saturn, and Caroline spied her 8 comets.

### Her 96th Birthday

When her brother William died, Caroline Herschel returned to Germany. She continued to use her smaller telescope to "sweep the heavens" and to write books and catalogues of stars. On her 96th birthday, the King of Prussia awarded her a Gold Medal for Science.

## Instructor's Guide:

### COMET IN A BAG Demonstration

### Background Information:

**A COMET IN A BAG** demonstrates how rock fragments, moisture, elements such as carbon and iron, and sub-zero temperatures combine in space to a create a comet. Essentially, comets are "giant snowballs."

(DO NOT TOUCH DRY ICE!! Wear your heavy-duty work gloves from the time you take the dry ice out of the cooler until you finish the experiment!!!)

### Instructions:

1. Into the plastic freezer bag combine the following items:
   - 3/4 cup regular sand
   - 1 1/2 cups water
   - 2 tablespoons of roughly grated charcoal square (This is the carbon ingredient.)
   - 30 seconds of metal shavings from a rusty nail
2. PUT ON YOUR "SERIOUS" WORK GLOVES.
3. Break the dry ice into smaller chunks (about the size of ping pong balls) and drop approximately 2 cups of dry ice into the plastic bag. Do not seal bag.
4. Hold the bottom of the bag for support but do not hide the "bubbling" activity.

**Ask . . .**

*What do you think is happening in the bag?*

If some students suggest that the comet is boiling,

**Ask . . .**

*How can our comet be "boiling" when the temperature of dry ice is -109.3 degrees Fahrenheit (or -78.5 degrees Centigrade)?*

[The bubbling activity hints of boiling but what we are actually seeing is the act of freezing.]

5. Continue to hold the bag until all of the items in the bag are fused into what appears to be a large dirty snowball (5 to 10 minutes). You are holding a comet.
6. Return the comet to the cooler. REMOVE YOUR GLOVES.
7. Distribute "My Notes" and give students time to discuss the questions with another student and to complete these sheets.
8. Ask students to share their responses to the "My Notes" questions.
9. As students share, jot down their insights and questions on the sheets of newsprint or butcher paper.
10. Collect "My Notes" and hold for next time.
11. Carefully clean-up.

### To Make The Collage:

1. Introduce the idea of the collage and explain that its purpose is to feature information about comets.

**Ask . . .**

*Where do you think we can find the answers to our questions?*

2. Together decide where and how to collect this information. (The class may decide to assign the questions, etc.)
3. Discover the answers and add this information to the collage.
4. When the collage is finished, redistribute "My Notes" and complete "Fun Facts about Comets."
5. Distribute ***The Scientific Gazette.***

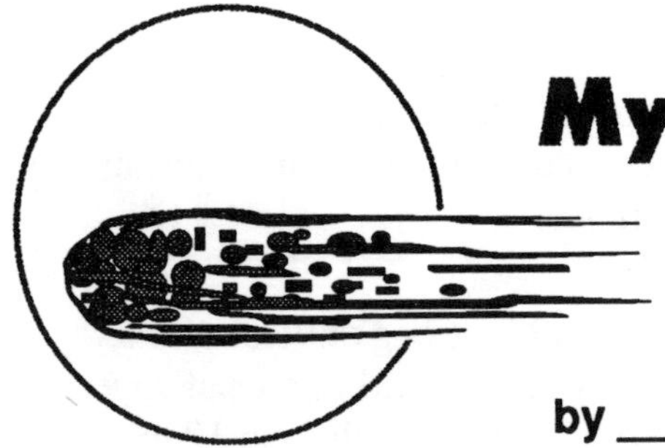

# My Notes

**A COMET IN A BAG Demonstration**

**by ______________________________, Scientist**

**Work with another student scientist.**

1. What did you learn from the comet-in-a-bag? ____________________

____________________________________________

____________________________________________

____________________________________________

2. What questions do you have about comets?

____________________________________________

____________________________________________

____________________________________________

____________________________________________

## Fun Facts About Comets

- A comet's tail may be thousands or millions of miles long.
- ____________________________________________
- ____________________________________________
- ____________________________________________
- ____________________________________________
- ____________________________________________
- ____________________________________________
- ____________________________________________
- ____________________________________________

## Noted Astronomer Honored on Her 96th Birthday

**HANOVER, Germany:** Not every 96-year old receives a Gold Medal in Science from a king on her birthday. But astronomer Caroline Herschel did. Born in Hanover on March 16, 1750, she was the fifth of six children and spent most of her childhood serving as the Cinderella of the household. Her mother, unable to read and write, believed girls did not need to be educated.

Caroline thought otherwise. In her early twenties, she moved to England to live with her brother William and to study singing, accounting, and mathematics. Caroline joined William in his work in astronomy. They became the only sister-brother astronomer team in the world.

During their fifty years of "sweeping" the heavens, they studied Saturn's rings, the polar ice caps on Mars, and the mountains on the moon. Her brother discovered Uranus and Caroline spied eight comets.

**Their 40' Newtonian telescope was called the Great Telescope, "the eighth wonder of the world..."**

To see the size of this telescope tube, find a tree or person that is about 5' tall. Use a yard-stick or measuring tape and measure 40' from the tree. Caroline Herschel made the large mirrors for this telescope.

*My Favorite Fun Fact About Comets*

______________________________

______________________________

______________________________

______________________________

*"The comet, a large ball of ice, gas, and rock . . ."* **The Oregonian** August 4, 1995

### At Home

Make a telescope. Homemade telescopes are less expensive and provide exciting night-sky viewing opportunities. In **175 Science Experiments to Amuse and Amaze Your Friends,** author Brenda Walpole describes how to make a simple telescope from a shaving mirror, a small flat mirror, and a magnifying glass. Check resources in your library or local science museum.

An asteroid is one of thousands of small planets between Mars and Jupiter. **The Lucretia Asteroid** is named for Caroline Lucretia Herschel.

The only biography of Caroline Herschel is an excellent juvenile book entitled **Sweeper of the Skies: A Story of the Life of Caroline Herschel, Astronomer**. The author is Frances Lowry Higgins.

Mary Anning, a 19th century paleontologist, examines the bones of a dimorphodon.

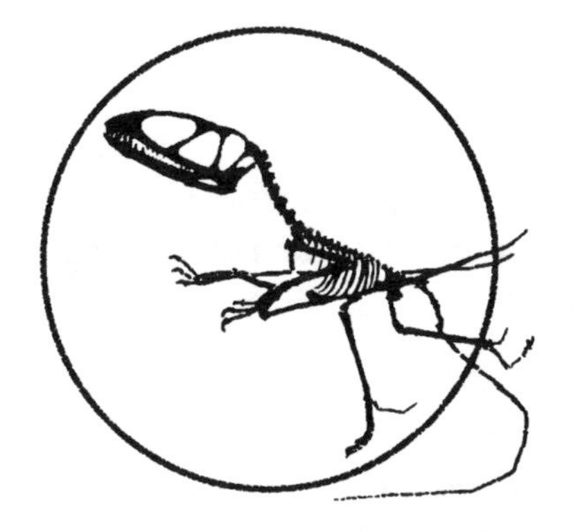

# Discovery Unit No. 9

## Mary Anning
## Dinosaur Paleontology

### PALEONTOLOGY PUZZLE

**Time-line:**

- **1799 - 1847 Mary Anning**
- 1835 - Halley's Comet reappears
- 1839 - An inventor in Scotland builds the world's first bicycle

**Pronunciation guide:**

- Dimorphodon [Die-MOR-foe-dawn]
- Ichthyosaurus [Ik-thee-o-SOAR-us]
- Paleontologist [Pay-lee-on-TAW-loe-gist]
- Plesiosaurus [Plee-zee-o-SOAR-us]
- Pterosaurs [TAIR-o-soars]

**Key points:**

☛ Mary Anning's career began when she was a young girl in Lyme Regis, England.

☛ She discovered, excavated, and sold dinosaur skeletons.

☛ From these dinosaur skeletons, Mary Anning and others imagined what these animals must have looked like.

☛ The PALEONTOLOGY Puzzle will help students realize that paleontologists must be receptive to new facts that may contradict earlier ideas.

**Supplies:**

✔ An overhead projector

✔ One blank 8 1/2 x 11 sheet of paper for each student

✔ Transparency showing the skeleton of a dimorphodon (See page 54.)

✔ Copy of dimorphodon skeleton for each student (See page 55.)

✔ *The Scientific Gazette* for each student

✔ Pencil, felt pens, crayons, and scissors

**Steps:**

1. Learn to recognize and pronounce the "difficult" words.
2. Point out Lyme Regis, England, on a map or globe. (See page 56.)
3. Share highlights of Mary Anning's biography.
4. Conduct the PALEONTOLOGY Puzzle. (See instructor's guide, page 53.)
5. Distribute ***The Scientific Gazette.***
6. Assist students in clean-up.
7. Add Mary Anning's name and a memento to the time-line.
8. Enrichment Activity (page 56) is optional.

**For next time:**

- Announce the next scientist.

**Bibliography:**


Alic, Margaret. **Hypatia's Heritage.**

Gordon, Mrs. **The Life and Correspondence of William Buckland**, 1894.

Holden, Raymond. **Famous Fossil Finds: Great Discoveries in Palaeontology.**

Ogilvie, Marilyn. **Women in Science.**

Sattler, Helen Roney. **The Illustrated Dinosaur Dictionary.**

## Biography of MARY ANNING 1799 - 1847

As a little girl, Mary Anning and her father explored the cliffs near their coastal village of Lyme Regis, England. Embedded in these chalk-like cliffs were shells and fossils that Richard Anning and his daughter carefully dug up and sold as souvenirs to tourists.

Among the fossils they collected were vertebrae, or pieces of bone from the spinal column, of ancient reptiles. Mary and her father called these pieces "verterberries."

When Mary was eleven years old, her father died. She continued to explore the cliffs for fossils and decided to make her living by collecting and selling the "verterberries" to scientists and tourists.

### Mary's Amazing Discovery

In 1811, 12-year-old Mary Anning was walking on the beach when she spied "something unusual, something dull white and streaky protruding" (Holden, **Famous Fossil Finds**) at the base of the cliff. There was not much time to waste; the tide was coming in.

Using the special tools she carried with her, she hurried to free the slab of rock containing the white, streaky object from the cliff. The slab was too large for her to move by herself so she ran to find people to assist her.

Once the rock slab was moved to higher ground, Mary chipped and brushed away the soft sedimentary rock; she became the first person to uncover a nearly complete skeleton of an extinct reptile called an ichthyosaurus.

Ichthyosaurus means "fish lizard." This marine reptile ranged from 15 to 30 feet in length.

### Thirteen Years Later

Now 25 years old, Mary Anning discovered an almost complete skeleton of a plesiosaurus. This name means "near lizards." They, like the ichthyosaurus, are not really dinosaurs but marine reptiles that grew 8 to 10 feet in length. Their paddle-like legs propelled them in the water much like marine turtles and on the land much like walruses.

### "Two-Form Teeth" Found

Three years later Anning uncovered a skeleton of a kind of pterosaur called a dimorphodon, meaning "two-form teeth."

***The overhead transparency (page 54) shows the skeleton of a dimorphodon.***

### Mary Anning's Legacy

Before Mary Anning discovered the skeleton of the ichthyosaurus, other scientists thought that animals like this might have existed a long time ago but they had no proof. Mary Anning's discoveries helped to provide that proof.

Technically, Anning was not a scientist since she lacked the formal education. (In the early 1800s in England, girls and women were not encouraged to attend school.) However, her knowledge of fossils and her ability to discover, unearth, and identify them qualify her as a scientist. Some historians call her an archeologist, some a geologist, and others a dinosaur paleontologist. Her knowledge spanned all three fields but "dinosaur paleontologist" seems most appropriate.

At the Fossil Reptile Gallery of the British Museum, visitors can see the dimorphodon and plesiosaurus skeletons that Mary Anning discovered.

## Instructor's Guide:

### The PALEONTOLOGY PUZZLE

### Background Information:

To a paleontologist, a dinosaur skeleton is a guide. Paleontologists realize that their ideas about the appearance of an animal based solely on its skeleton may have to change as they uncover additional information. This exercise is intended to help students understand how paleontologists must be receptive to new facts that may contradict their previous notions.

### Instructions:

1. Distribute the blank sheets, one per student.
2. Show the transparency of the dimorphodon skeleton (page 54).
3. Ask the students to draw what they think a dimorphodon looked like. Like a dinosaur paleontologist, they must use the skeleton as a guide.
4. Distribute sheet showing the light grey dimorphodon skeleton.
5. Instruct students to draw on top of the skeleton their idea of the dimorphodon after each new fact:

   A. **The dimorphodon had a mouthful of large and small teeth. It had a head like a turtle's.**

   Students draw their impression on top of the skull and neck bones of their skeleton.

   B. **Its tail was rat-like in length and appearance.**

   Students add this new information to their skeletons.

   C. **The dimorphodon was a flying reptile whose bat-like wings stretched from its hands to its hind legs.**

   Students add this new information.

   D. **Instruct students to "complete" their dimorphodons.**

6. Have the students compare this last impression with the first one they drew.

**Ask . . .**

*How did the second drawing compare with the freehand drawing you did first?*

*How did you feel knowing that new information might cause you to change your ideas?*

*How did you use your reasoning powers?*

*How did you use your imagination?*

7. Distribute ***The Scientific Gazette***.
8. Assist students in cleaning up.

### Add notes here:

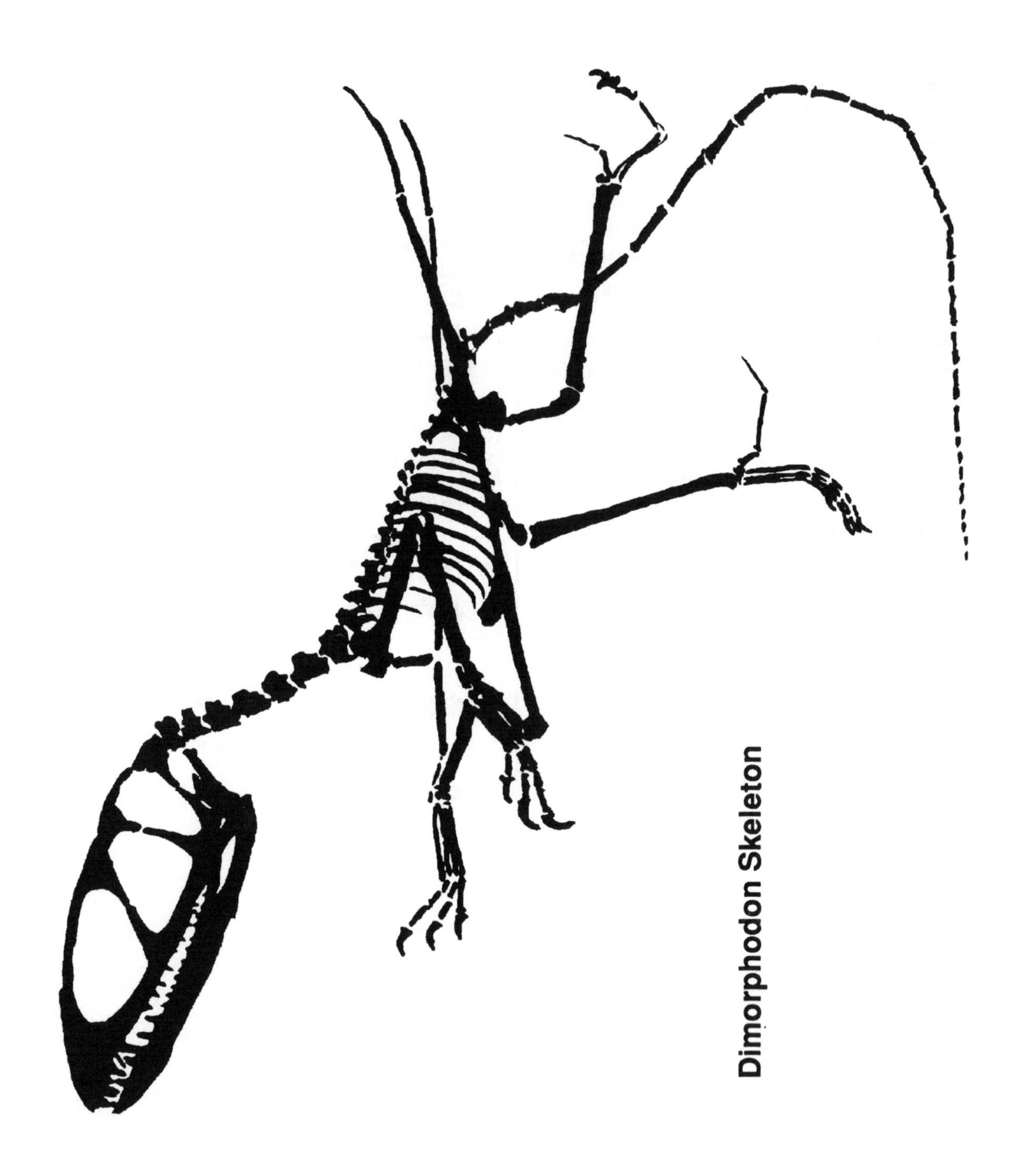

Dimorphodon Skeleton

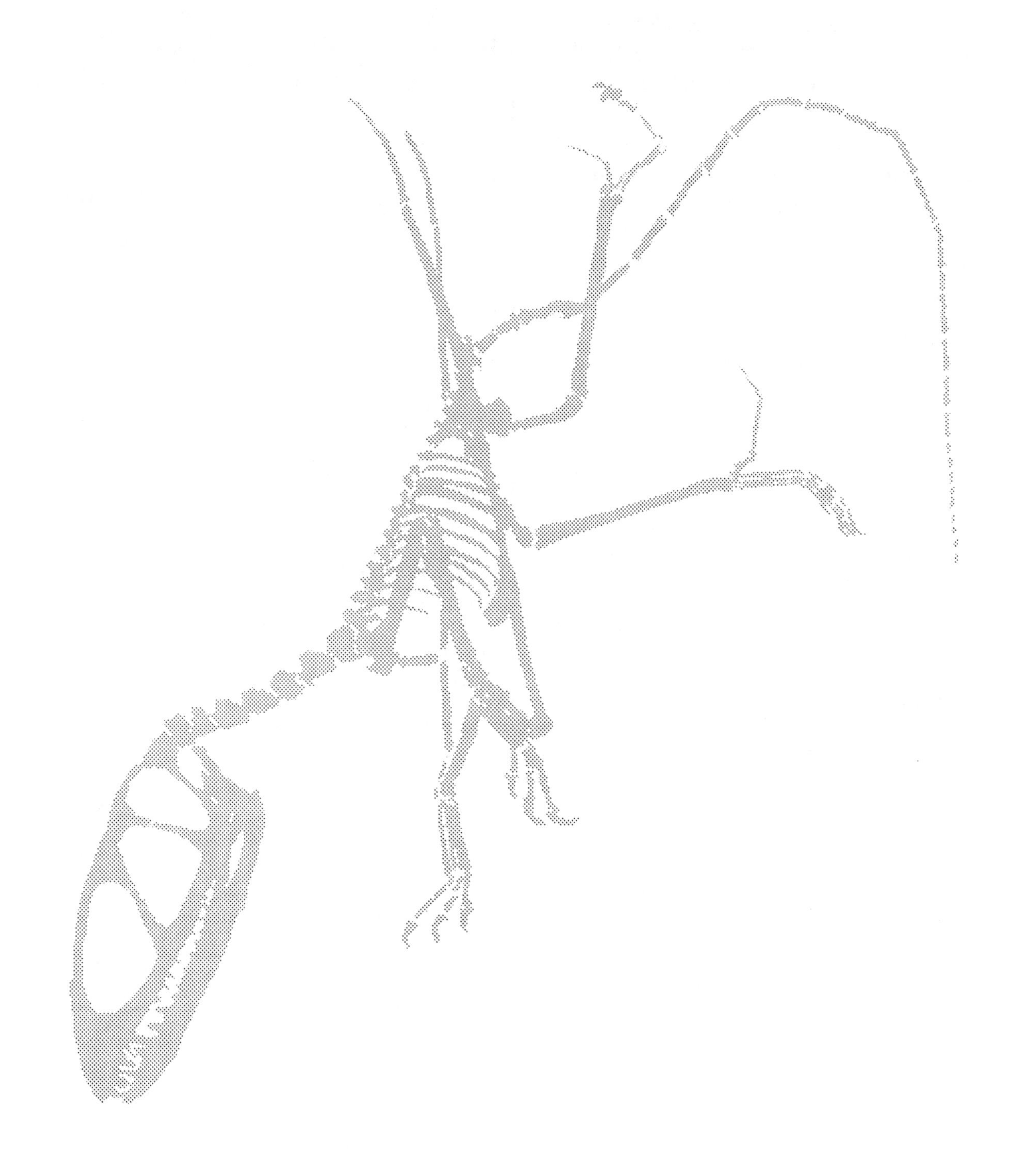

## Enrichment Activity:

[During the enrichment activities, the teacher is not an expert but a co-learner with students.]

The Mesozoic Geologic Era includes the Triassic, Jurassic, and Cretaceous Periods. This era dates back 70 to 225 million years and includes the Age of Reptiles.

Explore this era. Its dinosaurs, birds, mammals, sea creatures, and plant life were varied and exotic. The information gleaned from school, home, and community resources can be compiled and incorporated into other activities:

- trivia game
- spelling bee of Mesozoic terms
- art projects — Mesozoic diorama, dinosaur puppets, etc.
- Mesozoic time-line with illustrations
- "Twenty Questions" — a student thinks of an animal or plant from the Mesozoic Era and other students ask 20 questions (answers must be "yes" or "no") to determine this animal or plant.
- Mesozoic drama

## Add other ideas here:

*Research geology of area around Lyme Regis.*

## Lyme Regis, England:

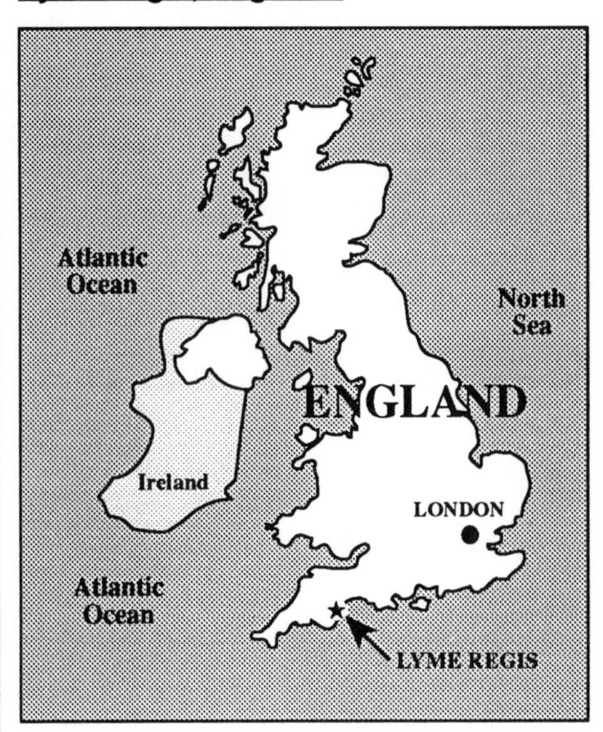


## Other dinosaurs from the Jurassic Period:

If you add muscle and skin to its skeleton, the ichthyosaurus probably looked like this:

A plesiosaurus could have looked like this:

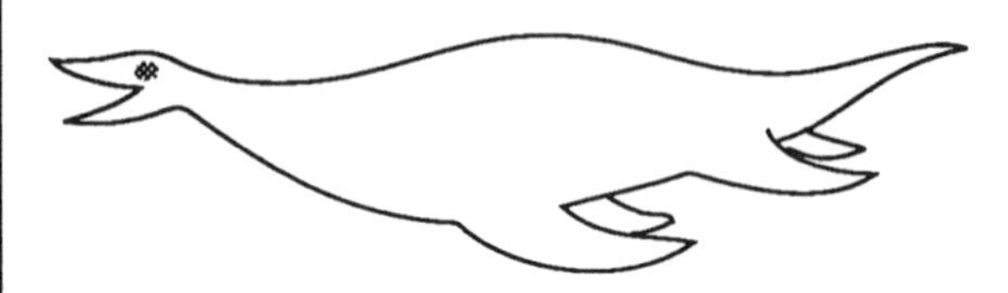

The Scientific Gazette
Dinosaur Paleontology Mary Anning

# Twelve-year-old Girl Discovers Sea Monster Skeleton by Cliff

**Dateline: 1811**

LYME REGIS, England: Mary Anning, daughter of the late Richard Anning, a carpenter of Lyme Regis, was walking on the shore east of Lyme when a white fragment near the base of a cliff caught her eye. She investigated and decided that the fragment was part of a skeleton belonging to a large animal.

The tide forced Anning to run for help. A group of men standing near the timber pier answered her cries. Returning to the site, Anning used her fossil-hunting hammer to loosen the slab of soft rock containing the skeleton. Once free, the rock with the embedded skeleton was carried to a site safe from the tide.

Who knows what the young Mary Anning will discover as she chips and brushes away the sedimentary rock! If it turns out to be the skeleton of a sea monster that once swam in these waters, the town of Lyme Regis and others will praise the twelve-year-old Mary Anning for finding such a creature. Her reputation as a fossil hunter will spread far and wide.

**Dateline 1992:**

Mary Anning's "sea monster" was really a marine reptile called an **ichthyosaurus** (from the Greek word **ichthys** which means **fish** and the Greek word **sauros** which means **lizard**). During her lifetime she found several skeletons of ichthyosaurs, and a **plesiosaurus**, and a **dimorphodon**.

## A Paleontologist's Puzzle

Here is a sketch showing my impression of a dimorphodon:

The word **dinosaur** means "terrible lizard."

## Examining a dimorphodon skeleton

Artist Helen Caroll drew this picture depicting Mary Anning examining the skeleton of a dimorphodon.

A **diomorphodon** was a pterosaur or "winged lizard" with bat-like wings. Pterosaurs were warm-blooded animals who varied in size from that of a hummingbird to a creature with a 50-foot wingspan. Pterosaurs were not dinosaurs.

For her discovery of a new comet, American astronomer Maria Mitchell received a gold medal from the King of Denmark.

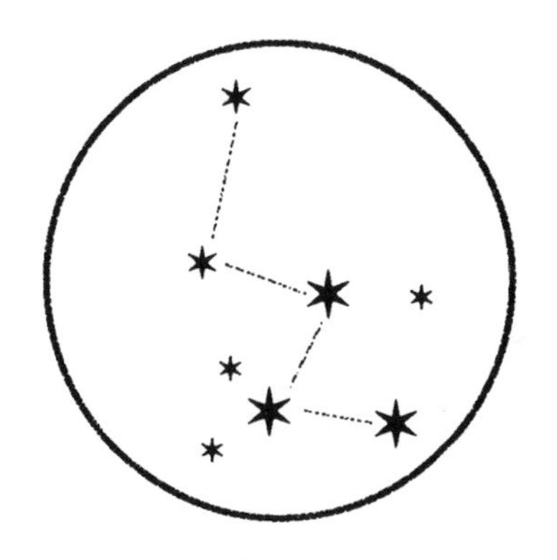

# Discovery Unit No. 10

## Maria Mitchell
## Astronomy

### MAKE YOUR OWN CONSTELLATIONS Project

**Time-line:**

- **1818 - 1889 Maria Mitchell**
- 1830 - Belva Lockwood is the first woman to run for President of the U.S.
- 1883 - Brooklyn Bridge in New York City opens for traffic

**Pronunciation guide:**

- Maria [Ma-RYE-uh]
- asterisms [AS-ter-is-ems]

**Key points:**

- Maria Mitchell was the first woman astronomer in the United States.
- On October 1, 1847, she observed a new comet. This discovery earned her a gold medal from the King of Denmark.
- Regarded as one of the leading astronomers in the U.S. and Europe, Mitchell agreed to become professor of astronomy at the newly-established Vassar College in Poughkeepsie, New York.
- In the MAKE YOUR OWN CONSTELLATIONS Project, students will imitate the tradition of creating and naming constellations.

**Supplies:**

- ✔ Overhead projector
- ✔ Two overhead transparencies of "Boötes." (Originals on pages 63 and 64.)
- ✔ An overhead projector pen (any color)
- ✔ "My Notes" sheets for each student
- ✔ *The Scientific Gazette* for each student

**Steps:**

1. Point out Nantucket Island, Massachusetts.
2. Share highlights of Maria Mitchell's life.
3. Conduct the MAKE YOUR OWN CONSTELLATIONS Project. (See instructor's guide, page 61.)
4. Allow time for students to complete their "My Notes."
5. Share constellations and stories.
6. Assist students in clean-up.
7. Distribute ***The Scientific Gazette***.
8. Add Maria Mitchell's name and a memento to the time-line.
9. Enrichment Activity (page 62) is optional

**For next time:**

- Announce the next scientist.

**Bibliography:**

Kass-Simon, G., and Patricia Farnes. **Women of Science: Righting the Record**.

Mammana, Dennis. **The Night Sky**.

McPherson, Stephanie Sammartino. **Rooftop Astronomer**.

Ogilvie, Marilyn Bailey. **Women in Science**.

Rey, H. A. **The Stars: A New Way to See Them.**

## Biography of MARIA MITCHELL 1818 - 1889

Mitchell Crater on the moon is named for Maria Mitchell, the first woman astronomer in the United States, who discovered a comet, received a medal from the King of Denmark, and taught astronomy at Vassar College for 23 years.

### Her Childhood

Maria's childhood was not typical of other girls. Her mother worked at two libraries so she could read all the books in both. Her father, William Mitchell, believed girls should be educated as well as boys.

Astronomy was William Mitchell's hobby. He created a model of the solar system in the attic and set up his telescope on the rooftop. His stellar observations checked the accuracy of the chronometers, or timepieces, of the local whalers. Maria shared his enthusiasm for astronomy and became his assistant.

### Opens School

Maria not only followed her father into astronomy but into teaching. His free school included field trips where students collected seashells and flowers. When she was 17 years old, Maria opened her own school. She charged 3 cents a day. Like her father, Maria stressed field trips; students arrived early to watch for birds or stayed late to study the stars. A year later Maria became the librarian at the Nantucket's Atheneum Library.

### The Comet

On October 1, 1847, Mitchell observed a new comet. The King of Denmark had offered a gold medal to the first person who found a "telescopic" comet — one not visible to the naked eye. A year after the siting, Maria received the medal whose Latin inscription meant, "not in vain do we watch the setting and rising of the stars."

Mitchell's siting of the comet made her famous. She became the first woman elected to the American Academy of Arts and Sciences and the American Association for the Advancement of Science.

### World Traveler

Mitchell traveled to New York City and Washington, D.C. for scientific meetings. A visit to England in 1856 included a trip to Greenwich Observatory where she stood at the point zero longitude. In Rome she was disappointed to learn that women were not allowed inside the Vatican Observatory. This famous astronomer finally obtained permission to enter but was not allowed to stay after dark!

### Vassar College

Beginning in 1865 Mitchell taught astronomy and directed the observatory at the newly-established Vassar College in New York. A devoted teacher and feminist, she convinced her students that they could excel at astronomy and mathematics.

### Honors

Maria Mitchell received three honorary doctorates. A public school in Denver, Colorado, bears her name as does a crater on the moon. Her name also appears on the front of the Boston Public Library. The Maria Mitchell Association of Nantucket honors the nation's first woman astronomer who began as her father's assistant and became one of the leading astronomers in the U.S. and Europe.

## Instructor's Guide:

### The MAKE YOUR OWN CONSTELLATIONS Project

#### Background Information:

Prior to international agreement, the shapes and names of constellations varied from country to country. What we in the U.S. called the Big Dipper was seen by the Greeks as the long tail of a bear and by the Europeans as a plow. This variety occurred because constellations are really "dot-to-dot" creations whose shapes and stories reflect the culture from which they originate.

The imaginary lines connecting stars are ***asterisms***. Asterisms can be drawn within a constellation (The Big Dipper is really an asterism within the ***Ursa Major*** [Great Bear] constellation) or can include stars from several constellations. The MAKE YOUR OWN CONSTELLATIONS Project allows students to imitate this ancient creative tradition. (A secret: The constellations featured in "My Notes" Pages 1 and 2 are Pegasus the Winged Horse and Orion the Hunter respectively.

#### Instructions:

1. Prepare the overhead projector. Have the two transparencies ready to show. Also have the overhead projector pen handy.

> **Explain . . .**
> *Thousands of years ago, storytellers traveled from village to village. At night they told stories of dragons, maidens in distress, kings, queens, and fierce animals. The night sky was like a screen across which the storyteller created shapes and characters by connecting stars with imaginary lines — like dot-to-dot pages in coloring books. We call these imaginary lines **asterisms** and the big pictures, constellations.*

> **Ask . . .**
> *Imagine you are a storyteller, what pictures do you see in this cluster of stars?*

2. Show the Star Cluster Transparency.
3. Invite students to share what pictures they see in the cluster. Perhaps some may wish to use the pen to draw their asterisms for the class.

> **Explain . . .**
> *The ancient Greeks looked at this cluster of stars, drew these asterisms, and created this constellation:*

4. Place the Boötes Constellation Transparency over the Star Cluster Transparency.

> **Ask . . .**
> *Are you surprised? How does their constellation compare with yours?*

5. Distribute "My Notes" sheets.

> **Explain . . .**
> *Here's another opportunity to draw asterisms and create constellations.*

6. Allow time for students to complete these sheets.
7. Share constellations and their stories.
8. Assist students in clean-up.

## Enrichment Activity:

*". . . we especially need imagination in science. It is not all mathematics, not all logic, but is somewhat beauty and poetry."*

**— Maria Mitchell, U.S. astronomer**

Explore and compare the stories behind the constellations. Examples include:

- **Boötes** has usually been seen as a man; to some Greeks, a wolf; and to the Hebrews, a barking dog.
- Since preclassical times, **Pegasus** has been identified as a winged horse whose action-packed Greek legend includes the constellations of the hero **Perseus**, King **Cepheus**, Queen **Cassiopeia**, their daughter **Andromeda**, and **Cetus**, the sea monster.
- To the Egyptians, **Orion** marked the resting place of their god Osiris; and, to the Greeks, he was the handsomest of men killed by a scorpion.
- The constellation **Ursa Major** (Great Bear) contains the **Big Dipper**, the best known group of stars in the Northern Hemisphere. The two stars at the tip of the bowl are called the pointers. These help locate the North Star (**Polaris**). The North Star is positioned at the end of the **Little Dipper** which pours its contents into the bowl of the Big Dipper.

◆ ◆ ◆

## Use for additional ideas:

## A Cluster of Stars

## Copy onto transparency

### Boötes constellation

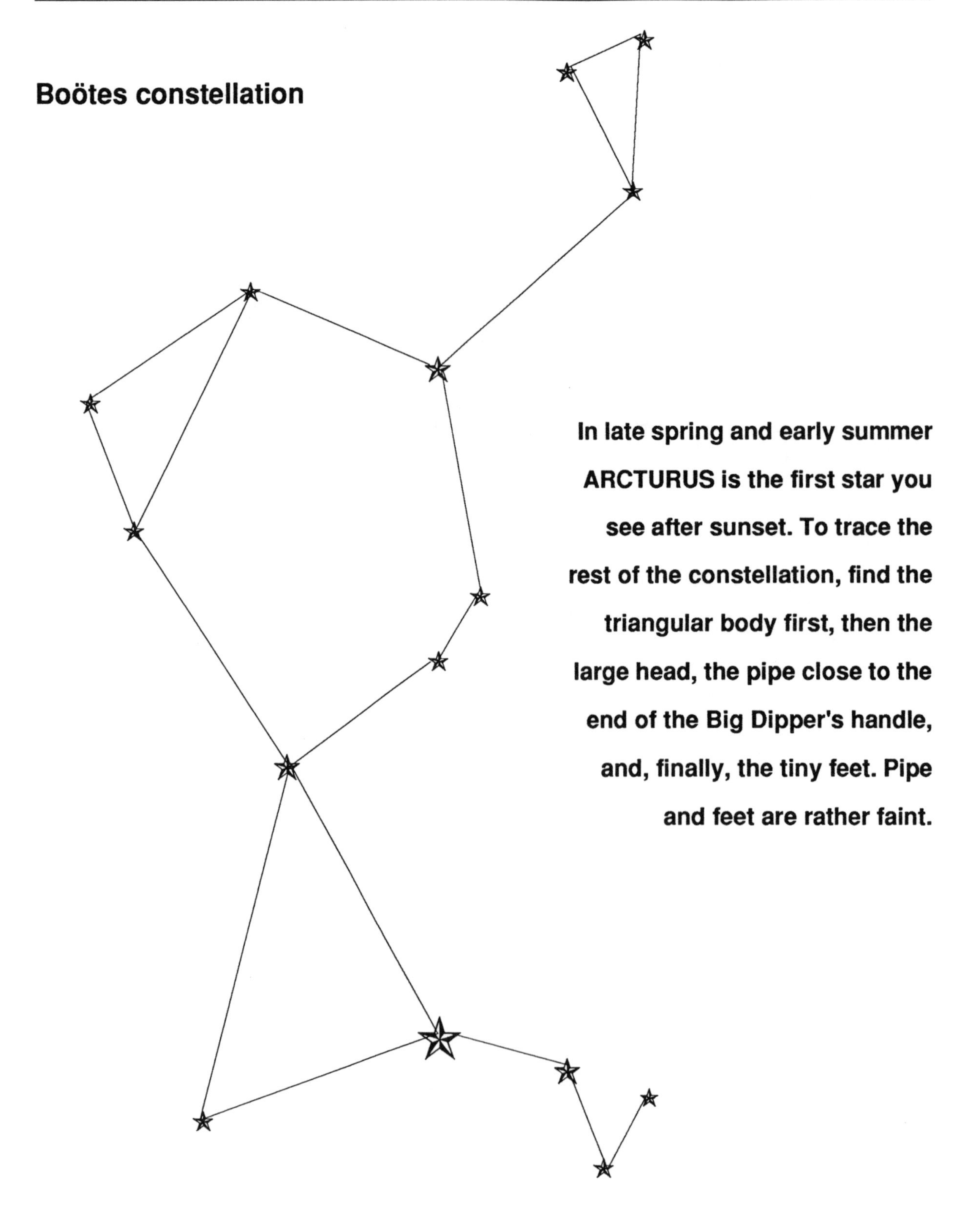

In late spring and early summer ARCTURUS is the first star you see after sunset. To trace the rest of the constellation, find the triangular body first, then the large head, the pipe close to the end of the Big Dipper's handle, and, finally, the tiny feet. Pipe and feet are rather faint.

**Boötes (The Herdsman) looks like a man sitting and smoking a pipe. Its main star, orange-colored ARCTURUS, is 24 times bigger than our sun.**

# My Notes

by ______________________________, Scientist

MAKE YOUR OWN CONSTELLATION Project

My Constellation, Page 1

## My Story

______________________________

______________________________

______________________________

______________________________

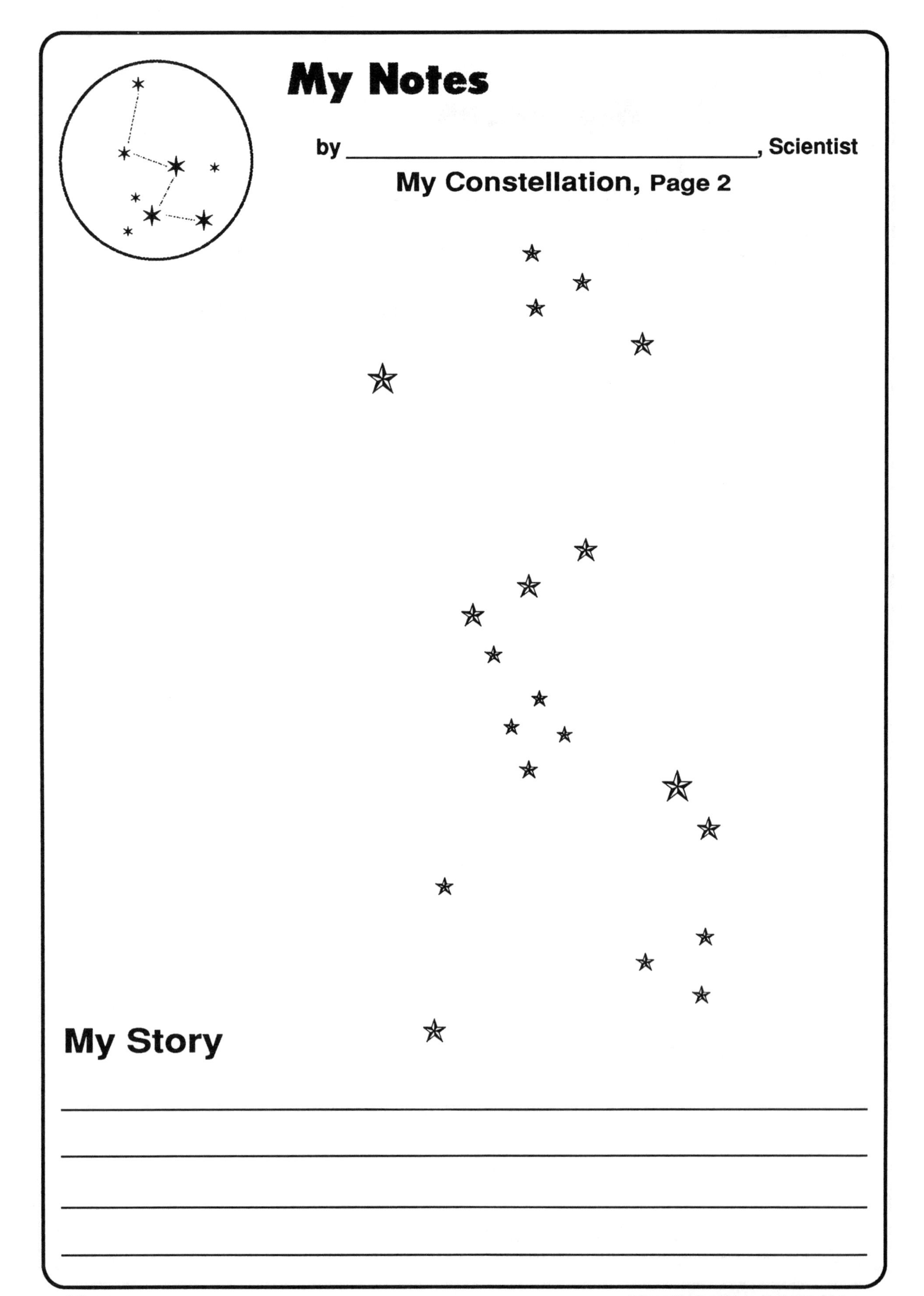
My Notes
by ____________________, Scientist
My Constellation, Page 2
My Story

# The Scientific Gazette

*"It is lifetime added to lifetime that leads to the discovery of law."*

*—Maria Mitchell*

Mark (✓) these statements true or false.

☆ Maria Mitchell was the first woman astronomer in the U.S. T ❒ F ❒

☆ When she was 17, Maria opened her own school. She charged 3¢ a day. T ❒ F ❒

☆ On October 1, 1847, Maria observed a telescopic comet. T ❒ F ❒

☆ For 23 years Maria Mitchell taught astronomy at Vassar College. T ❒ F ❒

☆ A crater on the moon is named for Maria Mitchell. T ❒ F ❒

## Data about the Sun

Maria Mitchell enjoyed learning about stars including our solar system's one star — the sun. She observed several solar eclipses, studied sunspots, and collected data — or facts — about the sun. Did you know? . . .

- The sun is 93 million miles away from earth.
- At its core, the sun's temperature is 25 million degrees Fahrenheit.
- The sun's diameter is approximately 864,000 miles. The earth's diameter is approximately 8,000 miles.
- The sun is all gas but weighs two octillion tons. An octillion is: 1,000,000,000,000,000,000,000,000,000, and a ton is 2,000 pounds.
- Storms on the sun are called sunspots. They may last for days or months and measure 500 to 50,000 miles wide. Sunspots may affect our weather and interfere with radio transmissions.

## YEARLY PARTY HELD AT BASE OF TELESCOPE

Professor Maria Mitchell taught at Vassar for 23 years. Each year she and her students enjoyed a party in the observatory at the base of the telescope. Students spread "sun-shaped balls of butter on rolls that looked like crescent moons." (McPherson, **Rooftop Astronomer**)

Here's a recipe for crescent-moon rolls:

1 package yeast
1 1/2 cups warm water
1 Tablespoon sugar
1/2 teaspoon salt
4 cups flour

In a large bowl mix together yeast and warm water. Add the sugar and salt. Stir in flour until the dough is too stiff to stir. Knead dough until smooth — about 5 minutes. Divide into portions about the size of tennis balls, shape into crescents, and bake at 450 degrees 15 minutes. Serve with butter, peanut butter, jam, or honey.

### At Home

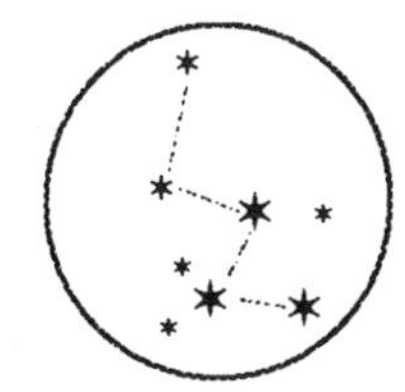

★ Like Maria Mitchell and her father, create a model of the solar system.

★ Visit your library to explore books on stars and space. **Rooftop Astronomer** by Stephanie Sammartino McPherson is a juvenile biography of Maria Mitchell. **The Night Sky** by Dennis Mammana provides sky maps of constellations, astronomy experiments, calendars of upcoming solar and lunar eclipses and meteor showers, and an excellent glossary.

(All statements in the true/false section are true.)

Dr. Sonya Kovalevskaya, a 19th century Russian mathematician, was called the "Princess of Science."

# Discovery Unit No. 11

## Dr. Sonya Kovalevskaya
## Mathematics

### PATTERN IN A PAPER SNOWFLAKE Activity

**Time-line:**

- **1850 - 1891 Dr. Sonya Krukovsky Kovalevskaya**
- 1866 - Alfred Nobel invents dynamite
- 1883 - First skyscraper is built in Chicago

**Pronunciation guide:**

- Krukovsky [Crew-COFF-ski]
- Kovalevskaya [Coe-vah-LEFF-sky-yuh]
- Ostrogradsky [Oss-tro-GRAD-ski]

**Key points:**

☛ Dr. Sonya Kovalevskaya was born and raised in Russia.

☛ As a young girl Sonya spent hours studying notes from a mathematics lecture pasted on her bedroom wall.

☛ By the time Dr. Kovalevskaya was 33 years old, she was such a famous mathematician in Europe that people called her the "Princess of Science."

☛ Patterns exist in both mathematics and nature. In the PATTERN IN A PAPER SNOWFLAKE Activity students will see a pattern unfold before their eyes.

**Supplies:**

✔ An overhead of the Ostrogradsky-Hermite formula (page 73)

✔ 3 to 4 copies of star template (page 72)

✔ Blank sheets of paper — at least one per student

✔ A pair of scissors for each student

✔ Hole punches

✔ "My Notes" sheet for each student

✔ *The Scientific Gazette* for each student

**Steps:**

1. Point out Russia and Sweden on a map.
2. Share highlights of Dr. Kovalevskaya's life. Show transparency of formula during highlights.
3. Distribute supplies and "My Notes."
4. Conduct the PATTERN IN A PAPER SNOWFLAKE Activity. (See instructor's guide, page 71.)
5. Discuss other patterns students have observed.
6. Distribute *The Scientific Gazette.*
7. Add Dr. Sonya Kovalevskaya's name and a memento to the time-line.

**For next time:**

- Announce the next scientist.

**Bibliography:**

Kovalevskaya, Sonya. **Her Recollections.**

Leffler, Anna Carlotta. **Sonya Kovalevsky.**

Perl, Teri. **Math Equals.**

## Biography of DR. SONYA KRUKOVSKY KOVALEVSKAYA 1850 - 1891

Sonya Krukovsky grew up feeling she was the least loved of the three children in the family. Her sister was six years older than she, and her brother was three years younger.

### Instead of Wallpaper

When Sonya was a young girl growing up in Russia, the family moved into a large house — almost a castle — in the country. They remodeled the large dwelling but misfigured the amount of wallpaper needed for Sonya's room. Her parents covered the bare spot with notes from a mathematics lecture by Professor Ostrogradsky. Sonya spent hours staring at these pages trying to make sense of the mysterious numbers, letters and squiggly lines. This is an example of one of Ostrogradsky's formulas:

***The overhead transparency shows the Ostrogradsky-Hermite formula being used to solve a problem.***

Sonya's love of mathematics did not originate with her mathematics teacher or her strict English governess but with her fun-loving, eccentric Uncle Peter. From him Sonya acquired a "reverence of mathematics."

### Universities Closed to Women

When Sonya was 17 and wanting to attend college, there was no university in Russia that accepted women students. Four years earlier, in 1863, the Russian government had prohibited higher education to women. How was Sonya to get the education she needed and wanted?

Through marriage! This was a desperate solution, but many Russian women were resorting to it in order to obtain a travel visa to study in another country. (Single young women from respectable families were not free to travel.)

### To Germany

Sonya Krukovsky married Vladimir Kovalevsky and left Russia to study higher mathematics in Germany. In 1874 Sonya Kovalevskaya received her doctorate from the University of Gottingen.

### The Princess of Science

By the time she was 33 years old, Dr. Kovalevskaya was so famous as a mathematician that she was called the "Princess of Science." In November 1883, she arrived in Stockholm to begin a distinguished teaching career at the newly-established University of Stockholm.

### Other Interests

In addition to teaching mathematics and winning a prestigious prize granted by the French Academy of Science (1888), Dr. Kovalevskaya studied the rings around the planet Saturn, wrote poetry in French and a novel in Russian, and sewed for her daughter Fouzi.

Unfortunately, at the young age of 41, Dr. Sonya Kovalevskaya, the first woman lecturer in Sweden, died of pneumonia.

## Instructor's Guide:

### PATTERN IN A PAPER SNOWFLAKE

### Background Information:

Dr. Kovalevskaya found patterns intriguing. To discern a pattern, a mathematician becomes a detective. The numbers given are the clues and the mathematician must detect the pattern.

### Instructions:

1. On a chalkboard write the following numbers:

   2, 4, 6, 8, 10, ___, ___, ___, . . . ?

   10, 9, 8, 7, ___, ___, ___, . . . ?

   1, 6, 5, 10, 9, 14, 13, 18, 17, 22, 21, ___, ___, . . . ?

> **Explain . . .**
>
> *Dr. Kovalevskaya enjoyed working with patterns in mathematics.*

2. Ask students to identify the pattern in each of the examples written on the chalkboard.

   [answer to third pattern is +5, -1]

> **Explain . . .**
>
> *The dots after the last number mean that the pattern could go on forever. Some patterns are infinite and some are not.*
>
> *Sometimes the pattern is easy to detect. At other times the mathematician might have to collect several clues before detecting the pattern. In the PATTERN IN A PAPER SNOWFLAKE Activity we will collect clues together and try to detect a pattern between the number of folds in a paper snowflake and the subsequent number of holes.*

3. Distribute supplies and "My Notes."
4. Instruct students to trace and cut out the six-pointed star.
5. Lead students through these instructions:
   - Fold "snowflake" in half and punch a hole near the center point.

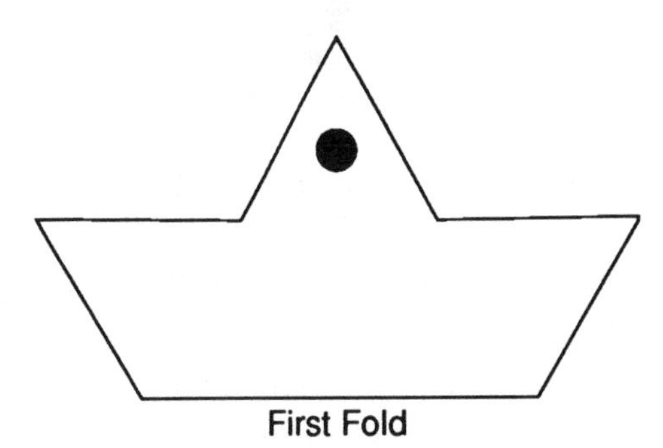

First Fold

   - Open snowflake and on the "My Notes" sheet record the number of holes. (Should be 2) Refold the snowflake like it was folded when you cut the first hole.
   - Fold the snowflake in half again and punch a hole in the designated spot.

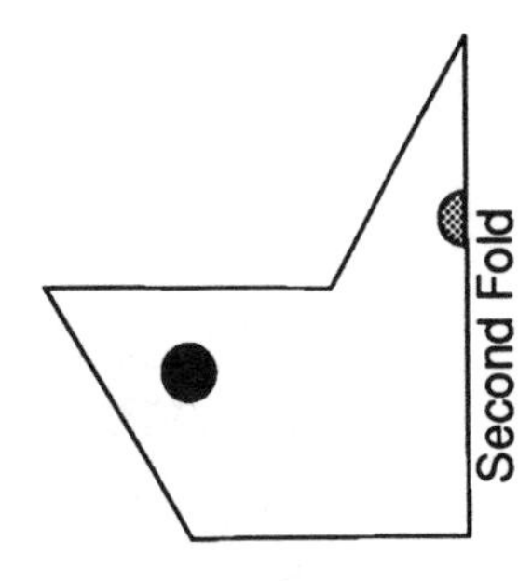


   - Before opening the snowflake, take a guess at how many holes you will have. Open; record number (should be 6) on "My Notes."
   - Refold; fold in half again; punch a third hole.

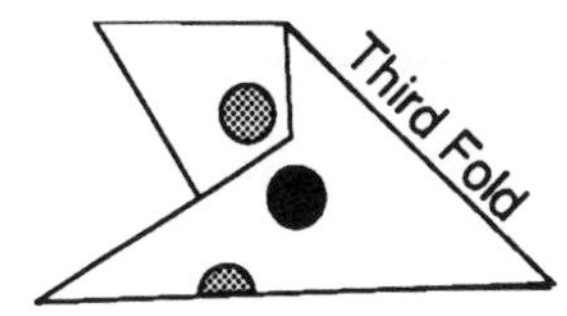


   - Guess the total number of holes you will find when you unfold the snowflake. Open; record number (should be 14) on "My Notes."

- Refold; fold in half one last time; punch a fourth hole.

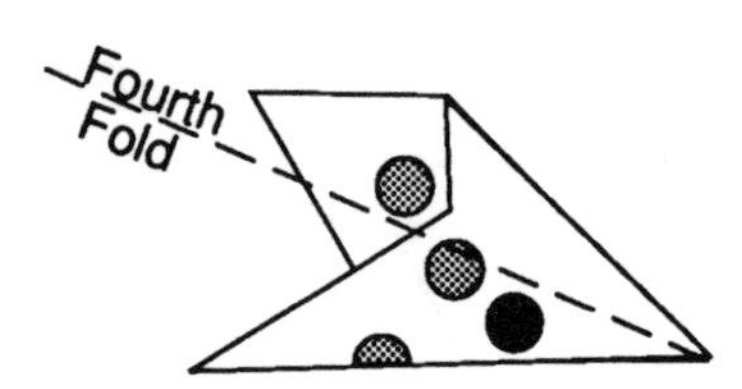


- Guess the total number of holes you will find when you unfold the snowflake. Open; record number (should be 30) on "My Notes."

6. Ask if anyone has identified the pattern yet. Once the pattern is detected, ask students to complete their "My Notes" sheet.
7. Assist students in clean-up.

**Answers (for the instructor):**

| fold | total holes | pattern |
|---|---|---|
| 1 | 2 | |
| 2 | 6 | (2 x 2) + 2 |
| 3 | 14 | (2 x 6) + 2 |
| 4 | 30 | (2 x 14) + 2 |
| *5* | *62* | *(2 x 30) + 2* |
| *6* | *126* | *(2 x 62) + 2* |
| *7* | *254* | *(2 x 126) + 2* |
| *8* | *510* | *(2 x 254) + 2* |
| *9* | *1022* | *(2 x 510) + 2* |
| *10* | *2046* | *(2 x 1022) + 2* |

**Use this six-pointed star as a template for the paper snowflake.**

**Let each student trace one on a sheet of paper.**

The Ostrogradskii-Hermite formula:

$$\int \frac{\phi(x)}{f(x)}dx = \frac{\omega(x)}{d(x)} + \int \frac{w_1(x)}{D_1(x)}dx$$

$$\int \frac{dx}{(x^3+1)^2} = \frac{ax^2+\beta x+\gamma}{x^3+1} + \int \frac{\delta x^2+\varepsilon x+\eta}{x^3+1}dx$$

$$\frac{1}{(x^3+1)^2} = \frac{(2ax+\beta)(x^3+1)-3x^2(ax^2+\beta x+y)}{(x^3+1)^2} + \frac{\delta x^2+\varepsilon x+\eta}{x^3+1}$$

$$1=(2ax+\beta)(x^3+1)-3x^2(ax^2+\beta x+\gamma)+(\delta x^2+\varepsilon x+\eta)(x^3+1)$$

$$\varepsilon - a = 0; \eta - 2\beta = 0; 2a+\varepsilon = 0; \beta + \eta = 1$$

$$a=\gamma=\delta=\varepsilon=0; \beta=\frac{1}{3}; \eta=\frac{2}{3}$$

$$\int \frac{dx}{(x^3+1)^2} = \frac{x}{3(x^3+1)} + \frac{2}{3}\int \frac{dx}{x^3+1}$$

$$\frac{1}{x^3+1} = \frac{A}{x+1} + \frac{Mx+N}{x^2-x+1}$$

$$1 = A(x^2-x+1)+(Mx+N)x+1$$

$$M=-\frac{1}{3}; N=\frac{2}{3}$$

$$\frac{1}{x^3+1} = \frac{1}{3(x+1)} - \frac{x-2}{3(x^2-x+1)}$$

$$\int \frac{dx}{x^3=1} = \frac{1}{3}\int \frac{dx}{x+1} - \frac{1}{3}\int \frac{x-2}{x^2-x+1}dx =$$

$$= \frac{1}{3}\log(x+1) - \frac{1}{6}\log(x^2-x+1) + \frac{1}{\sqrt{3}} arc\ \tan\frac{2x-1}{\sqrt{3}} + C$$

$$\int \frac{dx}{(x^3+1)^2} = \frac{x}{3(x^3+1)} + \log(x+1) - \frac{1}{9}\log(x^2-x+1)$$

$$+ \frac{2}{3\sqrt{3}} arc\ \tan\frac{2x-1}{\sqrt{3}} + C$$

# My Notes

by ______________________________, Scientist

PATTERN IN A PAPER SNOWFLAKE Activity

The question we are going to answer is: ______________________________

| Number of Folds | Number of Holes |
|---|---|
| 1 | |
| 2 | |
| 3 | |
| 4 | |
| 5 | |
| 6 | |
| 7 | |
| 8 | |
| 9 | |
| 10 | |

What is the pattern? ______________________________

# The Scientific Gazette



## A Decorating Tip from Russia?

$$a_k = \frac{1}{\pi}\int_0^{2\pi} f(x)\cos(kx)\,dx$$

$$= \frac{1}{\pi}\int_0^{2\pi} x^2\cos(kx)\,dx = \frac{1}{\pi}\int_0^{2\pi} \frac{u^2}{k^2}\cos u\,\frac{du}{k}$$

$u = kx$, $du = k\,dx$

$$= \frac{1}{\pi k^3}\Big[2(kx)\cos(kx) + ((kx)^2 - 2)\sin(kx)\Big]_0^{2\pi} = \frac{4}{k^2}$$

This is what some of the wallpaper may have looked like in Sonya Krukovsky's childhood home. When her parents remodeled their country home in Russia, someone misfigured how much wallpaper was needed for Sonya's room. To solve the problem of the bare spots, pages from a mathematics lecture were glued onto the unpapered wall.

"What could these lines and numbers mean?" Sonya wondered when she went to bed. For hours she stared at the assorted pages trying to make sense of the mysterious drawings.

Who could have imagined that twenty years later that little girl would be such a famous mathematician in Europe that people called her the Princess of Science?

Dr. Kovalevskaya loved mathematics and believed that mathematicians use their intelligence as well as their imagination.

---

Patterns exist in mathematics, nature, and art. I have noticed patterns in: ____________

________________________________

________________________________

________________________________

________________________________

________________________________

## Pennies in a Pattern

You and a friend are playing miniature golf and doing your homework at the same time. Your assignment is to begin with a penny and double the amount every time you putt the ball into a hole. There are 18 holes on the miniature golf course.

This is your homework sheet:

**Fill in the missing amounts:**

Start with 1¢

after the 1st hole you have ________,
after the 2nd hole you have ________,
after the 3rd hole you have ________,
after the 4th hole you have ________,
after the 5th hole you have ________,
after the 6th hole you have ________,
after the 7th hole you have ________,
after the 8th hole you have ________,
after the 9th hole you have ________,
after the 10th hole you have ________,
after the 11th hole you have ________,
after the 12th hole you have ________,
after the 13th hole you have ________,
after the 14th hole you have ________,
after the 15th hole you have ________,
after the 16th hole you have ________,
after the 17th hole you have ________,

How many pennies after the 18th hole?

__________

How many dollars is this? ____________

Dr. Florence Bascom, first woman geologist in the United States, taught at Bryn Mawr College during the school year and mapped land formations for the United States Geological Survey during the summer.

# Discovery Unit No. 12

## Dr. Florence Bascom
## Geology

### VOLCANO IN THE CLASSROOM Demonstration

**Time-line:**

- **1862 - 1945 Dr. Florence Bascom**
- 1876 - Alexander Graham Bell invents the telephone
- 1938 - Ballpoint pen is invented

**Pronunciation guide:**

- Bascom (BASS-come)
- igneous (IG-knee-us)

**Key points:**

- ☛ Dr. Florence Bascom was the first woman geologist in the United States.
- ☛ A geologist studies rocks in order to learn the history of the earth.
- ☛ **Igneous** rocks harden from a molten state, such as lava from an erupting volcano.
- ☛ The VOLCANO IN THE CLASSROOM Demonstration will illustrate how volcanoes have shaped our landforms. The Volcano Cards will help students see the worldwide distribution of volcanoes.

**Supplies:**

- ✔ One 8 oz. jar
- ✔ 1/2 cup white distilled vinegar
- ✔ Several drops of red food coloring
- ✔ One Tablespoon baking soda
- ✔ One fairly deep dinner plate
- ✔ Packet of Volcano Cards and masking tape (See pages 81-84.)
- ✔ Political or topographical map
- ✔ *The Scientific Gazette* for each student

**Steps:**

1. Point out Massachusetts and Pennsylvania.
2. Share highlights of Dr. Bascom's life.
3. Conduct the VOLCANO IN THE CLASSROOM Demonstration.
4. Assist students in clean-up.
5. Divide class into groups of 3 or 4 students.
6. Distribute Volcano Cards and locate volcanoes. Share observations.
7. Distribute ***The Scientific Gazette***.
8. Add Florence Bascom's name and a memento to the time-line.

**For next time:**

- Announce the next scientist.

**Bibliography:**


Decker, Robert W. and Barbara B. **Mountains of Fire: The Nature of Volcanoes.**

James, Edward T., Editor. **Notable American Women: A Biographical Dictionary, Vol. I.**

Lambert, David, and the Diagram Group. **The Field Guide to Geology.**

Ogilvie, Marilyn Bailey. **Women in Science.**

Kass-Simon, G., and Patricia Farnes. **Women of Science: Righting the Record.**

## Biography of
## DR. FLORENCE BASCOM
## 1862 - 1945

Florence Bascom traced her mother's ancestry to Miles Standish of ***The Mayflower***. Her father's ancestors came to Massachusetts about a decade later — in 1634.

Florence was born in Massachusetts in 1862. Her mother, Emma Bascom, was a feminist, a former schoolteacher, and a charter member of the Association for the Advancement of Women. John Bascom, Florence's father, believed in women's suffrage and equal education. When Florence was 12 years old, John Bascom became the president of the University of Wisconsin, and the family left Massachusetts to move west to Wisconsin.

### College Degrees

At age 16, Florence enrolled at the University of Wisconsin. The year was 1878, and women had been attending this university for only 6 years. There were special rules, such as men and women students could not use the library at the same time.

In six years Florence earned three bachelor degrees (the first and second in Arts and Letters, and the third in Science). She remained at the university with geology becoming her favorite subject. In 1887 she received a master's degree in geology.

Geology is a "very young science dealing with old rocks." Geologists study rocks to learn the history of the earth. This is geological history — not political history in which you learn the names of kings and queens and the dates of famous inventions. Political history goes back thousands of years while geological history includes three billion years.

### Earns Ph.D.

After teaching for two years, Florence Bascom enrolled at Johns Hopkins in Baltimore, Maryland. In 1893 she was awarded her Ph.D. and became the first woman to receive a doctorate from Johns Hopkins.

### First Woman Geologist

Dr. Florence Bascom became the first woman geologist in the United States. She joined the science department at Bryn Mawr College in Pennsylvania and remained on the faculty for 33 years. Despite opposition, she established the geology department. A popular teacher, her classes at this women's college were well attended. During the summer she traveled on horseback, or with horse and buggy, through Pennsylvania, Maryland, and New Jersey mapping land formations for the United States Geological Survey, a federal agency that prepares maps.

### Her Legacy

Through her enthusiasm and encouragement, other women entered the field of geology. They taught in universities and worked for the United States Geological Survey. By the 20th century, women geologists were employed by state surveys, museums, businesses, and oil companies. Dr. Florence Bascom paved the way for their entry into this "very young science dealing with old rocks."

## Instructor's Guide

### The VOLCANO IN THE CLASSROOM Experiment

### Background Information:

Dr. Florence Bascom studied rocks to learn the history of the earth. Rocks are nature's building blocks. This means that all landforms, e.g., mountains, valleys, river beds, are made of rock. Basically, there are three kinds, or classes, of rocks. One class is **igneous** (the other two are sedimentary and metamorphic). Igneous rocks are formed from a molten state, such as lava that erupts from a volcano. Dr. Bascom studied landforms made from igneous rocks. The VOLCANO IN THE CLASSROOM Demonstration will show how some volcanic eruptions create landforms.

### Instructions:

1. Set up the experiment:
   - Place the 8 oz. jar on the fairly deep dinner plate
   - Pour 1/2 cup vinegar into the jar
   - Add 3 drops of red food coloring
2. Ask the students to imagine that the reddish vinegar is magma or rock that is so hot it is liquid; that the jar is a pipe through which the magma travels; that the mouth of the jar is the volcano vent; and that the dinner plate is the ground around the volcano. (Magma becomes ash, gases, and/or lava when it escapes from the volcano.)
3. Announce that the volcano is about to erupt!
4. Drop the Tablespoon of soda quickly into the vinegar.
5. Observe the volcanic eruption.

**Ask . . .**

*What can this "eruption" tell us about lava?*

[When a volcano erupts, lava flows may collect around the base of the volcano. When the lava cools, igneous rocks are formed and the landscape changes — maybe drastically.]

**Ask . . .**

*Suppose the volcano erupts several times?*

[The lava builds up. Hot lava covers the old lava, or igneous rock, and then cools making more rock. In time, the land around the volcano builds up.

In addition to lava, volcanic eruptions send out ash and gases into the atmosphere.]

6. Assist students in clean-up.
7. Work with VOLCANO Cards.

## VOLCANO CARDS

### Background Information:

Each card features the name of a volcano and its general geographic location. Additional information appears on some cards, although not all historical eruptions are listed. The purpose of attaching the cards to a map is to help students see the worldwide distribution of volcanoes. The Himalayas and Alps contain no volcanoes.

### Instructions:

1. Photocopy and cut cards.
2. Divide the class into groups of 3 or 4 students.
3. Distribute Volcano Cards.

> **Explain . . .**
>
> *Today we are going to see where there are volcanoes in the world. Some of these volcanoes are* ***extinct*** *(not expected to erupt again); some are* ***dormant*** *("sleeping" — not erupting now but probably will in the future); and some are* ***active*** *(have erupted in human history or currently erupting).*

4. Allow sufficient time for students to locate the countries (or states) in which the volcanoes are located and to **attach** their Volcano Cards to the map.
5. Share observations: volcanoes are in the ocean as well as on land; volcanoes are young and old; above and below water; in warm and cold climates, etc.

### Pronunciation Guide:

- Caldera (Call-DARE-ah) — A caldera is a large depression formed when a volcanic eruption is so violent that the summit of the volcano is blown away or collapses.

### Bibliography:

Asimov, Isaac. **How Did We Find Out About Volcanoes?** (Juvenile)

Decker, Robert W. & Barbara B. **Mountains of Fire.**

Harris, Stephen L. **Fire & Ice: The Cascade Volcanoes.**

Milne, Lorus J. & Margery, and The Editors of LIFE. **The Mountains.**

Poynter, Margaret. **Volcanoes: The Fiery Mountains.** (Juvenile)

### Add notes here:

**VOLCANO Cards — Photocopy and cut apart.**

| | |
|---|---|
| Volcano: ACONCAGUA<br>Location: Argentina | Volcano: EL MISTI<br>Location: PERU |
| Volcano: ARENAL<br>Location: COSTA RICA, Central America<br>• Fact: Erupted 1968 and showered the area with volcanic blocks and "bombs" | Volcano: GALAPAGOS SERIES of Underwater Volcanoes<br>Location: Near the GALAPAGOS ISLANDS, west of Ecuador<br>• Fact: These are active volcanoes whose heat and gases support exotic sea life. |
| Volcano: ASAMA<br>Location: JAPAN<br>• Fact: Remains active — First eruption was in 685 A.D. | Volcano: ILOPANGO LAKE (A caldera)<br>Location: EL SALVADOR<br>• Fact: Erupted about 300 A.D. |
| Volcano: BEZYMIANNY<br>Location: KAMCHATKA PENINSULA on the Bering Sea<br>• Fact: Kamchatka Peninsula has 127 volcanoes. | Volcano: IRAZU<br>Location: COSTA RICA, Central America<br>• Fact: Erupted in 1723 |
| Volcano: CERRO NEGRO<br>Location: NICARAGUA, Central America<br>• Fact: Erupting off and on since its birth in 1850 | Volcano: KATMAI<br>Location: ALASKA — Aleutian Peninsula<br>• Fact: Ash from Katmai's June 6, 1912 eruption was 6 feet deep in some locations. |
| Volcano: COTOPAXI<br>Location: ECUADOR, South America<br>• Fact: At 19,344 feet, this is the world's highest volcano. | Volcano: KILAUEA<br>Location: HAWAII — Hawaii Island<br>• Fact: Between 1924 - 1990, Kilauea erupted 41 times. |
| Volcano: EL CHICHON<br>Location: MEXICO<br>• Fact: Erupted March & April 1982 | Volcano: KILIMANJARO<br>Location: TANGANYIKA, Africa<br>• Fact: Located 200 miles from the equator |

**VOLCANO Cards — Photocopy and cut apart.**

Volcano: KRAKATAU ISLAND
Location: INDONESIA
- Fact: Krakatau's August 27, 1883 eruption was the largest volcanic eruption in human history. It was heard 3,000 miles away, created 120' high waves, and spread volcanic dust around the world.

Volcano: MAUNA LOA
Location: HAWAII — Hawaii Island
- Fact: Mauna Loa is about a million years old.

Volcano: MAYON
Location: PHILIPPINES
- Fact: Its last eruption was February 1993.

Volcano: LA SOUFRIERE
Location: GUADELOUPE ISLAND in the Caribbean Sea

Volcano: MIHARA
Location: JAPAN

Volcano: LAKE NYOS
Location: CAMEROON, Africa
- Fact: A cloud of carbon dioxide gas "erupted" from the lake on August 21, 1986. The gas came from a volcano at the bottom of the lake.

Volcano: LAKI
Location: ICELAND
- Fact: Beginning in 1783, this volcano erupted for two years.

Volcano: MONT PELEE
Location: MARTINIQUE ISLAND in the Caribbean Sea
- Fact: Its eruption on May 8, 1902 "sounded like thousands of cannon," wrote Purser Thompson from the Steamship *Roraima.*

Volcano: LOIHI
Location: HAWAII — near Hawaii Island
- Fact: Loihi is an underwater volcano that is only 1,000 years old.

Volcano: MOUNT ADAMS
Location: State of WASHINGTON, USA
- Fact: This volcano is dormant or "sleeping."

Volcano: MAUNA KEA
Location: HAWAII — Hawaii Island
- Fact: About 1,000,000 years old, this volcano has not erupted for 3,000 years.

Volcano: MOUNT BAKER
Location: State of WASHINGTON, USA
- Fact: Erupted at least 7 times in the 1800s

**VOLCANO Cards — Photocopy and cut apart.**

Volcano: MOUNT EREBUS
Location: ANTARCTICA

Volcano: MOUNT ETNA
Location: SICILY
- Fact: Erupted March 1669 and August 1979

Volcano: MOUNT MAZAMA
Location: State of OREGON, USA
- Fact: Mt. Mazama erupted 6,900 years ago. The eruption was so violent that a caldera, or large crater, formed. This caldera filled with water and is now Crater Lake, the deepest lake in the United States.

Volcano: MOUNT FUJIYAMA
Location: JAPAN
- Fact: Last eruption was 1707

Volcano: MOUNT MISERY
Location: ST. KITTS ISLAND in the Caribbean Sea

Volcano: MOUNT GARIBALDI
Location: BRITISH COLUMBIA, Canada

Volcano: MOUNT PINATUBO
Location: PHILIPPINES
- Fact: Erupted July 6, 1992

Volcano: MOUNT HOOD
Location: State of OREGON, USA
- Fact: Erupted about 6 times in the 1800s and again in 1907.

Volcano: MOUNT RAINIER
Location: State of WASHINGTON, USA
- Fact: Erupted 1879 and 1882

Volcano: MOUNT JEFFERSON
Location: State of OREGON, USA
- Fact: Scientists do not know if Mt. Jefferson is extinct or dormant.

Volcano: MOUNT REDOUBT
Location: Near Anchorage, ALASKA
- Fact: Erupted in 1966 and 1993.

Volcano: MOUNT LASSEN
Location: State of CALIFORNIA, USA
- Fact: Erupted 1914 - 1921.

Volcano: MOUNT ST. HELENS
Location: State of WASHINGTON, USA
- Fact: Erupted around 1800, 1831, 1835, 1842-1857, and in 1980. This volcano remains active.

**VOLCANO Cards — Photocopy and cut apart.**

Volcano: MOUNT SHASTA
Location: State of CALIFORNIA, USA
- Fact: Last eruption may have been around 1855.

Volcano: RUAPEHU
Location: NEW ZEALAND
- Fact: Its summit contains a lake of hot water.

Volcano: MOUNT TABOR
Location: PORTLAND, OREGON — USA
- Fact: This is the only extinct volcano in a big US city.

Volcano: SANTORINI
Location: SANTORINI ISLAND in the Aegean Sea
- Fact: During its main eruption in 1600 B.C., the center of the island collapsed 1/2 mile below sea level.

Volcano: MOUNT VESUVIUS
Location: POMPEII, ITALY
- Fact: Erupted August 24, 79 AD. By 1944 Mt. Vesuvius had its 18th recorded major eruption.

Volcano: MOUNT WASHINGTON
Location: State of OREGON, USA
- Fact: Became extinct over 1,000 years ago

Volcano: SHISHALDIN
Location: ALASKA — Aleutian Peninsula
- Fact: Since 1775, this volcano has erupted about 30 times.

Volcano: NEVADO DEL RUIZ
Location: COLOMBIA, South America

Volcano: STROMBOLI
Location: LIPARI ISLANDS (between Sicily and Italy)
- Fact: For the last 2,500 years, this volcano has erupted about every 30 minutes.

Volcano: PARICUTIN
Location: MEXICO
- Fact: Its February 20, 1943 eruption killed vegetation within a 7 mile radius of the volcano.

Volcano: SURTSEY
Location: ICELAND
- Fact: Beginning in 1963, this volcano erupted for 3 years and formed Surtsey Island.

Volcano: THE PEAK
Location: TRISTAN DA CUNHA (An island in the South Atlantic Ocean between Africa and South America)
- Fact: Erupted 1961

Volcano: TAMBORA
Location: INDONESIA
- Fact: Its eruption was heard more than 1,000 miles away.

# The Scientific Gazette

**Geology** — **Dr. Florence Bascom**

## Geologist travels by horseback

To map land formations for the U.S. Geological Survey, Dr. Florence Bascom (1862-1945) spent her summers riding horseback through Pennsylvania, Maryland, and New Jersey. During the remaining nine months of the year, she taught geology at Bryn Mawr College in Pennsylvania.

Dr. Bascom was the first woman to earn a doctorate from Johns Hopkins in Baltimore, Maryland, and the first woman in the United States to become a geologist, a scientist who studies rocks to learn the history of the earth. She taught at Bryn Mawr for 33 years and established the geology department there. Her classes were well attended and Dr. Bascom, like her colleague, mathematician Dr. Emmy Noether, was a popular professor.

## Largest Volcano in Human History Erupted in 1883 in Indonesia

The eruption of Krakatau (or Krakatoa), a volcano in Indonesia, on August 27, 1883, was the largest volcanic eruption in human history. It was heard 3,000 miles away, created 120' high waves, and spread volcanic dust around the world.

In his book **How Did We Find Out About Volcanoes?**, Isaac Asimov wrote, "If Krakatoa had exploded in Kansas, everyone in the United States would have heard the noise, and so would many people in Canada and Mexico."

### Fun Fact

Indonesia has 127 "live" volcanoes, and Japan has 100.

## A Volcano in our Classroom

To honor Dr. Bascom, our class watched a volcano erupt in our classroom. The eruption was sudden as the magma (vinegar and food coloring combined with baking soda) shot up through the pipe (a glass jar), rolled over the volcano vent (the rim of the jar) and, becoming lava, covered the surrounding countryside (a dinner plate). The class remained calm.

Our earth has approximately 1,300 active volcanoes. About 50 of these erupt each year. The United States has the most "potentially active" volcanoes.

## Building Blocks

Rocks are the building blocks of land formations. There are three major classes of rocks. Find one fact about each kind:

Igneous ______________________

______________________________

Sedimentary ___________________

______________________________

Metamorphic __________________

______________________________

**At Home:**

**Adventures with Rocks and Minerals** by Lloyd H. Barrow contains 30 fun, simple experiments ranging from "What are the Color Properties of Minerals?" to "How Can We Clean up Dirty Water?" Written with elementary and middle-school students in mind, Barrow's experiments include common materials and easy-to-read instructions.

Dr. Marie Sklodowska Curie, the "mother of atomic physics," received two Nobel Prizes.

# Discovery Unit No. 13

NOBEL

Dr. Marie Sklodowska Curie
Chemistry/Physics

**NOW YOU SEE IT, NOW YOU DON'T Demonstration**

## Time-line:

- **1867 - 1934 Dr. Marie Sklodowska Curie**
- 1874 - The typewriter is invented
- 1933 - Ruth Wakefield of Massachusetts invents the chocolate chip cookie

## Pronunciation guide:

- Sklodowska [Sklow-DOW-skaw]
- Sorbonne [SOAR-bahn]
- thorium [THOR-ee-um]
- polonium [Pah-LOW-knee-um]
- distillation [dis-tah-LAY-shun]

## Key points:

☛ Dr. Curie's work with radioactivity was the beginning of atomic physics.

☛ Atomic physics is the study of atoms "in motion."

☛ Dr. Marie Curie is the only woman scientist in history to receive two Nobel Prizes: one in physics (1903) and another in chemistry (1911).

☛ The NOW YOU SEE IT, NOW YOU DON'T Demonstration will illustrate **distillation**, a process Dr. Curie used in her scientific work.

## Supplies:

✔ One saucepan
✔ A cup of water
✔ Blue, green, or red food coloring
✔ A hot plate
✔ A metal lid large enough to collect condensation (A pizza pan works well.)
✔ A small bowl (clear glass or white)
✔ A "My Notes" sheet for each student
✔ ***The Scientific Gazette*** for each student

## Steps:

1. Point out Warsaw, Poland, and Paris, France, on a map or globe.
2. Share highlights of Dr. Curie's life.
3. Distribute "My Notes" sheet.
4. Conduct the NOW YOU SEE IT, NOW YOU DON'T Demonstration (page 89).
5. Complete "My Notes."
6. Assist students in clean-up.
7. Distribute ***The Scientific Gazette.***
8. Add Dr. Marie Curie's name and a memento to the time-line.

## For next time:

- Announce the next scientist.

## Bibliography:


Birch, Beverly. **People Who Have Helped The World: Marie Curie.**

Curie, Eve. **Madame Curie.**

Halacy, Daniel S. **Radiation, Magnetism, and Living Things.**

Keller, Mollie. **Marie Curie.**

McGrayne, Sharon Bertsch. **Nobel Prize Women in Science.**

Milne, Lorus J. & Margery. **Understanding Radioactivity.**

## Biography of DR. MARIE SKLODOWSKA CURIE 1867 - 1934

Marya Sklodowska was born in Warsaw, Poland. Her father was a professor of physics and mathematics, and her mother was a musician and a director of a private school.

### Excellent Student

The youngest of five children, Marya was reading by the time she was 4 years old. Learning was easy and school fun. Once she confessed to a friend, "Perhaps you will make fun of me, but nevertheless I must tell you that I like it [school], and even that I love it."

At age 15, Marya graduated first in her all girls' high school. She wanted to attend college, but universities in Poland did not admit women. Marya — or "Marie" in French — Sklodowska decided to attend college in France but had to work 3 years before moving to Paris to study at the Sorbonne.

### In Paris

To save money, Marie lived in an apartment without electricity and running water, and spent one dime per day on expenses. In 1894 she graduated first in her class with a degree in physical sciences. One year later she placed second in her class with a degree in mathematics. Marie became a scientific researcher at the Sorbonne, married physicist Pierre Curie, and began work on her doctoral degree.

### The Mystery of X-Rays

To earn a doctorate, Marie Curie had to make a scientific discovery or solve a scientific problem. She chose to study atoms and to discover why some rocks gave off mysterious waves or rays. The Curies called these rays "radiation" and the rocks emitting radiation, "radioactive." Marie hypothesized that motion inside atoms caused radiation. Her work with radioactivity was the beginning of **atomic physics**, the study of atoms in motion.

### Mystery Solved

Four years and hundreds of experiments later, Marie Curie solved the mystery of radiation and earned her doctorate. From a black rock named pitchblende ore, Dr. Curie discovered several radioactive elements: **uranium, thorium, polonium** (named after her native Poland), and **radium**. Polonium proved 400 times more radioactive than uranium and radium 900 times. These radioactive elements decay. They are unstable and may release energy for billions of years before becoming the stable element called lead.

### Nobel Prizes

For these discoveries Marie Curie not only received her doctorate in 1903, but she and her husband shared the Nobel Prize in physics. Although Pierre Curie died in 1906, Dr. Curie continued her work in radioactivity and in 1911 received a Nobel Prize in chemistry. Dr. Marie Curie is the only woman in history to receive two Nobel prizes.

Her longtime exposure to high doses of radiation caused her to feel tired all of the time, to become easily sick, and to suffer from "badly burned and cracked fingers." (Keller, **Marie Curie**) On July 4, 1934, Dr. Marie Sklodowska Curie, the "mother of atomic physics," died from leukemia.

## Instructor's Guide:

### The NOW YOU SEE IT, NOW YOU DON'T Demonstration

(A demonstration in distillation)

**Background Information:**

To separate the radioactive elements from an ore called pitchblende, Dr. Curie used different processes including **distillation**. She took sackloads of pitchblende and "began an endless process of mixing, dissolving, heating, filtering, distilling, crystallizing, on and on and on . . ." (Birch, **People Who Helped the World: Marie Curie.**) This demonstration will show how distillation changes a liquid (water, in this case) to a gas (evaporation) and back to a liquid (condensation).

## Instructions:

1. Add several drops of food coloring to approximately one cup of water in the saucepan.
2. Turn on the hot plate.
3. Give students adequate time to answer questions # 1 and 2 on "My Notes."
4. Conduct the demonstration.
   - Place saucepan on hot plate and bring solution to full boil.
   - When solution is boiling, hold pizza lid at an angle above the saucepan so the condensation "rolls" down the lid and into the bowl.

5. Invite students to file by so they can see the colorless cooled liquid (or condensation).
6. Give students adequate time to answer question # 3.

**Explain . . .**

*Dr. Curie did not start with water and food coloring. She began with soil containing pitchblende which she knew held radioactive elements. Through heating the soil, some elements changed from a solid to a gas and back to a liquid. Dr. Curie collected the cooled liquid (or condensation), tested it for radiation, and then discarded the liquid should it prove non-radioactive.*

7. Discuss question # 4 and give students adequate time to answer both #4 and 5.
8. Assist students in cleaning up.

## Add notes here:

# My Notes

by ______________________________, Scientist

**NOW YOU SEE IT, NOW YOU DON'T Demonstration**

**Answer questions #1 and #2 before the experiment.**

1. What color is the solution in the saucepan?

______________________________

2. If you boil this solution and the steam rises and cools on a lid, what color will the cooled liquid (condensation) be?

______________________________

Your answer is your **hypothesis**.
The NOW YOU SEE IT, NOW YOU DON'T Demonstration will test your hypothesis.

---

**Answer questions #3 and #4 after the experiments.**

3. What color is the condensation?

______________________________

4. Complete this sentence: **Distillation is**

______________________________

5. I think the experiment was named NOW YOU SEE IT, NOW YOU DON'T because:

______________________________

______________________________

# The Scientific Gazette

**Chemistry/Physics** **Dr. Marie Sklodowska Curie**

## A Woman of Many "Firsts"

Born in Warsaw, Poland, in 1867, Marya Sklodowska grew up to become Dr. Marie Sklodowska Curie, one of the most famous women in history. Her life held many "firsts."

She was the first woman to:

- receive a Nobel Prize
- work as a professor at the Sorbonne
- be elected to the Academy of Medicine

She is the only woman to:

- receive two Nobel Prizes (one in physics and another in chemistry)
- have a daughter who also won a Nobel Prize

She is the first person to:

- study atomic physics, the study of atoms "in motion"
- discover the radioactive elements of thorium, polonium, and radium
- use the word "radioactivity"
- decide that the unit for measuring radium would be called "the Curie"

Marie Curie conducted most of her work in France.

## Ingredients = Elements

A baked cake does not look like its ingredients — the eggs, flour, baking powder, sugar, etc., that went into the batter. Pitchblende ore is like that baked cake. The pitchblende rock looks like one thing but really has many ingredients, or elements, e.g., uranium salts, polonium, and radium. Marie Curie set out to discover the radioactive elements in pitchblende ore. She knew that these elements would tell her the source of the mysterous X-rays coming from pitchblende.

## *Wedding Announcement*

On July 26, 1895, Marie Sklodowska married Pierre Curie, a famous physicist. Although they were too poor to buy wedding rings, they purchased bicycles before their wedding and spent their honeymoon cycling through the French countryside. After their honeymoon Marie returned to the difficult task of earning her doctorate.

### At Home

Work with an adult and conduct these experiments in distillation:

1. Dissolve 1 tsp. salt in warm water. Taste. Bring solution to a boil, collect and taste the condensation.
2. Add 2-3 Tbs. vinegar to water. Taste. Bring solution to a boil, collect and taste condensation. What might the results tell you about the boiling points of water and vinegar?

Beginning in 1925 Ynes Mexia collected botanical specimens in Mexico, Alaska, and South America.

# Discovery Unit No. 14

## Ynes Mexia
## Botany

### ALL PRESSED UP Project

**Time line:**
- **1870 - 1938 Ynes Mexia**
- 1898 - The microphone is invented
- 1914 - Panama Canal opens

**Pronunciation guide:**
- Ynes [Ee-NEZ] Mexia [mah-HE-ah]
- *Hacienda* [oss-ee-EN-dah] — a large estate in a Spanish-speaking country

**Key points:**
- ☛ Mexia did not consider herself a scientist but a botanical collector.
- ☛ Mexia began collecting plants when she was 55 years old. In 10 years she collected approximately 137,600 specimens — more plants than any other woman collector.
- ☛ Most of these specimens came from Mexico and South America.
- ☛ In the ALL PRESSED UP Project, students will collect flowers and preserve these specimens by pressing them.

**Supplies — Before the first day:**
- ✔ "My Notes" sheet

**Steps — Before the first day:**
1. Discuss guidelines for collecting flowers.
2. Record guidelines on "My Notes."

**Supplies — Today:**
- ✔ "My Notes" sheet
- ✔ Fresh flowers
- ✔ A sheet of newspaper for each student
- ✔ Heavy books — approximately 10
- ✔ ***The Scientific Gazette*** for each student

**Steps — Today:**
1. Point out western Mexico, Ecuador, Peru, Brazil, the Amazon River, Chile, Argentina, the Straits of Magellan, and the Andes Mountains on a map.
2. Share highlights of Ynes Mexia's life.
3. Collect fresh flowers.
4. Begin the ALL PRESSED UP Project. (See instructor's guide, page 95.)

**Supplies — 3 to 5 days later:**
- ✔ Pressed flowers
- ✔ Construction paper cut into strips approximately 2" x 6".
- ✔ Self-adhesive plastic cut into strips 1/4" - 1/2" larger than the paper strips.
- ✔ Scissors
- ✔ "My Notes" sheet

**Steps — 3 to 5 days later:**
1. Complete ALL PRESSED UP Project.
2. Assist students in clean-up.
3. Distribute ***The Scientific Gazette***.
4. Add Ynes Mexia's name and a memento to the time-line.
5. Ongoing Activities (page 95) are optional.

**For next time:**
- Announce the next scientist.

**Bibliography:**


Bonta, Marcia Myers. **Women in the Field.**

Duff, Gail. **Natural Fragrances.**

Ehrhardt, Eleanor. **Charlie Brown's Super Book of Things to Do and Collect.**

## Biography of YNES MEXIA 1870 - 1938

For the sake of plants, Ynes Mexia scaled cliffs, shot rapids, fractured ribs, and battled insects. She was not a botanist, a scientist who studies plants, but a botanical collector who loved nature and craved adventure.

### Troubles

Ynes had an unhappy childhood. Born in Washington, D.C. to Enrique Antonio Mexia, an agent for the Mexican government, and Sarah Wilmer Mexia, Ynes spent much of her youth separated from her father. With her mother and six siblings, Mexia lived in Texas, Pennsylvania, Ontario Province in Canada, and Maryland. From 18 to 28 years of age, she resided in Mexico City living on her father's *hacienda* which she inherited after his death.

Married in 1897, Mexia was widowed 7 years later. She continued to live at the *hacienda*, started a poultry and pet stock-raising business, remarried, sold her business, divorced, and moved to California where she became a social worker. She was unhappy. At times she would withdraw "from the world, read books, and overeat." (Bonta, **Women in the Field**)

### A Purpose in Life

In 1920, at the age of 50, Ynes Mexia traveled with the local Sierra Club (an organization whose members work to protect wilderness areas) and enrolled as a special student at the University of California in Berkeley. Studying natural sciences, Mexia soon realized that her favorite subject was botany. In 1925, following a course in flowering plants, Mexia signed on for her first botanical collection trip.

Despite a fall from a cliff that left Mexia's hand injured and some ribs broken, this trip to western Mexico changed her life. She now had a purpose in life: to collect plants in Mexico. Her familiarity with the language and customs, her interest in botany, and her love for adventure combined to make this an ideal career to which she devoted the rest of her life.

### 137,600

Mexia returned from Mexico with 500 specimens some of which were new to botanists in the United States. One year later she returned to Mexico and collected 33,000 specimens. In 1928 she traveled to Alaska's Mount McKinley and acquired 6,100 plants. Beginning in 1929 Mexia spent over two years in Brazil and Peru exploring 3,000 miles of the Amazon River and collecting 65,000 specimens. In the mid-1930s she collected 5,000 specimens in Ecuador, 15,000 from Peru, and 13,000 from Mexico. The grand total: 137,600 specimens! In 10 years Ynes Mexia collected more plants than any other woman collector.

### From Ticks to Monkey Stew

Despite ticks ("about the size of the dot of the letter i"...), mosquitoes, and sand flies, a primitive camp in a banana grove, floods, headhunters, and meals of parrots, toucan or monkey stew, Mexia no sooner finished one trek before she was planning another. She had, in her own words, "found a task where I could be useful and really produce something of lasting worth, while living out among the flowers." (Bonta, **Women in the Field**)

Bad health forced her to return to California from Mexico in May 1938. She was hospitalized and died of lung cancer two months later.

## Instructor's Guide:

### The ALL PRESSED UP Project

#### Background Information:

Ynes Mexia's ability to discover a career that encompassed her love of nature, her desire for honest-to-goodness adventure, and her knowledge of flowers and their preservation is an admirable model. (On her second collecting expedition in Mexico, not one of the 33,000 specimens was spoiled despite the tropical heat.) The ALL PRESSED UP Project is an opportunity to combine a love and knowledge of nature and art.

#### Instructions:

**Before the first day**

1. Hand out "My Notes" sheet.
2. Discuss where and how to collect flowers. Perhaps a nearby homeowner or two would be willing to allow students to collect flowers on their property. (Small flowers, such as violets and lobelia, would be perfect.)
3. Create guidelines, e.g., pick the flower only if many of the same kind are present.

   Ask students to write these guidelines on their "My Notes" sheets.
4. Collect supplies: scissors, identification guidebooks, etc.

**Today**

After sharing highlights of Ynes Mexia's life:

1. Collect flowers. (Review guidelines from "My Notes.")
2. Students select one or two flowers to press.
3. Distribute newspaper sheets.
4. Instruct students to:
   - Write their names on the folded news paper sheets.
   - Place their flowers inside the newspaper sheet. Pedals and leaves should be facing up.
   - Refold the sheets very carefully.
   - Stack sheets (very carefully).
   - Add the heavy books to the stack of newspaper sheets.
   - Wait patiently 3 to 5 days.

**3 to 5 days later**

1. Remove books.
2. Distribute scissors, strips of construction paper, strips of self-adhesive plastic, and newspaper sheets containing pressed flowers.
3. Instruct students to:
   * Open their newspaper sheets carefully.
   * Gently remove the pressed flower(s) and place on a strip of construction paper.
   * Print or write the name of the flower(s) (optional).
   * Peel the paper from the back of the self-adhesive plastic.
   * Patiently, critically, lovingly (There is no second chance!) place the plastic adhesive sticky-side down over the flower and onto the strip of construction paper.
   * Trim the plastic.
   * Repeat process (optional)
4. Distribute and complete "My Notes." Identify each flower.
5. Assist students in clean-up.

**Ongoing**

- Display pressed flowers.
- Research each flower. Discover its history and folklore.
- Create a garden. Feature wildflowers, herbs, produce, exotic wonders, newly-developed hybrids, or plants indigenous to your area.

# My Notes

by ______________________________, Scientist

The ALL PRESSED UP Project

**Guidelines for picking flowers:**

______________________________

______________________________

______________________________

______________________________

**The flowers I collected:**

# The Scientific Gazette

**Botany** | **Ynes Mexia**

**Ynes Mexia, botanical collector**

## Peppers and Poinsettias

While exploring the Amazon River Basin in 1931, Mexia celebrated Christmas by decorating a palm tree with red peppers and poinsettias.

**The Amazon River** is 4,131 miles long. It is the longest river in the world.

**The Amazon River** drains one-sixth of the globe's runoff into the ocean.

**The Amazon Rain Forest** supports 3,000 varities of trees.

## Create Your Own Great Adventure

Ynes Mexia created a job that combined her love and knowledge of nature and her desire for adventure. One of her greatest adventures was exploring the Amazon River. By selling her plant specimens to university and museum scientists, Mexia paid her living and traveling expenses. These sales made her adventures possible.

What would be a great adventure to you?

## An Outstanding Collection

In 1925 Ynes Mexia took her first botanical collection trip. She was 55 years old and very unhappy. But this first of many trips to collect plants gave her life new purpose. Over the next 13 years, Mexia collected plants in Mexico, Alaska, South America's expansive Amazon River Basin south to the Straits of Magellan, and southwestern United States.

Despite ticks, mosquitoes, floods, and meals of monkey stew, Mexia no sooner finished one trip before she was planning another. In 13 years she collected approximately 137,600 plant speimens, a total greater than any other woman collector.

## Fun Things to do at Home

- ✔ Find Titia Joosten's **Flower Drying with a Microwave** and learn a new method of preserving flowers.
- ✔ Contact the local Sierra Club to learn what activities they sponsor.
- ✔ Tour a local nursery, botanical garden, or arboretum.
- ✔ Begin a collection. The possibilities are endless:
  - pinecones
  - autographs
  - stamps
  - pencils
  - paper clips
  - ______________________
  - ______________________
  - ______________________

Mathematician Dr. Emmy Noether was, in Albert Einstein's words, "the most significant creative mathematical genius thus far produced since the higher education of women began."

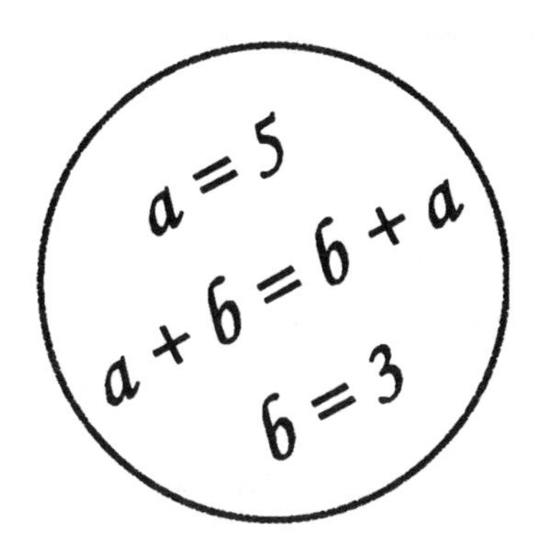


# Discovery Unit No. 15

## Dr. Emmy Noether
## Mathematics

**BIG IDEAS Activity**

### Time-line:
- **1882 - 1935 Dr. Emmy Noether**
- 1891 - The zipper is invented
- 1932 - Vitamin D is discovered.

### Pronunciation guide:
- Noether [NO-tur]
- eponym [EP-ah-nim]

### Key points:
☛ Dr. Emmy Noether was a famous mathematician who lived in Germany before moving to the United States in the 1930s.

☛ Dr. Noether believed mathematics should be studied "for the fun and intellectual interest of it."

☛ Using her imagination to see relationships beyond numbers and operational signs, Dr. Noether founded abstract algebra.

☛ Through creating simple math problems in the BIG IDEAS Activity, students will use their imaginations and common sense to discover a general mathematical concept.

### Supplies:
✔ To each group of 2 students give nine slips of paper that they number 1 through 9. Also distribute to each group a set of directions (page 102) for the math experiment.

✔ "My Notes" sheet for each student

✔ *The Scientific Gazette* for each student

### Steps:
1. Conduct the BIG IDEAS Activity. (See instructor's guide, page 101.)
2. Point out Germany and Pennsylvania on a map or globe.
3. Share highlights of Dr. Noether's life.
4. Distribute ***The Scientific Gazette.***
5. Assist students in clean-up.
6. Add Dr. Noether's name and a memento to the time-line.
7. Enrichment Activity (page 104) is optional.

### For next time
- Announce the next scientist.

### Bibliography:
McGrayne, Sharon Bertsch. **Nobel Prize Women in Science: Their Lives, Struggles and Momentous Discoveries.**

Perl, Teri. **Math Equals.**

## Biography of DR. EMMY NOETHER 1882 - 1935

*". . . she was by far the best woman mathematician of all time, and one of the greatest mathematicians (male or female) of the twentieth century."*

**— Jean Dieudonne**
**French mathematician**

Emmy Noether believed that mathematics should be studied "for the fun and intellectual interest of it." As a young girl, Emmy played number games at the dinner table, and, as a young woman, she hosted teas at which guests played mathematical guessing games. Numbers intrigued her, but it wasn't until she was 21 years old that Emmy Noether decided to study mathematics.

### Few Women Students

When Noether decided to study mathematics in 1903, most of the universities in Germany did not admit women. The University of Erlangen in Erlangen, Germany, did and Emmy Noether enrolled. She was one of five women in the university and one of 80 women in Germany who were full-time university students.

### Not Paid

After earning her doctorate, Dr. Emmy Noether spent the next 8 years teaching without pay at the University of Erlangen. Then she moved to Gottingen, Germany, and taught without pay at the famous University of Gottingen for 18 years. While in Gottingen, Dr. Noether worked on the mathematical calculations for Dr. Albert Einstein's general theory of relativity.

### Abstract Algebra

During the 1920s Dr. Noether changed algebra, the language of mathematics. Algebra allows us to work with formulas, discuss unknowns, graph ideas, and even write computer programs. Dr. Noether looked beyond numbers and operational signs (like *plus, minus* etc.) and thought about the ideas beyond those numbers and signs. These ideas (or governing principles) were the beginning of abstract algebra. Dr. Emmy Noether was a "big idea" person.

### Illegal Classes

Even though Dr. Noether was one of the most famous mathematicians in Europe, she was forced to quit teaching when Hitler fired all Jewish professors. Dr. Noether stayed in Germany and taught illegal math classes in her apartment.

### Moves to Pennsylvania

In the early 1930s, Bryn Mawr College in Pennsylvania offered Dr. Noether a teaching position. She accepted and moved to the United States. For the first time, she was paid a respectable salary.

Dr. Noether was a popular professor. On Saturday afternoons she took her students on walks and became so involved in discussing mathematics she forgot to watch the traffic. Her students watched for her.

### Dr. Noether & Dr. Einstein

Weekly Dr. Noether traveled to the Institute for Advanced Studies in New Jersey to teach students and visit her friend, Dr. Albert Einstein, who also had left Germany. When Dr. Noether died suddenly in 1935, Dr. Einstein said of her: . . . "Fraulein Noether was the most significant creative mathematical genius thus far produced since the higher education of women began."

## Instructor's Guide:

### The BIG IDEAS Activity

## Background Information:

The BIG IDEAS Activity demonstrates that behind numbers and operational signs are governing principles (or properties) that apply irrespective of the size of the numbers.

A "big" idea that this experiment is designed to help students discover is called the **commutative property of addition**. This fancy phrase only means that in **addition** you can add numbers in any order and still get the same answer. Since algebra is a language of numbers and operations, symbols are used to express ideas. The **commutative property** is expressed this way:

$$a + b = b + a$$

There is no commutative property in subtraction: 5 - 3 will not give you the same answer as 3 - 5.

## Instructions:

1. Divide the class into groups of 2 students.
2. Distribute supplies including the "My Notes" sheet for each student.
3. Instruct the students that they are to conduct the first part of the activity in these two-person work groups. If they have questions during the activity, they are to come to you rather than asking the questions aloud. Your task is to circulate, answer questions, and encourage.
4. Give them adequate time (approximately 10 minutes) to read the directions, conduct the math experiment, and complete "Part A" of "My Notes."
5. Have each two-person group combine with another to share their discoveries. While these four-person groups are working collaboratively and answering "Part B" of "My Notes" (allow 7 - 10 minutes), circulate and appoint two boys and two girls to share their groups' results.
6. If there is time and interest, conduct experiments to learn if the **commutative property** holds true in multiplication and division.

   (Hint: a x b = b x a)
7. As for the suggestion that they add "even" and "odd" numbers to learn if there is a pattern, the results are: "even" + "even" = "even"; "odd" + "odd" = "even"; and "even" + "odd" = "odd".

## Make notes here:

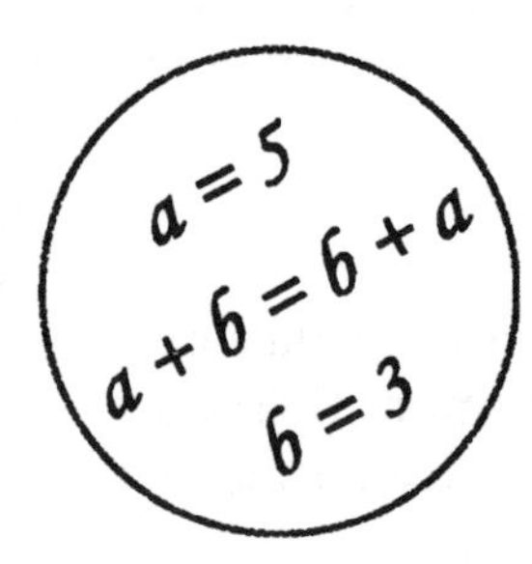


## Student's Directions

## BIG IDEAS Activity

You are going to explore some math ideas that a famous woman mathematician named Dr. Emmy Noether would have enjoyed. She liked to use her imagination to find "big ideas" beyond numbers and math signs.

**To conduct the activity:**

- ➡ Number your nine pieces of paper 1 through 9. Put only one number on each piece of paper.
- ➡ Create and solve some problems in addition.
- ➡ Use the same problems but change the order of the numbers.
- ➡ Create some problems in subtraction. Find the answers.
- ➡ Change the order of the numbers in your subtraction problems.
- ➡ Do you see any "big idea" yet? Keep looking. Relax. Use your imagination. Talk with your partner.
- ➡ When you are ready, fill in Part A of "My Notes."

---

- ➡ Your instructor will now have you work with two other students. When you are ready, fill in Part B of "My Notes."
- ➡ If you have time, look for other big ideas. For example, add only "even" numbers, or add only "odd" numbers.

*Dr. Emmy Noether thought math should be studied "for the fun" of it. Do you agree?*

$a = 5$

$a + b = b + a$

$b = 3$

# My Notes

by ______________________________, Scientist

**BIG IDEAS Activity**

## Part A

**This is a "Big Idea" that the two of us discovered:**

____________________________________________

____________________________________________

____________________________________________

**Mark "X" in front of the statement that you think is true:**

______ This "Big Idea" is true in addition.

______ This "Big Idea" is true in subtraction.

______ This "Big Idea" is true in both addition and subtraction.

---

## Part B

**This is a "Big Idea" that the four of us discussed:**

____________________________________________

____________________________________________

____________________________________________

____________________________________________

**We found other "Big Ideas." They are:**

1. ____________________________________________

____________________________________________

2. ____________________________________________

____________________________________________

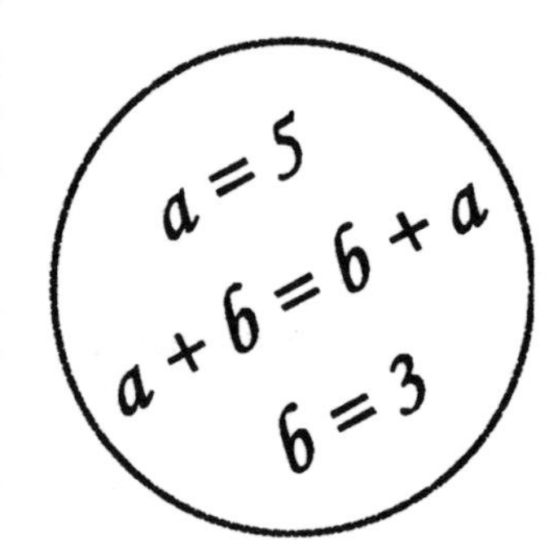


# Enrichment Activity

## Another BIG IDEA

In algebra a set is a collection of "objects" (called elements) put together for a reason. Sets and elements are found outside mathematics, e.g., a collection of cows (objects) is a herd (set). Draw lines to connect the set to its elements:

| Set | Elements |
|---|---|
| class | apple trees |
| orchestra | stores |
| gaggle | sister, mother . . . |
| U.S. Senate | whales |
| country | lions |
| family | Thanksgiving |
| skulk | students |
| orchard | carbon, tin, oxygen . . . |
| a mall | fish |
| gam | houses |
| hive | violins |
| holiday | geese |
| neighborhood | U.S. Senators |
| pound | states |
| school | foxes |
| basic elements | bees |
| pride | ounces |
| whole integers | -5,4,3,127,-39,0 |

Name other sets and elements:

| | |
|---|---|
| ______________________ | ______________________ |
| ______________________ | ______________________ |
| ______________________ | ______________________ |
| ______________________ | ______________________ |
| ______________________ | ______________________ |
| ______________________ | ______________________ |

# The Scientific Gazette

**Mathematics** **Dr. Emmy Noether**

**Dr. Emmy Noether was a famous German mathematician who discovered abstract algebra.**

$$a(1+5)+b(6+3)=b(6+3)+a(1+5)$$

Algebra is the language of mathematics. Just as there are rules in English (we call this *grammar*), there are rules in algebra. These rules (or properties) in algebra may look peculiar because they contain letters. These letters are symbols. Each symbol represents a range of numbers — not just one number. A rule in algebra is: $a + b = b + a$.

This rule is the **commutative property in addition.** We discovered this rule when we conducted the BIG IDEAS Activity.

In my own words, this rule means:

______________________________

______________________________

______________________________

______________________________

______________________________

## New School Named for Famous Mathematician

**Erlangen, GERMANY:** In 1983 the city of Erlangen, Germany, dedicated the Emmy Noether Gymnasium, a new school in honor of one of Germany's greatest mathematicians. Dr. Emmy Noether received her doctorate and graduated with highest honors from the University of Erlangen in 1907.

Following graduation she taught at the university but was not paid. Later, she taught at the University of Gottingen in Gottingen, Germany. While in Gottingen, she worked on some of the mathematical calculations for Dr. Albert Einstein's general theory of relativity. Dr. Noether enjoyed discovering the big ideas behind mathematical signs and numbers.

### Eponyms . . .

When a mathematician or scientist discovers a new law or principle, that discovery is usually named for that person. This is called an eponym (ep-ah-nim). The list of eponyms named for Noether is very long and includes: ". . . Noetherian rings, Noetherian theorem, Noetherian problems, Noetherian modules, Noetherian scheme, Noetherian space, and Noetherian factor systems." (McGrayne, **Nobel Prize Women in Science**)

Eponyms are not limited to science and math. How many eponyms do you know? (Hint: geographic places, diseases or medicines, company names, commercial products...)

*My Eponym*

**I would like this object or idea named after me.**

From 1939 until 1954, Winifred Goldring served as the State Paleontologist of New York.

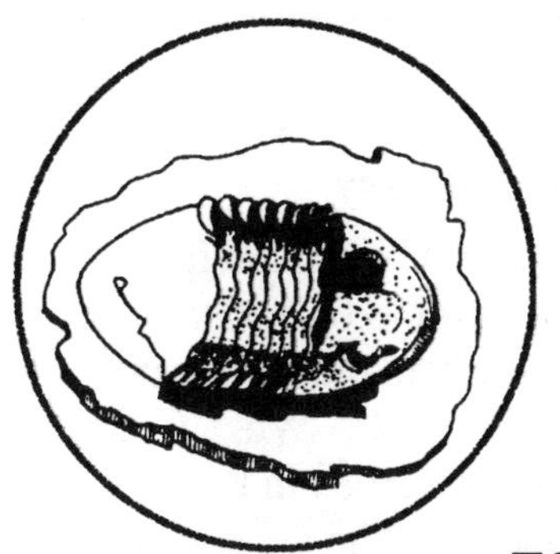

# Discovery Unit No. 16

## Winifred Goldring
## Paleontology

### FOSSILS in the EARTH are like EGGS in the MUD Dig

**Time-line:**

- **1888 - 1971 Winifred Goldring**
- 1903 - Wright Brothers fly their airplane at Kitty Hawk, North Carolina
- 1969 - U.S. astronauts land on the moon

**Pronunciation guide:**

- Paleontologist [Pay-lee-on-TAW-loe-gist]
- Devonian [Dee-VO-knee-un]
- crinoids [CRY-noids]

**Key points:**

☛ Winifred Goldring was a paleontologist who specialized in Devonian fossils.

☛ At a time when few women worked in paleontology, Winifred Goldring became State Paleontologist of New York.

☛ The paleontologist's work site and excavation of fossils is called a "dig."

☛ The FOSSILS in the EARTH are like EGGS in the MUD Dig will demonstrate the patience required to be a successful paleontologist.

**Supplies:**

✔ An "Egg Dig" for each student. These are made two days before. You need:
- a 4" square cardboard or plastic flower pot for each student
- mud to fill the flower pot
- 1 egg per student: one-third of the eggs are raw; one-third, hard-boiled; and one-third, hollow. To hollow out an egg, take a nail and make holes the size of a small pea at both ends. Blow out contents and rinse egg thoroughly. With a permanent marker, write an "H" on the hard-boiled eggs and an "R" on the raw eggs.

✔ To make the "Egg Dig," cover the bottom of the flower pot with mud. Add egg and cover with mud. Allow mud to harden.

✔ Newspapers to cover desks or floor unless the "Egg Dig" is an outdoor activity

✔ Toothpicks, small paint brushes, and spoons

✔ A "My Notes" sheet for each student

✔ ***The Scientific Gazette*** for each student.

**Steps:**

1. Point out Albany, New York, on a map.
2. Share highlights of Winifred Goldring's life.
3. Enjoy the Dig! (See instructor's guide, p. 109.)
4. Distribute, complete, and discuss "My Notes."
5. Assist students in clean-up.
6. Distribute ***The Scientific Gazette***.
7. Add Winifred Goldring's name and a memento to the time-line.

**For next time:**

- Announce the next scientist.

**Bibliography:**


Kass-Simon, G., and Patricia Farnes. **Women of Science: Righting the Record.**

Strahler, Arthur N. **Physical Geography.**

Warren, Rebecca Lowe, and Deborah Totten. **"In Their Footsteps."** (Curriculum Department, Portland Public School District)

## Biography of WINIFRED GOLDRING 1888 - 1971

In a time when few women were earth scientists, Winifred Goldring became a paleontologist, an earth scientist who studies fossils of plants and animals to learn the history of the earth. This history is a mind-boggling 3 billion years old.

### Fossils Are Clues

Being a paleontologist is like being a detective. A fossil becomes a clue to help the scientist learn what the earth was like millions, if not a billion or two, years ago. Goldring worked in New York State. Approximately 285 to 325 million years ago, the area we now call the state of New York was covered with widespread, shallow seas. In geologic time this was the Devonian Period.

Over time these seas receded or dried up, and deposits of dead marine animals called crinoids remained. (Crinoids were not big animals like sharks or whales but marine animals smaller than starfish and sea urchins.) The crinoids were covered with sand, silt, and dirt many feet thick. When the ground hardened, a fossil of the crinoid sometimes formed.

Winifred Goldring specialized in Devonian fossils, both plants that grew during that period and crinoids. Each fossil she uncovered in the field was another clue that provided her with more information about the history of the earth.

### NY State Museum

Goldring earned BA and MA degrees from Wellesley, a women's college in Massachusetts. She did graduate work at Johns Hopkins in Baltimore, Maryland, and Columbia University in New York City.

Beginning in 1914 Winifred Goldring worked at the New York State Museum in Albany, New York. She organized creative museum exhibits and published handbooks for the public.

### Controversy

Scientists who want to be successful paleontologists must travel to the mountains, valleys, and riverbeds where the fossils are. Scientists call this "field work." When Goldring was alive, field work for women in the earth sciences was controversial. The general belief was that women should work in laboratories, offices, or museums since field work posed problems of inappropriate attire, poor health, disapproval of colleagues, and personal safety. Some women in the field carried guns.

Goldring opposed the general belief against women in the field and trekked through New York mapping terrain and recovering fossils. Her work was so outstanding that from 1939 until she retired in 1954, she served as the State Paleontologist of New York.

## Instructor's Guide:

### The FOSSILS in the EARTH are like EGGS in the MUD Dig

## Background Information:

The purpose of this project is to help students experience the patience and skill required to dig successfully for fossils. Some fossils, being fairly accessible and sturdy (like hard-boiled eggs), may be easy to discover and retrieve while others may be fragile (like hollow eggs). Other fossils fall between these two extremes (like raw eggs).

This dig requires more preparation by the teacher than is usually asked for in these units. If this seems extreme, make the preparation (or a portion of it) a class project.

## Instructions:

1. After sharing highlights of Winifred Goldring's life:

> **Explain . . .**
>
> *A paleontologist's work site and excavation of fossils is called a "dig." Today you will be working in an "egg dig." The ground rules are :*
>
> *— You are to use the "excavating tools" (toothpicks, paint brushes, etc.) to remove the egg from the "egg dig" container. Do not tip the container over to free the egg.*
>
> *—You are to try to remove the egg without breaking it. Some of your eggs are hard-boiled, some raw, and some hollow.*

2. Distribute the newspapers and "Egg Digs."
3. Allow time for students to conduct the "dig" and to complete Part A of "My Notes."
4. Discuss experience and allow time for students to complete Part B of "My Notes."
5. Assist students in clean-up.

## Add other ideas for "digs":

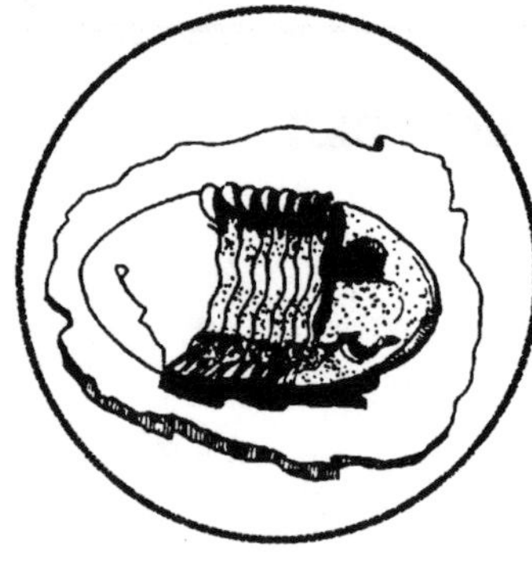

# My Notes

by ______________________________, Scientist

**FOSSILS in the EARTH are like EGGS in the MUD**

**Part A.**

Describe the soil in your "Egg Dig." Was it hard, soft, wet, dry, sandy, clayey, red, brown, clean, dirty . . . ?

______________________________________________

What strategy (plan of action) did you use to retrieve the egg? Were you successful?

______________________________________________

______________________________________________

Which tools did you use and for what purpose?

______________________________________________

______________________________________________

Was your egg a raw one, hard-boiled, or hollow?

______________________________________________

**Part B.**

Compare your strategies and observations with others.

______________________________________________

______________________________________________

Determine how many eggs of each kind (hard-boiled, raw, and hollow) were successfully removed.

______________________________________________

______________________________________________

How do you think fossils in the earth are like eggs in the mud?

______________________________________________

______________________________________________

# The Scientific Gazette

**Paleontology** **Winifred Goldring**

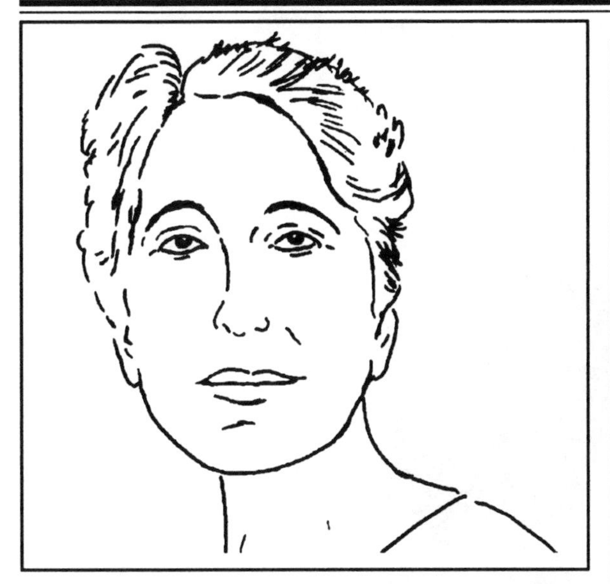

## History studied through fossils

Paleontologist Winifred Goldring (1888 - 1971) studied fossils of small marine animals called crinoids (CRY-noids) to learn the history of the earth. She specialized in the Devonian (Dee-VO-knee-un) Period (approximately 285 to 325 million years ago) when the area we now call New York was shallow sea.

When this sea receded or dried up, crinoids — similar in size to starfish and sea urchins — died. Over millions of years, sand, silt, or mud built up and covered the remains of these dead marine animals. The ground hardened and a fossil, or imprint, of the crinoid, often formed.

Goldring climbed hills, scoured valleys, and explored riverbeds to discover crinoids and other fossils from the Devonian Period. Her work was so exceptional that from 1939 until her retirement in 1954, Winifred Goldring served as the State Paleontologist of New York.

Explore the history of the earth in your area. Learn about its ancient seas, retreating glaciers or raging rivers, the exotic plant life, and extinct animal life forms. A local university or historical society might have information.

## Paleozoic Means "Ancient Life"

Scientists who study the history of the earth have created a "Table of Geological History" that estimates the length of geologic eras in millions of years. The Paleozoic Era spans more than 300,000,000 years and is divided into seven periods with one of these being the Devonian Period.

From youngest to oldest, the seven geologic periods are Permian, Pennsylvanian, Mississippian, Devonian, Silurian, Ordovician, and Cambrian. Discover at least one fact about each of these geologic periods:

Permian ____________________

Pennsylvanian ____________________

Mississippian ____________________

Devonian ____________________

Silurian ____________________

Ordovician ____________________

Cambrian ____________________

◆◆◆

## A Simple Quiz

A paleontologist's work site is called a "dig."
True ❑ False ❑ Maybe ❑

In the "Egg Dig" my egg did not break.
True ❑ False ❑ Maybe ❑

I would like to learn more about crinoids.
True ❑ False ❑ Maybe ❑

When paleontologists work "in the field," they plant gardens.
True ❑ False ❑ Maybe ❑

The earth is several thousand years old.
True ❑ False ❑ Maybe ❑

Fossils in the earth are like eggs in the mud.
True ❑ False ❑ Maybe ❑

Dr. Barbara McClintock, geneticist, received the Nobel Prize for Medicine in 1983.

# Discovery Unit No. 17

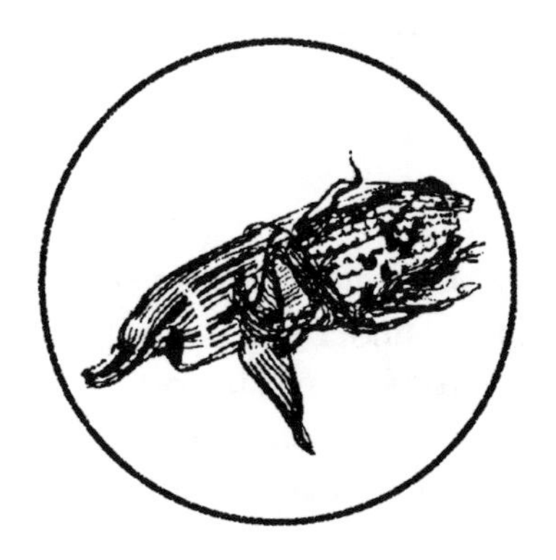

Dr. Barbara McClintock
Botany/Genetics

**The PROBABILITY Project**

## Time-line:

- **1902 - 1992 Dr. Barbara McClintock**
- 1910 - Halley's Comet returns
- 1937 - First jet engine built

## Pronunciation guide:

- chromosome [CROW-mah-soam]

## Key points:

- Dr. McClintock was a geneticist (a scientist who studies how parents pass on different characteristics to their offspring) who worked and lived for more than 50 years at a research laboratory on Long Island, New York.
- For 69 years Dr. McClintock studied Indian corn cells and discovered "jumping" genes.
- This idea of "jumping" genes was so controversial that most geneticists disagreed with Dr. McClintock's findings.
- Dr. Barbara McClintock received the Nobel Prize for Medicine (or Physiology) in 1983.
- The PROBABILITY PROJECT will help students understand how probability and genetics are related.

## Supplies:

- ✔ Two different coins (a nickel and a penny), a pencil, and a tally sheet for each team of student scientists
- ✔ A "My Notes" sheet for each student
- ✔ A couple sheets of newsprint and felt pen
- ✔ ***The Scientific Gazette*** for each student

## Steps:

1. Point out Long Island, New York, on a map.
2. Share highlights of Dr. McClintock's life.
3. Divide students into teams of two.
4. Distribute supplies.
5. Conduct the PROBABILITY Project. (See instructor's guide, page 115.)
6. Distribute ***The Scientific Gazette***.
7. Add Dr. McClintock's name and a memento to the time-line.

## For next time:

- Announce the next scientist.

## Bibliography:


Keller, Evelyn Fox. **A Feeling for the Organism.**

Kittredge, Mary. **Barbara McClintock.**

McGrayne, Sharon Bertsch. **Nobel Prize Women in Science: Their Lives, Struggles and Momentous Discoveries.**

## Biography of DR. BARBARA McCLINTOCK 1902 - 1992

*"She was a giant figure in the history of genetics."*

**— James Shapiro**
**University of Chicago**

As a young girl, Barbara McClintock enjoyed ice- and roller-skating, bicycling, "pitch and catch," and boxing. Her mother provided Barbara with trousers to wear under her skirts so she could climb trees. Her father told Barbara's teachers not to assign her homework so she would be free to do other activities after school.

### Indian Corn

After high school Barbara attended Cornell University in Ithaca, New York. She studied botany. While working toward her masters degree, she began working with Indian corn. In 1927 she completed her doctoral degree.

Dr. McClintock only wanted to research corn but businesses, colleges, and even the U.S. government usually hired men as researchers. She unhappily juggled teaching and research until 1941 when the Carnegie Institute hired her as a researcher. She spent the next 50 years, until her death in 1992, growing and studying Indian corn at the Cold Spring Harbor Research Center on Long Island, New York.

### Corn Cells and Heredity

Why did she study corn? Dr. McClintock was a geneticist. She wanted to know how parents pass on different traits or characteristics to their offspring. This "passing on of traits" is called "heredity." Because corn cells and human cells are similar, what Dr. McClintock learned about heredity in corn was also true for heredity in humans.

The basic units of heredity are chromosomes and genes. Dr. McClintock examined thin slices of corn kernels under a microscope and identified the 10 chromosomes in corn. Genes are smaller than chromosomes and could not be seen under Dr. McClintock's microscope.

### Jumping Genes

Sometimes a corn kernel, corn cob, or a leaf on the corn plants had an unusual appearance. "How could this happen?" Dr. McClintock asked herself. Finding the answer took her six years. Even though she could not see the genes, she concluded that a gene sometimes leaves its place on the chromosome and "jumps" to a new location on that same chromosome. When that happens, the "jumping gene" affects its new neighbors in such a way that the kernel, cob, or leaf has an unexpected, unusual appearance.

Most geneticists at this time thought that genes never moved and Dr. McClintock could not change their minds. Some of these geneticists called Dr. McClintock "crazy," but she knew she was right. Twenty-five years passed before most geneticists agreed that genes do "jump."

In 1983 Dr. Barbara McClintock received the Nobel Prize in Medicine. Her research helped explain heredity in humans, the cause of some diseases, and bacteria's ability to change and resist antibiotics. "Jumping genes" may also be the key to understanding cancer.

## Instructor's Guide

### The PROBABILITY Project

### Background Information:

In the 1860s, before scientists understood how parental traits or characteristics were transmittted to their offspring (heredity), an Austrian teacher by the name of Gregor Mendel conducted plant-breeding experiments with garden pea plants. When he crossed a pure-bred tall garden pea plant with a short one, all of the offspring (first generation) were tall. However, when he crossed these offspring with one another, their offspring (second generation) were both tall and short.

Usually three out of four of the second generation offspring were tall and one was likely to be short. Mendel concluded that inherited traits appear in some mathematical pattern. This mathematical pattern is called "probability."

As a geneticist Dr. Barbara McClintock understood probability. An unusual appearance in a corn kernel or cob was an improbable, unlikely event that required an explanation. Finding the answer — McClintock's "jumping gene" theory — took her six years.

In the PROBABILITY Project, teams of students will toss two coins 100 times, tally the results, and compare their findings with the principle of probability as it relates to garden pea plants. The principle of probability and genetics are indeed related.

### Instructions:

1. Distribute tally sheet, coins, pencils, and "My Notes" sheets.
2. Ask science teams to read instructions under Part A of their "My Notes" sheets. Answer students' questions.
3. Give students adequate time to conduct the PROBABILITY Project. While students are tossing coins and tallying results, draw the following grid on the newsprint. Leave room to record the results from all teams.

| | Hh | Ht | Th | Tt |
|---|---|---|---|---|
| Team #1 | | | | |
| Team #2 | | | | |
| Team #3 | | | | |
| etc. | | | | |
| Totals | | | | |

4. Post newsprint grid.

**Ask . . .**

*Let's go around the room and share results. How Many times did both coins come up "heads" (Hh)?* [Record results on newsprint.]

**Ask . . .**

*How many times did the nickel come up "heads" and the penny come up "tails" (Ht)?* [Record results.]

**Ask . . .**

*How many times did the nickel come up "tails) and the penny come up "heads" (Th)?* [Record results.]

**Ask . . .**

*How many times did both coins come up "tails" (Tt)?* [Record results.]

5. Allow time for the students to study the results.

**Ask . . .**

*Do you observe any mathematical pattern?* [Each of the four combinations should have "come up" around 25 times each.]

**Ask . . .**

*How do you explain this pattern?*[When you threw one coin, you had an equal chance of getting heads or tails. The probability was 1 out of 2 or 50%. When you threw the other coin, you also had an equal chance of getting heads or tails.

Remember, there were four possible combinations you could get when you tossed both coins. With two coins, the probability became 1 out of 4 or 25% of getting a particular combination, e.g., both coins coming up heads.]

6. Instruct students to look at Part B of "My Notes."

**Explain . . .**

*Garden pea plants are either tall or short. Each plant inherits a "tall" or "short" gene from each parent plant. If a garden pea plant inherits a tall gene from one parent and a short gene from the other parent, the offspring plant will be tall because that gene is dominant.*

*Geneticists use symbols to note dominant genes. In this case we will use "T" for a tall gene and "t" for a short gene.*

7. Encourage student teams to work together to complete Part B. Be available to answer questions.
8. Discuss their results. (The four possible gene combinations are TT, Tt, tT, and tt.)

**Ask . . .**

*Imagine you are a geneticist like Dr. Barbara McClintock, what mathematical pattern do you observe?*

[One of the four plants would probably be short.]

**Ask . . .**

*Why does that pattern occur?*

[There are four possible genetic combinations — remember the coins — but three of those have a "T" gene so those plants would be tall. One of the four combinations is a plant with two short genes (tt). According to the principle of probability, this combination would likely occur one out of four times or 25% of the time.]

**Add notes here:**

**Tally Sheet (one per team):**

| | | | |
|---|---|---|---|
| 1. ____ | 26. ____ | 51. ____ | 76. ____ |
| 2. ____ | 27. ____ | 52. ____ | 77. ____ |
| 3. ____ | 28. ____ | 53. ____ | 78. ____ |
| 4. ____ | 29. ____ | 54. ____ | 79. ____ |
| 5. ____ | 30. ____ | 55. ____ | 80. ____ |
| 6. ____ | 31. ____ | 56. ____ | 81. ____ |
| 7. ____ | 32. ____ | 57. ____ | 82. ____ |
| 8. ____ | 33. ____ | 58. ____ | 83. ____ |
| 9. ____ | 34. ____ | 59. ____ | 84. ____ |
| 10. ____ | 35. ____ | 60. ____ | 85. ____ |
| 11. ____ | 36. ____ | 61. ____ | 86. ____ |
| 12. ____ | 37. ____ | 62. ____ | 87. ____ |
| 13. ____ | 38. ____ | 63. ____ | 88. ____ |
| 14. ____ | 39. ____ | 64. ____ | 89. ____ |
| 15. ____ | 40. ____ | 65. ____ | 90. ____ |
| 16. ____ | 41. ____ | 66. ____ | 91. ____ |
| 17. ____ | 42. ____ | 67. ____ | 92. ____ |
| 18. ____ | 43. ____ | 68. ____ | 93. ____ |
| 19. ____ | 44. ____ | 69. ____ | 94. ____ |
| 20. ____ | 45. ____ | 70. ____ | 95. ____ |
| 21. ____ | 46. ____ | 71. ____ | 96. ____ |
| 22. ____ | 47. ____ | 72. ____ | 97. ____ |
| 23. ____ | 48. ____ | 73. ____ | 98. ____ |
| 24. ____ | 49. ____ | 74. ____ | 99. ____ |
| 25. ____ | 50. ____ | 75. ____ | 100. ____ |

Totals: Number of Hh ________

Number of Ht ________

Number of Th ________

Number of Tt ________

Grand Total 100

# My Notes

by ________________________________, Scientist

The PROBABILITY Project

**Part A — Instructions:**

1. Decide who will toss the coins and who will record the results. Use the following symbols:

   "H" = when the nickel comes up heads  "T" = when the nickel comes up tails

   "h" = when the penny comes up heads  "t" = when the penny comes up tails

2. Record each toss as it is made.
3. When finished, tally the results at the bottom of the tally sheet.

**Part B:**

Determine the four possible gene pairs for an offspring of Parent Plant A [Tt] & Parent Plant B [Tt].

(1) __________  (1) __________  (1) __________  (1) __________

Draw a tall or short pea plant for each of your four gene pairs. Remember that "T" stands for "tall" and "t" stands for "short."

tall pea plant

short pea plant

| [______] | [______] |
|---|---|
| [______] | [______] |

**Dr. Barbara McClintock, winner of the Nobel Prize in Medicine in 1983, spent 69 years studying Indian corn. Her research helped explain heredity in humans. She discovered "the jumping gene."**

## Probability

Probablity is the likelihood that an event will take place. If I toss a coin, the probability it will come up "heads" is 1 out of _____. If I throw a die, the probability it will come up a "five," is 1 out of _______.

Describe other probabilities. If I __________

______________________________________

______________________________________

______________________________________

______________________________________

______________________________________

Even though Dr. Barbara McClintock was only 5' tall, she was *"a giant figure in the history of genetics."*

— **James Shapiro, University of Chicago**

## Nobel Winner Loves Privacy

On October 10, 1983, Dr. Barbara McClintock learned over the radio that she had received the 1983 Nobel Prize in Medicine (or Physiology). Usually winners are contacted by telephone, but Dr. McClintock chose not to own a phone. She believed that whoever wanted to contact her, could write her a letter.

Dr. McClintock wanted to know how parents pass on traits or characteristics to their offspring. This "passing on of traits" is called heredity. Since corn cells and human cells are similar, what Dr. McClintock learned about heredity in corn was also true for heredity in humans.

Her research explained the cause of some diseases and bacteria's resistance to antibiotics. Her "jumping gene" discovery may be the key to understanding cancer.

Dr. McClintock was the **seventh** woman in history to receive a science Nobel, the **third** woman not to have to share the prize with another scientist, and the **first** woman awarded an unshared Nobel in Medicine.

## At Home

Check your library for books on Dr. McClintock. An excellent resource, with many photographs, is Mary Kittredge's **Barbara McClintock** (1991).

Called the "Gentle Genius," Dr. Dorothy Crowfoot Hodgkin received a Nobel Prize in 1964 for her discovery of the atomic structure of penicillin and vitamin B-12.

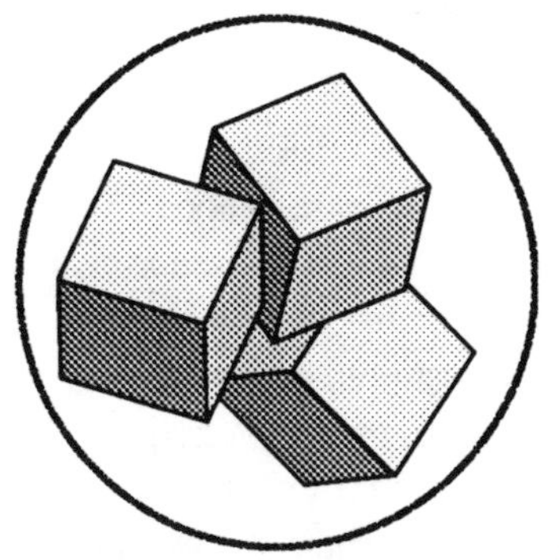

# Discovery Unit No. 18

## Dr. Dorothy Crowfoot Hodgkin
## Biochemistry

### GROWING SUGAR-SWEET CRYSTALS Experiment

**Time-line:**

- **1910 - Dr. Dorothy Crowfoot Hodgkin is born in Cairo, Egypt.**
- 1912 - The word "vitamine" is coined
- 1951 - U.S. produces almost 400,000 pounds of penicillin

**Pronunciation guide:**

- crystallography [kris-tah-LOG-rah-fee] — process of "shooting" x-rays through crystals to identify their atomic structures

**Key points:**

☛ Dorothy Hodgkin became interested in crystals when she was 10 years old.

☛ Crystals occur when atoms, like miniature building blocks, arrange themselves in patterns. Millions of atoms make one crystal large enough for us to see, e.g., a salt or sugar crystal.

☛ Dr. Hodgkin learned crystallography and discovered the atomic structures of penicillin, vitamin B-12, and insulin. In 1964 she received the Nobel Prize in Chemistry.

☛ The GROWING SUGAR-SWEET CRYSTALS Experiment will provide an opportunity to watch crystals "grow."

**Supplies:**

✔ A hot plate
✔ One saucepan
✔ A stirring spoon
✔ A heat-tempered transparent cup
✔ One chopstick
✔ A piece of string or yarn several inches longer than the height of the cup
✔ A paper clip
✔ Measuring cups
✔ 1/2 cup water
✔ 1 to 1 1/2 cups granulated sugar
✔ Food coloring (optional)
✔ "My Notes" for each student
✔ ***The Scientific Gazette*** for each student

**Steps:**

1. Point out Cairo, Egypt, and Oxford, England.
2. Share highlights of Dr. Hodgkin's life.
3. Set up the GROWING SUGAR-SWEET CRYSTALS Experiment. (See instructor's guide, page 123.)
4. (Next 4 - 5 days) Distribute "My Notes" and observe experiment.
5. Distribute ***The Scientific Gazette.***
6. Add Dr. Dorothy Crowfoot Hodgkin's name and a memento to the time-line.

**For next time:**

- Announce the next scientist.

**Bibliography:**

Berry, James. **Exploring Crystals.**

Kass-Simon, G., and Patricia Farnes. **Women of Science: Righting the Record.**

McGrayne, Sharon Bertsch. **Nobel Prize Women in Science.**

Stangl, Jean. **Crystals and Crystal Gardens You Can Grow.**

## Biography of DR. DOROTHY CROWFOOT HODGKIN b. 1910

Dorothy Crowfoot Hodgkin's friends and professional associates called her "the Gentle Genius" who unlocked the mysteries of penicillin, vitamin B-12, and insulin.

### World War I

Born May 12, 1910, in Cairo, Egypt, Dorothy Crowfoot lived in northern Africa until she was 4 years old. Her father worked with the Ministry of Education, and her mother was a self-taught expert in ancient and contemporary textiles. When World War I broke out, the family was vacationing in England. The parents found a home for Dorothy, her two sisters, and a nursemaid, but they returned to Africa. Since wartime travel was dangerous, Dorothy and her sisters saw their mother once during the next four years.

After the war the parents remained in Africa during the school year but spent the summers in England with their daughters.

### A Lab in the Attic

Dorothy discovered crystals when she was 10 years old. She set up a small lab in the attic and grew crystals. Crystals, she learned, were solids made of up atoms, like miniature building blocks, arranged in patterns. These patterns are of seven different types or shapes. Salt crystals are like square boxes or cubes while quartz crystals are always six-sided. Other types include rectangles, pyramids, and hexagons.

Crystals are everywhere. Some, like salt and sugar, are edible. Others, like sand, diamonds, and rocks, are not.

### Off to Study Chemistry

In high school a female chemistry instructor made an exception to the school rule that girls could not take chemistry and welcomed Dorothy and a friend into her class. By graduation in 1928, Dorothy decided to enroll at Oxford University in Oxford, England, and study chemistry.

### X-Rays and Crystals

While in college, Dorothy learned about crystallography, a new procedure that used x-rays to determine the atomic structure of crystals. X-rays "shot" into crystals were scattered before they hit a photographic plate leaving an ornate pattern of spots. There might be thousands of spots on one photographic plate. Dozens of photographs and thousands of mathematical calculations were necessary to determine the atomic structure of just one crystal!

### Fighting Disease

Learning that the structure of protein crystals could be discovered through crystallography created new challenges for Dr. Hodgkin. Penicillin is a protein crystal. By learning the structure of this protein, scientists could create synthetic penicillins. Discovering the structure of penicillin took Hodgkin and an associate, Barbara Rogers Low, four years.

In 1948 Dr. Hodgkin began to work on red crystals called vitamin B-12. Discovering the structure of this vitamin took seven years.

For deciphering the penicillin and vitamin B-12 crystals, Dr. Dorothy Crowfoot Hodgkin received the Nobel Prize in Chemistry in 1964.

### A Bigger Challenge

In 1969 Dr. Hodgkin and her research team succeeded in finding the structure of the insulin crystal. This success helped scientists better understand the disease diabetes and how insulin works.

### The Order of Merit

Hodgkin's work in crystallography unlocked the mysteries of protein crystals. This knowledge has saved millions of lives. In 1965 the Queen of England awarded the Order of Merit to Dr. Dorothy Hodgkin. Prior to Dr. Hodgkin, the only female recipient had been Florence Nightingale.

## Instructor's Guide:

### The GROWING SUGAR-SWEET CRYSTALS Experiment

## Background Information:

Although studying the atomic structure of crystals may be impossible for most amateur scientists, watching crystals grow is not. The following experiment can serve as an introduction to crystals — a springboard for additional information and colorful experiments. If possible, include magnifying glasses and microscopes in this unit.

## Instructions:

**Today**

1. Distribute "My Notes."
2. Sprinkle several grains of sugar onto a sheet of black construction paper. Allow students time to look at these grains through magnifying glasses or microscopes. (optional)
3. Set out items for the experiment.
4. Tie the paper clip onto one of the ends of the piece of string or yarn. Tie the other end of the string to the chopstick. Set aside.

Caution. Boiling water can cause severe burns. The instructor should do this part of the experiment.

5. Place the saucepan on the hot plate. Pour 1/2 cup water into the saucepan and bring to a boil. Turn off the heat, add one cup sugar, and stir for one minute.

**Explain . . .**

*Sugar grains are crystals. In science the chemical name for the granulated sugar we use in baking and sprinkling on our cereal is* ***sucrose****. In one sugar grain are millions of atoms held together in bundles, or "little masses," called molecules. These molecules are packed closely together. When I pour the sugar into the boiling water, the sugar dissolves.*

**Ask . . .**

*Why do you think the sugar dissolves?*

[Water molecules (two hydrogen and one oxygen atom make a water molecule) attract and surround the sugar molecules causing them to break away from each other. Hot water dissolves more sugar than cold water because hot water has more energy. Energy is necessary to break molecules apart.]

6. If all the sugar dissolves, add 1 to 2 tablespoons more and stir for 30 seconds. (Option: add 2 drops of food coloring.)

**Explain . . .**

*I am adding more sugar than the water can dissolve at room temperature since this solution must be "super-saturated."*

7. Pour the solution into the cup. Dampen the string and rub a few grains of sugar onto the string. Lower the paper clip and string into the solution until the chopstick rests on the cup's rim.

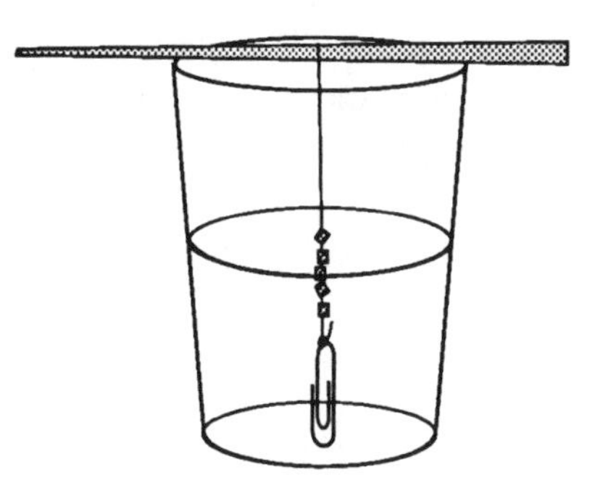

8. Give students time to answer #1 and 2 on "My Notes."

**Continued Next Page**

## Instructor's Guide continued:

**Explain . . .**

Your answer to question #2 is your **hypothesis** about the outcome of the experiment. Each day we will observe the sugar-water solution and record our findings.

9. Assist students in clean-up.

### Next 4 to 5 Days

1. Find time each day to distribute "My Notes" and observe the experiment. There should be changes daily. On the last day, allow adequate time for students to make, record, and discuss their observations and answers to question #3.

**Ask . . .**

*How does the experiment's outcome compare with your hypothesis?*

*What do you think caused the sugar crystals to grow?*

[As the solution cooled, the sugar molecules could no longer be kept apart by the water molecules. The sugar molecules became attracted to each other and began to group together. This grouping together, or "growing of crystals," is called **crystallization**.]

## Additional Notes:

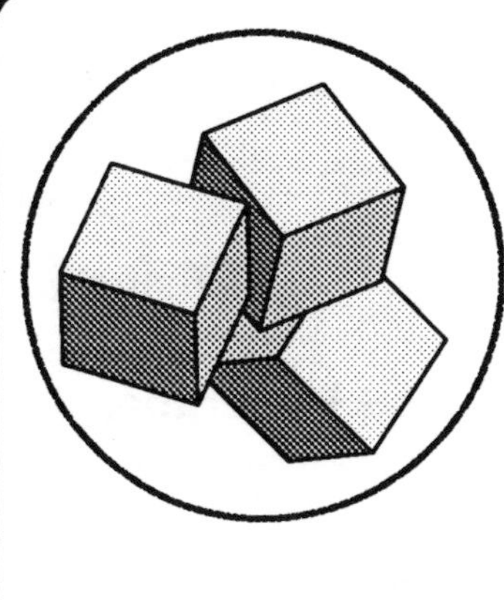

# My Notes

**by** ________________________________, **Scientist**

**GROWING SUGAR-SWEET CRYSTALS Experiment**

1. Draw the cup, string, and sugar-water solution. Space is provided for any notes you wish to write down.

| **ILLUSTRATION** | **NOTES** |
| --- | --- |
| | ______________________ |
| | ______________________ |
| | ______________________ |
| | ______________________ |
| | ______________________ |

2. Since the hot water dissolved, or broke apart, the sugar (**sucrose**) molecules, what do you think will happen when the sugar-water solution cools?

______________________________________________

______________________________________________

______________________________________________

(This answer is your **hypothesis** - or "educated guess" about the outcome of the experiment.)

---

**Day 2**

| **ILLUSTRATION** | **NOTES** |
| --- | --- |
| | ______________________ |
| | ______________________ |
| | ______________________ |
| | ______________________ |
| | ______________________ |

# My Notes

by ______________________________, Scientist

GROWING SUGAR-SWEET CRYSTALS Experiment

**Day 3**

**ILLUSTRATION**

**NOTES**

______________________________

______________________________

______________________________

______________________________

**Day 4**

**ILLUSTRATION**

**NOTES**

______________________________

______________________________

______________________________

______________________________

**Day 5**

**ILLUSTRATION**

**NOTES**

______________________________

______________________________

______________________________

______________________________

3. What do your latest observations tell you about your hypothesis?

______________________________

______________________________

______________________________

**For her extraordinary work with penicillin and vitamin B-12, Dr. Dorothy Crowfoot Hodgkin received the Nobel Prize in Chemistry in 1964. She was the sixth woman in history to receive a Nobel and the third in chemistry.**

## "The Gentle Genius" Wins a Nobel Prize

From the time Dorothy Crowfoot Hodgkin was 10 years old, she was curious about crystals. She set up a lab in the attic of the family home and grew crystals from a variety of solutions. Her first experiments were with copper sulfate and alum crystals.

Dorothy studied chemistry in college and earned a doctorate from Oxford University. In the 1940s Dr. Hodgkin decided to use X-rays to discover the atomic structure of penicillin, a protein crystal. This process is called **crystallography**. This task took four years. Seven years later Dr. Hodgkin understood the structure of vitamin B-12, and in 1969 she and her research team discovered the atomic structure of insulin.

In 1965 the Queen of England awarded the Order of Merit to Dr. Hodgkin, the second woman in England's history to receive this award. The first was Florence Nightingale.

In the 1940s one of Dr. Hodgkin's students was Margaret Thatcher, former Prime Minister of England.

## ❅ CRYSTALS ❅

- Crystals are solids.
- The atoms in crystals are arranged in a pattern.
- Crystals are everywhere—in food (sugar and salt are crystals), on the ground (igneous rocks and sand), in caves (stalagmites and stalactites), in display windows (diamonds and gold), in the air (snowflakes), and in computers, televisions, lasers, and communication satellites
- Growing crystals is possible. In class we grew **sucrose**, or __________, crystals.
- **Crystallization is** ________________

________________

## Diagnosis: Rheumatoid Arthritis

When Dorothy Hodgkin was 24 years old, the joints in her hands became quite painful. A doctor diagnosed rheumatoid arthritis. No cure existed for this condition, and Dr. Hodgkin's hands became gnarled and her fingers twisted. She did not let the arthritis interfere with her work.

Upon meeting Dr. Hodgkin, the artist Henry Moore was so moved by her hands that he asked to sketch them. She agreed. Dr. Hodgkin's official portrait and Moore's sketch of her hands hang side-by-side in the Royal Society. Dr. Hodgkin's favorite is Moore's sketch.

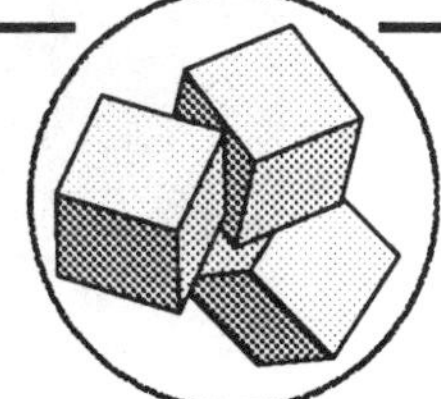

## At Home

- Experiment with crystals. Jean Stangl's **Crystals And Crystal Gardens You Can Grow** (1990), offers 50-plus pages of simple experiments.
- Each afternoon Dr. Hodgkin enjoyed tea with her co-workers. Explore this English tradition and make or purchase the customary treats.

Experimental nuclear physicist, Dr. Chien-Shiung Wu, disproved the law of parity in subatomic particles.

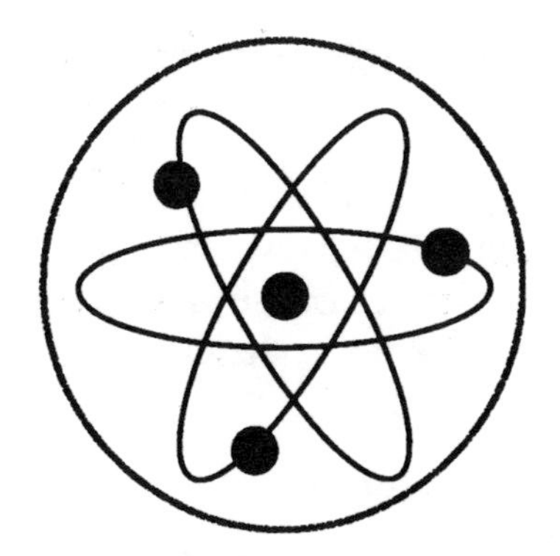

# Discovery Unit No. 19

## Dr. Chien-Shiung Wu
## Atomic Physics

### ATOMIC STATIONS

**Time-line:**

- **1912 - Dr. Chien-Shiung Wu is born in Liuhe, China.**
- 1932 - Amelia Earhart flies solo across the Atlantic Ocean
- 1951 - Color TV "arrives" in the U.S.

**Pronunciation guide:**

- Chien [Chin] - Shiung [Shing] Wu [Woo]

**Key points:**

☛ Dr. Chien-Shiung Wu is a retired experimental nuclear physicist who studied atoms.

☛ Atoms are everywhere!

☛ Atomic particles include the nucleus, protons, neutrons, and electrons.

☛ Although atoms and their particles are not visible, students at the ATOMIC STATIONS will see what happens when atoms, or some of their particles, move.

**Supplies:**

✔ Equipment for the ATOMIC STATIONS:

**BENDING WATER**
— one balloon, blown up and tied
— a sink and faucet

**INVISIBLE ATTRACTION**
— a plastic comb (or children can use their own combs for this experiment)
— one ping pong ball

**SEEING & HEARING IS BELIEVING**
— One balloon, blown up and tied
— Flavored gelatin sprinkled on a dinner plate

**LPs AND OATS**
— one long-playing record album
— 1/4 cup dried oats cereal sprinkled on a dinner plate

✔ Directions for each Atomic Station. (See page 132.)

✔ Equipment for Instructor:

**STICKY SOAP BUBBLES**
— one balloon, blown up and tied
— bottle of soap bubble mix with bubble ring

✔ "My Notes" sheets for each student

✔ ***The Scientific Gazette*** for each student

**Steps:**

1. Distribute "My Notes" sheets.
2. Visit Atomic Stations.
3. Conduct STICKY SOAP BUBBLES. (See instructor's guide, page 131.)
4. Point out Liuhe, China, and New York City on a map.
5. Share highlights of Dr. Wu's life.
6. Distribute ***The Scientific Gazette***.
7. Add Dr. Wu's name and a memento to the time-line.

**For next time:**

- Announce the next scientist.

**Bibliography:**


Herbert, Don. **Mr. Wizard's Supermarket Science.**

Hewitt, Paul G. **Conceptual Physics.**

Mebane, Robert C., and Thomas R. Rybolt. **Adventures with Atoms and Molecules: Chemistry Experiments for Young People.**

## Biography of DR. CHIEN-SHIUNG WU b. 1912

Dr. Wu is thought by many to be the "Queen of Nuclear Physics." As an experimental nuclear physicist, Dr. Wu created experiments testing theories about subatomic particles.

### "Courageous Hero"

Born in Liuhe, China, near Shanghai on May 29, 1912, her father gave her a name meaning "Courageous Hero." He believed in equal rights for women and wanted his newborn daughter to become a courageous woman. He provided her with an excellent education and advised her "to ignore the obstacles."

When she was 9 years old, Chien-Shiung left home to study at the Soochow Girls School. In high school she was enrolled in the teachers training school but soon realized that she preferred the science textbooks her friends were studying. Wu taught herself mathematics, physics, and chemistry. Physics became her favorite subject. In 1930 Wu graduated from Soochow with the highest grades in her class.

### Father's Encouragement

Before entering the National Central University in Nanjing, China, Wu thought she would study education. She felt unprepared to study physics. Her father disagreed and encouraged her to study advanced mathematics, chemistry, and physics on her own before starting the university in the fall. Wu studied on her own, majored in physics, and graduated as the university's top student.

### To the United States

In 1936 Wu left China to study at the University of Michigan. She got as far as San Francisco and enrolled at the University of California at Berkeley, the center of physics in the United States. Wu studied with Dr. Ernest O. Lawrence who would win the Nobel Prize in physics in 1939.

Wu earned her doctorate in 1940. In 1942 she married Luke Yuan, also a physicist, and moved East to teach at Smith College and Princeton University. Dr. Wu was the first woman to teach at Princeton.

### Testing Theories

From 1944 until her retirement in 1981, Dr. Wu lived in New York City and worked at Columbia University. She created experiments that tested ideas and theories about subatomic particles. (Almost 200 subatomic particles have been discovered.) One particular experiment finished in 1957 earned her worldwide attention. Dr. Wu proved that the law of parity does not hold for subatomic particles inside the nucleus — that some particles, like people, are right-handed or left-handed and favor one direction over another as they "leave" the nucleus.

### Awards

Dr. Wu did not win the Nobel Prize for her experiment (althought the two scientists who proposed testing the theory did) but did receive many awards including election to the National Academy of Science. In 1976 President Gerald Ford awarded her a National Medal of Science. She is the first living scientist to have an asteroid named in her honor.

### Bibliography:

McGrayne, Sharon Bertsch. **Nobel Prize Women in Science.**

McLenighan, Valjean. **Women and Science.**

## Instructor's Guide:

### ATOMIC STATIONS
### and
### STICKY SOAP BUBBLES

## Background Information:

There are about 100 different kinds of atoms and millions of ways these atoms combine. When two or more atoms combine, the result is a molecule. ("Molecule" is an Italian word meaning "little bundle.")

The nucleus is at the center of an atom. Inside the nucleus are protons (positively charged) and neutrons (neutrally charged). Outside the nucleus (but still inside the atom) are electrons (negatively charged). In a sense, electrons are not as closely bound to an atom and, therefore, more likely to "escape" to another object or person.

## Instructions:

**Prior to Class**

1. Set up Atomic Stations. Directions for each station are on page 132.

**In Class**

2. Distribute "My Notes."

> **Explain . . .**
>
> *Today we are going to visit Atomic Stations. You are to read the directions at each station, conduct the experiment, and write down your observations and explanations on the "My Notes" sheets.*

3. Divide class into 4 groups.
4. Visit ATOMIC STATIONS.
5. Bring the group together by demonstrating STICKY SOAP BUBBLES.

## Directions for Sticky Soap Bubbles:

a. Charge the balloon by rubbing it through your hair about 30 times.

b. Hold the balloon with one hand while you dip the bubble ring into the soap bubbles with the other.

c. Blow bubbles toward the balloon while you move the balloon toward the bubbles.

> **Explain . . .**
>
> *We cannot see atoms but we can see what happens when atoms and parts of atoms move. These parts are called "particles" and include protons, neutrons, and electrons.*
>
> *When I rubbed the balloon through my hair, electrons jumped from my hair to the balloon. When that happened, there were more electrons on the balloon than there were protons. This imbalance made the balloon electrically charged so it pulled the "polar ends" of the soap molecules toward it.*

> **Ask . . .**
>
> *What were some of your observations at the ATOMIC STATIONS?*
>
> *What do you think was happening?*
>
> [At **THE ATOMIC STATIONS** electrons were transferred to the balloons, your combs, and the record. These objects became electrically charged —with negative charges— and "attracted" objects that were either neutrally or positively charged. When the balance of electrons and protons was restored, the "attraction" ended, e.g., the ping pong ball no longer moved toward the comb, the cereal fell off the record, etc.]

6. Assist students in clean-up.

## Directions for each Atomic Station

**Station No. 1 — Bending Water:**

1. Turn the water on but not too hard.
2. Take the balloon and rub it on top of your head about 20 times.
3. Hold the part of the balloon you rubbed on your head next to the stream of water coming out of the faucet. Make sure that the balloon does not touch the water.

**Station No. 2 — Invisible Attraction:**

1. Run your comb through your hair about 20 times.
2. Hold the comb close to, but not touching, the ping pong ball.

**Station No. 3 — Seeing and Hearing is Believing:**

1. Rub the balloon on top of your head about 20 times.
2. Hold the balloon one inch above the gelatin sprinkled on the plate.

**Station No. 4 — LPs and Oats:**

1. Rub the record on top of your head about 20 times.
2. Hold the side of the record you rubbed on your head one inch above the cereal sprinkled on the plate.

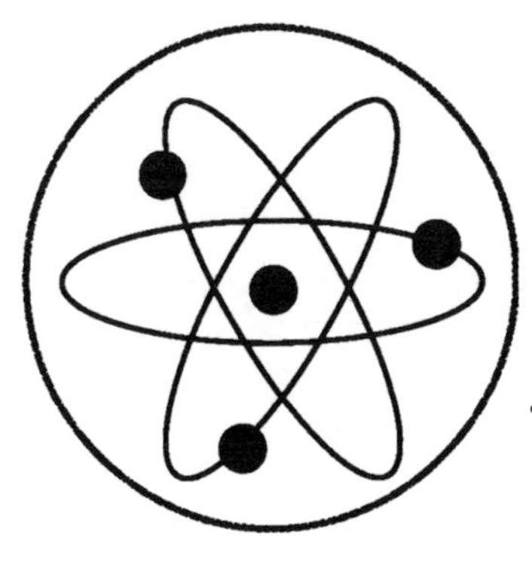

# My Notes

by ______________________________, Scientist

**The ATOMIC STATIONS, Page 1**

"Science is not static, but ever-growing and dynamic"
— Dr. Chien-Shiung Wu

**Station No. 1:**

Title ______________________________

My Observations ______________________________

______________________________

______________________________

My Explanation ______________________________

______________________________

______________________________

______________________________

**Station No. 2:**

Title ______________________________

My Observations ______________________________

______________________________

______________________________

My Explanation ______________________________

______________________________

______________________________

______________________________

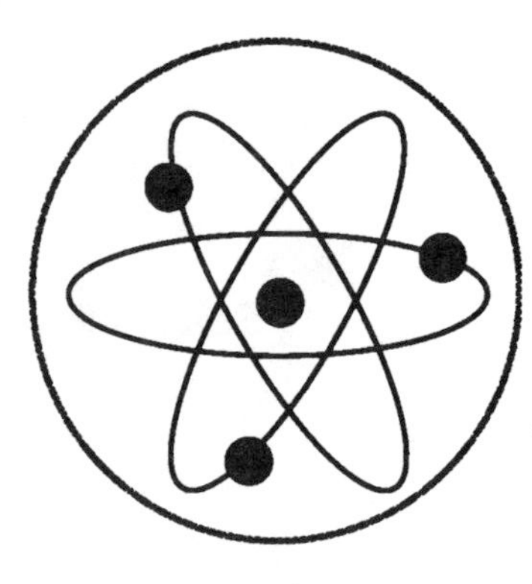

# My Notes

by ______________________________, Scientist

The ATOMIC STATIONS, Page 2

**Station No. 3:**

Title ______________________________

My Observations ______________________________

______________________________

______________________________

My Explanation ______________________________

______________________________

______________________________

______________________________

**Station No. 4:**

Title ______________________________

My Observations ______________________________

______________________________

______________________________

My Explanation ______________________________

______________________________

______________________________

______________________________

# The Scientific Gazette

**Atomic Physics** | **Dr. Chien-Shiung Wu**

## Atoms Are Everywhere

**Dateline: EARTH**

Atoms are in our food, in our hair, and in our clothes. We eat them, breathe them, walk through them, and even stomp on them. Atoms are in our pencils, in our papers, in our eyelashes and in the water we drink. In one tablespoon of water, there are as many atoms as there are drops of water in the Atlantic Ocean.

We may not be able to see atoms or their particles, but we can see what happens when they move. When bed covers are thrown back and little sparks suddenly appear and disappear, those dots of light are electrons moving from one blanket to another. If the sparks tickle, then the electrons are moving from the blanket to you!

At our ATOMIC STATIONS in class, we saw what happens when electrons move from one object to another. This is a picture of me at one of the Atomic Stations.

**In this picture I am** ______________________

______________________________________

______________________________________

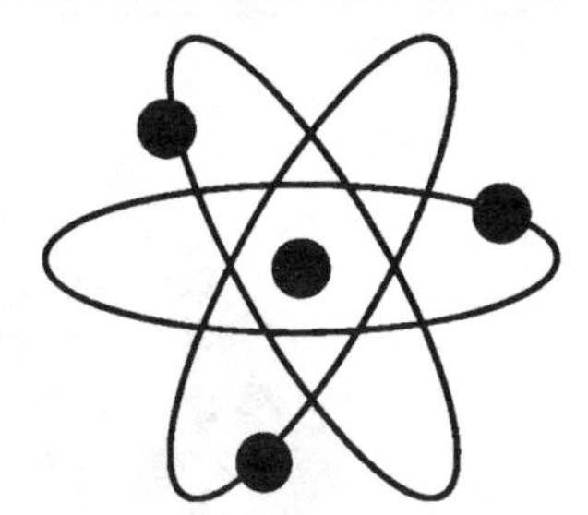

Physicists create drawings to help them understand how atoms work. One drawing compares an atom to a solar system.

### Learning About a Famous Scientist

Dr. Chien-Shiung Wu is a retired experimental nuclear physicist who studied atoms. How many of the following true or false questions can you answer correctly?

**Dr. Chien-Shiung Wu**

| T | F | | |
|---|---|---|---|
| ❑ | ❑ | 1. | In Chinese, Dr. Wu's name means "Courageous Hero." |
| ❑ | ❑ | 2. | Many scientists call Dr. Wu "The Queen of Nuclear Physics." |
| ❑ | ❑ | 3. | Dr. Wu was born in San Francisco, California. |
| ❑ | ❑ | 4. | She was the first woman to teach at Princeton University. |
| ❑ | ❑ | 5. | In an experiment finished in 1957, Dr. Wu disproved the law of parity in subatomic particles. |

❄❄❄

*"Ignore the obstacles. Just put your head down and keep walking forward."*

— Wu Zhongyi, Dr. Wu's father

❄❄❄

(Questions 1,2,4,5 are true. Question 3 is false.)

Dr. Jewel Plummer Cobb, cell biologist, is a third-generation scientist.

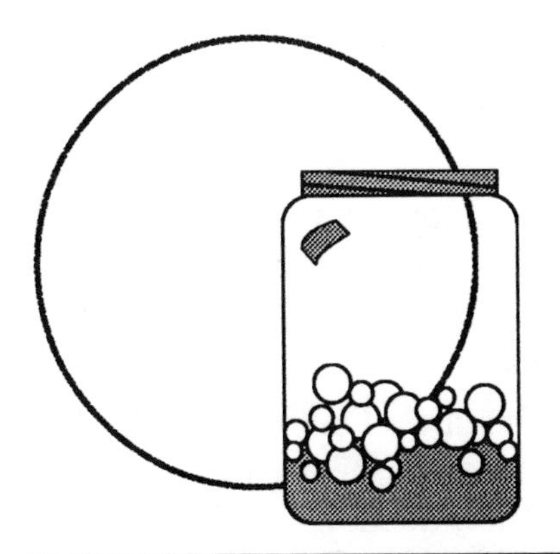

# Discovery Unit No. 20

## Dr. Jewel Plummer Cobb
## Biology

### FRIENDLY FUNGUS Experiment

**Time-line:**

- **1924 - Dr. Jewel Plummer Cobb is born in Chicago, Illinois.**
- 1954 - U.S. children receive polio inoculations
- 1966 - Color television becomes popular

**Pronunciation guide:**

- melanoma [mell-uh-NO-mah]

**Key points:**

☛ Dr. Cobb is a third-generation scientist. She is a cell biologist.

☛ Her interest in biology goes back to her sophomore year in high school.

☛ Believing "no career was out of bounds," Dr. Cobb wants other women and minorities to pursue careers in the sciences and mathematics.

☛ The FRIENDLY FUNGUS Experiment will offer the student an opportunity to study yeast, a single-celled fungi.

**Supplies:**

✔ Two 1-pint canning jars

✔ 1 cup warm tap water

✔ 2 teaspoons sugar

✔ 1 Tablespoon active dry yeast

✔ Measuring cups and measuring spoons

✔ Microscopes, if available, so that students can watch yeast cells divide

✔ "My Notes" for each student

✔ *The Scientific Gazette* for each student

**Steps:**

1. Point out Chicago, Illinois, and Fullerton, California, on a map.
2. Share highlights of Dr. Cobb's life.
3. Distribute "My Notes" sheet.
4. Conduct the FRIENDLY FUNGUS Experiment. (See instructor's guide, p. 139.)
5. Assist students in clean-up.
6. Distribute ***The Scientific Gazette***.
7. Add Dr. Cobb's name and a memento to the time-line.

**For next time:**

- Announce the next scientist.

**Bibliography:**

Cloyd, Iris, Editor. **Who's Who Among Black Americans.**

National Women's History Project Archives. Windsor, California.

Sammons, Vivian Ovelton. **Blacks in Science and Medicine.**

Smith, Jessie Carney, Editor. **Notable Black American Women.**

## Biography of
## DR. JEWEL PLUMMER COBB
## b. 1924

*"Our most important task is the guidance and inspiration we can give to young people through the process of education."*

**— Dr. Jewel Plummer Cobb**

Dr. Cobb is a third-generation scientist. Her grandfather, a freed slave, was a pharmacist; her father, Dr. Frank V. Plummer, practiced medicine in Chicago; and she became a cell biologist.

### Home Life

Jewel Plummer was an only child. Since her father was a physician and her mother a physical education/dance instructor, science discussions and cultural events were common in the Plummer household. A large home library contained material about black Americans, scientific journals, and assorted magazines including current news periodicals.

### High School Biology

Dr. Cobb's interest in biology began in high school during her sophomore year when her biology teacher gave the students microscopes. This experience opened "an entirely new world beyond my normal viewing capacity." (Cobb in **SAGE**, Vol. VI, no. 2 [Fall 1989]) Botany and zoology followed, but biology remained Jewel's favorite subject.

### College, College, and more College

Biology became her major in college. She graduated in 1944 from Talladega College in Alabama and then studied for six years at New York University where she earned her master's and doctoral degrees in cell physiology.

### Research and Education

Dr. Cobb entered research. A cell biologist watches living cells and how they interact with other living cells. A molecular biologist studies the atoms and molecules of cells. Dr. Cobb's interest was in cell biology and cancer research. She studied how cancer drugs act on human cancer cells particularly melanoma, cancer (or tumors) of the skin.

In addition to research, Dr. Cobb began teaching college students. She taught at University of Illinois Medical School, New York University, Sarah Lawrence College, Connecticut College, and Douglass College (women's division of Rutgers University). Her classes included biology, anatomy, and zoology. At Connecticut and Douglass Colleges, Dr. Cobb served as a dean and professor.

### College President

In 1981 Dr. Cobb became the president of California State University in Fullerton, California. She was the first black woman president of a major public university in the western U.S. During her presidency, the student body grew from 22,000 students to 25,000, and the college obtained money for a computer science building and funding for a $22 million science building. Believing "no career was out of bounds," Dr. Cobb recruited more women and minorities to the campus and encouraged them to pursue careers in the sciences and mathematics.

In 1990 Dr. Cobb retired as president and returned to writing books and articles about higher education. She is the author of 46 publications and the recipient of 16 honorary doctorate degrees.

## Instructor's Guide:

### The FRIENDLY FUNGUS Experiment

### Background Information:

For her master's degree, Dr. Jewel Plummer Cobb studied the effects of organic molecules on the respiration of yeast cells. Students will work with active dry yeast, a "friendly" single-celled fungi.

### Instructions:

**Several days before**

- Decide format most suitable for your class, e.g., one central experiment using two jars, or 4 to 5 experiment centers with students divided into groups. If available, include magnifying glasses and/or microscopes.

**Today**

1. Distribute "My Notes."
2. Organize class into the format of your choice.

**Explain . . .**

*When Dr. Cobb was studying for her master's degree, she studied yeast cells. Yeast cells are a fungus.*

3. To conduct the experiment:
   - Place the two jars side-by-side. Label one jar "A" and the other "B".
   - Into each jar pour 1/2 cup warm tap water.
   - Add 1 teaspoon sugar to each jar. Stir gently to dissolve sugar.

**Explain . . .**

*We are now going to add active dry yeast to jar "A". One Tablespoon of yeast contains millions of these one-celled fungi.*

   - Add yeast to jar "A" and stir gently to dissolve.

**Ask . . .**

*What is the independent variable in The FRIENDLY FUNGUS Experiment?* [The yeast]

*How do active dry yeast cells react when put in a warm sugar-water mixture?*

4. Allow 5 - 10 minutes to observe the experiment. Remind students to jot down their observations and to answer the questions on their "My Notes" sheets.
5. Give students time to discuss their observations/answers in their experiment groups or in pairs.
6. Discuss observations/answers as a class.

**Explain . . .**

*Yeast cells jump into action when placed in a warm, moist environment. When yeast cells take in — or absorb — water, they begin to digest the sugar in the water and then release alcohol and carbon dioxide. The bubbles are carbon dioxide. If we add flour to our yeast mixture, we make bread dough. During the baking of the dough, the yeast cells die from the heat, the alcohol evaporates, and the carbon dioxide makes holes in the bread.*

7. Assist students in clean-up.

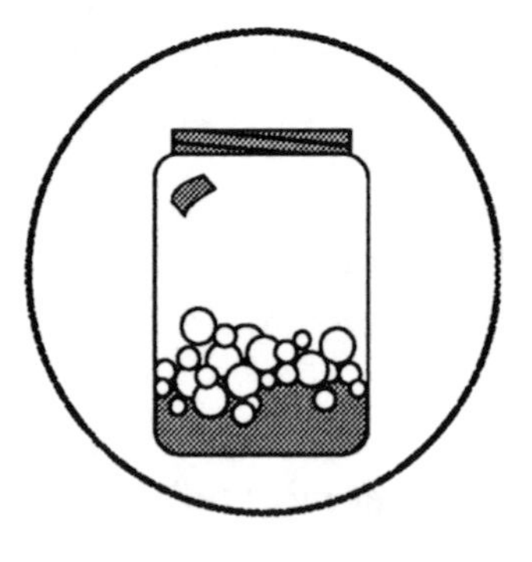

# My Notes

by ______________________________, Scientist

**FRIENDLY FUNGUS Experiment**

| **JAR "A"** | **JAR "B"** |
| --- | --- |
| 1/2 cup warm water | 1/2 cup warm water |
| 1 teaspoon sugar | 1 teaspoon sugar |
| 1 Tablespoon yeast | |

1. What is the **independent variable** in this experiment? ____________________
2. What question will this experiment answer? ____________________

______________________________________________

## My Observations of the Experiment

(Drawings or Notes — or both!)

3. From this experiment I learned that ____________________

______________________________________________

______________________________________________

*In one pound of yeast, there are 3,200 billion yeast cells. In one tablespoon, there are millions.*

# The Scientific Gazette

**Biology** **Dr. Jewel Plummer Cobb**

## A Shore-to-Shore Journey

**Dr. Jewel Plummer Cobb, cancer cell biologist and college administrator, believed "no career was out of bounds." She is a third-generation scientist.**

Born in Chicago, Illinois, Jewel's mother was a physical education/dance instructor, and her father was a physician. Her interest in biology began her sophomore year of high school. Cobb attended the University of Michigan at Ann Arbor before transferring toTalladega College in Alabama to study biology.

From 1944-1969 Dr. Cobb entered New York University where she earned master's and doctoral degrees in cell physiology, did research work at the National Cancer Institute in New York, and taught at several colleges including the University of Illinois, Hunter College, and Sarah Lawrence College.

For the next seven years, Dr. Cobb was a Professor of Zoology and Dean at Connecticut College in New London, Connecticut, followed by a five-year deanship at Douglass College in New Jersey. Her next job was President of California State University in Fullerton, California.

Upon retiring in July 1990, Dr. Cobb returned to writing books and articles. She is the author of 46 publications and the recipient of 16 honorary doctorate degrees.

## At Home:

- As a child, Dr. Cobb "became familiar with the aspirations, successes, and talents of black people" (**Notable Black American Women**, Jessie Carney Smith, Editor) including historian Carter G. Woodson, writer/librarian Arna Bontemps, anthropologist Allison Davis, and YWCA director Alpha White. Her uncle was musician Bob Cole. Begin with your local library and explore the lives of these notable Americans.
- From molds and mushrooms to "imperfect fungi" used to make penicillin and to flavor cheeses, the 81,500 species of the kingdom Fungi are everywhere. Check out the world of fungi at your local library.

> *"I think I'd like to be remembered as a black woman scientist who cared very much about what happens to young folks, particularly women going into science."* — **Dr. Jewel Plummer Cobb**

## AMAZING YEAST

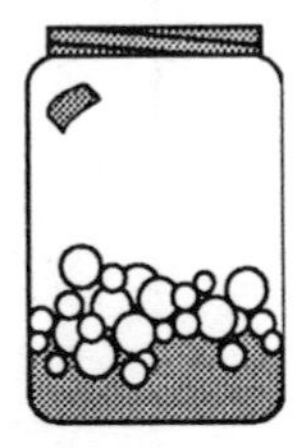

For her master's degree, Dr. Cobb studied the respiration of yeast cells. Yeast cells are a single-celled fungi. In our FRIENDLY FUNGUS Experiment, we studied how active dry yeast expands.

### Fun Fungi Fact

Although some yeast cells cause disease, others ferment beverages, synthesize antibiotics, and raise bread dough.

Breadmaking was popular among the ancient Egyptians: they combined yeast, flours, water, and salt; kneaded the dough well (sometimes with their feet); and baked the loaves in beehive-shaped clay ovens.

Dr. Reatha Clark King, former chemist and college professor, now serves as the Executive Director of the General Mills Foundation.

# Discovery Unit No. 21

## Dr. Reatha Clark King
## Chemistry

### CANDLE, CANDLE BURNING BRIGHT Experiment

**Time-line:**

- **1938 - Dr. Reatha Clark King is born in Pavo, Georgia.**
- 1960 - U.S. launches its first weather satellite
- 1982 - Cray computer does 100,000,000 operations in a second

**Key points:**

- ☛ Dr. Reatha Clark King is the Executive Director of the General Mills Foundation whose grants support education, health, social action, the arts, and cultural affairs.
- ☛ From 1977 to 1988, Dr. King was president of Metropolitan State University in St. Paul/ Minneapolis, Minnesota.
- ☛ Dr. King earned a doctorate in chemistry and worked as a research chemist and professor of chemistry.
- ☛ Chemistry studies how chemicals form everything in the world.
- ☛ In the CANDLE, CANDLE BURNING BRIGHT Experiment, students will observe a surprising chemical reaction.

**Supplies:**

- ✔ A candle and candle holder
- ✔ Matches
- ✔ Two identical 8 oz. jars (transparent)
- ✔ 2 Tablespoons distilled vinegar
- ✔ 1 teaspoon baking soda
- ✔ A "My Notes" sheet for each student
- ✔ ***The Scientific Gazette*** for each student

**Steps:**

1. Point out Pavo, Georgia, and St. Paul/ Minneapolis, Minnesota, on a map.
2. Share highlights of Dr. Reatha Clark King's life.
3. Distribute "My Notes" sheet.
4. Conduct the CANDLE, CANDLE BURNING BRIGHT Experiment (See instructor's guide, page 145.)
5. Complete and discuss "My Notes."
6. Assist students in clean-up.
7. Distribute ***The Scientific Gazette***.
8. Add Dr. Reatha Clark King's name and a memento to the time-line.

**For next time:**

- Announce the next scientist.

**Bibliography:**

Cloyd, Iris, Editor. **Who's Who Among Black Americans.**

King, Reatha Clark. "Becoming a Scientist: An Important Career Decision," **SAGE**, Vol. VI, No. 2 (fall 1989)

National Women's History Project Archives. Windsor, California.

## Biography of DR. REATHA CLARK KING b. 1938

*"Our destiny as Black children was to make something out of ourselves...."*

— Dr. Reatha Clark King

### Because of Science

Dr. King has lectured in Japan, Israel, the Philippines, Tanzania, India, and Bangladesh. She has received honorary doctorate degrees from seven colleges/universities and serves on corporate and community boards.

She is the Executive Director of the General Mills Foundation in Minneapolis, Minnesota. Grants from this foundation support education, health programs, social action, the arts, and a variety of cultural affairs.

Dr. King credits the knowledge and discipline she learned in science for her success.

### From Home Ec to Chemistry

When Reatha Clark entered Clark College in Atlanta, Georgia, she was planning to study home economics. Her family, neighbors, teachers, and church people encouraged her to make good use of her brains, although no one suggested she become a scientist.

That was before Dr. Alfred Spriggs, the Chair of the Chemistry Department at Clark College, told Reatha about the requirements for becoming a research chemist and described the work and the pay. Reatha changed her major to chemistry.

### A Doctorate

After graduating from Clark College, Reatha attended the University of Chicago where she earned a master's degree in science in 1960 and a doctorate in chemistry three years later.

Dr. Reatha Clark King became a research chemist at the National Bureau of Standards in Washington, D.C. She analyzed, tested, and measured chemicals in different substances like fuel oils. The work was demanding and had to be of the highest quality.

After working at the Bureau for almost six years, Dr. King left to begin her career as a chemistry professor and associate college dean.

From 1977 to 1988, Dr. King was president of Metropolitan State University in St Paul/ Minneapolis, Minnesota. During this time enrollment increased from 1600 to 6000 students.

### Family

Family has always been important to Dr. King. She grew up in a sharecropper family in Pavo, Georgia, and spent time picking cotton and other crops. Her parents were not formally educated, but their love and concern guided Reatha and her sister Mamie who majored in nursing at Dillard University in New Orleans.

In 1961 Reatha Clark married Dr. N. Judge King, Jr. They live in Maplewood, Minnesota, with their two sons, N. Judge King III and Scott. Dr. Reatha King acknowledges that her family is a source of strength and optimism.

## Instructor's Guide:

### The CANDLE, CANDLE BURNING BRIGHT Experiment

#### Background Information:

In this experiment, students will observe a chemical reaction. By holding the vinegar (Step 1) and then the baking soda (Step 2) to the candle with no subsequent "ill effects" to the flame, the demonstration of a chemical reaction when both substances are combined (Step 3) will be more impressive.

#### Instructions:

1. Assemble all equipment needed for the experiment.
   - A candle and candle holder
   - Matches
   - Two 8 oz. glasses or jars (transparent)
   - 2 Tablespoons distilled vinegar
   - 1 teaspoon baking soda
2. Distribute "My Notes."
3. Light the candle.
4. Measure 2 Tablespoons vinegar into one of the 8 oz. jars.
6. Give students time to answer Part A. 1. on "My Notes."

#### Conduct Step 1 of Experiment:

1. Tilt the jar with the vinegar so both the jar and vinegar are approximately 1/2" from the candle flame. Hold for 15 seconds.
2. Give students time to complete Part A.
3. Measure 1 teaspoon baking soda into the other 8 oz. jar.
4. Give students time to answer Part B. 1.

#### Conduct Step 2 of Experiment:

1. Tilt the jar with the baking soda so both the jar and the soda are approximately 1/2" from the candle flame. Hold for 15 seconds.
2. Give students time to complete Part B.
3. Give students time to answer Part C. 1.

#### Conduct Step 3 of Experiment:

1. Pour the vinegar into the baking soda. Immediately tilt the jar so its rim and bubbling mixture are 1/2" from the candle flame. Hold for 15 seconds. (The flame should extinguish in 8-12 seconds.)
2. Share answers and discuss.

**Explain . . .**

*Fire needs oxygen to burn. Sometimes firefighters will use water to put out a fire and sometimes they smother a fire by putting another chemical over it so oxygen can't get to the fire. A chemical that smothers fires is carbon dioxide. Carbon dioxide is a gas. Fire extinguishers are filled with carbon dioxide.*

**Ask . . .**

*What caused the candle's flame to be extinguished?* [When vinegar and baking soda are combined, carbon dioxide is produced.]

**Explain . . .**

*When two substances, like vinegar and baking soda, combine and another substance, like carbon dioxide, is produced, you have a* ***chemical reaction****. When you work with and study chemical reactions, you become a* ***chemist*** *like Dr. Reatha Clark King.*

3. Give students time to complete Part C.
4. Assist students in clean-up.

# My Notes

by ______________________________, Scientist

**CANDLE, CANDLE BURNING BRIGHT Experiment**

A. 1. When the vinegar is held next to the candle flame, I think the flame will:

______________________________

Your answer is your *hypothesis*.

2. What happened when the vinegar was held next to the flame?

______________________________

3. Was your *hypothesis* correct? ______________________________

B. 1. When the baking soda is held next to the candle flame, I think the flame will: ______________________________

2. What happened when the baking soda was held next to the flame?

______________________________

3. Was your *hypothesis* correct? ______________________________

C. 1. When the baking soda and vinegar are combined and held next to the candle flame, I think the flame will: ______________________________

______________________________

2. What happened when this mixture was held next to the flame? __________

______________________________

3. Was your *hypothesis* correct? ______________________________

# The Scientific Gazette

**Chemistry** | **Dr. Reatha Clark King**

**Reatha Clark King, Executive Director, college president, and research chemist**

## Credit Given to Science

Dr. King believes her work in chemistry prepared her to be a college president, worldwide lecturer, community worker, and Executive Director of the General Mills Foundation.

Growing up in a sharecropper family in Georgia, King picked cotton and other crops. Her parents were not formally educated, but they loved Reatha and her sister and encouraged both girls to make something of themselves.

Reatha Clark King went to college with the idea of studying home economics but changed to chemistry. After earning a doctorate from the University of Chicago, Dr. King worked as a research chemist at the National Bureau of Standards in Washington, D.C. Science taught her to work hard and to do a good job at whatever she undertook.

## Na - Au - Sn - C - O - Fe

**Na**
**Au**
**Sn**
**C**
**O**
**Fe**

Chemists have their own language. They use special symbols, **chemical symbols**, instead of writing out the names of elements. All matter, including solids, liquids, and gases, is made up of elements. There are approximately 100 known elements, and each has its own chemical symbol. A symbol may have one, two, or three letters. The first letter is always capitalized.

Look in a dictionary under ***element.*** Complete the chart below.

| Element | Symbol |
|---|---|
| Carbon | C |
| | Au |
| | H |
| Iron | |
| | Ni |
| Oxygen | |
| | Na |
| Tin | |
| | U |
| Zinc | |

**Chemical Symbols** come in handy when chemists write formulas. Instead of writing out "carbon dioxide," a chemist writes "$CO_2$". The formula for baking soda is $NaHCO_3$. Look at your chart. What elements are in baking soda?

**Fun things to do at Home:**

- **175 More Science Experiments To Amuse and Amaze Your Friends** by Terry Cash, Steve Parker, and Barbara Taylor features simple chemistry experiments (pages 89 to 128).
- Explore careers in chemistry.
- Read ingredient labels on packaged foods.

Biologist Dr. Elma Gonzalez is the first Mexican-American woman scientist to achieve the rank of Full Professor in the University of California nine-campus system.

# Discovery Unit No. 22

## Dr. Elma Gonzalez
## Biology

### CAN'T GROW WRONG Experiment

**Time-line:**

- **1942 - Dr. Elma Gonzalez is born in Mexico.**
- 1954 - Scientists develop a measles vaccine

**Pronunciation guide:**

- Gonzalez [Gone-ZAH-less]

**Key points:**

- ☛ From the time Dr. Gonzalez was a young girl, she enjoyed asking questions. Now a research scientist, she still asks questions.
- ☛ Dr. Gonzalez's research projects include work with castor bean seeds.
- ☛ In July 1993, Dr. Elma Gonzalez became the first Mexican-American woman scientist to achieve the rank of Full Professor in the University of California system.
- ☛ In the CAN'T GROW WRONG Experiment, students will germinate lima bean seeds and observe how they grow.

**Supplies:**

- ✔ 3 - 4 large lima beans for each student (Purchase from a bulk food bin. There are approximately 175 beans in 1/2 pound.)
- ✔ A clear plastic drinking glass/student
- ✔ One blank sticker label/student
- ✔ 2 - 3 paper towels for each student
- ✔ Plastic wrap to cover each glass
- ✔ Rubber bands to encircle the glasses
- ✔ Water
- ✔ Magnifying glasses (Days 2 - 10)
- ✔ Colored pencils or felt pens
- ➙ "My Notes" for each student
- ➙ *The Scientific Gazette* for each student

**Steps — Day 1:**

1. Begin the CAN'T GROW WRONG Experiment. (See instructor's guide, p. 151.)
2. Complete Day 1 of "My Notes."
3. Assist students in clean-up.
4. Point out Los Angeles, California, on a map.
5. Share highlights of Dr. Gonzalez's life.

**Steps — Day 2 to Day 9:**

1. Examine experiment and enter observations in "Notes and Illustration."
2. On Day 7, invert seed glasses.

**Steps — Day 10:**

1. Examine experiment.
2. Complete Day 10 "Notes and Illustration."
3. Assist students in clean-up.
4. Distribute ***The Scientific Gazette***.
5. Add Dr. Gonzalez's name and a memento to the time-line.

**For next time:**

- Announce the next scientist.

**Bibliography:**


Gonzalez, Dr. Elma. **UCLA Press Release.**

Gonzalez, Dr. Elma. **UCLA Biology Department Brochure.**

Ontario Science Centre. **Foodworks.**

Verheyden-Hilliard, Mary Ellen. **Scientist with Determination, Elma Gonzalez.**

## Biography of DR. ELMA GONZALEZ b. 1942

*"Education is a way out of being poor."*

**— Nestor and Efigenia Gonzalez**

### No School Bus

In 1942 Elma was born to Nestor and Efigenia Gonzalez, migrant workers in Mexico. When she was six, her family moved to Texas. They worked for a rancher and lived in a cabin on his ranch. In September the school refused to send a bus out to the ranch to pick up just one person — Elma. To attend school, Elma's parents sent her into the city to live with an older cousin. Soon Elma was back home. Her tendency to ask many questions caused the cousin to return the inquisitive child to her parents.

By nine years of age, Elma still had not attended school. To make this possible, the Gonzalez family moved into the city.

### 21 Years

From 1951 until 1972, Elma attended school. In junior high, she enjoyed math, especially algebra, and at Hebbronville High School in Hebbronville, Texas, she joined the science club, played basketball, and graduated third in her class. In the spring and summer, she picked fruit. A student loan made college possible.

At Texas Woman's University, Elma majored in biology and chemistry. After graduation she worked as a research technician at a medical school in Dallas. From 1968 until 1972, she attended Rutgers University in New Brunswick, New Jersey, and earned a Ph.D in cellular biology.

### UCLA

In 1974 Dr. Gonzalez was appointed to the faculty of the Department of Biology at the University of California in Los Angeles (UCLA). Her job as a research scientist is a perfect career for someone who loves to ask questions. Her research has included yeasts and castor bean seeds. She is now researching marine phytoplankton (fi-toe-PLANK-ton), single-celled algae that form their own crystals which settle to the bottom of the ocean. In millions of years, this accumulation of crystals may break the surface of the ocean and form chalk cliffs, like the White Cliffs of Dover, England.

Dr. Gonzalez is the author of over 35 research papers and articles published in notable scientific journals. At UCLA she directs the Center for Academic and Research Excellence and focuses on the academic needs of Native Americans, Mexican-Americans, Latinos, and African Americans.

### A Fellowship and Invitations

Dr. Gonzalez received a fellowship from the Ford Foundation in 1978, participated in a national meeting of Women in Higher Education Administration in 1987, and presented her research findings at international gatherings in England and France in 1993.

### A "First"

In July 1993, Dr. Elma Gonzalez became the first Mexican-American woman scientist to achieve the rank of Full Professor in the University of California (UC) nine-campus system. Approximately six Latina Full Professors in all disciplines are employed in the UC system. Her parents were right: "Education is a way out of being poor."

◆ ◆ ◆

## Instructor's Guide:

### CAN'T GROW WRONG Experiment

### Background Information:

Dr. Elma Gonzalez studied castor bean seeds which are poisonous. Students will study large lima beans (which they may think are poisonous but we know otherwise!). Although both the castor and lima are beans, they belong to different families.

From the organization of the castor bean seed's protein cells during germination, Dr. Gonzalez learned how the bean develops and protects itself from disease. She hopes this information will shed light on how human cells might more effectively fight disease. From the CAN'T GROW WRONG Experiment, students will learn how bean seeds germinate and seem to "know" that roots grow "down" and stems grow "up."

### Instructions:

Allow 10 days for this experiment. The purpose of the extensive use of "Notes and Illustration" in this unit is to sharpen the young scientist's powers of observation and verbal expression.

**(Have magnifying glasses and colored pencils available daily.)**

#### Day 1

1. Begin the CAN'T GROW WRONG Experiment.
   - Distribute lima beans, glasses (called seed glasses from this point on), and blank sticker labels. Students write their names on the labels and affix to seed glasses.
   - In the seed glasses, soak seeds in water 45 to 60 minutes.
2. Instruct students to pour off the water and examine the seeds.

**Explain . . .**

*All seeds have a seed coat on the outside. This coat protects the seed.*

**Ask . . .**

*What happened to the seed coat after you soaked it in water? How might this help the seed germinate?*

[By softening the seed coat, the seed can sprout.]

3. Distribute "My Notes."
4. Allow time to complete Day 1 "Notes and Illustration."
5. Distribute paper towels, dampen, and "scrunch" loosely into the seed glasses. Place the beans between the glass and the towels so beans are visible.
6. Cover seed glasses with plastic wrap and secure wrap with a rubber band. Puncture **several small holes** in the plastic wrap.

#### Days 2 to 6

1. Distribute seed glasses and "My Notes."
2. Allow time for "Notes and Illustration."

#### Day 7

1. Distribute seed glasses and "My Notes."
2. Complete "Notes and Illustration."
3. Invert the seed glasses. Keep inverted through Day 10.

#### Days 8 and 9

1. Distribute seed glasses and "My Notes."
2. Complete "Notes and Illustration."

#### Day 10

1. Distribute seed glasses.

**Ask . . .**

*Since you turned over the seed glasses, what has happened to the seeds?*

[Plants seem to know that roots grow down and stems grow toward the source of light. These bean plants CAN'T GROW WRONG even if we try to fool them!]

2. Turn seed glasses right-side-up.
3. Allow time for students to answer Question A in Day 10 "Notes and Illustration."
4. Carefully remove the seeds from the seed glasses.
5. Test hypotheses by carefully opening one or two seeds from each seed glass.
6. Students draw their illustrations and answer Question B.
7. Share answers and discoveries.

**Explain . . .**

*The inside of the bean is food for the baby plant or plant embryo. As the plant grows, the seed becomes smaller. In time, the plant will be fed through its roots.*

8. Assist students in clean-up. Discard seeds or plant them in soil.

◆ ◆ ◆

**Enrichment Activities:**

- Purchase a package of 15-bean soup. Select the 15 varieties. Try germinating some of these beans.
- Explore George Washington Carver's work with peanuts. Like the castor bean, Carver found many uses for the peanut and its byproducts.

**Add notes here:**

## My Notes — CAN'T GROW WRONG Experiment

by ______________________________, Scientist

**Day 1: Notes and Illustration**

Describe & illustrate seed's appearance before soaking:

______________________________

______________________________

______________________________

______________________________

Describe & illustrate seed's appearance after soaking:

______________________________

______________________________

______________________________

______________________________

**Day 2: Notes and Illustration**

______________________________

______________________________

______________________________

______________________________

**Day 3: Notes and Illustration**

______________________________

______________________________

______________________________

______________________________

# My Notes — CAN'T GROW WRONG Experiment

by ______________________________, Scientist

**Day 4: Notes and Illustration**

______________________________

______________________________

______________________________

______________________________

**Day 5: Notes and Illustration**

______________________________

______________________________

______________________________

______________________________

**Day 6: Notes and Illustration**

______________________________

______________________________

______________________________

______________________________

**Day 7: Notes and Illustration**

______________________________

______________________________

______________________________

______________________________

## My Notes — CAN'T GROW WRONG Experiment

by ______________________________, Scientist

**Day 8: Notes and Illustration**

______________________________

______________________________

______________________________

______________________________

**Day 9: Notes and Illustration**

______________________________

______________________________

______________________________

______________________________

Why do you think this is called the CAN'T GROW WRONG Experiment?

______________________________

______________________________

______________________________

**Day 10: Notes and Illustration**

**Question A:**

If you looked inside the seed, what do you think you would find? (Your answer is your *hypothesis*.)

______________________________

______________________________

______________________________

# My Notes — CAN'T GROW WRONG Experiment

by ______________________________, Scientist

Test your hypothesis. Gently open one of the seeds. Draw what you see inside the seed.

**Question B:** How does your discovery compare with your hypothesis?

_______________________________________________

_______________________________________________

_______________________________________________

_______________________________________________

*"Seeds found after several thousand years in the tombs of Egyptian pharaohs or kings were still able to germinate."* — **Foodworks by the Ontario Science Centre**

The Scientific Gazette

Biology — Dr. Elma Gonzalez

## Girl With Love for Questions Becomes Research Scientist

When Elma Gonzalez was a young girl and the school refused to send a bus out to the ranch to pick her up, her parents sent Elma into the city to live with an older cousin. Elma was soon returned home. She asked the older cousin too many questions!

Later, when Elma Gonzalez was in college and was thinking about becoming a teacher, a college professor suggested she become a research scientist instead. After all, Elma loved questions and a research scientist's job includes asking questions and then working to find the answers.

At the University of California in Los Angeles (UCLA), Dr. Elma Gonzalez is a research scientist who has studied yeasts and castor bean seeds. The organization of the seeds' protein cells during germination may help scientists understand how human cells can fight disease.

Dr. Gonzalez finds her work exciting. She is the first Mexican-American woman scientist to achieve the rank of Full Professor in the University of California nine-campus system. As Director of the Center for Academic and Research Excellence, she encourages other Native American, Mexican-American, Latino and African American students to enter scientific and research careers.

### The Amazing Castor Bean

Castor trees grow mostly in Brazil and India. Although the castor bean is poisonous, non-poisonous oil is pressed from the seed and used for medicine. The poisonous residue is processed and used in:

oil for race cars and airplane engines
paints, dyes, and varnishes
plastics
asphalt tile
electrical insulation
perfumes
nylon
biodegradable detergents

The ancient Egyptians used castor oil in embalming fluid and the Sumerians made soap from castor oil

*"Education is a way out of being poor."* —**Nestor and Efigenia Gonzalez**

### A Vine and A Stalk

Native Americans planted bean seeds beside a sprouting corn stalk. When the bean seeds germinated and grew, their vines wrapped around the corn stalks.

Harvested at the same time, the beans and corn were cooked together in water and flavored with oil or bear grease. This dish was called *sukquttahash*, the early version of our modern day *succotash* which includes carrots, turnips, and potatoes as well as beans. (Perl, Lila. **Slumps, Grunts and Snickerdoodles: What Colonial America Ate and Why.**)

**At Home:**

With an adult's assistance, make soup using a 15-bean mix.

Dr. Mae C. Jemison, medical doctor and astronaut, is the first woman of color to go into space.

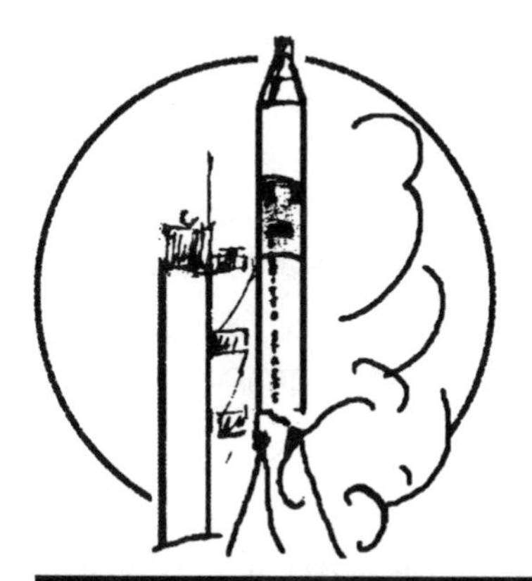

# Discovery Unit No. 23

Dr. Mae C. Jemison
Physics

## GRAVITY IS SERIOUS BUSINESS Experiment

### Time-line:

- **1956 - Dr. Mae C. Jemison is born in Decatur, Alabama.**
- 1965 - In the United States, $26.2 billion is spent for public education
- 1969 - Apollo 11 spacecraft travels through space at 25,000 m.p.h.

### Key Points:

☛ On September 12, 1992, Dr. Mae C. Jemison became the first woman of color to go into space.

☛ Dr. Mae C. Jemison is a physician, a general practitioner, who has practiced medicine in Sierra Leone and Liberia as well as in Los Angeles.

☛ Retired from NASA, Dr. Jemison has founded a company whose mission is to improve health care in West Africa.

☛ In the GRAVITY IS SERIOUS BUSINESS Experiment, students will explore the relationship between the distance an object falls and the speed of that object.

### Supplies:

✔ A round rock (approximately 1" in diameter) for each group

✔ A cookie sheet (or deep tray) for each group

✔ Mud spread thickly onto each cookie sheet *(Called "earth trays," these can be a class project prior to conducting the experiment. A good ratio of water:earth is 1: 6.)*

✔ A large spoon or trowel for each group

✔ A ruler marked in centimeters for each group

✔ A "My Notes" for each student

✔ Different heights up to and exceeding 10 feet. Consider using chairs, a platform on playground equipment, second-story balcony, etc., to reach these heights.

✔ ***The Scientific Gazette*** for each student.

### Steps:

1. Point out Chicago, Illinois, on a map.
2. Share highlights of Dr. Mae Jemison's life.
3. Conduct the GRAVITY IS SERIOUS BUSINESS Experiment. (See instructor's guide, page 161.)
4. Allow time for students to complete "My Notes." Share observations.
5. Assist students in clean-up.
6. Distribute ***The Scientific Gazette***.
7. Add Dr. Jemison's name and a memento to the time-line.

### For next time:

- Announce the next scientist.

### Bibliography:

**Biographical Profile**. Courtesy of Dr. Mae C. Jemison.

National Women's History Project Archives. Windsor, California.

## Biography of DR. MAE C. JEMISON b. 1956

*"I am just doing what I want to do: I don't think of myself as a role model."*

**— Dr. Mae C. Jemison**

When she was five years old, Mae dreamed of becoming an astronaut and rocketing into space. At age 36 this dream came true: on September 12, 1992, Dr. Mae Jemison became the first woman of color to go into space.

### Childhood in Chicago

Born in Decatur, Alabama, the Jemison family moved to Chicago when Mae was three years old. Her mother was a teacher and her father, a maintenance supervisor. Mae attended public schools and believes that the public school system must be kept strong. In 1992 a public school in Detroit, Michigan, was named The Mae C. Jemison Academy.

### College

At age 16 Mae entered Stanford University on a scholarship and graduated with a Bachelor of Science degree in chemical engineering. She also satisfied the requirements for a BA degree in African and Afro-American Studies.

Enrolled in Cornell Medical School, Jemison traveled to Thailand and Kenya where she provided primary medical care. In 1981 she earned her doctorate.

### In Africa

Dr. Jemison worked as a general practitioner in Los Angeles before spending two and a half years as an Area Peace Corps Medical Officer for Sierra Leone and Liberia in West Africa. Her responsibilities ranged from managing health care systems for U.S. Peace Corps and U.S. Embassy personnel to supervising the pharmacy and laboratory. Dr. Jemison taught health care classes, wrote health manuals, and developed research projects on Hepatitis B vaccine and rabies.

In 1985 Dr. Jemison returned to Los Angeles to resume her medical practice.

### NASA

In June 1987 the first step in her dream of becoming an astronaut came true. Out of 1,962 applicants, Jemison was one of 15 selected to become an astronaut candidate. At 30 years of age, Dr. Jemison became the first Black female astronaut trainee for NASA (National Aeronautics and Space Administration).

The demanding one-year training and evaluation program began in August and included land and water survival training. Once accepted as a full-fledged astronaut, Dr. Jemison sometimes worked 60-hour weeks. From monitoring the orbiter's thermal protection system to learning to move in a weightless environment, Jemison found the five-year routine vigorous, challenging, and exciting.

### September 12, 1992

Dr. Jemison was the mission specialist on the shuttle Endeavor in STS-47, Spacelab-J, an eight-day cooperative mission between the United States and Japan. Forty-four in-flight experiments were conducted including one with frog eggs that tested how well living things develop without gravity.

### Leaves NASA

Early in 1993 Dr. Jemison left NASA. She has founded a company whose mission is to improve health care in West Africa.

Dr. Jemison encourages all people who want to be scientists, especially women and minorities, to pursue those careers. They, like Dr. Jemison, can make their dreams come true.

## Instructor's Guide:

### The GRAVITY IS SERIOUS BUSINESS Experiment

## Background Information:

Isaac Newton (1642 - 1727) was not the first scientist to realize that gravity "makes" objects fall to the ground. Galileo and others had studied gravity but failed to make the creative leap that the same force that holds us to earth also holds the planets in their place. Earth's gravity holds the moon in place and the sun's gravity holds the earth and other planets in its solar system.

In the GRAVITY IS SERIOUS BUSINESS Experiment students work with gravity and the relationship between the distance an object falls and the speed of that object.

## Instructions:

1. Distribute "My Notes."
2. Divide class into groups and distribute supplies to each group. (The groups can share a chair, a platform, a second-story balcony, etc. The last two heights on the "My Notes" are blank to allow you to choose the heights and locations.)

> **Explain . . .**
>
> *In this experiment you will be dropping a rock into the "earth tray." On the "My Notes" sheet, you see "1 foot, 2 feet, 3 feet," etc. Those are the heights from which you will drop the rock.*

> **Ask . . .**
>
> *What are some good ways to figure out how far is 2 feet above the tray? 4 feet? etc.*
>
> [Discuss their suggestions and, as a class, determine which ways will work.]

3. Instruct students to complete Part A of "My Notes."

> **Explain . . .**
>
> *After you have dropped the rock, carefully remove it. Use the ruler to measure in centimeters the width and depth of the hole that the rock made. Before you drop the rock again, use the trowel to level out the mud so there is no hole.*

4. Allow adequate time for groups to conduct the GRAVITY IS SERIOUS BUSINESS Experiment. Remind them to complete Part B of "My Notes" as they conduct the experiment.
5. Share and compare observations.

   [Within limits, objects gain speed as they fall. Generally, the greater the fall, the faster the speed, and the bigger the hole.]

> **Ask . . .**
>
> *Why do you think gravity is "serious business" to astronauts?*
>
> [On takeoff, spacecraft must have enough power — or "thrust" — to overcome gravity; in space, astronauts must deal with weightlessness; and upon re-entry into the earth's atmosphere, spacecraft must be able to control the effect of earth's gravity . . .]

6. Assist students in clean-up.

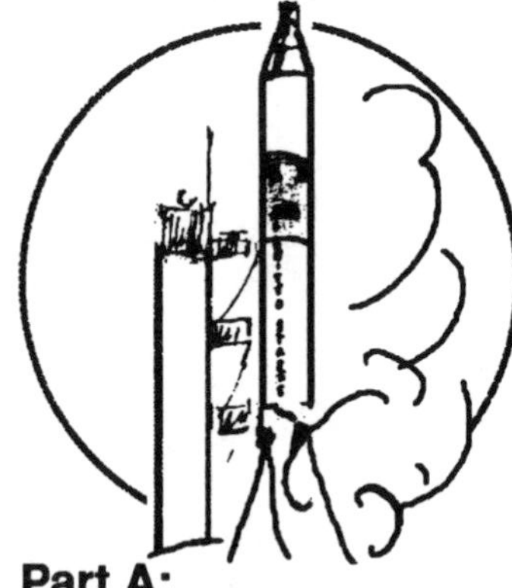

# My Notes

by ______________________________, Scientist

**GRAVITY IS SERIOUS BUSINESS Experiment**

**Part A:**

1. Do you think the hole made by the rock will get bigger or smaller as the height of its fall increases? _________________ This answer is your ***hypothesis*** — or "educated guess" about the outcome of the experiment.
2. Our rock is __________ centimeters in diameter.

**Part B:**

| HEIGHT | WIDTH OF HOLE (in centimeters) | DEPTH OF HOLE (in centimeters) |
|---|---|---|
| 1 Foot | ____________________ | ____________________ |
| 2 Feet | ____________________ | ____________________ |
| 3 Feet | ____________________ | ____________________ |
| 5 Feet | ____________________ | ____________________ |
| 7 Feet | ____________________ | ____________________ |
| 10 Feet | ____________________ | ____________________ |
| ____ Feet | ____________________ | ____________________ |
| ____ Feet | ____________________ | ____________________ |

Was your hypothesis correct? ______ Explain: ________________________________

________________________________________________________________________

________________________________________________________________________

Aboard the **Endeavor** Dr. Mae Jemison conducted experiments that tested how well living things develop without gravity.

# The Scientific Gazette

**Physics** | **Dr. Mae Jemison**

## Physician and Astronaut

Mae Jemison grew up in Chicago, Illinois. Her mother was a teacher and her father, a maintenance supervisor. From the time she was five years old, Jemison wanted to be an astronaut.

Jemison became a physician and worked as a general practitioner in Los Angeles before spending two and a half years as an Area Peace Corps Medical Officer in Sierra Leone and Liberia.

In June 1987 the first step in her dream of becoming an astronaut came true. Out of 1,962 applicants, Jemison was one of 15 selected to become an astronaut candidate. At age 30 Dr. Jemison became the first Black female astronaut trainee for NASA (National Aeronautics and Space Administration).

Five years later, on September 12, 1992, Dr. Mae C. Jemison rocketed into space aboard the **Endeavor** in STS-47, Spacelab-J. This was a cooperative mission between the U.S. and Japan. The astronauts conducted 44 in-flight experiments. They were testing how well living things develop without gravity.

**Dr. Mae Jemison, first woman of color to go into space**

Dr. Jemison left NASA in 1993: "I leave with the honor of having been the first woman of color in space, and with an appreciation of NASA — the organization that gave me the opportunity to make one of my dreams possible."

### Fun Facts about Dr. Jemison

| | |
|---|---|
| 1. _____ The name of her cat | a. The Mae C. Jemison Academy |
| 2. _____ Favorite TV show as a girl | b. Mars |
| 3. _____ Her sister, a psychiatrist | c. Russian, Swahili, and Japanese |
| 4. _____ TV show she appeared in | d. Astronomy |
| 5. _____ Her interests | e. ***Star Trek*** |
| 6. _____ Plants she enjoys growing | f. Dr. Ada Jemison Bullock |
| 7. _____ A place she'd love to visit | g. "Sneeze" |
| 8. _____ A favorite reading topic as a youth | h. African Art, weight training, sewing, skiing, photography, graphic arts, and reading |
| 9. _____ An alternative public school in Detroit, Michigan | i. ***Star Trek: The Next Generation*** |
| 10. ____ Besides English, languages spoken | j. Calla lilies, gardenias, herbs, poinsettias and vegetables |

Be creative! Describe an experiment you would like to conduct in space.

______________________________________

______________________________________

______________________________________

______________________________________

______________________________________

### At Home:

Explore the relationship between an object's weight and gravity's pull. 175 Science Experiments To Amuse and Amaze Your Friends by Brenda Walpole is a great place to begin. (If a spacesuit weighs 183 pounds on earth and weighs only 31 pounds on the moon, how much would you weigh on the moon?)

Nancy D. Wallace, manufacturing engineer, designs production systems for Digital Equipment Corporation.

# Discovery Unit No. 24

## Nancy D. Wallace
## Engineering

**STOP THE WATCH! Activity**

### Time-line:

- **1958 — Nancy Wallace is born.**
- 1960 - Rocket-powered airplane flies almost 2200 m.p.h.
- 1978 - Naomi Uemura, Japanese explorer, completes solo trip to North Pole
- 1992 - Digital Equipment Corporation unveils the Alpha chip

### Key points:

- ☛ Nancy D. Wallace is an American Indian of the Comanche and Creek Nations.
- ☛ Wallace studied industrial engineering at the University of Oklahoma and has worked as a manufacturing engineer for Digital Equipment Corporation.
- ☛ Wallace believes a "high-tech environment requires students to be well-grounded in problem solving and critical-thinking skills."
- ☛ In the STOP THE WATCH! Activity, students will become time-study engineers and use their problem-solving and critical-thinking skills.

### Supplies:

- ✔ A room large enough for students to stand in a circle.
- ✔ A light-weight ball that can be thrown indoors.
- ✔ A stopwatch
- ✔ ***The Scientific Gazette*** for each student.

### Steps:

1. Point out Faxon, Oklahoma, on a map.
2. Share highlights of Nancy Wallace's life.
3. Conduct the STOP THE WATCH! Activity. (See instructor's guide, page 167.)
4. Distribute ***The Scientific Gazette***.
5. Add Nancy Wallace's name and a memento to the time-line.
6. Enrichment activity (page 168) is optional.

### For next time:

- Announce the celebration!

### Bibliography:

Verheyden-Hilliard, Mary Ellen. **Engineer from the Comanche Nation, Nancy Wallace.**

Wallace, Nancy. **Letter** dated October 25, 1993.

Wallace, Nancy. **Telephone Interview,** November 5, 1993.

## Biography of NANCY D. WALLACE b. 1958

*"You must never stop learning. Technology changes so rapidly that you need to drive yourself to keep up."* — **Nancy D. Wallace**

Nancy Wallace grew up on a farm in Faxon, Oklahoma, a small town with one post office, one gas station, and one hundred seventy people. She now lives in the populated San Francisco Bay Area and works for a company that employs 124,000 people nationwide.

### Comanche and Creek

Her father's family were members of the Comanche Indian Nation and her mother's were from the Creek Indian Nation. As a young girl, Nancy collected arrowheads.

### A Reader and Leader

Faxon, Oklahoma, did not have a library. Every two weeks a library in a bus rolled into town. During the summer that Nancy was eight years old, the library sponsored a contest: anyone reading 25 books during summer vacation would receive a prize. Nancy read 50 books and still believes that reading broadens one's understanding.

In high school, she worked at a hospital sterilizing medical equipment; earned letters in basketball, volleyball, and softball; and, in her senior year, served as president of the student council and graduated second in her class.

### The University of Oklahoma

After talking with her high school counselor and reading the book **Women in Engineering**, Nancy decided to study industrial engineering at the University of Oklahoma. Engineers can perform a variety of occupational jobs. They build bridges, conduct time-motion studies, design ships, assemble printing presses — the list is endless.

### Digital Equipment Corporation

Digital Equipment Corporation designs, makes, and services computers and software. Nancy Wallace began work as an entry-level engineer and in five years worked through the ranks to become the Manager of Manufacturing Engineering. Her field was still industrial engineering but her specific occupation title was manufacturing engineer.

As a manufacturing engineer, Nancy Wallace designed production systems. She decided how to organize people and machinery to make printer products and mid-range computers. Some of the questions she asked were: What are the steps required to build the product? What is their order? How much time do these steps take? What task needs to be done at each workstation? What tools must each worker at each workstation have in order to complete the task? Will the worker stand? Will the worker sit?

"It's like following a recipe," Wallace explains.

### Santa Clara, California

In May 1990 Nancy Wallace and her daughter Toy moved to California so Wallace could work in Sales and Consulting for Digital Equipment Corporation. As a Customer Program Manager, Wallace pulls together individuals who create computer hardware and software for other companies. These projects may span two to five years and include aerospace companies, transportation systems, and state and local governments.

How does she use her engineering background in her new job? "I take the logical thought process of engineering and integrate that with customer satisfaction and perception." Future plans include a move to Washington, D.C. Her life, like technology, never stops changing.

## Instructor's Guide:

### The STOP THE WATCH! Activity

*"A high-tech environment requires students to be well-grounded in problem-solving and critical-thinking skills."*

— **Nancy D. Wallace**

## Background Information:

Industrial engineers are concerned with production. They want to find the most efficient and effective use of personnel, materials, and machines. Occupation titles for industrial engineers are many and their job descriptions are varied. In the STOP THE WATCH! Activity, students will "become" time-study engineers. Your job is to work the stopwatch and facilitate their suggestions on how to speed up the activity and still follow the guidelines.

For the Enrichment Activity (page 168), there may be a particular time-study problem/situation for students to study. Their suggestions could be shared with appropriate personnel.

## Instructions:

1. Move to a room large enough for the class to form a circle.

**Explain . . .**

*Industrial engineers have many occupation titles. Some are safety engineers, some production engineers, and some are time-study engineers.*

**Ask . . .**

*What do you think a time-study engineer does?*

[Tries to reduce the amount of time it takes to do an activity]

**Explain . . .**

*We're going to imagine we are time-study engineers. We are going to do an activity and then reduce the amount of time it takes us to do this activity.*

2. Have the students form a large circle. Hand the ball to one of the students.

**Explain . . .**

*(Name of student) is going to throw the ball to another student who then will throw the ball to another Everyone must receive and throw the ball but only once. I will start the stopwatch as soon as (name of student) throws the ball. Remember to whom you throw the ball.*

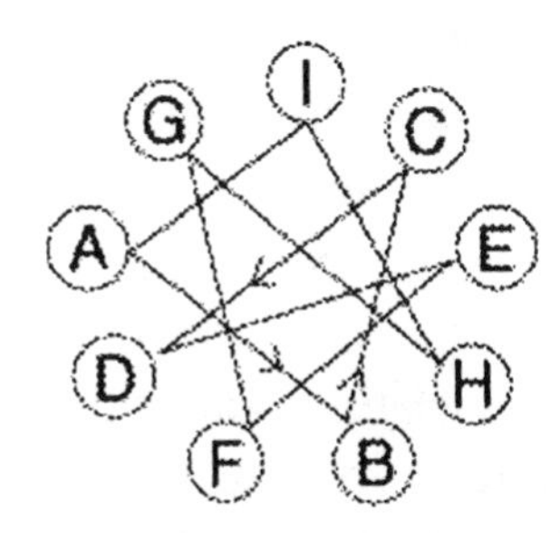


3. Time the activity. Announce the length of time.
4. Ask them to repeat the activity. Time the activity. Announce the time.

**Ask . . .**

*How can we keep the same throwing order and the same shape (a circle) but reduce the time this activity takes?*

[Ask for their suggestions and try some of them. A great solution is to reorganize the circle so everyone is standing next to the person that he/she threw the ball to. Standing close together, the ball is quickly passed from person to person yet the same throwing order and shape remain!! See diagram.]

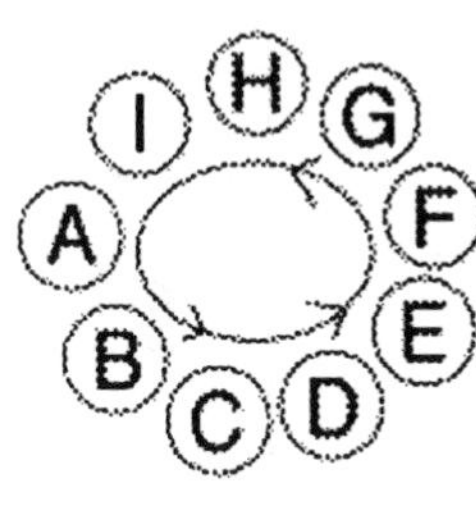


5. Return to the classroom.

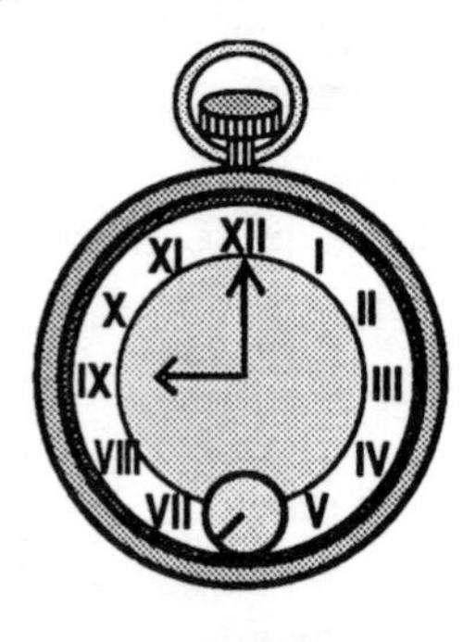


# Enrichment Activity

An **industrial plant** includes the buildings and land used by a company to produce products and services. **Departments** are divisions of an industrial plant. Each department has its responsibilities but must work with other departments if the company is to do its work efficiently and effectively. Examples of departments are personnel, research, sales, product development, and maintenance. **Workstations** exist in each department. A workstation may be a desk, a workshop, a countertop, a computer, or a closet.

When Nancy Wallace was trying to produce a new computer product, she had to find the answers to these questions:

- What are the steps required to build this product?
- What is the best order for these steps?
- How much time does each step take?
- What tools are needed at each workstation?
- Will the worker sit? Will the worker stand?

## The School is the Plant: The Desk is the Workstation

Imagine you are an industrial engineer. Think of your school building as being an industrial plant. Its departments are the office, cafeteria, gymnasium, classrooms, and playground. Workstations include desks, shelves, countertops, closets, etc.

- Draw the layout of all or part of your school. (Use the following drawing as a guide.):

Classroom
Lunch Room
Classroom
Classroom
Boys Rest Room
Office
Library
Classroom
Girls Rest Room

- How could your plant and its departments and workstations be run more efficiently?

**Nancy D. Wallace, whose family includes members of the Comanche and Creek Indian Nations, is an industrial engineer.**

## "Never Stop Learning"

After high school Nancy Wallace attended the University of Oklahoma and graduated with a degree in industrial engineering, a science that studies how an industrial plant (a factory) can efficiently and effectively organize its staff and machines to make products.

Wallace was hired by Digital Equipment Corporation (DEC), a large company that designs and makes computer products. This was exciting work. In five years Nancy Wallace worked her way from an entry-level engineer to Manager of Manufacturing Engineering.

In 1990 Wallace accepted a new job at DEC. As a Customer Program Manager, she organizes teams of individuals to create computer hardware and software packages for other companies.

Wallace continues to use her engineering skills. "I take the logical thought process of engineering and integrate that with customer satisfaction and perception." Wallace follows her own advice and "never stops learning."

## Industrial Engineers Have Many Occupation Titles

An industrial engineer may work with safety issues (a safety engineer), or fire-prevention (a fire-prevention research engineer). Some industrial engineers make the best use of space inside a building or room (a factory lay-out engineer) or make the best use of time (a time-study engineer).

In STOP THE WATCH! we became time-study engineers. Our best time was ________ seconds.

Our solution was: ____________________

________________________________

________________________________

________________________________

*"Technology changes so rapidly that you need to drive yourself to keep up."*
**— Nancy D. Wallace**

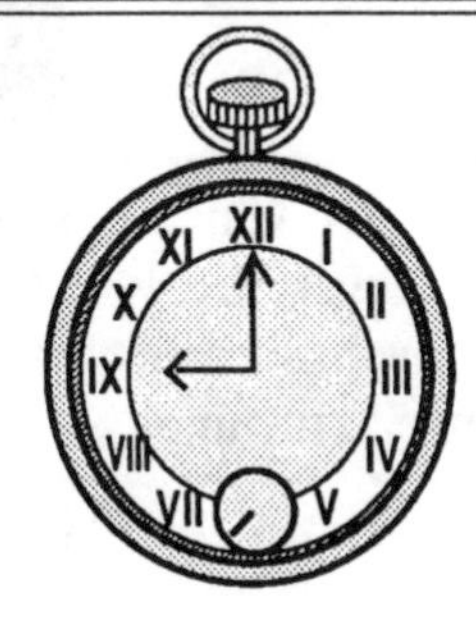


### At Home

- Conduct time-motion studies on a variety of activities, e.g., setting the table, vacuuming, folding clothes, raking leaves....
- Explore careers in engineering.
- Enjoy **Cheaper by the Dozen**, a fun book describing the homelife of industrial engineers Lillian and Frank Gilbreth, and their 12 children.

# Celebration Bingo

**Directions:** Each student may sign the Bingo Sheet once. The challenge is to have a signature in every square.

| | | | | |
|---|---|---|---|---|
| Like Mary Anning, I like to dig in the dirt. | Both Martine de Beausoleil and I have names that are difficult to spell. | I have used a double boiler, an invention by Miriam the Alchemist. | I, like Dr. Jewel Plummer Cobb, have been to California. | Like Dr. Barbara McClintock, I spend a lot of time by myself. |
| Like Nancy D. Wallace, I am part American Indian. | Like Dr. Emmy Noether, I like to have guests visit my home. | I follow Trotula's advice and get plenty of exercise. | Like Caroline Herschel, I have seen a comet. | I, like Dr. Elma Gonzalez, have grown bean plants from seed. |
| Like Hypatia, I like math. | Dr. Marie Sklodowska Curie liked to go bicycling. So do I. | **Dinosaur Bones to Labs in Space** | Like Dr. Florence Bascom, I have an ancestor that sailed to America on ***The Mayflower***. | Like Ynes Mexia, I have ridden a horse. |
| I, like Hildegard of Bingen, write poetry. | Like Dr. Chien-Shiung Wu, my name has a special meaning. | Like Dr. Reatha Clark King, my family is very important to me. | Like Winifred Goldring, I have held rocks that are 1,000,000 years old. | Like Maria Sibylle Merian, I like insects. |
| Like Dr. Mae C. Jemison, **Star Trek: The Next Generation** is one of my favorite shows. | I, like Dr. Sonya Kovalevskaya, know more than one language. | Maria Mitchell enjoyed reading. So do I. | I, like Dr. Dorothy Crowfoot Hodgkin, own a chemistry set. | **Like all these women scientists, I like science** |

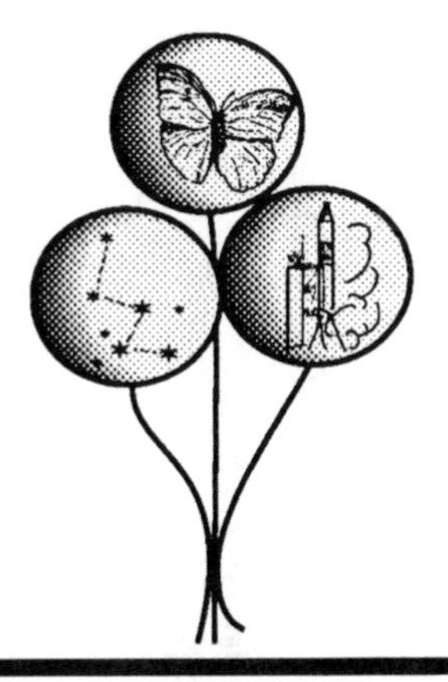

# Discovery Unit No. 25

## A Celebration!
## Dinosaur Bones to Labs in Space

### and — Where do we go from here?

**Instructor's Guide:**

A celebration proclaims that an event or person is important to us. In "Dinosaur Bones to Labs in Space" Celebration, students will:

- Celebrate the scientist within themselves.
- Celebrate these women in science whose contributions range from discovering dinosaur bones to conducting experiments in space.

**Activities** for this celebration are left to the instructor and students. A Celebration "Bingo" Game Sheet is included as an entertainment option. Other possibilities include:

- **An Invention Convention** — Supplies are provided and students invent theme items, e.g., robots, spacecraft, computers...
- **A New Century Science Fair** — Students bring their completed science projects. These could be individual or collaborative projects.
- **Experiments We Have Known and Loved** — Prior to the celebration, list all the experiments conducted in these units. Students vote for their favorite and the top 4 or 5 become the celebration's entertainment. For variety, a couple of new experiments might be the instructor's "gift" to the celebration.
- **Writer, Producer, Actor** — Students (collaboration is optional) create a play, poem, or video featuring one or several of the women scientists. A video of a science project/experiment completed at home would also be a possibility.

**Refreshments** for the celebration can highlight the contributions of women:

- **Chocolate Chip Cookies** -- In 1933 Ruth Wakefield, owner of the Toll House Inn in Whitman, Massachusetts, created the chocolate chip cookie.
- **Ice Cream Cone** — A woman at the Louisiana Purchase Exposition in 1904 invented the ice cream cone when she took half a cookie wafer and wrapped it around an ice cream portion. Her name is not known.

**Celebration Props** can include balloons with the names of the women scientists and students written in permanent pen. Also consider:

- **Time-Line Update** — Under the year 2000 A.D., add the names of the students and you, the instructor, to the time-line.
- **Student-Made Placemats** — Laminated, these party favors with a science theme can be taken home and enjoyed for months.
- **Cone Party Hats** — Honor Hypatia. Create and decorate conic hats.

**The "Scientist Within You" Certificate** may be given to each student at the close of the "Dinosaur Bones to Labs in Space" Celebration. (See certificate on page 172.)

# *Certificate of Achievement*

*to*

______________________________, *scientist*

***for having successfully completed***

**"The Scientist Within You"** ***Discovery Units***

***"The more one learns about that which one knows nothing of, the more one gains in wisdom..***

**— Hildegard of Bingen**
**1098-1170 A.D.**

## A Few Suggestions:

Now you have successfully introduced your students to science and mathematics in a fun and easy way. So where do you go from here?

- Take your students on field trips to science museums, college and university science labs, research facilities, pharmacies, engineering offices, assembly plants, etc.
- Involve students in Science and Project Fairs.
- Watch and discuss science-related videos.
- Explore science topics through computer software and CD-ROMs.
- Create a science lab in your room. Add the resource books listed in the bibliographies of each Discovery Unit.
- Invite community scientists and mathematicians (especially women and ethnic minorities) to become role models for your students.
- Encourage community involvement by asking an organization to sponsor one (or more) of the programs mentioned on the following pages.

## What About Costs?

Some costs might include:

- Rental of space and/or equipment
- Transportation costs for field trips
- Expenses for speakers, visiting scientists, high school and university science students
- Supplies and equipment
- Purchases of resource books for a classroom library
- Rental or purchase of science videos, software, and/or CD-ROMs
- Classroom subscriptions to science magazines
- Costs related to participation in science fairs

## Where can you find the money?

Although money for additional programs, equipment, and materials are in short supply, many organizations/businesses are willing to make a contribution to help young people enhance their learning experiences. Some sources to approach are the following:

- Local utility companies
- Local banks
- Cable television companies
- Telephone companies
- Service organizations such as Rotary, American Association of University Women (AAUW), Business Professional Women (BPW), Soroptomists, etc.
- Parent/Teacher/Student organizations

For more extensive projects, you may wish to write for a grant. There are people in your education district who are trained in writing grants and who could help you. Some of the grants available can be applied for through

- National Science Foundation
- American Chemical Society
- American Association of University Women Educational Foundation*
- State and federal equity grants

* **AAUW Community Action Grants** provide seed money for programs promoting education and equity for women and girls. **Eleanor Roosevelt Teacher Fellowships** for female public school teachers emphasize increasing girls' participation in math- and science-related endeavors and providing educational opportunities for at-risk girls. For information and applications, contact: **AAUW Educational Foundation,** 1111 16th Street NW, Washington, DC 20036-4873.

## Draft of sample fundraising letter:

- Prior to writing, contact the company/organization and ask to whom you should send the letter.
- Type letter on letterhead stationery of your school or organization.

Dear ___________:

The ___________ at ____________ is working with the ideas and experiments in "The Scientist Within You" — a hands-on science program. To give the students more experience in the field of __________, I would like ____________ (to go on a field trip to...., invite a speaker, conduct a major experiment, etc.). I estimate the cost to be __________. Outside funding is necessary.

Are you willing to underwrite or contribute to this ________(type of event)?

I will be calling you within two weeks to learn your response. Thank you for the consideration you give this request.

Sincerely,

Name and phone/FAX #'s

- Provide your telephone number and FAX number (if available).
- Be sure to call within two weeks!
- Follow-up contribution with a personal thank-you note from you and/or from students. A photograph of the event would be a thoughtful gesture.

**Operation SMART** (**S**cience, **M**ath **a**nd **R**elevant **T**echnology) excites girls to pursue math and science in order to master the knowledge and skills needed for financial independence. Established by Girls Incorporated in 1985, SMART programs are developed through extensive research, evaluation and consultation with expert advisory committees. They are hands-on, participatory, and experiential. From going on a worm hunt to designing a circuit, Operation SMART challenges girls to ask questions, make predictions, keep their options open and plan for the future. For information about **Operation SMART**, contact:

**National Headquarters**
30 East 33rd Street
New York, NY 10016
(212) 689-3700

**Girls Incorporated**

**National Resource Center**
441 West Michigan Street
Indianapolis, IN 46202
(317) 634-7546

The goal of **Expanding Your Horizons** in Science and Mathematics Conferences (EYH) is to excite young women, grades 6 through 12, about math and science and encourage them to pursue middle and high school courses that provide more options in their future work lives. Conference participants interact with women who are mathematicians, statisticians, physicists, engineers, chemists, electricians, architects etc. The day's schedule also includes panel discussions, hands-on workshops, and career discussions. Established in 1976 by the Math/Science Network, a non-profit membership organization that promotes the advancement of women in science, mathematics, and technology, almost 250,000 young women have participated in EYH Conferences. As of 1992 there are more than 100 EYH sites in the U.S. A new program, **Expanding More Horizons**, encourages young minority women in science and math. For information on EYH Conferences in your area or on organizing an EYH site, contact:

MATH SCIENCE NETWORK
Math/Science Resource Center
Reservation Park
678 13th Street, Suite 100
Oakland, California 94612
(510) 893-MATH

**EQUALS** is a mathematics/equity inservice and curriculum program that focuses on increasing the numbers of female and minority students who participate successfully in mathematics education. Since 1977 EQUALS has worked with K-12 teachers to address equity issues of racism, sexism, and economic status through mathematics methods and materials. Programs assist teachers and parents to create greater success in mathematics for *all* students. **Family Math**, a major project of the EQUALS program, helps parents and children to enjoy doing mathematics together. **Matemática Para La Familia** enables Spanish-speaking families to participate fully in the program. For more information about EQUALS' programs and publications, contact:

**Equals**
Lawrence Hall of Science
University of California
Berkeley, CA 94720
(510) 642-1910 FAX (510) 643-5757

**Posters, photo displays, books, and curriculum materials on**

# American Women in Science and Mathematics

**are among the many multicultural women's history materials available from the**

**National Women's History Project**
**7738 Bell Road**
**Windsor, CA 95492**
**707-838-6000**
**Call or write today for a free catalog.**

The **Association for Women in Science** (AWIS) is a non-profit organization dedicated to increasing the educational and employment opportunities for girls and women in all fields of science. The 5,200 AWIS members are organized into a network of 66 chapters across the country. Members network with one another, problem-solve, develop leadership skills, and "project a voice" on such national issues as education and employment equity. They also promote opportunities for women in science and **exercise a commitment "to foster the next generation of women in science."** Their publications include:

- AWIS Magazine
- Grants at a Glance
- A Hand Up: Women Mentoring Women in Science
- Mentoring Means Future Scientists
- Taking the Initiative: Report on a Leadership Conference for Women in Science and Engineering

For more information, contact the National Office, Association for Women in Science, 1522 K St. NW, Washington, D.C. 20005. PH: (202) 408-0742, Fax: (202) 408-8321, E-mail: awis@awis.org

The **American Chemical Society**'s (ACS) materials and programs for elementary and middle school students include:

- ***WonderScience***, a monthly publication for students grades 4 - 6
- Bilingual ***WonderScience***, a 32-page Spanish/English publication
- "Operation Chemistry," a training program for teams of teacher educators
- **FACETS**, science curriculum for grades 6 - 8
- "Tracing the Path/Inventing the Future," a videotape/activity book series that examines the contributions of African and African-American scientists, mathematicians, and inventors over the centuries
- "The Science Discovery Challenge," a videotape/teachers guide highlighting Latino Scientists.

Through Community Science Grants, ACS funds programs promoting adult/child involvement in hands-on science. For information, contact:

**The American Chemical Society**
Education Division
1155 16th St., NW
Washington, D.C. 20036.

The **American Society of Microbiology** (ASM) provides programs designed to improve the quality of education in the life sciences at all levels. The following materials are available:

- **Career Materials** provides information about the microbiology careers in medicine, biotechnology, industry, and environmental sciences. Salaries, scope of work and preparation of degrees are included.
- **Fellowships and Travel Grants** are offered to undergraduate, graduate and post-doctoral students as well as undergraduate faculty in the microbiological sciences.
- **Focus on Microbiology Newsletter** is an 8-page publication for undergraduate faculty in the microbiological sciences. It contains discussion articles, how-to section, and classroom activities.
- **Microbiology Network** is a database listing microbiologists in your geographical area who are available to answer questions about research projects, academic courses and degrees in the microbiological sciences.
- **Orientation Handbook for Volunteers in the Classroom** is a how-to manual for volunteers in science education to enhance your outreach efforts, especially with middle and high school students and teachers.
- **Conferences, Audioconferences, and Workshops** for microbiology practitioners and undergraduate teaching faculty.

For more information, contact the American Society for Microbiology, 1325 Massachusetts Ave., NW, Washington, DC 20005; (202) 942-9283; e-mail: EducationResources@asmusa.org.

The **National Science Foundation** (NSF) provides grants for research, education, and related activities in science, engineering, and mathematics (SEM). To encourage the full participation of girls and women in SEM, and help to reverse their disproportionately low current representation, special efforts are underway at NSF, primarily in the Directorate for Education and Human Resources, especially its Human Resources Development Division. The Program for Women and Girls includes the following components to effect changes in the representation of women in SEM education and careers:

- **Model Projects** to encourage the design and implementation of innovative, relatively short-term, highly-focused activities;
- **Experimental Projects** to create positive, permanent changes through comprehensive, collaborative projects; and
- **Information Dissemination Activities** to facilitate widespread dissemination of strategies and information.

A comprehensive description of the Foundation's programs is included in its annual *Guide to Programs*. The program announcement describing the above-noted efforts, as well as program-specific application information is entitled *EHR Activities for Women and Girls*. The *Grant Proposal Guide* provides general application instructions and forms. These may be obtained from the Forms and Publications Unit at NSF (4201 Wilson Boulevard, Arlington, VA 22230; Ph: 703/306-1130; E-mail: pubs@nsf.gov). For program inquiries, call the Program for Women and Girls, Division of Human Resource Development (703/306-1637).

## American Association for the Advancement of Science

(AAAS) has a variety of materials available:

✓ ***Science Education News*** and ***Parent Enlightenment*** are free newsletters highlighting, respectively, resources and events in science education and strategies to help parents stimulate children's interest and achievement in science and mathematics

✓ ***Science Books and Films*** includes reviews by scientists and educators of trade science, math, and technology books and films and produces special issues focused on textbook reviews and specific content areas

✓ Training program for adults who work with girls in hands-on science and mathematics: ***Girls and Science: Link up with the Future.*** Also, ***Girls and Science*** newsletter.

✓ ***IDEAAAS*** is a source book which includes information on scientific organizations, state and federal agencies, education associations, museums, and a wide variety of programs and materials for educators. ($24.95 + 4.00 S&H)

✓ ***Status of Women Scientists and Engineers in the United States.*** Statistical information on women and girls. Useful for proposals and report preparation. ($7.50 + S&H)

Contact: Directorate for Education & Human Resources Programs, AAAS
1333 H Street, NW, Washington, DC 20005
(202) 326-6690 for these and other resources.

## Order Form

**Mail Orders To:**

ACI Publishing
Post Office Box 40398
Eugene, OR 97404-0064

**Credit Card Orders To:**

ACI Publishing
800/935-7323
Or by mail

| Quantity | Book | | Amount |
|---|---|---|---|
| _______ | **The Scientist Within You:** Experiments and Biographies of Distinguished Women in Science. **Volume 1** Ages 8 - 13, (192 pages) | $21.95 | _________ |
| _______ | **The Scientist Within You:** Women Scientists from Seven Continents — Biographies and Activities. **Volume 2** Ages 10 - 15, (224 pages) | $24.95 | _________ |
| | | Shipping: $4.00 first book $1.50 each additional book | _________ |
| | | TOTAL | _________ |

❑ Paid by check ❑ Paid by VISA ❑ Paid by MasterCard

Card Number ______________________ Exp. Date ______________

Name on Card ______________________ Signature ______________

Please ship to:

Name ____________________________________________

School or Organization ____________________________

Address __________________________________________

City/State/Zip ____________________________________

Wk. Ph. ____________ Hm. Ph. ____________ Fax ____________

Additional Instructions or Comments ________________________

____________________________________________________

____________________________________________________

# SPEAKING PROFESSIONALLY

## A Concise Guide

ALAN JAY ZAREMBA

Northeastern University

Australia · Brazil · Canada · Mexico · Singapore · Spain · United Kingdom · United States

**Speaking Professionally: A Concise Guide, First Edition**

Alan Jay Zaremba

**VP/Editorial Director:**
Jack W. Calhoun

**VP/Editor-in-Chief:**
David Shaut

**Senior Publisher:**
Melissa S. Acuña

**Acquisitions Editor:**
Neil Marquardt

**Developmental Editor:**
Taney Wilkins

**Senior Marketing Manager:**
Larry Qualls

**Production Project Manager:**
Amy Hackett

**Manager of Technology, Editorial:**
Vicky True

**Technology Project Editor:**
Kelly Reid

**Web Coordinator:**
Scott Cook

**Manufacturing Coordinator:**
Diane Lohman

**Production House:**
GEX Publishing Services

**Printer:**
Transcontinental
Louiseville, QC

**Art Director:**
Stacy Jenkins Shirley

**Cover and Internal Designer:**
Grannan Graphic Design, Ltd.

**Cover Photo Credit:**
Getty Images

**Photography Manager:**
John Hill

**Photo Researcher:**
Rose Alcorn



Printed in Canada

1 2 3 4 5 08 07 06 05

Student Edition: ISBN 0-324-37762-2



Library of Congress Control Number: 2005928285

For more information about our products, contact us at:

Thomson Learning Academic Resource Center

1-800-423-0563

**Thomson Higher Education**
5191 Natorp Boulevard
Mason, OH 45040
USA

For Donna

*An artist and an educator to whom*
*and with whom I raise glasses*

# Brief Contents

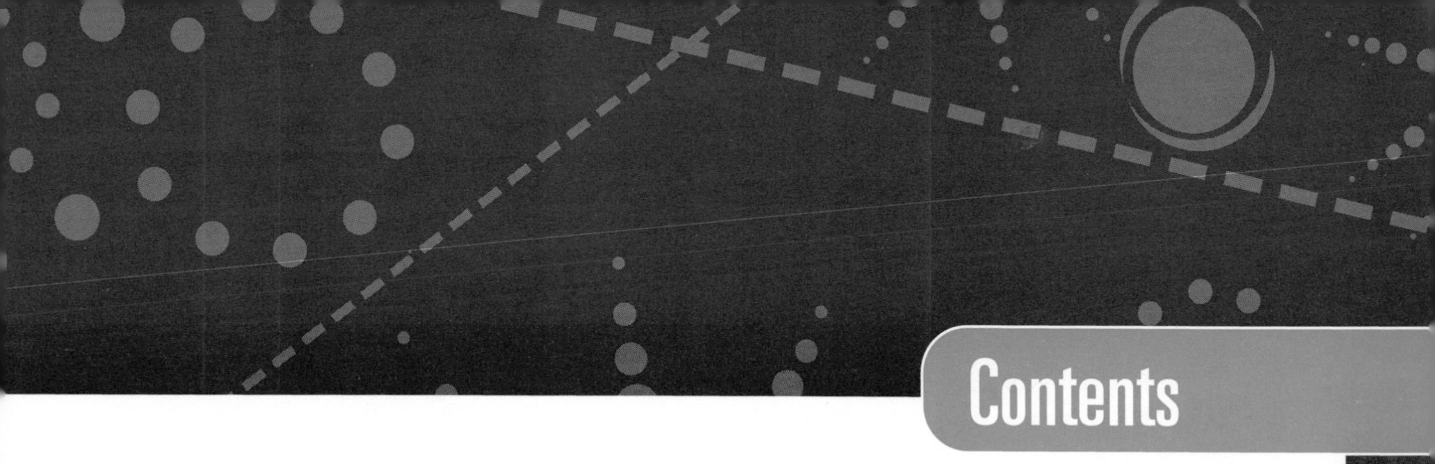

# Contents

## CHAPTER 3 Ethical Decisions and Public Presentations 35



## CHAPTER 4 Addressing Presentation Anxiety 55



## CHAPTER 5 Audience Analysis: Taking a Receiver-Centered Approach 72

## CHAPTER 6 Selecting an Appropriate Speaking Style 93



## CHAPTER 7 Structuring the Message 109



## CHAPTER 8 Visual Support for Your Presentation 126

## CHAPTER 9 Teams and Team Presentations 140



## CHAPTER 10 Persuasive Messages 162



## CHAPTER 11 Verbal and Nonverbal Aspects of Delivery 179

# Preface

This book is based on the premise that competence and confidence in presentation settings is personally empowering and can advance professional careers. Intelligent and educated individuals who are able to express what they know are advantaged. Those who cannot communicate skillfully are unlikely to become as successful as they otherwise could be.

I am often asked to listen to managers deliver presentations and then comment on the quality of their talks. It may not surprise the reader to learn that, frequently, intelligent and thoughtful individuals are unable to speak effectively. However, it may be surprising to learn that many successful managers who aspire to become executives confide their fears about making presentations and acknowledge the importance of overcoming these anxieties for career success.

*Speaking Professionally: A Concise Guide* identifies and describes principles that will help readers who desire to become more efficient in speaking settings. You may be enrolled in a class dedicated to improving speaking skills, or you may be in a class with a section devoted to professional speaking. In either case, this book can be used as a resource to help you prepare, deliver, and evaluate presentations. Specifically, the book can be used to address speaking anxiety, conduct audience analyses, structure presentations, improve speaking delivery, use visual complements, deliver team presentations, persuade those who listen to you, consider ethical issues pertaining to persuasive messages, and prepare for question-and-answer sessions.

Speaking is a skill that can be learned. It is not a skill that you either have or do not have. The goal of the book is to help you become more skillful in an area that is very important for personal and professional fulfillment.

I am grateful to many people for their assistance with this project. To those who have not worked on a book-length writing project it may seem as if the acknowledgments section of a preface reflects the completion of an obligatory task and is merely a formality. I can assure the uninitiated that the work of even an individually authored book requires the help of many dedicated others.

Taney Wilkins served as the developmental editor for *Speaking Professionally*. Taney has also been the developmental editor for my other books published by Thomson. It is difficult to overstate her value to this project. She is a dedicated professional—an unusually responsible, perceptive, and approachable individual. I am very fortunate that she was assigned to this book and am grateful for her hard work, tact, and insights.

Amy Hackett, the production editor for *Speaking Professionally: A Concise Guide*, and Jeny Roehrig of GEX, the production house for the project, were both as efficient as they were meticulous. It was wonderful to work with people so committed to the success of the project. These two dedicated professionals are responsible for the aesthetic quality of the book you now hold in your hands.

Jennifer Codner, formerly of Thomson, was the acquisitions editor who signed me to write *Speaking Professionally*, and I am grateful to Jennifer for her support of my work with this book as well as the others I have written with Thomson. Neil Marquardt has replaced Jennifer and has been a very supportive member of the Thomson team. Larry Qualls has been the marketing director for my books, and I am impressed with Larry's energy, ideas, and knowledge. I am grateful for his work in ensuring that my books reach those who may be interested in them. Erin Berger was another vital member of the Thomson group that helped make this book a reality.

Several colleagues at Northeastern University were very helpful and offered encouragement as this project evolved. Specifically, I would like to thank Susan Picillo and Walter Carl, who allowed me to use some of their evaluation materials for this text. Tom Downard, Murray Forman, David Marshall, Julie Hall, Alan Gellin, Michelle Lee, Ed Wertheim, Sam Lotuff, Chuck Fountain, Vincent Rocchio, Greg Kowalski, Marcus Breen, Julie Hertenstein, Elise Dallimore, Tony Buglio, Jacqui Sweeney, Michael Woodnick, and Carey Noland also offered words of support throughout my involvement with this project. Meaghan Sinclair and Jonathan Cunha in our department office were extraordinarily helpful and resourceful. Meaghan and Jonathan saved me hours of time as I worked on the final stages of the book. I am grateful also to Angela Chin, our department administrative assistant, who tolerated my inquiries in a manner that reflects either tremendous patience or considerable experience working with university faculty members.

Several professionals gave graciously of their time to relay experiences they have had that were germane to the principles discussed in the book. I am grateful to Ken Weiss, John Amicangelo, Ken Baltin, Bob Whitaker, Gabe Smallman, Francis Battisti, Leslie Donnell, Ken Berk, Ken Turow, David Murray, Marcia Meislin, Roberta Reich, Hillel Zaremba, and Robert Zaremba. Thank you also to Tom Daly of *Vital Speeches of the Day* for his permission to use excerpts from the publication he edits for the sample speech features that appear at the end of each chapter. Bill Wilhelm of Indiana State University was kind enough to allow me to excerpt a portion of an excellent paper he delivered at an ABC meeting, and I thank him for his support and permission.

All textbooks are reviewed before publication by colleagues in the field. I was very fortunate to have had many reviewers who supported the project and made remarkably insightful comments that served to strengthen this manuscript. I am indebted to the following: Judy Jones Tisdale, University of North Carolina; Richard Linge, Arizona Western College; Glenda Stewart-Langley, New Mexico Tech; Carter A. Daniel, Rutgers Business School; Barbara D. Davis, University of Memphis; Scott D. Troyan, University of Wisconsin–Madison; Susan E. Picillo, Northeastern University; Jim Lindsey, Ferris State University; Maryann Roeske, Three Lakes School District; Bob Stowers, The College of William & Mary; Rod G. Haywood, Indiana University Bloomington; Thomas S. Brice, University of Michigan–Flint; and Liddy Tuleja, University of Pennsylvania.

Finally, I am grateful to members of my immediate and extended family who have been supportive of my energy and efforts. A foundation of love is important for anyone to do anything, and I have been blessed with loving and supportive parents, a brilliant sibling, a precious companion, and many dear relatives who have encouraged my work.

No doubt, I have forgotten to include one or several others who were crucial to the success of this project even though I have tried hard not to do just that. For all those who have helped me, I thank you sincerely.

# SUPPLEMENTS

The Instructor's Resource CD (0-324-31225-3) includes a PowerPoint® presentation created by Barbara D. Davis; an author-created Instructor's Manual including teaching tips, answers to end-of-chapter content, and other resources useful for preparing lecture and classroom materials; and an author-created Test Bank for each chapter.

This comprehensive Test Bank is available in Word files and makes test preparation and grading easy. The book support Web site, **http://zaremba.swlearning.com**, contains the PowerPoint®, Instructor's Manual, and other useful resources for students and instructors.

# About the Author

***Alan Zaremba*** earned his Ph.D. from the University of Buffalo and his undergraduate and master's degrees from the State University of New York at Albany. Since 1981, Dr. Zaremba has been on the faculty at Northeastern University. From 1976 to 1981, he worked at the State University of New York College at Fredonia.

On four occasions, Dr. Zaremba has received a university's most competitive award for excellence in teaching. He has twice been a recipient of Northeastern University's Excellence in Teaching Award; before leaving the SUNY system, he was honored with a SUNY Chancellor's Award for Excellence in Teaching; and in 2001, he was fortunate to be one of two alumni to receive his undergraduate alma mater's award for excellence in education.

In addition to his responsibilities on the faculty in the Department of Communication Studies, Dr. Zaremba created and is the academic director for Northeastern University's master's, bachelor's, and certificate programs in Corporate and Organizational Communication.

Dr. Zaremba is also the author of three other books:

- *Mass Communication and International Politics*, 1988
- *Management in a New Key*, 1989; second edition, 1993
- *Organizational Communication: Foundations for Business and Collaboration*, 2003; second edition, 2006

Chapter in a Nutshell

*Presentation skills can be learned and are crucial for professional advancement and personal empowerment.*

# 1 Foundations

*If all my possessions and powers were to be taken from me with one exception I would choose to keep the power of speech, for by it I could soon recover all the rest.*[1]

-Daniel Webster

*To know how to say what others only know how to think is what makes people poets or sages.*[2]

-Elizabeth Rundle Charles


## Abstract

The difference between a successful career and a pedestrian one can have less to do with native intelligence or even industry than with the ability to communicate. Perhaps it is for this reason that surveys repeatedly indicate that employers identify communication as the number one skill they look for when evaluating college graduates for hire. Project managers, trainers, salespersons, union representatives, executives, department heads, meeting participants, and nearly all employees are duty-bound to make presentations periodically to various audiences. The quality of these presentations can affect individual advancement and organizational success. When you have completed this chapter, you should be able to do the following:

- Explain why presentation skill is important for organizational and individual success
- Discredit common misconceptions about presentation skill competence
- Describe typical problems in presentation contexts
- Discuss what is meant by communication competence and identify speaking competencies
- Describe the range of topics and scope of the book

# Jensen's Presentation

Ron Jensen had a problem that was keeping him up at night and troubling him in his day hours as well. For months, he and a group of others had been working hard on an engineering project that had been yielding gratifying results. The project involved complicated research that would, eventually, assist meteorologists in their attempts to predict weather more accurately. Jensen and his group had enjoyed nearly total autonomy as they pursued their research.

However, the project was funded by a government grant and it was time to prove to the granting agency that the money invested in the research had been spent wisely. Jensen had been selected to deliver a presentation to members of the granting agency to explain the progress of the studies.

Jensen knew more about his area of research than anyone else on the planet. However, the problem was that he was far more adept at conducting research than at explaining it. In college and throughout his entire professional life, he had avoided presentational speaking whenever he could. Jensen's self-assessment of those few times when he had been compelled to speak was that he was "a disaster behind a podium." Nevertheless, he was the leader of the research group and clearly acknowledged as the keenest mind on the team.

There was quite a bit at risk. Not only did he have to explain the research, he also had to persuade the body that it should continue to support the project. To complicate matters, some of the attendees would not be subject matter experts. Jensen's colleagues told him he would have to "dumb down" much of what he needed to relay to reach these people. For all Jensen knew, the least knowledgeable in the attending group could be the most powerful decision makers. Jensen was so involved in the complexities of his research that he frequently had trouble recognizing what a layperson might or might not understand. On occasion, he found himself using obscure words and acronyms when speaking to friends and family about his work. He realized that he was incomprehensible only when he noticed the glazed looks of his listeners.

Finally, Jensen felt added pressure from his peers. He didn't want to disappoint his colleagues who needed the continued support as much as he did. He did not want to be a "disaster behind a podium" in front of them.

- Have you ever been in a situation that is similar to the one Ron Jensen faced?
- How would you recommend that Jensen prepare for his talk?
  - Should Jensen write his talk out word for word?
  - Should he pass out a copy of his talk?
  - Should Jensen explain his work to another who will act as spokesperson for the group?

## INTRODUCTION

A 1999 article published in the *Journal of Business Communication* reported what appeared to be startling findings. Two researchers, Paul Gamble and Clare Kelliher, studied managers who were required to deliver daily briefings to their sales staffs. These presentations were short 5- to 9-minute speeches and, taken collectively, were intended to meet three organizational objectives.

Management desired to do the following:

- Disseminate information to employees
- Motivate employees to meet sales targets
- Establish a sense of common goals within the workforce[4]

Gamble and Kelliher evaluated the effectiveness of the managers' presentations by distributing questionnaires to the employees who had been briefed. Subsequently, the researchers analyzed the completed questionnaires.

The results of their study indicated almost no correlation between what the employees contended had been the content of the briefings and what the managers contended were the messages that had been relayed. These findings prompted the authors to comment that if the managers had been aware of the results, they would have likely remarked: "I might as well be talking to myself."[5]

Are you surprised by these findings? Does your experience suggest that managerial presentations of this nature are, essentially, valueless?

In the article, three additional points were made about the organization and the briefings:

1. The organization considered the briefings to be a very important part of a manager's overall responsibility.
2. Only one of the nine managers involved in the study had any form of presentation skill training.
3. The organization's formal evaluations for managers did not include an assessment of a manager's speaking abilities.

These aspects of the study are significant for those who study business presentations. Despite an awareness of the importance of speaking for success, the organization apparently did not think it needed to train the employees to be effective speakers nor assess how effectively they presented information. Two incorrect assumptions had been made: The first was that all managers could and would deliver these important presentations effectively. The second was that the receivers in these contexts could and would be industrious and attentive listeners. (Note: The researchers had contacted the organization and had requested access to conduct the study. The organization had not requested an assessment of their managers' presentations).[6]

The results of this study highlight common problems related to presentations in organizational contexts. Management often presumes that otherwise capable people should and will be comfortable and capable speakers. Presenters often assume that what they say has been consumed and digested by those who are allegedly listening to their presentations.

## The Importance of Presentation Skill Competence

### Speaking Skill Can Affect Career Success

Nearly all members of an organization are required to make presentations

- Salespersons pitch the product to prospective customers
- Managers brief their staffs during department meetings
- Team leaders explain the status of their work to related departments to gain the necessary buy-in
- Union representatives present employee perspectives to top management
- Trainers orient prospective employees with introductory presentations about the company
- Executives make state-of-the-organization talks to stockholders
- Company representatives brief the media during times of crisis

Given these organizational responsibilities, it behooves organizational women and men to become capable communicators in presentation contexts. Regardless of your particular organizational responsibility—and regardless of your place on the organizational chart—your successes and failures are likely to be a function of how well you can speak to your internal and external audiences. Florida State University's Dr. Donnalyn Pompper captures the sentiments of practitioners and academics alike when she writes, "In the trenches, one's ability to sell ideas to clients and internal audiences can make or break a career."[7]

Many organizations identify communication skills in general and presentation skills in particular as primary considerations when evaluating potential candidates for positions. One study ranked communication skills ahead of work experience, motivation, and academic credentials as criteria when selecting candidates.[8]

### Speaking Skill Can Be Personally Empowering

Beyond the work environment, we are obliged to make presentations when attending town meetings, accepting or presenting an award, making a toast at a wedding, announcing the state of the fund drive, explaining our credentials for town representative, or when speaking to the little league team before the big game. Our jobs beyond our jobs require presentation skills. Being able to meet these personal obligations can be empowering. Being incapable to meet these obligations can be limiting. If eloquence is power, as President John Quincy Adams suggested, then becoming eloquent is empowering.[9]

All persons—from national leaders who address their constituents, to sports fans who call in to make their points on talk radio—desire to clearly explain their perspectives. Citizens who are enraged that the school superintendent has decided to merge two elementary schools will be empowered by their ability to express their fury in an effective and appropriate manner. Club leaders will be empowered by their abilities to motivate other members and will feel debilitated if they are unable to articulate the urgency of their requests. Even in our family and romantic relationships, we are empowered by our eloquence and frustrated when we cannot convey what we wish we could.

Pericles, the great Greek leader, was so revered that *The Age of Pericles* has come to refer to the high point of ancient civilization. His comment on the value of eloquence speaks directly to the point of empowerment. Pericles said that those "who can think and do not know how to express what they think are at the same level of those who cannot think."[10]

How do you react to this perspective?

- Are those who can think but unable to express their thoughts reduced to the level of those who cannot conceive of ideas?
- Is frustration, tension, and a sense of inadequacy an inevitable by-product of being unable to express your feelings?
- Are those who can eloquently articulate their reactions to the previous two questions more empowered than those who cannot?

In *How to Write and Deliver an Effective Speech,* Judith McManus argues that good presentation skills foster "a more positive self-image and improved self-confidence and esteem."[11] Do you agree?

## Improving Speaking Skills Can Result in Better Listening Skills

We are inundated with messages from various sources, and our healthy survival requires us to assess the quality of these messages. Practicing and studying presentations help us critically consider not only what we say, but how to evaluate what we hear. In workshops or classes like the one you are taking, participants will listen to far more presentations than they will deliver. Typically, participants are asked to critique these other presentations. This analysis and evaluation can be valuable in that it requires the industrious student to hone listening skills. Even those who are not enrolled in speaking courses will become better listeners by virtue of studying how to express their perspectives to listeners.

College recruiters, automobile manufacturers, computer salespeople, and financial managers all send messages to us that require our analysis. By examining presentations and the presentation context, we become more adept at critically assessing the messages that we ourselves are compelled to consume, digest, and evaluate. (Listening and presentation evaluation is discussed in detail in chapter 13 of the book.)

### Reverse the Perspective

Throughout the text you will see recurring boxed inserts entitled *Reverse the Perspective.* In these segments, you will be asked to evaluate various issues pertaining to the nature, importance, and quality of presentations from the vantage point of the listener. This book is about improving presentation skills. However, thinking about how you feel when you listen to presentations may generate an awareness of what you wish to avoid and adopt when you are speaking. Therefore, reversing the perspective may help speakers become sensitive to the importance and nuances of successful professional presentations.

Below is the first *Reverse the Perspective* from the vantage point of listeners:

### Reverse the Perspective

- Should presentation skill be a criterion that makes or breaks a job candidate? That is, should otherwise bright and industrious candidates be eliminated from consideration if they can not demonstrate skill in presentation settings? Companies regularly screen employees for reading and writing literacy. Should speaking skill be a similar screening criterion?
- Are there some positions that would require such skills and others that do not?
- If your answer to the previous question is yes, which types of positions do not require speaking skill competence?

## Myths Regarding Presentation Skill Competencies

Several misconceptions about presentation skill proficiency should be dispelled before we proceed further. The perpetuation of these impressions reduces the chances of becoming more adept in speaking contexts.

### Six Misconceptions

#### *Some people have the gift of gab. Others are not as fortunate*

The ability to speak well is not a gift any more than the ability to divide by seven is a gift. Those of us who can divide numbers by seven learned how to do so and then were compelled to do many exercises to reinforce what we had learned. We were not born with the gift of arithmetic.

Similarly, presentation skills can be, and are, learned. Some people may be more naturally adept at speaking than others, but learning how to speak effectively requires understanding principles, and then practice applying the principles. As DeVito comments, "Speakers aren't born; they are made. It is through instruction, exposure to different speeches, feedback, and individual learning experiences that you become a better speaker." [12]

#### *Effective speakers are not apprehensive*

People, all people, are apprehensive in speaking situations. Edward R. Murrow, the famous broadcaster, remarked that "the best speakers know enough to be scared.... The only difference between the pros and the novices is the pros have trained the butterflies to fly in formation."[13] We will discuss speech anxiety in detail in Chapter 4. However, in this introductory chapter, we must correct the notion that effective speakers are fearless. There might be something a bit abnormal about a person not feeling any anxiety prior to making an important presentation.

#### *Educated persons can, and should, be able to speak effectively*

Depth of knowledge does not necessarily translate into speaking prowess. Advanced degrees certainly do not, even when the advanced degree may be in a communication-related field. Ask your instructors if they have ever attended an academic conference and heard a poor presentation. No doubt, they could keep you occupied for hours with tales of weak presentations delivered by knowledgeable, intelligent, and perhaps even responsible individuals. Accrued knowledge does not guarantee the ability to communicate that knowledge.

### Creating a PowerPoint® presentation eliminates other speaking concerns

Most of us know intuitively that the above statement makes no sense. Yet, often business presentations seem to be nothing more than fancy bells and whistles in the form of computer-generated graphics. We will discuss visual supplements in Chapter 8, but it is important to understand, right from the beginning, that PowerPoint® slides can aid a presentation, but these slides do not become the presentation. If people are under the misapprehension that such slides do become the presentation, then they are almost guaranteed to be unsuccessful.

### Any person can teach presentation skills

Some people assume that speaking is a natural ability and, therefore, any competent person can be trained to teach others to be proficient speakers. This assumption is dangerous. Presentation skill workshops, like other classes, require instruction by those who have studied in their field. Scientists at universities will not phone the Communication Studies department when they seek an instructor to teach an open section of Introduction to Biology. Engineers within organizations do not contact members of the Corporate Communication department if they need assistance designing a building. It is illogical to believe that persons who are untrained in speaking can be appropriate candidates to teach presentation skills regardless of their responsible nature or even their speaking competence.

### Some people can simply never improve their speaking skills

All readers can become more effective presenters. Regardless of how little experience you have had, how uninformed you sense you may be, or how fearful you are, you can become an effective speaker. After thirty years of conducting executive workshops, managerial training sessions, and graduate/undergraduate courses in presentation skills, I can assure readers that only two groups of people do not become more adept in speaking situations: those who are convinced they have no need to improve and those who are afraid to try. Deanna Sellnow makes this point when she writes that effective speakers "are those who choose to work at developing their skills and ineffective speakers are those who choose not to do so." [14]

American politician Norman Thomas once commented, "More than once I have heard good people come out second best to demagogues because they have depended on their righteous indignation and neglected to do their homework."[15] To become efficient speakers, business leaders, students, and instructors need to do their homework and not assume that expertise, native intelligence, righteous indignation, technological gimmickry, or any natural capabilities will be sufficient.

## Common Problems with Presentations

Business professionals typically identify several problems in presentation skills contexts. The following is a list of these recurring issues with comments made by individual managers who have identified the problems.

### Lack of organization

"It bothers me when a presentation is unorganized. There are times when someone is knowledgeable but is nevertheless 'all over the place' when they speak. I can't follow what's being said. They know what they're talking about but apparently can't express it coherently."

### Overestimating or underestimating the audience

"Often I go to hear a presentation from technical support people and they are speaking way over my head, using terminology that only computer people are familiar with. Maybe one or two in the audience can understand the conversation but the rest of us are lost and I wonder why I'm wasting my time. The opposite occurs as well. I go to an in-house training program and feel they're speaking to me as if I'm a child. That is particularly exasperating. I don't like being condescended to even if I do need the information they are presenting."

### Reading off PowerPoint® slides

"I'll often attend a session and the speakers will have prepared elaborate and impressive PowerPoint® slides. However, occasionally speakers read from these slides verbatim. We can read. They do not need to say what we could be reading in our offices."

### Ums, ers, ahs, and you knows

"It is difficult to remain focused when someone intersperses junk words throughout. You tend to focus on these fillers and not the message itself. I have on occasion (I'm embarrassed to say but it's true), begun to tabulate the frequency of these ums. There is a fellow in Accounting who once uttered forty-three ums in a ten-minute talk."

### Time

"It's difficult to pay attention when a speaker seems to spend more time than necessary on a topic. Typically, there is too much redundancy. My time is valuable. Get to the point, so I can get back to my desk."

These problems reflect bad habits but not permanent conditions. Each of these counterproductive tendencies is relatively easy to address.

## Presentation Skill Competencies

Communication competencies, as the label suggests, refers to those skills that when acquired by individuals, render those individuals proficient communicators. The National Communication Association (NCA) and individual scholars have, for at least the last twenty-five years, worked toward identifying these competencies.[16] (Table 1-1 on page 10, "Communication Competencies," presents several sets of competencies that have been created by individual scholars working independently or with organizations like the NCA.)

Let's review the various competencies that have been identified and discuss those most applicable to speaking in professional contexts. Consider the list that appears on the following pages as a set of desired outcomes for those studying how to create, deliver, and evaluate professional presentations.

A competent speaker in professional contexts can do the following:

- **Analyze Audiences**
  When speakers use jargon that is unfamiliar to their audiences, they apparently have not taken the time necessary to discover who they will be addressing. A competent speaker takes that time, knows how to analyze the audience, and completes the analysis prior to creating the message.
- **Structure a Message**
  A competent speaker knows how to organize a message effectively. As indicated previously, a common complaint audience members identify is that speakers are "all over the place" when they make presentations.

- **Deliver a Message**
  Structuring a message efficiently does not guarantee that a presentation will be delivered competently. Knowing the correct route is not the same as driving the car. Competent speakers can effectively deliver the message they have constructed to identified audiences.
- **Address Speaking Anxiety**
  Some polls suggest that people fear making presentations more than they fear their own demise. Speaking anxiety is normal. Competent speakers can address their anxiety so that it does not interfere with the quality of their presentations.
- **Use Visual Complements**
  Most business presentations are delivered with visual support. Visual complements can be distractions if used ineffectively. Competent speakers know how to use visual aids to support and not hinder their presentations.
- **Develop and Evaluate Persuasive Arguments**
  Presentations typically include some element of persuasion. Even if speakers are simply making a status report, they are implicitly persuading the others that work is progressing well. A competent speaker is aware of methods for persuading and can identify fallacious arguments.
- **Recognize the Advantages of Speaking Styles for Particular Situations**
  When speakers are asked to make presentations, they have a number of options regarding how they will prepare and deliver the talk. They can employ some note system, write the talk out and deliver it verbatim, or even memorize what they wish to say. A competent speaker considers the advantages and disadvantages of the various styles for the presentation situation and the audience.
- **Respond to Questions During Q&A**
  A presentation is not over until the question and answer (Q&A) session is completed. An outstanding delivery during the formal portion of the talk can be undermined by a poor reaction to questions during the post-presentation Q&A session. Competent speakers know how to prepare and respond to questions during Q&A.
- **Prepare for and Deliver Team Presentations**
  Variables that affect team presentations are different from those that affect the individual speaker. These variables involve both the preparation and the delivery of the talk. Five speakers may do well individually but be a disaster if they have to work and present collectively. In professional contexts particularly, a competent speaker is aware of the factors that contribute to effective team presentations and can efficiently participate in these presentations.
- **Demonstrate an Awareness of a Speaker's Ethical Responsibilities**
  The Non Sequitur cartoon that appears on page 41 suggests that business people are unconcerned with ethical issues. One cannot monolithically characterize all business persons as either ethical or unethical. However, one can identify ethics as a central characteristic of the competent speaker. Even the most amoral individual will have to acknowledge that an ethical speaker is likely to be perceived as more credible than one who is seen as unethical. Therefore, a competent speaker is one who understands the ethical dimensions associated with speaking and adheres to ethical responsibilities.
- **Understand Fundamental Principles that Affect Communication Success**
  Speaking is a type of communication activity. Certain principles that pertain to the communication context are important to internalize if one wishes to be an effective presenter. For example, a basic principle of communication is that it is a receiver or audience-centered phenomenon. The goal when communicating is not to spew esthetically but to ensure that what is said is understood by intended receivers. Competent speakers are aware of such principles and reflect this awareness when they speak.

## Communication Competencies — Table 1.1

Several lists of communication competencies have been generated by associations, their representatives, and scholars working independently. Below is a collection of four such lists.

**A competent speaker:**
- Expresses ideas clearly
- Organizes messages for understanding
- Expresses ideas concisely
- Expresses and defends a point of view with evidence
- Uses speaking voice effectively
- Controls communication apprehension or anxiety
- Listens effectively
- Demonstrates social skills
- Asks effective questions
- Gives complete and appropriate answers to questions
- Uses language accurately and appropriately
- Uses appropriate nonverbal cues[17]

**Speakers should exhibit the following competencies. They should be able to:**
- Determine the purpose of oral discourse
- Formulate a thesis statement
- Provide adequate support material
- Select a suitable organizational pattern
- Demonstrate careful choice of words
- Provide effective transitions
- Employ vocal variety in rate, pitch, and intensity
- Demonstrate nonverbal behavior that supports the verbal message[18]

**College graduates should be able to:**
- Speak clearly and expressively using appropriate articulation, pronunciation, volume, rate, and intonation
- Decode verbal and nonverbal cues accurately and listen effectively and detect errors in the communication of others
- Assess the communication context and adapt the message to the audience
- Present ideas in an organizational pattern that allows others to understand
- Distinguish between different purposes and goals in communicating
- Convey enthusiasm for one's topic
- Structure a message with an introduction, main points, useful transitions, and a conclusion[19]

**Speaking competencies include the ability to:**
- Narrow a topic appropriately for an audience and occasion
- Communicate the objective appropriately for the audience and occasion
- Provide supporting materials
- Use an organization pattern appropriate to the topic, audience, occasion, and purpose
- Use language appropriate to audience and occasion
- Use vocal variety to heighten and maintain interest appropriate to audience and occasion
- Use pronunciation, grammar, and articulation appropriate to the audience and occasion
- Use physical behaviors that support the verbal message[20]

## Book Scope and Features

Each chapter in this text addresses one or more of the competencies identified in the previous section. The chapters provide information that will make it easier for you to prepare, deliver, and evaluate the presentations you make and observe.

In addition, several supplementary features have been included to clarify points, challenge the reader, and describe applications of the text content. In this initial chapter you have been introduced to the feature entitled *Reverse the Perspective*. The following other features appear in each chapter throughout the text.

### Stand Up & Deliver

The late Thoreau scholar Dr. Wendell Glick commented that he never was completely certain of how he felt or what he knew until he was compelled to write his thoughts down. The *Stand Up & Deliver* features were conceived with Professor Glick's comment in mind. Each *Stand Up & Deliver* segment requires the preparation and delivery of short talks related to presentation success. Completing the exercises will compel readers to examine, refine, and express their opinions. Typically, the exercises ask readers to articulate these opinions and to evaluate their own speaking tendencies as it relates to these perspectives.

The first *Stand Up & Deliver* segment appears below.

**Stand Up & Deliver**

Assume you will be making a presentation to classmates in this course. Prepare a two-minute to three-minute talk that responds to the following questions.

- Which five of the speaker traits listed below do you consider most significant for presentation success? Why have you selected these?
  - Vocal enthusiasm
  - Clear statement of objective and speaking agenda
  - Following the stated agenda
  - Respect for and knowledge of audience
  - Appropriate dress
  - Knowledge of subject
  - Use of visual complements
  - Eye contact
  - Appropriate body motions
  - Word choice
  - Content knowledge
  - Others
- In preparing for this presentation, what have you done to improve your chances of exhibiting the behaviors that you have identified as crucial?

## Sample Presentations and Review Questions

Each chapter concludes with a series of questions and a sample presentation. The review questions are provided to help students test their recollection of the chapter content. The sample presentations include discussion points that may facilitate class analysis of the selected presentations.

## Ethical Probe

As will be discussed in detail in Chapter 4, ethical considerations and decisions affect presentation success. In each chapter, readers are asked to take a position on an ethical question pertaining to presentations. Below is the first probe in the series.

### Ethical Probe

**Power and Speaking Competence**

Do people in power, with no power to lose, have an ethical responsibility to become competent presenters?

Assume the following scenario. Assume that speakers regularly address employees, own the company, and cannot possibly lose their jobs on the basis of weak presentations.

Do they still have an ethical responsibility to become competent speakers?

If your answer is no, explain why not.

If your answer is yes, explain specifically why becoming a competent speaker is an ethical responsibility as opposed to being a wise practical business decision.

Football coaches like to claim that they attempt to do everything they can to put their team in a position to win. Similarly, the goal of this book is to get you ready to do your best in presentation situations and improve your presentation skill competencies.

## Summary

- Communication competence can be learned.
- Speaking skill
  - Is important for professional success
  - Can be personally empowering
  - Can result in improved listening and analytical skills
- Myths regarding Speaking Skill include the following:
  - Effective speakers are not apprehensive
  - Educated persons can, should, and will speak effectively
  - A PowerPoint® presentation eliminates other speaking concerns
  - Any person can teach presentation skills
  - Some people will never improve their speaking skill levels

- Communication competencies include the abilities to do the following effectively:
  - Structure a message
  - Deliver a message
  - Analyze audiences
  - Address speaking anxiety
  - Use visual complements
  - Develop persuasive arguments
  - Recognize the advantages of speaking styles for particular situations
  - Respond to questions during Q&A sessions
  - Prepare for and deliver team presentations
  - Demonstrate an awareness of a presenter's ethical responsibilities
  - Understand the fundamental principles that affect communication success
- This text addresses each of these competency issues, and each chapter includes the following:
  - Reverse the Perspective
  - Stand Up & Deliver
  - Ethical Probe
  - Practitioner Perspective
  - Review Questions and Exercises
  - Sample Presentations for Analysis

## Sample Presentation for Analysis

### Sell Your CEO

*John J. McGrath was a speechwriter in the department of public affairs at the Argonne National Laboratory. The late Mr. McGrath delivered* SELL YOUR CEO *on March 21, 1995, to members of the Corridor Group, a consulting company. As you read through this excerpt please consider the following questions.*

1. *Is the quote attributed to Norman Augustine consistent with your image of the speaking skills of CEOs?*
2. *Are "boundary publics" influenced by the presentation skills of CEOs?*
3. *Do audiences indeed "abhor a vacuum"? Explain.*
4. *Does the depiction in the last paragraph of this excerpt seem to be more common than abnormal?*

"There are many excellent speakers in the United States. There also are many business executives. Apparently, the policy is not to intermingle the two."

Those are the words of Norman Augustine, chairman and CEO of Martin Marietta Corporation. I've known Norm Augustine for more than a decade. He is that rarest of creatures—an American chief executive who speaks common English, and speaks it well…even in public. When you consider that he's also a brilliant engineer, it's all the more remarkable because engineers (like doctors and lawyers) seemingly must shed the ability to speak common English in order to be licensed to practice.

The same might be said for CEOs. True, most CEOs earned their positions. True, they tend to be bright and fairly decisive. But in public, well…

OK, so what?

Why should we care? Why should CEOs care? If they turn a respectable profit, so what if they aren't especially charming and persuasive at the Rotary Club meeting...if they can be persuaded to attend at all!

Here are two reasons why we should care:

1. Organizations, like people, are not islands. Their ability to function...to succeed...to turn that profit...is directly affected by other organizations and groups at their boundaries. Like individual pieces of glass in a stained-glass window, each is both constrained and supported by its neighbors. For one to grow, for one to even move, its neighbors must cooperate.
2. Organizations don't speak. They can't. Nor can they attend that Rotary Club meeting. Only people can do that. So the image projected by the individual tends to become in the audience's mind the image of the organization that person represents. And if that individual happens to be the CEO, the depth to which that image is impressed grows markedly.

So the CEO's public image is the organization in the audience's mind. And strategic audiences, which we can call "boundary publics," directly influence the organization's ability to succeed.

Then why go at all?

After all, there's obvious risk in this image-transference business. Wouldn't it be better to avoid all risk and hide in the corporate office? Perhaps. If you, the communications executive, and your CEO were the only people interested in crafting an image for your organization. But you're not.

Many others would like to handle that task for you. And if you don't...Audiences, like nature, abhor a vacuum—so the image of your organization that is impressed upon them will be an image created by others. Who? The government, for one. Your unions, for another. Mike Wallace and his troops, maybe. Your competitors, perhaps. And how about those pesky environmentalists trained at the knee of Ralph Nader and Saul Alinsky?...

...International management and organization-design expert Henry Mintzberg says every CEO has three essential duties: 1) Direct supervision; 2) Development of the organization's strategy; and 3) Management of the organization's boundary conditions—its relations with its external environment...

...We can agree, I think, that top management's responsibility at and beyond the organization's boundaries is largely a communication responsibility. However, no commonly accepted model exists for decision, execution and assessment of communication opportunities. Within even some of the largest and most venerable organizations, the process used is haphazard and inconsistent at best, and nonexistent at worse. Decisions frequently are made at the middle-management level, and sometimes lower, by persons acting with neither strategic guidance nor a "big picture" perspective on the organization's situation and external environment.

**Source**: McGrath, John. "Sell your CEO! Winning the Corporate-image Battle in the '90s," *Vital Speeches of the Day*, May 1, 1995, 61, no. 14: 444(4).

## Review Questions

1. What were the results of the Gamble and Kelliher studies?
2. How can improving speaking competence affect professional and personal success?

3. How has speaking competence affected your academic, professional, and/or personal successes?
4. What are four myths about professional speaking competence?
5. Identify four issues that are identified when professionals are asked to list problems pertaining to business presentations.
6. This chapter lists and describes several competencies associated with professional speaking. What are ten of these competencies?

## InfoTrac Question

Use InfoTrac to find Robert Brody's article entitled "Podium Power." What points does Brody make that are consistent with the points made in this opening chapter? Does anything strike you as peculiar about the author given the nature of his audience?

---

1 Daniel Webster cited in James McCroskey, *An Introduction to Rhetorical Communication* (Allyn and Bacon, 2001), 19.

2 Elizabeth Rundle Charles, cited in *The Quotable Woman: The First 5000 Years*, ed. Elaine T. Partnow (New York: Checkmark Books, 2001), 185.

3 Dan O'Hair, Rob Stewart, and Hannah Rubenstein, *A Speaker's Guidebook: Text and Reference* (Boston: Bedford/St. Martin's, 2001), 7.

4 Paul Gamble and Clark Kelliher, "Imparting Information and Influencing Behavior, An Examination of Staff Briefing Sessions," *Journal of Business Communication* 36 (July 1999): 261–277.

5 Ibid, 261.

6 This is not clear from the article, but was confirmed in e-mail correspondence with one of the authors, Paul Gamble, in July 2003.

7 Dr. Donnalyn Pompper, professor at Florida State University, made this comment in her review of the prepublication manuscript of this textbook. Used with permission of Dr. Pompper.

8 The specific study that ranked communication skills ahead of experience, motivation, and academic credentials was reported in the December 29, 1998, *Wall Street Journal*, A1. Nearly five hundred companies were surveyed for the study. There are companies that attempt to address deficiencies with what amounts to remedial skill training in presentation skills. Whirlpool, Chrysler, and Motorola are three such companies. See Watson, Arden and James Bossley, "Taking the Sweat Out of Communication Anxiety," *Personnel Journal* (April 1995): 111. Also Robert Galvin, "Communication: the Lever of Effectiveness and Productivity," *Daedalus* (Spring 1996): 137. Also Donald McNerney, "Improve your Communication Skills," *HR Focus* (October 1994): 22 and Susan Greco, "How can I improve employees' presentation skills," *Inc.* (January 1998): 83.

9 Notre Dame Professor Sandra Gustafson entitled her book, *Eloquence is Power,* University of North Carolina Press, 2000. She refers to Adams's perspective on page xiii in the book's introduction.

10 The identification of *The Age of Pericles* has been made by Donald Kagan in encyclopedic entries as well as in Kagan's book, *Pericles of Athens and the Birth of Democracy* (Touchstone, 1991), 1. The Pericles quotation is found in Berko, Wolvin and Curtis, *This Business of Communicating,* 2nd ed. (Wm. C. Brown, 1983), vii.

11 Judith McManus, *How to Write and Deliver an Effective Speech,* 4th ed. (Thomson, Arco, 2002), 1.

12 Joseph DeVito, *Human Communication: The Basic Course,* 9th ed. (Allyn and Bacon 2003), 286.

13 Cited in Joe Ayres and Tim Hopf, *Coping With Speech Anxiety* (Ablex Publishing Company, 1993), 49.

14 Deanna Sellnow, *Public Speaking a Process Approach* (Media Edition 2003), xxi.

15 Norman Thomas was born in the late 1800s and was active in the American political arena during the first half of the twentieth century and until his death in 1968. While described at times as an American socialist (and as a six-time presidential nominee of the Socialist party), Thomas vigorously opposed Communism and was active in the American Civil Liberties Union. This quote not only reflects his disdain for demagoguery, but also his sense of the importance of effective advocacy.

[16] Beginning in the late 1970s the National Communication Association (then called the Speech Communication Association) developed lists of speaking and listening skills essential for students completing elementary school, high school, and the sophomore year of college. In addition, the NCA created a list of communication competencies that businesses expected employees to possess as well as competencies essential for specific communication situations. Interested readers can review the publication *Communication Is Life: Essential College Sophomore Speaking and Listening Competencies.* Richard Quianthy is identified as the project director for this 1990 Speech Communication Association publication. More information pertaining to communication competencies can be found on the NCA Web site: **http://www.natcom.org**.

[17] Adapted from a paper entitled *Problem-Based Assessment Speaking,* by Amanda W. Borden Ph.D., dean of Freshmen and Assistant Professor at Samford University. Borden's list of competencies is identified as an adaptation of the University of Colorado's public speaking assessment program. **http://www.samford.edu/groups/quality/CommunicativeLiteracy.pdf**.

[18] Adapted from op. cit. Quianthy 1990.

[19] See **http://www.natcom.org/instruction/DiversityMono/college_competencies_table2.htm**. This site contains several competency lists. This particular list is an adaptation from Table 3, I. C. found on the site. Readers who are interested in the evolution of such competencies should see Rebecca Rubin and Sherwyn Morreale, "Setting Expectations for Speech Communication and Listening" in *Preparing Competent College Graduates: Setting New and Higher Expectations for Student Learning,* ed. Elizabeth Jones (Jossey-Bass Publishers, 1996), 19–29. This volume is part of a series called *New Directions for Higher Education.*

[20] Adapted from the University of North Carolina at Greensboro Web site. **http://www.uncg.edu** page entitled "Eight Public Speaking Competencies and Criteria for Assessment." These eight competencies in slightly different forms are found elsewhere. For example at **http://pegasus.cc.ucf.edu** page entitled, "The Competent Speaker."

**Chapter in a Nutshell** *Presenters who understand communication principles have an advantage when they conceive, construct, practice, and deliver their presentations.*

# Communication Principles and Presentation Success

*Often beauty grows dull or common when speech breaks the mask.*[1]

-*Mary Renault from* The Mask of Apollo

*In the marketplace of ideas, the person who communicates clearly is also the person who is seen as thinking clearly.*[2]

-*D. Uchida*


## Abstract

David Murray, the editor of the *Journal of Employee Communication Management*, once commented that communication involves "getting what is in my head into your head."[3] This is a simple but not inaccurate depiction of the goal in all communication activity. It is important to understand the factors that either impede or facilitate the process of "getting what is in my head into what is in your head." In this chapter, we will review basic characteristics of the communication process and discuss their applications to the presentation setting. Specifically, at the end of this chapter, you should be able to do the following:

- Define communication
- Define public communication
- Identify elements of the communication process
- Discuss basic characteristics of communication that affect the presentation context
- Compare presentations settings to other communication settings
- Explain the distinction between presentations and speeches

## A Shrinking Audience

Thirty managers gathered in a presentation room to hear a talk about interactive video teleconferencing. The managers, all from the same pharmaceutical company, had not been compelled to attend the session, but enticing advertisements for the presentation had been distributed through interoffice mail and bulk e-mail. The notices suggested that the to-be-demonstrated video technology could save thousands of dollars for units within the organization. Interactive video was portrayed as an alternative to travel and many of the managers were looking for ways to reduce expenses. In addition, some people without any budgetary concerns decided to attend the presentation simply because the advertisements had piqued their intellectual curiosity.

The talk was billed as a demonstration as well as an explanation. A colleague of the assembled would address the audience live, but concurrently an on-screen person—actually located in another time zone—would also be seen and heard. The cohort was a representative of the vendor and would help illustrate how easy it could be to converse across regions using video teleconferencing.

Within fifteen minutes of the start of the presentation, audience members began departing courteously but regularly. The presentation never got off the ground. At the very beginning there was a brief technical problem. Once that had been addressed, the speaker began to explain the snag and the equipment itself, using terminology that was far beyond the understanding of many of the managers. In addition, both the live speaker and the screen presence almost immediately departed from whatever planned talk they had prepared and began entertaining questions from those few in the audience who had familiarity with technology. What ensued were three-way discussions addressing esoteric issues peripheral to the advertised session objectives. Initially, the live speaker appeared not to notice the people from the audience who were leaking from the group. But, at one point, the speaker looked up at the diminished audience, saw that over half the group had departed, and appeared genuinely perplexed.

- What did the live speaker desire to communicate to his audience?
- What did he communicate to his audience?
- What factors created the problem?
- Does this scenario surprise you?

- Assume that a second presentation was scheduled for the following week for all those managers who could not attend the first one. What would you recommend to the live and on-screen speakers to prevent the same situation from repeating?

## INTRODUCTION

*Half a lifetime among senior corporate policymakers offers convincing proof that when it comes to getting ahead in business—communication is **everything**.*[4]

(emphasis in original)

Burton Kaplan in *The Manager's Complete Guide to Speech Writing*

The word *communication* has been defined in many ways. Over 50 years ago, at an MIT-sponsored conference, S.S. Stevens remarked: "Although no phenomenon is more familiar to us than communication, the fact of the matter is that this magical word means many things to many people."[5] Half a century later, Stevens's comment remains true. When people desire to improve communication, their efforts are often, and ironically, frustrated because the communicators are not speaking about the same phenomenon.[6]

Kaplan in the quote above asserts that "half a lifetime" among senior executives convinces him that "communication is everything." What is he referring to by "everything"?

Take a moment to complete a simple exercise. Write down what the words *communication* and *communicator* mean to you in the following two sentences.

1. "Where I work, we need better communication."
2. "Pat is an excellent communicator."

Compare what you've written for statement 1 with the culled list of possible interpretations provided below.

Better communication (where you work) means the following:

- More timely notification about project deadlines
- More efficient public presentations
- More effective coordination of meetings
- More subordinate-to-superior communication channels
- Greater communication between departments
  - the complete elimination of the company grapevine
- More efficient interpersonal communication
- Fewer memos
- More efficiency with e-mail
- Better performance reviews
- More efficient software for teleconferencing
- More honest and less ambiguous interactions

Similarly, compare what you wrote for statement number 2, *Pat is an excellent communicator*, with this list of potential interpretations for the word in that context.

*Does* Pat

- deliver excellent presentations
- listen well
- lead a meeting effectively

- write excellent memoranda
- negotiate well for her department
- have an excellent vocabulary
- read nonverbal messages carefully
- use eye contact meaningfully; is she aware of how space, scent, dress, and time can reflect professionalism
- read quickly with outstanding comprehension
- respond effectively to questions
- communicate tactfully
- have integrity

Communication is a multifaceted concept and, apparently, can mean various things to different people. To understand the principles of communication as they pertain to the presentation setting, it is necessary to clearly define the word *communication*.

## Defining Communication

Rancer, et al, in *Building Communication Theory*, defines communication as the "manipulation of symbols to stimulate meaning in other humans."[7] Newcomb, in his "An Approach to the Study of Communicative Acts," describes communication as the "transmission of information, consisting of a discriminatory stimuli [sic], from a source to a recipient." Andersen, in the *Journal of Communication*, writes that it is "the process by which we understand others and in turn endeavor to be understood by them."[8]

Academic definitions can be cumbersome and occasionally can be more confusing than clarifying. However, all of the above definitions have merit. Communication is a "process," it does involve "source[s]," "symbols," "recipient[s]," and the "transmission of information." Those who intentionally communicate do "endeavor to be understood" by others.

Let's distill these and other similar definitions to construct a description of communication that is useful for our purposes. Below are three related statements about communication. Taken collectively, they define the concept. Following the bulleted list is a description of each of the key phrases in the defining statements.

- Communication is an audience-centered and nonlinear process
- It occurs when a receiver perceives meaning from verbal and nonverbal symbols that are intentionally or unintentionally transmitted by a source
- It is not synonymous with understanding

### Communication Is a Nonlinear Process

Theorist Harold Lasswell argued that communication could be analyzed by examining "Who Says What to Whom, (In Which Channel) With What Effect."[9]

For example, if you were listening to a sales representative describing a new product, the "Who" would be the salesperson, the "What" would be the information contained in the address, the "Whom" would be the members of the audience who listened to the presentation, and the "Effect" would be the reactions the audience members had to the talk.

A problem with this model is that it appears to be linear.

Lasswell may not have intended it to be interpreted this way, but the model implies that communication goes one way and is over when it reaches the receivers. Communication, in fact, is not linear and is not a one-way phenomenon.

Assume the sales representative in the example speaks too long, and the length appears to be particularly inappropriate given that all attendees prior to the session had been asked to read a detailed report that described the entirety of the presentation.

Further, assume that the speaker appears to be intent on using dozens of superfluous PowerPoint® slides and is reading verbatim from each of them.

If the speaker notices that some in the audience have reacted to the most recent slide reading by rolling their eyes and looking at their watches, he or she may respond to the observed reactions by ceasing to read the slides.

This scenario is not unusual (although some readers may wish that offending speakers were more typically willing to pick up on nonverbal cues). Nevertheless, we know that speakers often respond to nonverbal as well as verbal reactions from an audience. In the above example, listeners thought the talk was too long and reacted. The speaker noticed the reaction and then altered the presentation. The speaker (originally the Who) became the receiver (the Whom) when she or he noticed the nonverbal response. The listeners became the Who when they glanced at their watches.

The process of communicating is two-way and nonlinear.

## Communication Can Be Intentional or Unintentional

*"Anyone who says he isn't going to resign four times, will."*[10]

John Kenneth Galbraith

A message does not have to be intentionally sent to be communicated. For example, speakers who want to appear enthusiastic may boom their voices during their talks in the hope of sounding eager. They may state repeatedly how excited they are to be present in front of the group. It is possible, however, that audience members may wonder about the excessive volume and interpret it as inconsiderate, aggressive, or generally inappropriate. Audience members might even feel as if repetitive statements about enthusiasm suggest an absence of enthusiasm.

Ralph Waldo Emerson once quipped, "The louder he talked of his honor, the faster we counted our spoons."[11] People who incessantly tell you they are honest may make you wonder if you can trust them around your possessions. Speakers who use graphics that contain misspelled words may be communicating that they are poor spellers, or are careless, or have overworked assistants. The fact that speakers do not desire to convey such messages is irrelevant to whether the messages were relayed. What is communicated to audiences, therefore, may be unintentional.

## Communication Involves both Nonverbal and Verbal Messages

Most people in the twenty-first century are aware of the importance of nonverbal messages. We know that messages are not only communicated by language but by factors such as body movement, the use of time, and eye contact. Nevertheless, some presenters behave as if they are unaware of how nonverbal messages can complement or undermine the quality of their presentations.

Managers who make the claim that they are eager to hear about the problems of the staff can make that claim with appropriate language and reinforce that claim by looking and sounding as if they mean it. Similarly, spokespeople who announce "the financial future is bright" undermine that message if their voice sounds gloomy and their facial expressions seem to be screaming, "Someone is making me say this."

The word "verbal" is often used inappropriately to mean face-to-face or oral communication. Verbal communication simply means communication that uses words. Speakers who refer to their home as their "crib" are likely to be relaying a different message than people who talk of their "house." The use of technical terms—even if used correctly—can make it difficult for receivers to understand a message.

When we think of the word communication, we need to remember that the process involves both verbal and nonverbal dimensions. We will discuss in detail these verbal and nonverbal factors in Chapter 11.

## Communication Is an Audience-Centered Phenomenon

Robert Hopper has written that, "Communication can be said to have taken place only when messages are received and interpreted."[12] Similarly, James McCroskey states that communication "occurs when one individual stimulates meaning in the mind of another by means of a message."[13] In more technical terms, S.S. Stevens writes that communication requires "the discriminatory response of an organism to a stimulus.... If the stimulus is ignored by the organism, there has been no communication. The test is a differential reaction of some sort."[14]

In common language, these three quotes mean simply: You have not communicated by virtue of sending a message. You have only communicated when someone has received the message. When you prepare for your presentations, keep that defining characteristic of communication front and center on your radar screen.

If you have written a brilliant speech and the audience could not understand it, you have only communicated to them that your presentation was unclear. You have not communicated what you intended to send. Even if you distribute a text version of your presentation, you have not necessarily communicated any of the sentiments contained therein.

Arnold "Red" Auerbach is the author of a number of books, including *MBA: Management by Auerbach*, He is better known for his remarkable achievements as coach, general manager, and president of the Boston Celtics. His perspective on the subject of communication reflects his awareness of taking an audience-centered approach. "When it came to communications," he wrote, "my rule of thumb was very simple: It's not what you tell them, [it's] what they hear."[15] More academic sorts have put it this way: "...the eloquence of a speaker's words are irrelevant if the words are not understood or do not affect the people in the audience." [16]

Communication is an audience-centered phenomenon.

When you prepare for and deliver a presentation remember communication is an audience-centered phenomenon. You will only have communicated when someone has received a message. You do not communicate what you say. You communicate what the audience hears.

## Communication Is Different from Understanding

Some people think of communication as being synonymous with understanding. People who are engaged in an argument will sometimes remark, "We're just not communicating." This seems to imply, "We do not understand one another," or "We can't seem to explain to each other what we'd like to explain."

Even when two people who are conversing have trouble understanding each other, they are still communicating. The word *communication* does not imply that what has been intended to be received has been received as intended. If a team of speakers attempt to explain a project to superiors, there is no guarantee that the explanation will be understood.

We would like our communications to result in understanding, but when messages are received, we have communicated regardless of whether we have been understood.

In sum we have defined communication as

- An audience-centered phenomenon
- A nonlinear process
- A result of
  - Intentional and unintentional behaviors
  - Verbal and nonverbal behaviors
- Different from understanding

**Stand Up & Deliver**

Who is the best speaker you have ever heard in person? Did his or her speaking reflect an awareness of any of the defining characteristics of communication identified in the bulleted list above?

Assume you will be making a presentation to classmates in this course. Construct a two-minute to three-minute presentation that does the following:

- Identifies the best speaker you have ever heard in person
- Describes what made the person successful
- Indicates whether her or presentation reflected an awareness of any of the defining characteristics of communication identified in the bulleted list
- Demonstrates your awareness of the defining characteristics of communication identified in the bulleted list

## Elements of the Communication Process

Throughout the text there will be references to elements in the communication process. There are six such elements: the source, receiver, message, channel, feedback, and noise.

### The Source

The source refers to that person or persons who, intentionally or unintentionally, send the message. When a message is intentionally sent the source conceives, encodes, and then transmits the message.

In a presentation setting, the primary sources are those persons making the presentation. As indicated in the previous section, communication is a nonlinear process; and therefore, an audience member who responds—even nonverbally—to a speaker becomes the source when that response is observed by the speaker. However, the primary sources are those people who have conceived, constructed, and delivered the messages. Factors that affect a source's ability to be efficient include knowledge of the subject, expressive vocabulary, self-concept, and familiarity with the receiver or receivers.

### The Receiver

The receivers in the process are those persons who decode and perceive meaning.

When speakers walk into a lecture hall, some audience members may notice what the speakers are wearing. On the basis of the attire, these receivers might think, "very professional," "nice outfit," "better than usual," "must have money," or any of several different thoughts. Whatever they perceive, what they see is what has been communicated. A receiver who listens to a presentation that begins with a humorous anecdote will likely not only hear the story, but also make some determination about the speaker's sense of humor or sense of what is proper.

Some factors that affect a receiver's ability to decode include listening skills, selective perception, attitudes toward the speaker, attitudes toward the event, subject knowledge, and receptive vocabulary.

## Reverse the Perspective

The phrase *expressive vocabulary* refers to the words a speaker can use. *Receptive vocabulary* refers to the words a speaker can understand. One's receptive vocabulary tends to be larger than one's expressive vocabulary because individuals can typically understand more words than they can employ when writing or speaking.

When you listen to presenters who use words that you do not understand, how do you react?

When you listen to presenters who do not employ sophisticated vocabulary, do these speakers lose stature in your eyes?

Assume that you were in an audience when speakers made the following comments:

1. We are glad that Leslie has decided to join our team. We need someone in our group with such an **effervescent** energy along with a much needed ability to **perspicaciously** assess the proposals that come our way.
2. Effective presenters are aware that **digressions** in the speaking context are **transgressions.**
3. As I present the state of our department annual report, I want to remind you that we are a **fledgling** unit within this established organization.
4. I hope you had a chance to read through the article I had on reserve. I imagine you feel the piece is as clear as a **limpid** stream in a **rustic** area.

- If you heard these statements, what would have been communicated to you?
- Do you think any of the messages you received would be different than those the speakers intended?
- Assuming that the audience is your class, do you think the words employed would be the best words to use? Which would be inappropriate?

### The Message

The message is what the source intentionally or unintentionally, verbally or nonverbally, sends to the receiver. The president's state of the organization address is a message. A wave to an audience member is also a message, as is a smile or the nod to questioners who have their hands raised. Some factors that affect message quality are the organization pattern or structure, word choice, and nonverbal messages.

## The Channel

The message the receiver perceives has been sent through some channel. We can decode information by using any one of our senses or by using combinations of our senses. We can derive meaning by sound, sight, smell, touch, and taste. We hear what someone states. We see facial expressions that accompany the spoken words. We can smell a foul motor aroma suggesting that there may be a problem with a projector. If a speaker passes around an object that is being marketed, we may draw conclusions about the product by how it feels to the touch. We might assess a speaker's cooking skills by what samples we taste. Some factors that affect the channel relate to physical limitations or handicaps, visibility, health, weather, and drowsiness.

Some factors that affect the channel for communication include: physical handicaps, illumination, wellness, and external noise.

## The Feedback

Feedback refers to the responses we receive from our messages. If audience members laugh at our humor, that laughter is the feedback. If an employer frowns when you make a presentation about your group's progress, the facial expression is feedback and informs you that your supervisor disapproves of your progress assessment. The feedback can be verbal or nonverbal, immediate, or delayed.

Feedback often does, and should, influence the source of the message. *Feedback-induced response* refers to this phenomenon and illustrates why communication in presentation settings is best conceived of as nonlinear. Feedback-induced response means that feedback from the receiver induces a response from the source. If you are delivering a presentation and observe that listeners are spending more time reading the handout than listening to you, that feedback may induce you to request that listeners wait until after the presentation to read the handout. Figure 2-1 illustrates the non-linear nature of communication.

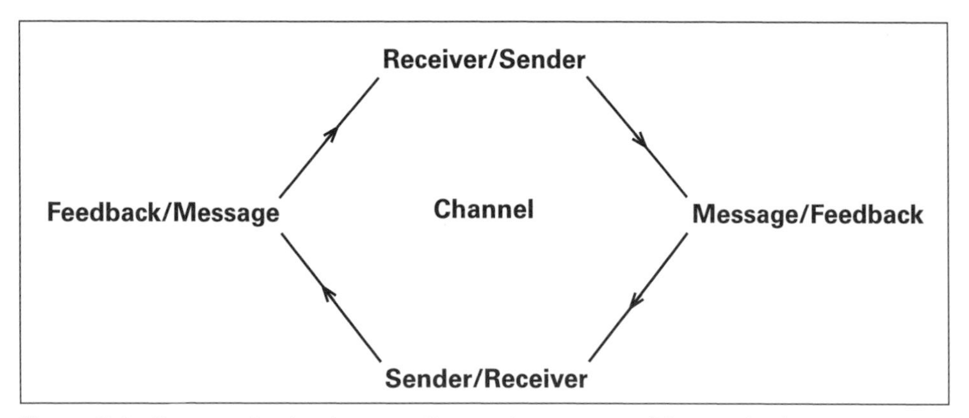


**Figure 2-1** Communication is a non-linear phenomenon. The sender becomes a receiver when the audience responds with verbal or nonverbal feedback.

Efficient speakers are proficient at reading feedback and responding appropriately. Were you to ignore people thumbing through the handout, you would be encouraging them to miss the messages you hoped they would receive. You might even find yourself distracted throughout your talk by the absence of attention. Since communication is a nonlinear phenomenon, the source/receiver components as well as the message/feedback components are essentially interchangeable. A person who is the source of the message also is, almost concurrently, a receiver as well. The feedback from the receiver can be seen as the receiver's message to the source.

## The Concept of Noise

Communication noise refers to the impediments that affect the ability to communicate effectively. Noise can literally be external noise such as distracting side conversations or rail traffic outside an opened window. Noise can also refer to psychological interference, such as being preoccupied with another matter while making or attending a presentation.

Unintentionally sent messages can inadvertently create communication noise. Receivers who decode these unwittingly sent messages may draw conclusions about the source that could affect future interactions. Senders, of course, may be unaware that a person harbors resentments derived from unconsciously communicated messages.

Imagine attending and nominally participating in a meeting while concurrently contemplating the various tasks that need to be accomplished during the day. You have to register your car in person at the Department of Motor Vehicles, write an important e-mail, and read a weighty document sent down from the Human Resources department. As you sit in this meeting, your thoughts are focused on how you will plan out the hours after the meeting so that you can accomplish your tasks and still have time to go to the gym.

While you are so engaged, a tardy colleague comes into the meeting room, sits across from you, appears to meet your eyes, and whispers a barely audible "Hello." You do not see nor hear this person, because as he sits, you are "in space" contemplating today's schedule—version three—which will permit your workout and the car registration at a time when the lines will not be too long. You can recall, too vividly, the last time you went to the registry when you had been stalled on an interminable queue standing behind someone who spoke loudly, nearly continuously, and apparently meaninglessly, on a cell phone.

Since you are preoccupied with your schedule and this unpleasant recollection, you do not notice your colleague nor acknowledge his presence. The absence of any acknowledgment from you registers with your colleague who thinks you are annoyed that he is late. The colleague thinks your reaction is inappropriate since he is, after all, busy and you have been late on several occasions as well. However, the reality is that you did not see him even though you appeared to be looking at him.

A few weeks later, you find yourself teamed with this colleague on another project. You cannot understand why, initially, he regards you with some disdain. It may irk you when he treats you this way. This tension could dissipate, but you two might remain at odds and you will not know why.

The attitudinal noise in this instance is related to the previous message your colleague received when you apparently ignored him. The example illustrates that noise is not always something generated at the time of a communication. Noise can be a residual of prior intentional or unintentional interactions.

As it relates to presentations, lingering resentments caused by unintentionally or intentionally sent messages can affect audience members' perceptions of speakers. These perceptions can become noises, i.e., impediments, which communicators need to identify and overcome to be successful.

## Presentation Effectiveness and Communication Noise

*Message fidelity* and *message distortion* are two phrases used to help conceptualize effective communication. When a receiver understands a message the way the source desired the message to be received, we say that there is message fidelity.[17] In the cases when senders unintentionally send messages, message fidelity could still occur. For example, assume that several speakers are preoccupied reviewing notes prior to a team presentation. These speakers may be sending unintentional messages to the audience. If audience members assume that the speakers are preoccupied, then the unintentionally sent message has been accurately decoded. Message distortion occurs when receivers do not accurately perceive the intended message or when receivers inaccurately decode unintentionally sent messages. Obviously, one would prefer message fidelity to message distortion.

Message fidelity can exist despite the presence of noise. Noise is omnipresent. Some writers define noise as that which creates distortion.[18] A better way to consider noise is to think of it as a factor that reduces the chances for successful communication but does not guarantee failure. If a train rushes by while you are speaking, you might have to increase your volume or receivers will have to work harder to hear your message, but it is still possible to understand what is being said. Another common example relates to the noise that accompanies distinctive speaking accents. Accents can be noises. Unfortunately, many listeners give up when they listen to someone who speaks with what, to them, is a foreign accent. However, if receivers are willing, they may get through the noise that accompanies an unusual speaking accent.

In short, noise should be viewed as an impediment, but like most impediments, noise can be overcome. Speakers and receivers have the responsibility to identify and overcome noise in order to increase the chances for message fidelity. The course you are taking is, in effect, a class that will help you recognize and reduce impediments to your success in the presentation setting.

### Ethical Probe

**Accents and Ethics**

Assume that a salesperson who does not speak English as a primary language delivers a presentation attempting to sell a product. Further assume that the speaker's accent is different than most of the listeners' accents and, therefore, the speaker is more difficult to understand than other salespersons.

- Do listeners have an ethical obligation to work harder to discern the messages of these salespersons?

# Presentation Skills and Other Contexts for Communicating

## Other Contexts

In addition to the presentation context, communication scholars examine interaction in four other areas.[19] These areas are discussed below.

### *Intrapersonal communication*

In simplest terms, intrapersonal communication means communicating with oneself. When we think about what we will be saying or writing to others, we are engaging in intrapersonal communication. When you consider how to respond to a questioner, your contemplations are categorized by intrapersonal communication.

### Dyadic communication

Dyadic communication refers to communication in groups of two. A formal performance appraisal interview is an example of dyadic communication. An informal conversation over the net on a tennis court is also an example of dyadic interaction.

### Group communication

Groups are a common and also very problematic context for communicating. As we will see when we discuss this in greater detail in Chapter 9, group interaction is often fraught with irritating noise. Many presentations in organizations are team efforts and/or delivered as a team. The noise that pervades group interaction must be addressed to facilitate effective presentations. Typically, groups are defined as bodies of anywhere from 3–15 people.

### Mass communication

Whether mass communication is printed or electronic, it involves disseminating information to large, sometimes unknown receivers. Typically, the feedback in mass communication is delayed. A problem with mass-communicated messages is that it is often difficult to assess if receivers are even aware of the messages being sent. A bulk e-mail, for example, can be distributed to thousands, but how many of those thousands read the e-mail can be a mystery to the message source. A broadcast political speech can reach millions of TV households. Yet, it is difficult to know how many of the viewers were focusing on the message and how many might have had the broadcast on as background noise while tending to other matters.

# Distinguishing Features of Presentation Contexts

Each communication context has distinguishing characteristics. Presentation skill contexts are distinctive from the others in a number of meaningful ways. As you begin working on improving your presentation skills, consider what makes the presentation setting distinctive.

## Preparation

As opposed to dyadic or group interaction, speakers have an opportunity to plan what they would like to send in presentation settings. This creates an enormous potential advantage. As opposed to dyadic situations in which you need to conceive, compose, and state your message without an opportunity to prepare, presenters have the opportunity to consider and plan what they would like to say.

However, this potential advantage also poses a problem. Not only does the speaker have an opportunity to prepare, but the audience typically knows that the speaker has had an opportunity to prepare. Therefore, an unprepared or poorly delivered presentation results in a double negative: The audience members will likely not receive the intended messages, and the audience members will likely hear that the speaker did not responsibly prepare for the event.

Speakers can prepare for their talk in several ways, and these will be discussed throughout the book. Some preparatory steps include analyzing the audience, researching the topic, selecting the right words to match ideas, and planning what visuals can be used and how they should be used to complement the message.

## Extent of Nonlinear Dynamic

Almost all communication is nonlinear but public communication contexts are more linear than group and dyadic contexts. Speakers may have an opportunity to present an uninterrupted message when making business presentations. This is an advantage, but the limited verbal feedback during the talk highlights the need for speakers to be adept at, and to be willing to, read the nonverbal feedback from the audience and adapt to that feedback.

In a group communication situation, a listener may interrupt a colleague to request a restatement of what has been said. A confused listener might interrupt a speaker in a presentation setting requesting clarification, but it is more likely that the speaker will have to read and react to the nonverbally communicated uncertainty.

## The Significance of Source Credibility

Source credibility is significant across communication contexts; however, the credibility of a source can undermine a public presentation before the speaker has an opportunity to utter a sound. In public discourse, who you are, in terms of credibility, may be more significant than what you have to say. If you are known to be honest, always prepared with a meaningful message, respectful of the audience, and effective when delivering a mesage, you have increased your chances of being successful. The opposite is also true. If your talk is brilliant, but you have previously earned a reputation as disrespectful, dishonest, and boring, it will be very difficult to engage your audience.

## Numbers of Receivers

The size of the audience in a business presentation can vary from three in a small room to hundreds who may be packed into an auditorium. Creating a message appropriate to large numbers of receivers is far more difficult than creating a message for one or two individuals. It is easier to investigate the nature of your audience if there are few persons in that group. This investigation is more difficult when there are numerous and diverse attendees.

## Anxiety Levels

Anyone who is compelled to give presentations is aware of speech anxiety. One may become nervous during interpersonal or group encounters, but that apprehension is likely to be relatively low when compared with the anxiety that surfaces when delivering a presentation. Speech anxiety will be discussed in detail in Chapter 4.

# Presentations vs. Speeches

There are differences—as well as many similarities—between a business presentation and a speech. A *Management Communication Quarterly* article suggests that since synonymous usage of presentations and speeches is "deeply embedded," there might be little value in attempting to perpetuate the distinction.[20] However, as this same article and others acknowledge, there are—at least subtle—differences.[21]

## Audience Composition

People who attend business presentations usually are required to be there. If you read a poster announcing that a speaker will come to the university to deliver a talk, you can choose to attend or avoid the event. If you are a department head and the vice president calls all department heads into a conference so that she can report the success of the last quarter, you can not decide to avoid the session. Therefore, business presentations are different from most public speeches because the audience is often compelled to be present.

### Topic Selection

In business contexts, the scope of the talk is confined to the organizational situation. Public speakers who are invited to address audiences may speak on various subjects. If former President Clinton is asked to deliver an after-dinner speech to conventioneers, he is normally given latitude regarding the speech topic. Business presenters are generally called in to meet specific objectives.

### Audience Participation

As discussed previously, presentations are more linear than interpersonal or group interactions. However, business presentations tend to be less linear than public speeches since there typically is more interactivity in a business presentation than there is in a public speech. Trainers and salespeople, for example, will have more questions and interruptions from audience members than an author who is invited to a group to deliver a speech. Often business presentations are linear. For example, a CEO's presentation to stockholders would be linear. However, speakers in organizational contexts should be prepared for an environment that may involve, if not require, interaction.

## A Game Conceptualization

Presenters might find it valuable to think of three games when considering communication principles and how these principles affect quality presentations. In meaningful ways communication is like the games of catch, pool, and chess.

When engaged in a game of catch, your objective is to throw an object so your partner can catch it. In catch, throwing the ball esthetically is not as crucial as throwing it so your friend can get it. Similarly, when presenting a message, your objective is to ensure receipt.

Pool players are aware that they have two objectives when striking the ball. They must attempt to sink the shot and they must set themselves up for the next attempt. Speakers can see an analogy here. The objective in speaking is not only to get an initial or even subsequent message across; speakers must continuously position themselves to increase their chances so that a subsequent message will be received as intended. Shouting derisively at subordinates during a presentation might succeed in "sinking the ball," which indicates disappointment. However, a tirade might increase the chances that subsequent messages, even relatively benign ones, will be affected by debilitating noise.

Chess is a complicated game. Competitors know that there are several ways to be victorious. Likewise, speakers should be aware that they have more than one way to convey a message. However, as in chess, rules govern the communicating process. Rooks cannot move diagonally. A King cannot move more than one space at a time. If a player was to move a King two spaces in apparent disregard of the rules, the opponent would balk. If the player insisted on breaking the rule, it is likely the opponent would cease to participate in the activity.

Audience members come to presentations with expectations. They may feel that speakers should be prepared, use appropriate vocabulary, speak to their level of expertise, use appropriate vocal energy, and demonstrate respect for the time the audience is spending being attentive. Should a speaker break these rules, reflecting ineptitude or disregard, then receivers are likely to disengage, or in the parlance of a game, stop participating and at least mentally quit. Speakers, therefore, must be aware of the rules that govern the presentation setting when they prepare for and deliver their addresses.

This game conceptualization of acknowledging the centrality of receipt, the importance of reputation, and the importance of audience analysis may be helpful to you as you prepare to improve your speaking abilities in presentation contexts.

## Summary

- Communication principles are applicable to the presentation context
- Communication can be characterized as
  - Nonlinear
  - Intentional or unintentional
  - Verbal or nonverbal
  - An audience-centered phenomenon
- Other communication contexts include the following:
  - Intrapersonal communication
  - Dyadic communication
  - Group communication
  - Mass communication
- Presentations differ from other contexts in the following terms:
  - The opportunity to prepare the message
  - The extent of the linear dynamic
  - The numbers of receivers
  - The extent to which unintended verbal and nonverbal messages can be communicated
  - Extent of speaking anxiety
- All contexts are similar in that all communication contexts have a
  - Source
  - Receiver
  - Message
  - Channel
  - Feedback

## Sample Presentation for Analysis

### A Just and Peaceful World

*George W. Bush delivered* "A Just and Peaceful World" *to the graduating class of the United States Military Academy. The speech was delivered at West Point, New York, on May 29, 2002. As you read through this excerpt please consider the following questions.*

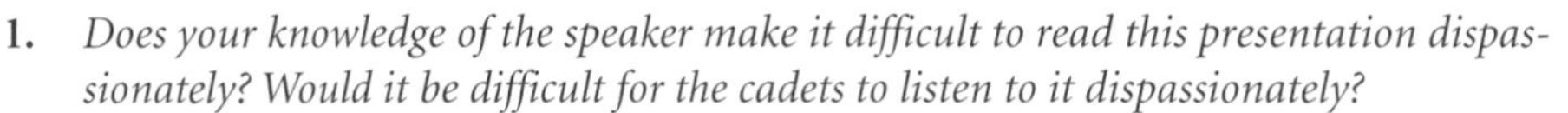

1. *Does your knowledge of the speaker make it difficult to read this presentation dispassionately? Would it be difficult for the cadets to listen to it dispassionately?*
2. *Does the allusion to being "a Grant man" increase or decrease the way the audience is likely to view the speaker?*
3. *Are the attempts at humor in the fifth and sixth paragraphs appropriate and effective?*
4. *Does the president establish a positive rapport with this audience? Has your perception of the president changed by virtue of having read this excerpt?*

...In every corner of America, the words "West Point" command immediate respect. This place where the Hudson River bends is more than a fine institution of learning. The United States Military Academy is the guardian of values that have shaped the soldiers who have shaped the history of the world.

A few of you have followed in the path of the perfect West Point graduate, Robert E. Lee, who never received a single demerit in four years. Some of you followed in the path of the imperfect graduate, Ulysses S. Grant, who had his fair share of demerits and said the happiest day of his life was "the day I left West Point." During my college years I guess you could say I was a Grant man.

You walk in the tradition of Eisenhower and MacArthur, Patton and Bradley, the commanders who saved a civilization. And you walk in the tradition of second lieutenants who did the same, by fighting and dying on distant battlefields.

Graduates of this academy have brought creativity and courage to every field of endeavor. West Point produced the chief engineer of the Panama Canal, the mind behind the Manhattan Project, the first American to walk in space. This fine institution gave us the man they say invented baseball and other young men over the years who perfected the game of football. You know this, but many in America don't. George C. Marshall, a VMI graduate, is said to have given this order: "I want an officer for a secret and dangerous mission. I want a West Point football player."

As you leave here today, I know there's one thing you'll never miss about this place: Being a plebe. But even a plebe at West Point is made to feel he or she has some standing in the world. I'm told that plebes, when asked whom they outrank, are required to answer this: "Sir, the Superintendent's dog, the Commandant's cat, and all the admirals in the whole damn Navy." I probably won't be sharing that with the Secretary of the Navy.

West Point is guided by tradition, and in honor of the "Golden Children of the Corps," will observe one of the traditions you cherish most. As the Commander-in-Chief, I hereby grant amnesty to all cadets who are on restriction for minor conduct offenses. Those of you in the end zone might have cheered a little early. Because, you see, I'm going to let General Lennox define exactly what "minor" means.

Every West Point class is commissioned to the Armed Forces. Some West Point classes are also commissioned by history, to take part in a great new calling for their country. Speaking here to the class of 1942—six months after Pearl Harbor—General Marshall said, "We're determined that before the sun sets on this terrible struggle, our flag will be recognized throughout the world as a symbol of freedom on the one hand, and of overwhelming power on the other."

Officers graduating that year helped fulfill that mission, defeating Japan and Germany, and then reconstructing those nations as allies. West Point graduates of the 1940s saw the rise of a deadly new challenge—the challenge of imperial communism—and opposed it from Korea to Berlin, to Vietnam, and in the Cold War, from beginning to end. And as the sun set on their struggle, many of those West Point officers lived to see a world transformed.

History has also issued its call to your generation. In your last year, America was attacked by a ruthless and resourceful enemy. You graduate from this Academy in a time of war, taking your place in an American military that is powerful and is honorable. Our war on terror is only begun, but in Afghanistan it was begun well.

I am proud of the men and women who have fought on my orders. America is profoundly grateful for all who serve the cause of freedom, and for all who have given their lives in its defense. This nation respects and trusts our military, and we are confident in your victories to come...

**Source**: Bush, George. "A Just and Peaceful World: Moral Truth is the Same in Every Culture," *Vital Speeches of the Day*, June 15, 2002, 68, no.17: 514(4).

## Review Questions

1. What does it mean to refer to communication as an audience-centered, nonlinear process?
2. How might presenters communicate information unintentionally?
3. What types of communication noise can affect the success of presenters and presentations?
4. Explain why presentations are nonlinear but more linear than other communication contexts. In what other ways do presentations differ from dyadic and group contexts?
5. What is the distinction between a presentation and a speech?
6. In what ways are presentations analogous to aspects of the games of catch, pool, and chess?

## InfoTrac Question

Use InfoTrac to find the Zielinski article in the August 2003 edition of *Presentations*. What does Zielinski identify as the values and problems associated with audience participation in business presentations?

---

[1] Mary Renault from *The Mask of Apollo*, cited in *Quotations by Women*, ed. Rosalie Maggio (Beacon Press, 1992), 304.

[2] Donna Uchida, Marvin Cetron, and Floretta Mckenzie, *Preparing Students for the 21st Century*, (American Association of School Administrators, 1996), 16.

[3] Conversation with David Murray at the IABC June 2002 Annual Meeting, Chicago, Illinois. As indicated in the text, Murray is the editor of the *Journal of Employee Communication Management.* Murray is also the editor of *Speechwriter's Newsletter*, a publication that has served corporate and political speechwriters for 25 years.

[4] Burton Kaplan, *The Manager's Complete Guide to Speech Writing* (The Free Press, 1988), xi.

[5] S.S. Stevens, "Introduction: A Definition of Communication," *Journal of the Acoustical Society of America* 22 (1950): 689. The article is part of the proceedings from a conference called the Speech Communication Conference held at the Massachusetts Institute of Technology from May 31 to June 3, 1950. This Speech Communication Conference is not to be confused with what became the annual conference of the Speech Communication Association. In 1950 that annual meeting was held in New York City.

[6] See Dance, Frank, "The Concept of Communication" in Applbaum, 1975, originally in *Journal of Communication* 20 no. 2 (June 1970): 201–210. In this article, Dance compiles over one hundred definitions of communication. Goldhaber is one of several others who comment that definitions of communication exist "by the dozens." Goldhaber, Gerald, *Organizational Communication 6th edition* (Brown and Benchmark, 1993), 128.

[7] Dominic Infante, Andrew Rancer, and Deanna Womack, *Building Communication Theory*, 4th ed. (Waveland Press, 2003), 340.

[8] Op. cit. Dance. Newcomb quote appears on: 7, Andersen quote on: 5.

[9] Harold D. Lasswell, "The Structure and Function of Communication in Society," in *The Communication of Ideas*, ed. Lyman Bryson (New York: Harper and Brothers, 1948), 37–51.

[10] This quote is sometimes referred to as "Galbraith's Law of Political Wisdom." John Kenneth Galbraith is a Canadian-born economist who has authored several books related to politics and economics. Galbraith also served as an ambassador to India in the Kennedy administration and is identified as a key advisor to President Kennedy.

[11] Ralph Waldo Emerson was a nineteenth century American essayist and philosopher.

[12] Robert Hopper, *Human Message Systems* (Harper and Row, 1976), 8.

[13] James McCroskey, *An Introduction to Rhetorical Communication*, 8th ed. (Allyn and Bacon, 2001), 21. Mortensen, Hopper, Timm and DeTienne, Hattersley, and McJannet all make similar claims. Mortensen comments that "communication occurs whenever persons attribute significance to message related behavior." Hopper writes, "Communication can be said to have taken place only when messages are received and interpreted." Tim and DeTienne write that "communication occurs whenever someone attaches meaning to a message." Hattersley and McJannet state, "Only what has actually been understood will have been communicated." C. David Mortensen, *Communication: The Study of Human Interaction* (McGraw Hill, 1972), 14. Robert Hopper, *Human Message Systems*, (Harper and Row, 1976), 8. Paul Timm and Kristen Bell DeTienne, *Managerial Communication: A Finger on the Pulse* (Prentice Hall, 1995), 15–17. Michael Hattersley and Linda McJannet, *Management Communication* (McGraw Hill, 1997), 7.

[14] Op. cit. Stevens 689.

[15] Auerbach, Arnold, and Joe Fitzgerald, *On and Off the Court* (MacMillan, 1985), 59.

[16] Verderber, Rudolph, and Kathleen Verderber, *The Challenge of Effective Speaking*, 12th ed. (Thomson Wadsworth, 2003), 5.

[17] Kathleen Krone, Fredric Jablin, and Linda Putnam, "Communication Theory and Organizational Communication: Multiple Perspectives," in *Handbook of Organizational Communication*, eds. Jablin, Putnum, Karlene Roberts and Lyman Porter (1987), 23.

[18] DeVito, for example, in *The Communication Handbook: A Dictionary* (Harper and Row, 1986), 209.

[19] One could argue that communication scholars explore dozens of contexts. For example, the National Communication Association is divided into several interest groups which reflect communication analysis in other contexts. In addition to the divisions mentioned in this section and earlier in the chapter the NCA has divisions in Spiritual Communication, Health Communication, and others. Interested readers might want to visit **http://www.natcom.org** or review a copy of the 2003 National Communication Association Directory, pages 24–30, to see the various areas of examination that are of interest to communication scholars.

[20] Frank Dance, "What Do You Mean by Presentational Speaking," *Management Communication Quarterly* 1 no. 2 (November 1987): 260–271. The part of the article that suggests that the terms have come to be nearly synonymous is on pages 270–271.

[21] In addition to the Dance article cited in note 20, see P.S. Rogers, "Distinguishing Public and Presentational Speaking," *Management Communication Quarterly* 2 no 1. (August 1988): 102–115. Rogers's article is essentially a counterpoint to Dance's. Dance suggests that the differences between public and presentational speaking are subtle if they exist at all. Rogers argues that the distinctions are significant.

Chapter in a Nutshell

*In presentation contexts, speakers as well as audience members have to make ethical decisions. These decisions are likely to have meaningful consequences.*

# 3 Ethical Decisions and Public Presentations

*Can there be a more horrible object in existence than an eloquent person not speaking the truth?*[1]

*-Thomas Carlyle*

*...This above all: to thine own self be true, and it must follow, as the night the day, thou canst not then be false to any man.*[2]

*-Polonius to his son Laertes:* Hamlet, *Act I Scene III*


## Abstract

Speakers are compelled to make ethical decisions when they conceive, create, and deliver their presentations. The great Roman rhetorician Quintilian defined the ideal speaker as "a good person speaking well."[3] Speakers must consider ethics because the repercussions of unethical behavior can be significant. Unethical speaking can dramatically affect consumers, organizations, nations, and even the careers of the unethical speakers themselves. This chapter examines why ethical considerations are central to the study of presentations and what it means to be an ethical communicator in presentation contexts. At the conclusion of the chapter, you should be able to do the following:

- Define ethics
- Identify speaking situations that require ethical decision making
- Explain why speakers need to consider ethical issues
- Describe several ethical perspectives for decision making
- List and describe characteristics of ethical speakers and listeners
- Identify resources for those who wish to examine the ethical dimensions of their presentations

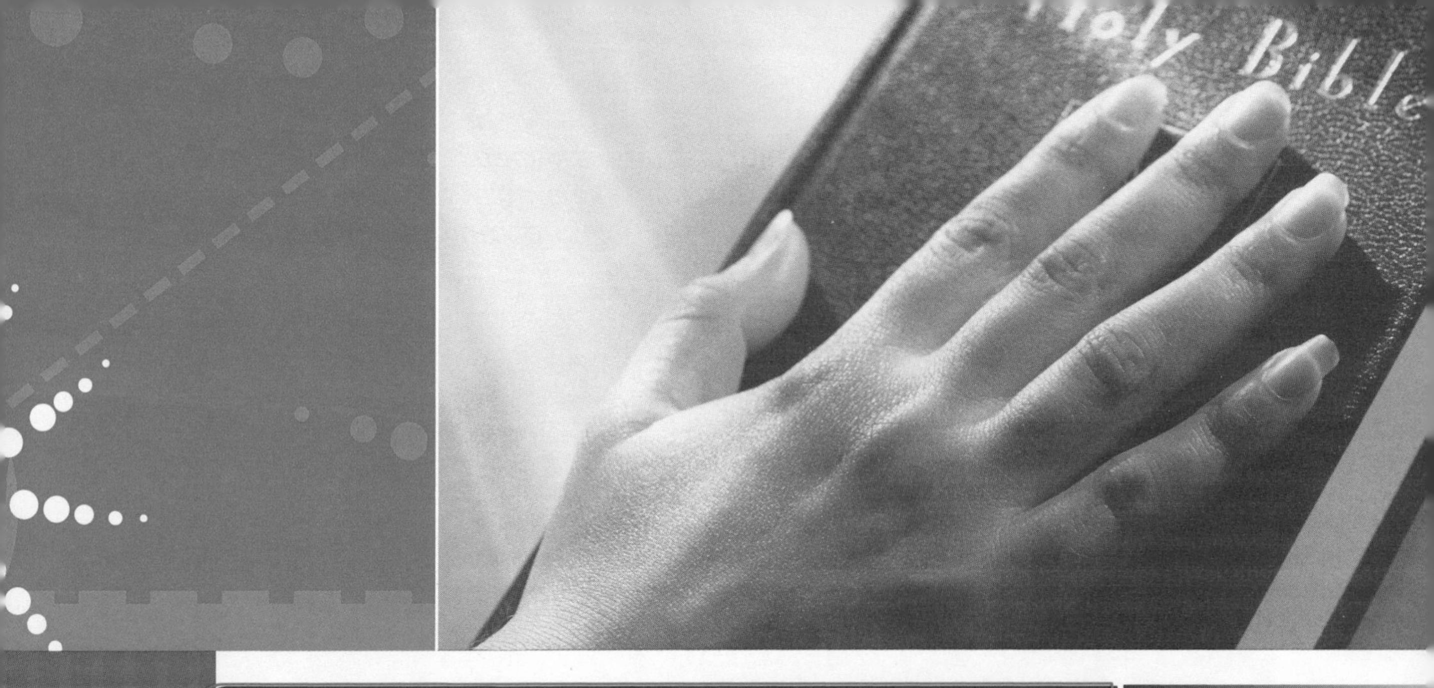


## Persuasive Weapons

In January of 2003, President George Bush addressed the United States Congress and the world when he delivered the annual State of the Union address. A section of that speech dealt with an impending confrontation between the United States and the sovereign country of Iraq ruled by Saddam Hussein. President Bush desired to convince Congress, the citizens of the United States, and the citizens of the world that Iraq's leader posed a threat to world safety. In March of 2003, the United States and its allies attacked Iraq. Baghdad fell in April of 2003. Saddam Hussein fled and was captured later. His sons were killed on July 22, 2003, eliminating the natural successors in any Hussein-led resurgence.

In the summer of 2003, President George Bush was criticized for a particular inclusion in the State of the Union address. Bush had alleged in the speech that Iraq had sought to procure uranium from African countries to strengthen its military arsenal. The reference supported the contention that Hussein was amassing weapons of mass destruction. That Hussein had or would soon have weapons of mass destruction (WMDs) was a major plank in the argument supporting military action. However, evidence surfaced in July suggesting that Bush might have known in advance of the talk that the assertion regarding the uranium might not be true.

On August 4, 1964, President Lyndon Johnson delivered a speech to the nation that alleged that two U.S. vessels had been destroyed by the North Vietnamese in the Gulf of Tonkin. Because of this action, the president asked Congress for the powers to take "all necessary measures to repel any armed attack against the forces of the United States and to prevent further aggression." Three days later on August 7, 1964, the United States Congress passed the Tonkin Gulf Resolution, giving President Johnson the power to extend United States involvement in Vietnam. In March of 1965, the first American ground troops arrived in Vietnam. By the end of the Vietnam War, close to 58,000 American soldiers were killed. Many historians contend that the alleged Gulf of Tonkin incident was a deliberate fabrication designed to gain support for increased U.S. involvement in Vietnam.[4]

Assume that both presidents had worthy objectives in that they were concerned about the destructive consequences of inaction. Assume that they both knew that important decision makers would be swayed by their claims. Finally, assume that both presidents knew that there were doubts regarding the veracity of their claims.

- Should the presidents have removed comments from their speeches if they thought the comments might not be true—even if they felt that their goals were laudable?
- Should the presidents have retained the references because they had an ethical responsibility to consider the welfare of the world?
- Do speakers have an ethical obligation to ensure that everything they claim in their talks is factual?
- Do speakers have an ethical obligation to consider their organization's larger good? If the larger good is served by deception, are speakers morally obliged to serve that larger good even if it means that the speakers will communicate deceptively?

# Ethical Decisions and Public Presentations

## Introduction

During a class discussion about ethics and communication, an MBA student made the following remark. "Isn't honesty overrated?" she asked.

The student's question was a statement more than it was an inquiry. She was asserting that the ideal of communicating truthfully is not as important as people tend to suggest. Another student, an undergraduate in a separate class, commented that unless she prefaced an assertion with the words, "This is the truth," then she was not bound to be honest with the words that followed. In both classes, other students were startled to hear these comments and sputtered reactions indicating that they were aghast.

Is honesty overrated? Should lying be condoned if speakers do not include a prefatory comment such as, "I'll be perfectly honest with you," "This is the truth," or "Trust me on this one"?

Consider the following scenarios. Should the speakers in these situations be honest?

**Does a salesperson have the moral obligation to be truthful when pitching a product to several potential customers?** If the salesperson's livelihood depended on sales, would that affect your decision? If the organization encouraged salespeople to "do whatever it takes," would that affect your decision? If competing salespersons routinely lie, would that affect your decision?

**Does a department head who is required to deliver a talk about the department's annual progress have the right to exaggerate accomplishments and omit information about unsuccessful projects?** If all department heads similarly exaggerate, would that affect your decision? If department heads are exaggerating to protect the job security of their subordinates, would that affect your decision?

**Is it ethical for a college admissions representative to come to a high school and distort the credentials of the university to attract quality students?** If the representatives have been given "the speech" to deliver by their supervisors and this prepared message contains the distortions, would that affect your decision?

**If you are asked to explain an idea to a group of supervisors, are you obliged to disclose that a colleague actually conceived of the idea if, by omitting this detail, you think you**

**might get promoted on the basis of your creativity?** If this colleague regularly steals others' ideas, would that affect your decision? If previously you had been passed over for a promotion that this colleague had received, would that affect your decision?

**If you are a company spokesperson for an organization that is experiencing a crisis, are you entitled to mislead the media to preserve the image of the organization you represent?** If you fear that the media will mislead the public unless you mislead the media, does that affect your decision?

**If you know that your audience is incapable of deciphering statistical information, is it unethical to mesmerize them with meaningless but nonetheless persuasive statistics?** Is it the audience members' "tough luck" if they are "too stupid" to know that the statistics are meaningless?

**If you are attending a presentation and you hear a spokesperson say something that you know to be incorrect, are you ethically responsible for correcting the speaker in front of the other listeners?** Are the other listeners responsible for their own critical thinking?

## Ethics: A Foundation for Effective Presentations

In *Ethical Issues in Business,* Peg Tittle defined ethics as "the study of what is right and wrong."[5] Potter Stewart, the former Supreme Court justice, commented that ethics refers to "knowing the difference between what you have a right to do and what is the right thing to do."[6] The perspective presented in this book is that speakers have a responsibility to their listeners, their organizations, and themselves to think about right and wrong and what is the right thing to do. For several related reasons, an ethical orientation provides a foundation for effective presentations and is consequently vital for effective professional speaking. These reasons are listed below and discussed in the pages that follow.

- A speaker's ability to engage, inform, and persuade listeners can be affected by a speaker's reputation as an ethical individual.
- Presenters are compelled to make ethical decisions. That is, speakers consciously or subconsciously make choices that are affected by ethical perspectives.
- The effects of unethical presentations can be economically, socially, and politically devastating to individuals and societies.
- Studies suggest that employers identify integrity as a primary employee attribute. If the employers surveyed have been candid and are representative, then unethical behavior is likely to diminish employee status.

### Reputation Affects Speaking Success

The Greek scholar Isocrates claimed that above all else an orator must be "a good person."[7] As stated earlier, the great Roman rhetorician Quintilian described the ideal orator as a "good person speaking well."[8] Readers may agree or disagree with the sentiments of Isocrates and Quintilian. However, one cannot dispute that credibility affects the speaker's ability to engage, inform, and persuade listeners.

Aristotle has been identified as the greatest theorist ever to write on the subject of rhetoric.[9] He claimed that ethos—a function of audience perception of speaker intelligence, character, and goodwill—was the most potent means of persuasion.[10] If ethos is the most potent means of persuasion and ethos is a function, at least in part of audience perception of character, then it follows that the ethical decisions speakers make will affect their successes and failures.

We all know this intuitively. When we listen to our supervisors speak, we accept or reject their messages depending on how honest they have been with us in the past. When we purchase products, we seek out sales representatives whom we feel we can trust. In an interview with Gabriel Smallman, the president of Getfused.com, a software company, Smallman commented that he does no marketing. All of his business comes from referrals.

"In the software business," he told me, "clients are unaware of how we do what we do. Often a client will agree to work with us and then tell us to go 'Do the voodoo that you do.' It is important to the client to trust the people who design the software because they do not want to become frustrated with poorly constructed product down the road. Because of the nature of software, clients have no way of knowing whether they are getting a solid foundation or a ticking bomb. Customers hire us because they have been told by others that we can be trusted. They are, in essence, not buying a product. They are buying us. We have a reputation of backing up what we say we can do. By the time we present our proposals to new clients we often have secured the account."

Sissela Bok concludes her comprehensive book entitled *Lying* with the following words: "Trust and integrity are precious resources, easily squandered, hard to regain. They can thrive only on a foundation of respect for veracity."[11] One hundred and fifty years earlier, Abraham Lincoln expressed similar sentiments when he remarked, "If you once forfeit the confidence of your fellow citizen, you can never regain their respect and esteem."[12]

If speakers do not address the ethical issues surrounding a presentation, they will find it difficult to regain the respect and esteem of their audiences. Without such respect, it is nearly impossible to meaningfully engage, inform, and persuade receivers.

## Presentations Require Making Ethical Decisions

When speakers conceive and construct messages, they are faced with ethical decisions. For example, they may need to consider whether they should

- Omit damaging information
- Exaggerate truths
- Deliberately attempt to confuse the audience with ambiguous language
- Use misleading statistics
- Be concerned with individual or societal repercussions of the message
- Present legitimate counterarguments
- Appropriate someone else's ideas
- Consider the value of an audience member's time
- Prepare thoroughly
- Blatantly lie

Each time your instructors prepare their lectures, they have to consider at least two of these issues. Each time sales representatives pitch their products, they may have to consider several. Similarly, whenever a recruiter addresses potential employees or students, she or he must consider many of these. Since these decisions nearly always surface for presenters, the consideration of ethical matters results in a necessary floorboard in the foundation for effective speaking.

## The Effects of Unethical Speaking Can Be Devastating

*The Power which has always started the greatest religious and political avalanches in history rolling has from time immemorial been the magic power of the spoken word, and that alone. The broad masses of the people can be moved only by the power of speech. All great movements are popular movements, volcanic eruptions of human passions and emotional sentiments, stirred either by the crude Goddess of Distress or by the firebrand of the word hurled among the masses....*

Adolf Hitler

Dan O'Hair, Rob Stewart, and Hannah Rubenstein comment that, "One of the most consistent expectations that we as listeners bring to any speech situation is that the speakers will be honest with us."[13] In addition, Robert Kraut has argued that people are not particularly adept at detecting lies.[14] Charles Ford makes corroborating comments in *Lies! Lies!! Lies!!! The Psychology of Deceit*. Not only are most people able to identify lies at a rate only "slightly greater than chance," but even those people who are coached to detect signs of deceit are unlikely to become more efficient at identifying lies and liars.[15]

Listeners are vulnerable. Audience members are not necessarily fools because they can be deceived. No person is omniscient. Even the brightest among us have been duped by people who have communicated unethically. Bok argues that those who are deceived become "resentful, disappointed and suspicious.... They see that they have been manipulated, that the deceit made them unable to make choices for themselves according to the most adequate information available."[16] She comments that even those who are inclined to deceive others desire to be treated without deceit.[17] Further, she argues that the damage of deceit transcends the effects on the deceived and includes the erosion of societal trust.[18]

The effects of some deceptions may be minimal, but some deceptions can be physically, emotionally, or financially damaging. An unethical presentation can result in the following:

**Consumers buying products that may be harmful.** A pharmaceutical company, for example, peddled an antidepressant drug by claiming that it was the only such drug that had not been proscribed for pregnant women. While this claim was superficially true, the company knew that the drug had simply not yet been banned.[19]

**Students deciding to attend universities that they cannot afford.** Some schools are notorious as bait and switch institutions. Prospective students are offered an attractive financial aid package in their first year and then subsequently financial aid is reduced. The affected students must decide whether to pull up roots and transfer or to absorb a cost that they cannot afford and could not have anticipated.

**Employees becoming unemployed when they thought their jobs were secure.** Employees who were assured of no impending layoffs may find themselves retrenched. They have lost time searching for a job, can be emotionally devastated, and may become financially drained.

**Employees accepting and moving to positions which, they discover subsequently, are quite different from the ones that had been described to them.** A deceptive presentation by a recruiter may result in a person selling the home, uprooting the family, and moving belongings across the country only to discover that the depiction of the position was deliberately misleading.

**Citizens supporting actions that have catastrophic consequences.** In democratic countries, citizens may, directly or through their representatives, participate in the decision making that affects their lives. Citizens, of course, can only meaningfully participate if they are provided with honest information.

## Studies Support that Employers Value Employee Integrity

As Figure 3-1 indicates, a number of studies have suggested that managers consider employee integrity to be a more important attribute than even employee literacy.[20]

If, as these studies indicate, integrity is more important to employers than employee basic skill sets, then speakers who are unethical may be sacrificing their future for short-term gains. The origin of the word *ethics* comes from the Greek word, *ethos*, which means "character." Apparently, the character of an employee is significant to those who make hiring decisions.

**Value Ratings of Employee Skill Sets**

| HARRIS, 1996 Skills | Scores | WILHELM, 1998 Skills | Scores* | HENDERSON, 2001 Skills | Scores* |
|---|---|---|---|---|---|
| Integrity/honesty | 9.24 | Integrity/honesty | 9.70 | Integrity/honesty | 8.88 |
| Listening | 9.21 | Reading | 9.50 | Reading | 8.50 |
| Serves clients | 8.77 | Participates a team | 9.40 | Listening/speaking | 8.42 |
| Responsibility | 8.35 | Responsibility | 9.30 | Responsibility | 8.24 |
| Participates as team | 8.35 | Works with diversity | 9.30 | Serves clients | 8.22 |
| Esteem | 8.12 | Serves clients | 9.20 | Knowing how to learn | 8.14 |
| Sociability | 8.06 | Listening | 9.10 | Participates | 8.12 |
| Reading | 7.97 | Sociability | 8.32 | Writing | 8.00 |
| Time management | 7.91 | Speaking | 8.30 | Works with diversity | 7.86 |
| Works with diversity | 7.91 | Knowing how to learn | 8.20 | Uses computers | 7.84 |
| Speaking | 7.88 | Arithmetic | 8.00 | Acquires and evaluates | 7.70 |
| Self-management | 7.88 | Writing | 7.90 | Decision making/solving | 7.56 |
| Interprets/Communicates | 7.77 | Self-management | 7.89 | Self-management | 7.42 |
| Organizes/maintains info | 7.50 | Problem solving | 7.80 | Self-esteem/sociability | 7.00 |
| Acquires and uses info | 7.47 | Allocates time | 7.70 | See things in mind's eye | 6.70 |
| Knowing how to learn | 7.38 | Self-esteem | 7.50 | Creative thinking | 6.48 |
| Problem solving | 7.35 | Decision making | 7.30 | Mathematics | 6.26 |
| Arithmetic/Mathematics | 7.06 | Reasoning | 7.20 | Teaches others | 6.22 |
| Teaches others | 7.03 | Creative thinking | 7.10 | Selects/applies technology | 6.14 |
| Writing | 6.94 | Uses computers | 6.90 | Indentifies, organizes, plans | 5.98 |
| Creative thinking | 6.94 | Mathematics | 6.60 | Leadership/negotiates | 5.70 |
| Decision-making | 6.91 | Interprets/communicates | 6.60 | Understands Systems | 5.66 |
| Reasoning | 6.85 | Acquires & evaluates info | 6.30 | Maintains/troubleshoots | 5.34 |
| Exercises leadership | 6.82 | Organizes/maintains info | 6.30 | | |
| See things in mind's eye | 6.50 | Exercises leadership | 6.10 | | |
| Manages materials | 6.50 | Negotiates | 6.10 | | |
| Understands Systems | 6.41 | Understands Systems | 6.10 | | |
| Uses computers | 6.32 | Teaches others | 5.90 | | |
| Negotiates | 6.21 | Improves or designs sys | 4.90 | | |
| Maintains/troubleshoots | 6.03 | Selects technology | 4.80 | | |
| Manages human resources | 5.88 | Applies technology | 4.80 | | |
| Monitors and corrects | 5.74 | Manages human resources | 4.60 | | |
| Improves or designs sys | 5.62 | Monitors/corrects | 4.60 | | |
| Manages money | 5.56 | Allocates money | 4.53 | | |
| Selects technology | 4.82 | Seeing things in mind's eye | 4.50 | | |
| | | Maintains/troubleshoots | 4.40 | | |
| | | Allocates materials | 4.20 | | |

*Scores in Wilhelm and Henderson studies were on a 5-point Likert scale. These scores were doubled for presentation in this table.

**Figure 3-1** As these studies show, employee integrity is valued more by employers than employee skill sets.

*Source:* Chart used with permission of William Wilhelm from his paper "Determinants of Moral Reasoning" presented at ABC national meetings in Cincinnati, October 2002.

## Reverse the Perspective

The following is an excerpt from a novel written in 1917 about the experiences and business successes of an immigrant. At one point, the main character comments on his observations of societal morality. Is this depiction accurate today, nearly a century later?

Does your sense of the morality of civilization affect how you listen to presentations by salespeople, lawyers, politicians, instructors, and peers?

> *My business life had fostered the conviction in me that, outside of the family, the human world was as brutally selfish as the jungle, and that it was worm-eaten with hypocrisy into the bargain. From time to time the newspapers published sensational revelations concerning some pillar of society who had turned out to be a common thief on an uncommon scale. I saw that political speeches, sermons, and editorials had, with few exceptions, no more sincerity in them that the rhetoric of an advertisement.... I saw that civilization was honeycombed with...conventional lies, with sham ecstasy, sham sympathy, sham smiles, sham laughter.... I imagined mountains of powder and paint, a deafening chorus of affected laughter, a huge heart, as large as a city, full of falsehood and mischief.*[21]

**David Levinsky** in *The Rise of David Levinsky,*
first published in 1917

# Ethical Presentation Behavior

## How Do Ethical Speakers Behave?

If ethical considerations provide a foundation for effective speaking, it is necessary to identify what makes a presentation an ethical one. What do ethical speakers do?

- They do not lie
- They have ethical presentation objectives
- They are fully prepared for the presentation
- They make sure that their message merits the audience's time and attention
- They disclose conflicts of interest
- They consider the ramifications of their actions
- They attribute their sources

## An Ethical Speaker Does Not Lie

### *The truth, the whole truth, and nothing but the truth*

What is a lie?

If you say you have a master's degree in biology and you do not, that is a lie. However, what if you mention during a talk that you attended Harvard University, and the truth is that you took two cooking classes there at night in the continuing education school? Have you lied? You did, after all, attend Harvard University. Certainly your objective was to mislead the receivers into thinking that you attended Harvard University as a regular, full-time, matriculating student. But, did you lie since what you said was, literally, the truth?

Ekman has defined a lie as "a deliberate attempt to mislead without the prior consent of the target."[22] If we use this definition, accepted by almost all persons who study deception,[23] then all of the following behaviors are lies.

### *Making a statement that is not true*

"For the class of 2005, the average SAT score for our freshman at this university is 1400."

If the average SAT score at the university is 1200 then, regardless of how many other colleges similarly inflate the average SAT score, the statement is a lie as it is a "deliberate attempt to mislead without the prior consent of the target."

**Omitting something from a message that will or could mislead the receiver.**
"I attended Harvard University before I began my work at Polaroid."

If you did not matriculate at Harvard, but simply took some evening classes, and you inserted the remark to mislead the audience, then you would be lying even though your words were literally true.

**Playing with the meaning of words to mislead a receiver.** A company once peddled its breakfast drink by arguing that the drink had more *food energy* than other breakfast drinks. Most people were unaware that food energy meant calories. The company would probably not have attempted to persuade by saying that its beverage had more calories than the competing product. This was a deliberate attempt to mislead the target.

**Using statistics to confuse the audience.** You may have heard the old cynical wheeze that there are "three types of liars: liars, damn liars, and statistics." Assume speakers ask-for your financial support by stating that "In the last 24 hours alone there has been a 100-percent increase in the number of contributors." This could mean, of course, that one person made a contribution prior to yesterday and now another person has made a contribution. This does represent a 100-percent increase. However, the objective of the speaker, apparently, was to mislead receivers into thinking that many individuals had joined the bandwagon. Since the statement is a deliberate attempt to mislead, regardless of the intelligence of the collective receivers or the truth of the claim, the statement is a lie and stating it is unethical.

**Employing strategic ambiguity.** Strategic ambiguity is an approach to communicating that attempts to "complicate the sense making apparatus of the receivers."[24] The supporters of strategic ambiguity suggest that it is advantageous because strategically ambiguous communication is deniable, preserves privileged positions in organizations, fuels creativity, and provides for something they call "unified diversity."[25] The notion of strategic ambiguity has been supported in some circles and criticized in others.[26] Regardless of your position on the issue, if you agree with the accepted definition of lying, strategic ambiguity must be construed as a euphemistic way to describe lying. When you attempt to "complicate the sense making apparatus of the receivers," you are engaged in a deliberate attempt to mislead without the prior consent of the target. Employing the word "strategic" is an attempt to create a membrane of legitimacy for lying.

**Avoiding brutal honesty and employing white lies.** Brutal honesty is a phrase used by some to mean complete honesty. It is often used by those who wish to argue in support of disingenuous communication. The word *brutal* becomes a convenient adjective if this is your goal. Brutal honesty sounds as if the act of being honest will have brutal consequences for the poor receiver who has to hear the complete truth. Similarly, the phrase *white lies* is used to describe mistruths that are likely to benefit the receivers more than the truth will. When avoiding brutal honesty or employing any white lie, the beneficiary of the largesse must indeed be the receiver and not the source or else the message is unethical. Usually, an audience is in a better position to determine what is for its own good than the speaker is. If the beneficiary is the source and not the receiver, then avoiding honesty because you allege that "to be honest would be to be brutal"—is brutally unethical.

## An Ethical Speaker Has Ethical Goals

Assume that you were hired by an organization that polluted the air. You were told by your employer to make presentations throughout the country describing the company's charitable and humanitarian activities. The goal of these presentations was to deflect attention from the company's polluting behavior. If you felt that the polluting behavior was unconscionable, you would not be an ethical speaker if you were to barnstorm, highlighting the company's altruistic efforts to deflect critical attention.

Consider this second example. Assume a group of neo-Nazis wanted to elect a Nazi for office. You were being considered for a job as a speechwriter for the Nazi. You were told to avoid any references to his racist ideologies and dwell on his dear mother, his career as a Cub Scout, and his record as a veteran. If you did this, your supportive words might be true, but they might contribute to the election of a person who believed in inherent inequality. Unethical communication behavior remains unethical regardless of whether it is one's job to behave unethically.

## An Ethical Speaker Is Fully Prepared

How do you feel when you attend an advertised lecture and you realize shortly after you arrived that the speaker has not prepared the message? How do you feel when you are compelled to attend a presentation and then arrive to hear nothing but garbled nonsense from the speaker? Would you be appeased if such speakers said they were busy? The speaker's professional obligations include the ethical obligation to prepare for a presentation.

## An Ethical Speaker Ensures that the Message Merits the Audience's Time

Organizational women and men are occasionally required to attend efficiently structured, well documented, carefully prepared, and expertly delivered presentations on subjects that are completely irrelevant to them. Readers may be able to recall instances when they have had to endure lengthy talks that seemed to serve the purpose of highlighting the speakers' authority or were insensitive to the receivers' collective time. Ethical speakers do not misuse the audience's time to demonstrate how smart, powerful, and attractive they may be.

## An Ethical Speaker Discloses a Conflict of Interest

If the audience's assessment of the speaker's message would be affected by the speaker's agenda, then that agenda should be relayed to the audience. If a speaker reports the advantages of building a new facility in the suburbs and urges the company to go through with the project, the speaker is obliged to inform the listeners that she or he has a financial interest in the construction company that will benefit from the expansion.

## An Ethical Speaker Considers the Possible Effects of the Presentation

As we discussed earlier, one reason for considering ethics when speaking is that the consequences of unethical speaking can be devastating. A business leader, for example, may encourage employees to invest retirement funds in the stock of a company in precarious economic straits without informing the employees of the company's financial plight. If the employees invest in this company, their entire life savings could evaporate overnight. An ethical speaker considers the possible effects of what he or she is saying. Speakers are not exonerated because they were just doing what they had to do or were told to do.

## An Ethical Speaker Does Not Plagiarize but Instead Gives Appropriate Attribution to Sources

Plagiarism involves the theft of ideas. If you need to give a talk, you are unethical if you lift the speech, or part of the speech, from another source without acknowledging the source. If you quote another, you need to give credit to the author. If you paraphrase a quote, you still must credit the source. If your assistant gave you the idea for a reorganization scheme, then you are obliged to credit the assistant.

### Ethical Probe

#### Justifications for Unethical Behavior?

In May 2000, an article in the *Journal of Employee Communication Management* described a study related to ethical communication in organizations.[27]

Graduate students who were full-time day managers were asked to complete a survey indicating whether specific communicative behaviors were ethical or unethical. In discussions that followed the completion of the survey, respondents identified factors that affected their decisions.

The list that follows includes three of the factors that emerged from these discussions.

- **Victimization**: If the respondents had been victimized by a particular unethical behavior in the past, they tended to consider that behavior unethical.
- **Job responsibilities**: If the respondents had jobs that (they claimed) required duplicity, then some unethical behaviors were condoned.
- **Personal tendencies**: Respondents tended to identify behavior as ethical if they themselves had a tendency to do it. Persons might comment, "It is okay to say that. I do that all the time."

Should any of these be considered when determining if a particular communication act is ethical or unethical?

# What Do Ethical Listeners Do?

To some extent, speakers are vulnerable to unethical audience behaviors. No individual desires to spend weeks working on a proposal, hours creating the PowerPoint® slides, anxious days practicing the delivery only to discover that the proposal had no chance of being accepted. No individual enjoys having a meticulously planned presentation interrupted by listeners who bounce up and out during the talk to take cell phone calls.

The effects of unethical listening may not be as devastating as the possible consequences of unethical speaking, but they are important. Ethical listeners do the following:

- **Think critically**
- **Behave courteously**
- **Listen dispassionately**

## Ethical Listeners Think Critically

> *There are four chief obstacles in grasping truth...namely submission to faulty and unworthy authority, influence of custom, popular prejudice, and the concealment of our own ignorance accompanied by an ostentatious display of our knowledge.*[28]

Ethical listeners think about what they hear and do not swallow any nonsense that comes their way. Edmund Burke once opined that "the only thing necessary for the triumph of evil is for good people to do nothing."[29] A listener who hears the ravings of someone like Nazi propagandist Joseph Goebbels is obliged to question the merit of what has been said. An ethical listener does not "do nothing" and passively facilitate the "triumph of evil." We will discuss in detail the specific responsibilities of critical listeners and listening in Chapter 13.

## Ethical Listeners Are Courteous and Attentive

When people attend a talk they are not given free rein to take phone calls or flee periodically to impress the speaker with their overall sense of importance or insensitivity. Such behavior is rude and distracts the speaker. An ethical listener does not talk with a colleague, do a crossword puzzle, or fall asleep during a speaker's presentation.

## Ethical Listeners Do Not Prejudge the Speaker

Keeping an open mind at all times is difficult, but an ethical listener attempts to do so. An ethical listener leaves ethnocentric tendencies as well as personal prejudices at the door to the conference room. Richard may be an unconscionable bore and less than personable, but listeners have an ethical responsibility to attempt to evaluate what Richard is saying despite who Richard may be.

## Does the End Justify the Means?

The word *dilemma* is frequently misused as a synonym for the word *problem.* When people are faced with a dilemma, they have a particular type of problem, one that has two unattractive alternatives. In common parlance, they have a choice between a rock and a hard place. Presenters are often faced with ethical dilemmas.

If speakers mislead employees about impending layoffs, then the employees will lose time that could be used to search for new work. If speakers honestly inform employees about impending layoffs, then during the next few weeks the employees may not be productive on the job, rumors may race through the organization, the company's stock price may plummet, and everyone in the company will need to endure painful consequences. Speakers may think that keeping the company afloat (the ends) is more important than the lie (the means) that kept it afloat.

If you believe that management might be justified in lying to employees, then you believe that when faced with an ethical dilemma, the end justifies the means.

The problem with the ends justifying the means argument is that it can be used relatively easily to rationalize behavior that is inconsiderate and damaging to others. Someone might think, for example, that the end of personal wealth is worth the means of deceiving consumers in order to obtain the wealth.

People have to consider whether there is a professional, civic, and personal obligation to be ethical when they make presentations. The case has been made in this chapter that

**NCA Credo for Ethical Communication**

---

**PREAMBLE**

*Questions of right and wrong arise whenever people communicate. Ethical communication is fundamental to responsible thinking, decision making, and the development of relationships and communities within and across contexts, cultures, channels, and media. Moreover, ethical communication enhances human worth and dignity by fostering truthfulness, fairness, responsibility, personal integrity, and respect for self and others. We believe that unethical communication threatens the quality of all communication and consequently the well-being of individuals and the society in which we live. Therefore we, the members of the National Communication Association, endorse and are committed to practicing the following principles of ethical communication:*

**PRINCIPLES**

- We advocate truthfulness, accuracy, honesty, and reason as essential to the integrity of communication.
- We endorse freedom of expression, diversity of perspective, and tolerance of dissent to achieve the informed and responsible decision making fundamental to a civil society.
- We strive to understand and respect other communicators before evaluating and responding to their messages.
- We promote access to communication resources and opportunities as necessary to fulfill human potential and contribute to the well-being of families, communities, and society.
- We promote communication climates of caring and mutual understanding that respect the unique needs and characteristics of individual communicators.
- We condemn communication that degrades individuals and humanity through distortion, intimidation, coercion, and violence, and through the expression of intolerance and hatred.
- We are committed to the courageous expression of personal convictions in pursuit of fairness and justice.
- We advocate sharing information, opinions, and feelings when facing significant choices while also respecting privacy and confidentiality.
- We accept responsibility for the short- and long-term consequences for our own communication and expect the same of others.

**Figure 3-2** NCA Credo for Ethical Communication

*Source:* "NCA Credo for Ethical Communication." *National Communication Association Convention Bulletin,* page 24. National Communication Association, 2003.

individuals become effective speakers when they become concerned with ethics. The Non Sequitur cartoon on page 46 seems to suggest that "anything goes" in the world of business. That may or may not be the case. In the course of our lives, we are likely to meet people who adhere to the "anything goes" philosophy and others who are offended by it. As you contemplate your ethical decisions, you might want to consider this: Regardless of how prevalent unethical communicative behavior might be, persons who have been deceived by lies and exaggerations are rarely placated by the balm that such behavior is normal.

## Codes of Ethics

To help individuals who are concerned with ethical behavior to make decisions, organizations have created codes of ethics for speakers. Figure 3-2 on page 47 and Figure 3-3 are such codes. It is important to remember that the adoption of codes, or even the acknowledgment that the items within the code are appropriate, does not guarantee ethical behavior. People who advocate "truthfulness, accuracy, honesty, and reason" will have to make difficult, ethical choices. When confronted with these choices, it can be difficult to be truthful,

**International Association of Business Communicators**
**Code of Ethics for Professional Communicators**

**Articles**

1. Professional communicators uphold the credibility and dignity of their profession by practicing honest, candid and timely communication and by fostering the free flow of essential information in accord with the public interest.
2. Professional communicators disseminate accurate information and promptly correct any erroneous communication for which they may be responsible.
3. Professional communicators understand and support the principles of free speech, freedom of assembly, and access to an open marketplace of ideas; and, act accordingly.
4. Professional communicators are sensitive to cultural values and beliefs and engage in fair and balanced communication activities that foster and encourage mutual understanding.
5. Professional communicators refrain from taking part in any undertaking which the communicator considers to be unethical.
6. Professional communicators obey laws and public policies governing their professional activities and are sensitive to the spirit of all laws and regulations and, should any law or public policy be violated, for whatever reason, act promptly to correct the situation.
7. Professional communicators give credit for unique expressions borrowed from others and identify the sources and purposes of all information disseminated to the public.
8. Professional communicators protect confidential information and, at the same time, comply with all legal requirementsfor the disclosure of information affecting the welfare of others.
9. Professional communicators do not use confidential information gained as a result of professional activities for personal benefit and do not represent conflicting or competing interests without written consent of those involved.
10. Professional communicators do not accept undisclosed gifts or payments for professional services from anyone other than a client or employer.
11. Professional communicators do not guarantee results that are beyond the power of the practitioner to deliver.
12. Professional communicators are honest not only with others but also, and most importantly, with themselves as individuals; for a professional communicator seeks the truth and speaks that truth first to the self.

**Figure 3-3** Code of Ethics for Professional Communicators

*Source:* "International Association of Business Communicators Code of Ethics for Professional Communicators." *Worldbook of IABC Communicators*, page 31A. International Association of Business Communicators, 2000.

accurate, honest, and reasonable. Therefore, the mere adoption of codes is insufficient. There must be a commitment to behaving consistently with the principles reflected by the codes. Also, if organizations wish to compel employees to adhere to identified ethical principles, then methods for enforcing the code must exist.

Stand Up & Deliver

## Ethical Philosophies

Richard Johannesen, author of *Ethics in Human Communication,* writes that ethical issues focus on the "degrees of rightness and wrongness in human behavior."[30] Yet, how does one determine what is right and wrong?

Below the bulleted items is a list of several approaches to examining ethical issues. Assume that you are to prepare a three-minute presentation on the subject of ethics and ethical behavior to your classmates.

- Which of the ethical perspectives below is most consistent with your own ethical orientation?
- What ethical decisions have you had to make when you have delivered presentations in this class or elsewhere?
- During prior presentations, did you communicate in a manner consistent with your declared ethical orientation?

**Ethical Relativism**

Ethical relativism assumes that all persons are bound by their own ethical framework and that each individual's ethical framework is legitimate for that person. What is right for you then, is likely to be different from what is right for me.

You may, for example, consider it reprehensible to tell employees that there will be no layoffs when you know that there will be layoffs. I may feel that my obligation is to the organization, and that I must keep the employees I am paying motivated.

Ethical relativists say that people develop and should respect their own ethical principles.

**Cultural Relativism**

Cultural relativism is similar to ethical relativism. However, this approach assumes that right and wrong depends not on individual philosophies but on the orientation of a group. What is right depends on what a particular culture believes is right. Cultural relativists would argue that if deception is appropriate within a particular society, then misleading an audience for members of that group is not unethical.

**Universalism—The Categorical Imperative**

This approach, often associated with Immanuel Kant, posits that there is nothing relative about ethical decision making. According to Kant and his followers, there are universal rights and wrongs. It is wrong to lie, period. It does not matter if your culture or you yourself consider certain types of lies justifiable. According to these theorists, lying is unethical because lying

(continues)

is categorically wrong. An ethical person then adheres to the universal rights and wrongs.

**Utilitarianism**

John Stuart Mill wrote of something that has been referred to as "The Greatest Happiness Principle." Essentially, Utilitarians contend that what makes an act right is whether the action benefits the greatest numbers of people affected by the action. Obviously, the categorical imperative is at variance with utilitarianism. The former argues that receivers' collective happiness is no yardstick. The yardstick for Kant is not negotiable regardless of the extent of collective happiness.

**Situational Ethics**

Situational ethics was developed by Joseph Fletcher and argues that every ethical decision depends on the situation and not on any absolute except for love. According to situational ethicists, determinations of what is right and wrong always depend on this lone criterion. "Whatever is the loving thing to do in any given situation is the right thing to do."[31]

For example, not resuscitating a monstrously deformed baby would be ethical if it is in the loving interests of the child and family.

## Summary

- Ethical considerations are important for speakers to consider because
  - Speakers have to make ethical choices
  - The repercussions of unethical activity are serious
  - Employers admire and hire persons with integrity
  - Ethical speaking can make someone more effective
  - Ethical listeners are courteous and attentive
- Ethical speakers must do the following:
  - Tell the truth
  - Consider the possible consequences of their message
  - Give credit to their sources
  - Critical thinkers
- Various philosophies of Ethics include the following:
  - Utilitarianism
  - Situational ethics
  - Cultural relativity
  - Ethical relativity
  - Universalism or the categorical imperative

## SAMPLE PRESENTATION FOR ANALYSIS

### Responsibility Lies In Leadership

*EMC Chairman Mike Reuttgers delivered* Responsibility Lies in Leadership *at the Raytheon Lectureship in Business Ethics at Bentley College in Waltham, Massachusetts. The presentation was delivered on October 8, 2003. As you read through this excerpt please consider the following questions.*

1. *Can an organizational culture be cultivated by the presentations of members within that organization?*
2. *Does the author make the point with the "boiled frog" parable? What is the point?*
3. *If Mr. Reuttgers and others at his organization delivered this presentation to members of his organization, would it affect the ethical culture?*

...My topic today is "the integrity of management and the management of integrity." I want to cover three things: First, the challenges of living a consistently ethical life; second, the causes of bad behavior in business, in my view often triggered by the lack of a proper frame of reference; and third, some recommendations on how to build an ethical business culture.

There is an old parable about the "boiled frog." Now I don't know why anyone would want to boil a frog, but the story goes that if you put a frog in a pot of boiling water, he'll try to jump out. But place him in room temperature water and gradually turn up the temperature, and he stays in and eventually is boiled. It seems to me that ethical confrontations are similar. When facing an obvious breach of ethics, you jump out to safety. But when the line between right and wrong is not so obvious, you can get boiled.

Life is full of ethical complexities and ethical challenges. In the game of life, there isn't a space you land on that says: "Draw an ethics card now." That means integrity is a lifelong task.

History shows us there will always be a few who are incorrigible and unteachable, and maybe even oblivious of what they are doing wrong. Even the best intentioned, most principled people have ethical lapses occasionally. But the great majority wants to act ethically. Unfortunately, among this majority, some number can be swayed to act against their better nature if they perceive that being honorable puts them at a financial or a career disadvantage...

...Edwards Deming, the quality expert who helped the Japanese transform their industrial management methods after World War II, was fond of saying: "Quality is made in the boardroom." The same is true about integrity. A company's commitment to integrity flows from the commitment, action, and credibility of its leaders. The litmus test becomes: How frequently and convincingly do they talk about integrity? Is it simply a bullet point on a PowerPoint® slide? Or a thread woven into the stories and observations they tell and retell when communicating the company's culture to employees, customers, and investors? Do they simply assume ethical behavior? Or do they go out of their way to regularly survey employee perceptions about whether the company conducts business in an ethical manner? And do they make it a point to publicize sound ethical decision making by employees, even when that good behavior has meant leaving some business on the table or walking away from a deal?...

...To this list of questions that get at a company's commitment to integrity, I would also add: Do the leaders subtly encourage an ends-justify-the means approach to business? Or do they weed out: great performers who may deliver great results but with no regard for the company's code of conduct?

And is integrity one of the core competencies used to recruit, assess, and develop senior executives? I heard a recruiting rule of thumb that's usually attributed to Warren Buffett. He said that in looking for people to hire, you look first for three essential qualities: integrity, intelligence, and energy. And if they don't have the first, the other two will kill you. Think about it. If you hire someone without integrity, you really would prefer them to be dumb and lazy.

Clearly there are a hundred dimensions to building a culture of integrity—and employees are sensitive to their presence or absence. In my experience employees can "feel" a company's integrity—as I did when I worked at Raytheon—by reflecting on:

- How they're treated
- How customers and suppliers are treated
- What's the priority given to shipping only the highest quality products
- How honest the company is with itself about its flaws and shortcomings
- How truthful the advertising is
- How attentive the board is to the goings on at the company
- And on and on.

So integrity goes all the way across and through an organization but it can be no better than the intent and behavior of the top people.

**Source:** Reuttgers, Mike. "Responsibility Lies in Leadership Vital Speeches of the Day," *Vital Speeches of the Day*, December 15, 2003, 70, no. 5.

## Review Questions

1. Why is ethics an important subject for a course in professional speaking? List three specific reasons.
2. What is the academic definition of lying? Why would deliberately omitting information be considered a lie given this definition? How could the deliberate use of ambiguity be considered a lie?
3. What are four characteristics of an ethical speaker?
4. What are three characteristics of ethical listeners?
5. What is meant by ethical relativism, utilitarianism, and the categorical imperative?

## InfoTrac Question

***Public Relations Quarterly***, Winter 1996 v41 n4 p42(4)

Use InfoTrac to find the Martinson article in *Public Relations Quarterly* entitled "Truthfulness in communication is both a reasonable and achievable goal for public relations practitioners." Do you agree with the points made by Martinson? Are professional communicators sometimes in a position that forces them to misrepresent the truth?

[1] Thomas Carlyle was a nineteenth-century essayist and historian. A collection of his works is called *On Heroes, Hero Worship, and the Heroic in History*. According to the 10th edition of Bartlett's *Familiar Quotations*, this particular comment was made in an address he made when he was Lord Rector at Edinburgh university.

[2] Polonius to his son Laertes in William Shakespeare's *Hamlet*, Act I Scene III.

[3] Marcus Fabius Quintilianus, known as Quintilian, lived in the first century A.D. He is famous for his *De Institutione Oratoria* (*On the Education of the Orator*). Sometimes this comprehensive treatise on oratory is simply referred to as the *Institutio*. The discussion germane to the referred to quote appears in book XII, Chapter I, sections 1, of the *Institution*.

[4] A description of the Gulf of Tonkin incident can be found in Marilyn Young's *The Vietnam Wars 1945–1990* (Harper Collins, 1991), 116–121. On page 120 the author quotes then Deputy Attorney General Nicholas Katzenbach as saying that the Tonkin Gulf incident "was an absolute nothing." The Tonkin Gulf resolution passed by an 88–2 margin in the Senate and a 416–0 margin in the House of Representatives.

[5] Peg Tittle, *Ethical Issues in Business: Inquiries, Cases and Readings* (Broadview Press, 2000), 20.

[6] Potter Stewart quoted in John Thill and Courtland Bovee (and elsewhere), *Excellence in Business Communication*, 6th ed. (Pearson–Prentice Hall, 2005), 23. What Stewart actually said may have been somewhat different. According to Fred Friendly on a television program broadcast on March 31, 1990, Stewart actually said the following "...the trouble with your profession—journalism—is that you fellows are all mixed up about the difference between what you have a right to do under the Constitution, under the First Amendment, and the right thing to do." **http://www.theopenmind.tv/tom/searcharchive_episode_transcript.asp?id=497**. Readers who visit this site will see that the discussion relates to what is ethical decision making specifically in the context of journalism.

[7] Isocrates was born in 436 B.C. and lived until he was 97. He was a prolific author of works related to rhetoric. Ironically, despite his knowledge of oratory, he himself was a nervous and shy individual and rarely spoke. See John Frederic Dobson, *The Greek Orators* [Books for Libraries Press, 1967 (originally published in 1919)], 128. On page 130, Dobson conjectures that Isocrates, a brilliant rhetorician, may "never have delivered a public speech."

[8] See op. cit. Quintilian, citation note 3. Quintilian's concern for the character of the orator actually transcends this phrase. In some translations, his sentiment is expressed as "a good man skilled in speaking." Quintilian writes that the first portion of this phrase is more significant than the second. That is, it is more important for an individual to be a good person than it is for that person to be skilled in speaking. He writes, "It is of importance that an orator should be good, because should the power of speaking be a support to evil, nothing would be more pernicious than eloquence..." Book XII Chapter 1 Section 1. Quintilian, *On the Education of the Orator*. In the translation by the Reverend John Selby Watson and published by George Bell and Sons in 1905, this section appears in volume 2, on page 392.

[9] Several writers have made this comment. In *Building Communication Theory*, 3rd ed. (Waveland Press, 1997), 508, the authors Infante, Dominic, Andrew Rancer and Deanna Womack, write that much of what is studied in academic communication programs is based on Aristotle's *The Rhetoric*.

[10] McCroskey makes these comments on pages 83 and 85 in the 2001 edition of an *Introduction to Rhetorical Communication*. James McCroskey, *An Introduction to Rhetorical Communication* (Allyn and Bacon, 2001). As it pertains to the components of ethos, Aristotle's own words are: "There are three things which inspire confidence in the orator's own character—the three namely, that induce us to believe a thing apart from any proof of it; good sense, good moral character, and goodwill." This quotation is found in the W. Rhys Roberts translation of Aristotle's *The Rhetoric*, (Modern Library, 1954), 91.

[11] Sissela Bok, *Lying: Moral Choice in Public and Private Life* (Vintage Books, 1999), 249.

[12] Quote referenced in Alexander McClure *Lincoln Yarns and Stories* published in 1904. According to McClure Lincoln made this comment to a visitor to the White House in 1865.

[13] Dan O'Hair, Rob Stewart, and Hannah Rubenstein, *A Speaker's Handbook* (Boston: Bedford: St. Martin), 38.

[14] Robert Kraut, "Humans as Lie Detectors: Some Second Thoughts," *Journal of Communication* 30, no. 4, page 209.

[15] Charles Ford, *Lies! Lies!! Lies!!! The Psychology of Deceit* (Washington D.C.: American Psychiatric Press, 1996), 211–214. The "slightly better than chance" characterization is used by op cit Kraut as well as Ford.

[16] Op. cit. Bok 23.

[17] Ibid, 20.

[18] Ibid, 23.

[19] This situation is discussed in Suzanne Taussig, "Strategic Ambiguity in Sales Communication," Master's Thesis (University of Houston May, 1999).

[20] Data from Harris, G. W. (1996). Identification of the workplace basic skills necessary for effective job performance by entry-level workers in small businesses in Oklahoma. (Doctoral dissertation, Oklahoma State University). Ann Arbor, MI. Dissertation Abstracts International. Henderson, D. K. (2001) Basic workplace and computer literacy skills for entry-level, non baccalaureate-degree employees of the Silicon Valley computer industry. (Doctoral dissertation, Utah State University). Ann Arbor, MI. Dissertation Abstracts International. Wilhelm, W. J. (1998). A Delphi study of desired entry-level workplace skills, competencies, and proof-of-performance products. (Doctoral dissertation, Arizona State University, Tempe, Arizona). Ann Arbor, MI: Dissertation Abstracts International.

[21] Abraham Cahan, *The Rise of David Levinsky* (Torchbook, 1960), 380. *The Rise of David Levinsky* was first published in 1917 by Harper and Brothers.

[22] Mary Frank and Thomas Feeley, "To Catch a Liar: Challenges for Research in Lie Detection Training," *Journal of Applied Communication Research* 31, no. 1 (February 2003): 60.

[23] Ibid.

[24] Eric Eisenberg, "Ambiguity as Strategy in Organizational Communication," *Communication Monographs*, 51 (1984): 236.

[25] Eric Eisenberg and H. Goodall Jr., *Organizational Communication: Balancing Creativity and Constraint*, 3rd ed. (Bedford/St. Martins, 2001), 24.

[26] Support can be found in textbooks written by Charles Conrad and Marshall Scott Poole in *Strategic Organizational Communication*, 5th ed. (Harcourt College Publishers, 2002), 238–239; Tom Dixon in *Communication, Organization and Performance* (Ablex Publishing Company, 1996), 181, and Thomas Harris in *Applied Organizational Communication*, 2nd ed. (Erlbaum, 2002), 144, 261. Critics include Philip Tompkins in *Organizational Communication Imperatives* (Roxbury Press, 1993), 137, and Alan Zaremba writing in *Organizational Communication Foundations for Business and Collaboration,* 2nd ed. (Thomson-Southwestern, 2006), 89–90, and in "Ethics and the Academic Advocacy of Strategic Ambiguity" paper presented at SWAC meetings March 28, 2003.

[27] Alan Zaremba, "Is Honesty Overrated?" *Journal of Employee Communication Management* (May/June 2000): 38–47.

[28] Roger Bacon lived in the thirteenth century A.D. He was an English philosopher and scientist. This quote appears in a book entitled *Opus Majus* written in 1266.

[29] This comment by Edmund Burke appears in many forms. There is some debate if the various permutations suggest that the often cited quotation bears little resemblance to what Burke actually may have said. Interested readers might enjoy visiting **http://www.tartarus.org/~martin/essays/burkequote2.html** which discusses this situation.

[30] Richard Johannesen, *Ethics in Human Communication*, 5th ed.(Waveland Press, 2002), 1.

[31] See **http://www.Gospel-herald.com/genesis_studies/situational_ethics.htm**.

Chapter in a Nutshell

*Speaking anxiety is common. Techniques can be employed to alleviate presentation-related tension.*

# 4 Addressing Presentation Anxiety

*I never made a speech until I was forty. A few hundred speeches later the fear hasn't lessened. But a thing that has helped me is realizing that if I fail utterly, if I rant, babble, or spew, if people walk out flinging the heavy linen napkins onto the big round tables in disgust—my life continues as good as it was.*[1]

*-Peggy Noonan*

*Whether you believe you can do a thing or not, you are right.*[2]

*-Henry Ford*

*Break on through to the other side.*[3]

*-The Doors*


## Abstract

Nearly everyone experiences public speaking anxiety. This anxiety can affect career development as well as academic performance.[4] Some people who experience high communication anxiety may be reluctant to accept positions that require making presentations. Students who are highly apprehensive may disguise their intelligence and industry when required to explain their work to instructors and peers. Presentation anxiety can be addressed and reduced. This chapter examines speech anxiety and identifies several methods for alleviating the apprehension that surfaces before and during presentations. Specifically, at the end of the chapter you should be able to do the following:

- Define speech anxiety and communication apprehension
- Identify types of communication apprehension
- Explain why communication apprehension is natural and predictable in presentation contexts
- List steps that can be taken to reduce speaking anxiety
- Implement steps to reduce your own levels of anxiety

## *Winston's Poise*

Sandra Winston enrolled in a speaking skills workshop I conducted. She told me before the first session that she had never spoken in front of a group before and was "deathly afraid" of doing so. Nevertheless, she wanted to address her fears. On the first day of presentations, Winston rushed to the lectern, determined to be the first speaker so she could (as she told me later) "get it out and get it over."

Her talk began quite well. Shortly after it began, a rude latecomer crashed through the door, making a racket like one would hear at a construction site. The tardy man glanced around the room looking for a chair and spotted one on the far side of the room. He then proceeded to walk directly in front of the speaker, swinging his coat as he hustled past her. While galumphing by he swiped the lectern with the coat. Then he noisily flopped into his seat.

The latecomer probably had not intended to maliciously sabotage the talk, but he could not have been more disruptive had he planned to be. However, I was pleased to observe that Winston was able to maintain her composure throughout the apparent rudeness. She delivered the talk with the equanimity of a seasoned speaker and did not appear flustered by the intruder.

At the end of the session, I suggested that delayed participants wait until a speaker is finished before entering the seminar room. I also commented that Winston had done a remarkable job of maintaining her poise despite the unfortunate and noisy intrusion. I asked Sandra Winston to stay after class and repeated then that I had been impressed with her poise given the rude latecomer.

"How did you keep going?" I inquired.

"I didn't even see him," she immediately replied.

## Introduction

An article in *The New York Times* about public speaking training for executives appeared under the following big, bold headline:

**"The Public Equivalent of a Root Canal"**[5]

This headline prompted an irate dentist to send a letter to the newspaper claiming that root canals should not be so maligned, because they are a relatively painless procedure.

"I take strong exception to the root-canal metaphor," wrote the dentist. "Root-canal therapy as it is practiced today is one of the least painful dental procedures...The bad press modern root-canal therapy receives is a disservice to dental health professionals, and creates a fear in the public that is unwarranted."[6]

Apparently, the dentist believed that the anxiety people felt about presentations **is** warranted. In fact, a large percentage of the population does fear making presentations. Lucas reports that more than 75 percent of even experienced speakers become apprehensive before their talks.[7] Max Isaacson, a former vice president of the Macmillan Oil Company, delivered a speech, subsequently published in *Vital Speeches of the Day*, entitled "Public Speaking and Other Coronary Threats." The title reflects the attitudes of many individuals. Some studies suggest that more than 40 percent of the population consider public speaking their greatest fear—greater than the fear of death.[8] This may be a grand exaggeration, but comedian Jerry Seinfeld used such reports as fodder for a joke when he quipped, "Apparently, most people would prefer to be in the casket at a funeral than deliver the eulogy."[9]

Speaking anxiety, however, is not humorous to those people for whom it is debilitating to the extent that they find promotion at work difficult or success in academic environments elusive.[10]

### Reverse the Perspective

From your perspective as a listener.

- When you notice that someone is apprehensive, do you
  - feel superior to the speaker?
  - hope they will become more comfortable?
  - attempt to nonverbally indicate your support?
  - silently ridicule the speaker?
  - feel uncomfortable yourself?
- What nonverbal or verbal behaviors suggest to you that a speaker is apprehensive?
- Do most speakers seem more or less apprehensive than you think you are when you speak?

## Types of Communication Apprehension

McCroskey defines communication apprehension as "an individual's level of fear or anxiety associated with either real or anticipated communication with another person or persons."[11] A high communication apprehensive is someone who experiences high levels of anxiety. A low communication apprehensive is relatively relaxed. Speech anxiety, or what is commonly called stagefright, refers to a particular type of communication apprehension—the tension associated with preparing for and delivering presentations.[12]

Types of communication apprehension have been categorized as follows.

## Traitlike CA

Traitlike apprehension is the label for oral communication anxiety that exists regardless of the communication context. A high traitlike apprehensive feels nervous in meetings, during interpersonal communication, and when making presentations. The venue is irrelevant. Tension may be greater in public speaking situations, but in any communication context there will be high levels of anxiety for those who have traitlike CA. The label for this category is "traitlike" and not "trait" for a very significant reason. Traitlike apprehension can be reduced. A trait, for example being a lefty versus a righty or eye color, is not likely to change once a person becomes an adult. However, the presence of traitlike apprehension can be altered with appropriate interventions.

## Context CA

Context apprehension is dependent on the communication situation. Many people have high apprehension in presentation settings, but experience relatively little anxiety when required to articulate opinions during meetings. For others, one-on-one interviews may be unnerving because of the proximity to the receiver and the impromptu nature of remarks, but presentation settings may be comparatively stress-free because of the relative anonymity of the receivers and the ability of speakers to prepare what they wish to say. Typically, public speaking contexts create the highest levels of communication apprehension.[13]

## Audience CA

Sometimes people are not traitlike or specific context apprehensives. They become apprehensive only on the basis of who is in the audience. A person may become anxious when speaking to peers, but not when speaking to subordinates. A person may become apprehensive when speaking to women, but not to men. Family members and friends in attendance may create more anxiety than strangers. Strangers may create more anxiety than friends except if a special friend is present. If the apprehension surfaces because of a particular listener or population of listeners, it is placed in this category.

## Situation or State CA

If the situation, not the context or audience, creates the tension, then the apprehension is referred to as situation or state. For example, if students are anxious when speaking in front of a tribunal that will determine if they can remain in school, they experience situation or state apprehension. This would be considered state CA and not audience CA if other circumstances involving the same tribunal would not create the same or any level of anxiety.

If you must take oral comprehensive exams at the end of a degree program, and if the success of your presentation will affect graduation, you are likely to experience situation apprehension.

As opposed to context apprehension, people who are situationally apprehensive could become anxious in dyads, groups, or presentations, depending on the perceived magnitude of the event. People could be relatively comfortable delivering a third presentation in a class, but experience anxiety when they must deliver a final presentation that counts for a higher percentage of the course grade.

Survey

**How would you categorize your level of communication apprehension?**

Several statements appear below that describe speaking situations. For each statement, indicate your typical level of anxiety in the situation. Use the following scale:

1—I am not anxious at all in these situations.
2—I am essentially relaxed in these situations but do have some sense of anxiety.
3—I would not describe myself as anxious or relaxed in such contexts.
4—I become nervous in these situations but am not very anxious.
5—I am very anxious in these situations.

a. Delivering a speech in a class with other students when you have never spoken to those students previously
b. Delivering a speech in a class when you have already addressed this group
c. Giving prepared remarks to club members at a weekly meeting
d. Talking during a job interview
e. Conversing during a first date when you are attracted to the other person
f. Speaking in class when called upon
g. Delivering a talk in a business context to fellow employees
h. Delivering a pep talk to your sports team
i. Conversing with a classmate about a project you are working on together
j. Delivering a speech when you are very well prepared
k. Delivering a speech when you are knowledgeable but not well prepared
l. Delivering an acceptance speech for an award
m. Delivering a eulogy for a relative or close friend
n. Delivering a sales pitch to potential clients
o. Delivering a speech to a large group (more than 100 people)
p. Delivering a speech to a midsized group (21–99 people)
q. Delivering a speech to a smaller group (10–20 people)
r. Delivering a speech to a few people (fewer than 10)
s. Speaking inside in an auditorium
t. Speaking outside
u. Speaking using PowerPoint® slides
v. Speaking when there is "a lot on the line"
w. Speaking when there is "not a great deal on the line"
x. Speaking to an audience of your superiors
y. Speaking when the message delivered will be upsetting to the receivers

To clarify the parameters of speech anxiety, and the types of communication apprehension, consider the following three points.

- Speech anxiety is a form of communication apprehension that occurs in the presentation context.
- Individuals can experience speech anxiety even if they would not be labeled as context apprehensives since these people might experience the anxiety only when speaking to certain audiences (audience CA) or on certain occasions (situational/state CA).
- People who experience speech anxiety may be, but are not necessarily, traitlike apprehensives.

## Reducing Speech Anxiety

Most people who take speaking courses are eager to address the anxiety they feel. Below is a list of nine recommendations for reducing anxiety. Some of these approaches are conceptual; that is, they involve *thinking* about the presentation context in a manner that is conducive to reducing anxiety. Other methods require activities designed to alleviate speech anxiety.

- Recognize the normalcy of presentation anxiety
- Acknowledge that presentation anxiety is often not detected
- Prepare thoroughly
- Visualize success
- Address physical manifestations of apprehension
- Use your nervous energy
- Make the presentation context less uncommon
- Employ Rational Emotive Techniques and/or cognitive restructuring
- Employ the intervention known as systematic desensitization

### Recognize the Normalcy of Presentation Anxiety

An initial step involves acknowledging that anticipating or experiencing apprehension does not reflect any sort of deficiency. You are not an underachiever because you feel tense.

Regardless of intelligence, knowledge, or socioeconomic class, people become nervous when they approach a lectern. Even people who speak beautifully are likely to have anxiety, and those who have no anxiety almost certainly experienced presentation-related tension at some point. Thriving executives have enrolled in presentation skills workshops to reduce speaking anxiety. (It is not uncommon for these executives to request to "go first" when several participants are scheduled to speak, claiming that otherwise they will not be able to concentrate on anyone else's talk.)

If you did not experience tension before you delivered an important presentation, the absence of anxiety might reflect a deficiency. Mark Sanborn is a professional speaker who has spoken to organizations throughout the world. His comment about the natural presence of speech anxiety is unequivocal. "Successful speaking doesn't mean eliminating anxiety; it means controlling it. If you aren't a little nervous before you speak it could be a warning you're overconfident or cocky. The trick is to channel nervous energy into passion and enthusiasm."[14]

Several reasons explain why communication apprehension in speaking contexts is and should be normal.[15]

- **When presenting, speakers are the centers of attention.**
  When you are in front of a group, the focus is on you. Ostensibly, people are paying attention to what you say and what you do and only to what you say and do. In actuality, the listeners may not be concentrating on you, but that is the way it seems. People typically are not subjected to the spotlight, and the focus can create discomfort. Consciously or otherwise, logically or illogically, people at the center of attention assume they are being scrutinized. It makes sense that the perception of such scrutiny would produce anxiety.
- **Speakers may consider themselves to be different from the members of the audience**.
  You may, in fact, be different from the members of your audience. They could all be salespeople, engineers, or members of the business club of Montreal. This difference could create some anxiety. It is also conceivable that you may not be so different from other members but believe that you are. If you think your listeners are more composed, sophisticated, or emotionally together, this—likely inaccurate—perception can create anxiety.
- **Speakers may be subordinate to the members of the audience**.
  A presentation to executives is likely to create tension if the speakers assume that how they present could affect career advancement. Student presentations to classmates will likely create less anxiety than the same presentations to potential employers or even faculty members. You may have been in a situation when you were all prepared for a talk and were told at the last minute, "Marsha and Chuck will be there." If Marsha and Chuck are your superiors and have declared that they are evaluating personnel for retrenchment, the announcement of their presence will understandably spike your anxiety level.
- **Speakers may have had difficult experiences making presentations previously**.
  A previous unpleasant experience speaking might overwhelm more positive recollections. If you delivered a talk that was unsuccessful, memories of the incident may make anticipating another very frightening. Since many of us have had some negative speaking experiences, the fact that these memories may dwarf the others renders presentation anxiety normal.
- **Speakers may have had few speaking opportunities.**
  A very understandable reason for presentation anxiety is based on the reality that speaking in a formal setting is something most people do not do regularly. If making a presentation is unusual, it makes sense that you might feel tense when compelled to do that which is unfamiliar—particularly because you will be doing it in front of an audience that may be, or you believe may be, evaluating you.

For all these reasons it is understandable that people become apprehensive when they speak. The foundation for reducing presentation anxiety is comprised of two conceptual planks: Speaking anxiety is normal. Speaking anxiety can be surmounted.

## Acknowledge that Anxiety Often Goes Undetected

A second step toward reducing anxiety involves accepting a simple proven fact. Audience members typically do not see speakers as the apprehensive persons they may be.[16] That is, often when you are certain that people are aware of your fear, audience members are looking at you wishing they possessed your poise. I have listened to thousands of presentations delivered by executives, managers, blue- and white-collar employees, graduate students, and undergraduate students. Well over half of the speakers comment that they were very nervous when they presented. Almost always—almost always—listeners comment that the apprehension was not discernible.

You may have witnessed this phenomenon yourself if you have ever had a presentation videotaped. Speakers while viewing tapes of their presentations often comment that it is "better than I thought" and that the apprehension they felt is not apparent through the lens of the camera.

## Prepare Thoroughly

Thorough preparation is consistently identified as a significant factor in reducing speech anxiety. Zarefsky asked five students who had completed a public speaking course to identify what had contributed most to a reduction in speaking anxiety. All five said preparation was the key.[17] The results from this small sample are supported with research based on much larger groups.[18] Walters, in her practitioner-based book, *Secrets of Successful Speakers*, writes that preparation reduces speech anxiety by 75 percent.[19]

Preparation involves studying the subject, analyzing the audience, crafting and practicing the delivery of the message, and examining the speaking location.

### Subject Preparation

If you have researched your subject thoroughly, you are likely to feel much better about your presentation than if your knowledge is limited. Michael H. Mescon, a former dean of the College of Business Administration at Georgia State University and an internationally known speaker and consultant, comments simply, "The best way to conquer stage fright is to know what you're talking about."[20]

### The Audience

Audience analysis can reduce tensions that may otherwise spike because of unanticipated audience composition, background, and expectations. We discuss in detail the various dimensions of audience analysis in Chapter 5.

### The Message

Preparation involves thoroughly planning how you will say what you intend to say. Anxiety is reduced when you have confidence not only in what you know, but in

- what you intend to say about what you know,
- how you have organized what you intend to say,
- and how you will deliver the organized message.

Speakers may know everything about the pros and cons of the state government's antismoking policy, but unless they have distilled what they know into an organized message and have planned how to communicate that message, they will become more anxious when they approach the lectern than they need to be.

### Preparing Delivery for the Room

Practicing delivering your message before you speak can help debug the presentation and reduce tension. Several rehearsals in the actual room where you will be speaking will acclimate you to the environment as well as to the nuances of the room—for example, placement of the outlets, screen location, and seating configuration. It is wise to conduct these rehearsals with all the visual complements you plan to use during the actual presentation. (We discuss presentation style, structure, and delivery in detail in subsequent chapters.)

Below is some additional counsel related to preparation and tension reduction.

- **Don't procrastinate.**
  Tuman and Fraley and others have argued that procrastinating increases anxiety.[21] Not only does procrastinating reduce the time for preparation, but it tends to build the tension that you need to reduce before the presentation.
- **Set realistic goals.**
  Creating objectives that are unlikely to be realized will, consciously or otherwise, increase anxiety levels.[22] As you ponder an improbable outcome, you will accrue anxiety thinking about the difficulties of attaining it.
- **Practice the introduction.**
  Several authors comment that honing the introduction can reduce anxiety.[23] By feeling secure initially you can begin with confidence, and then gain confidence with what you anticipate will be a positive response to the carefully prepared introduction. Suggestions for constructing introductions to presentations are found in Chapter 7.

## Ethical Probe

### Anxiety and Preparation

A consultant arrived at a seminar complex to conduct her typical speaking program. She had been hired by an agent to run a three-session presentation skills workshop for eleven foreign executives who worked for a company in the steel industry. The executives were attending a series of workshops while in the United States, one of which pertained to improving presentation skills. Having conducted this type of course scores of times, the consultant was prepared with the program, but she had not studied the audience as carefully as she needed to. She knew only the number of participants and that all were executives, as opposed to lower-level personnel.

When she arrived, she discovered that the participants were all men and all from a Middle Eastern country. It seemed to her that the men did not expect a female trainer and doubted her capabilities because she was a woman. This was unnerving, but her apprehension level really soared when each participant began delivering a short presentation. The trainer had promised to critique these individual talks and provide feedback. However, as each person approached the lectern and began to speak, she discovered, to her horror, that because the speaker accents were so atypical and thick and because the rate of speech was so rapid, she could not discern more than a few words from any one presentation. Nor could she make any meaningful distinctions between the presentations. After the eleven talks were completed, the participants—all eager to improve their speaking ability—waited to hear feedback from the trainer.

- Did the trainer have an ethical responsibility to acknowledge her inability to make intelligent comments about the presentations?
  - How would pretending to be knowledgeable affect her level of apprehension?
  - How would acknowledging her inability to evaluate the presentations affect her level of apprehension?

## Visualize Success

Visualization is not for everyone, but this technique—employed by athletes and stage performers—is an approach to consider before categorical rejection. In essence, visualization techniques involve imagining success prior to performance. Proponents argue that creating a mental picture of achievement facilitates performance that is consistent with the visualization.

As it relates to presentation settings, several studies suggest that "walking through" the speech cerebrally and imagining a positive result can reduce anxiety.[24]

Thomas Faranda is a professional speaker who commands $12,000 for a keynote address. He claims that to remove stage fright speakers should "visualize the end of the program with 5000 people standing up and applauding your ideas and presentation."[25] Similarly, the counsel in the *Successful Manager's Handbook* is that apprehensive speakers contemplate prior successes and visualize subsequent achievement by asking themselves the following questions.

- When have I given a successful presentation in the past?
- How did I feel at the beginning and at the end of that presentation?
- In what way was that occasion similar to the current situation?
- Are there any tactics that I used in the past presentation that I could draw on for this occasion?[26]

## Address Physical Manifestations of Apprehension

High communication apprehension can have physiological effects. Recommendations for reducing physical tension include running or exercising before the presentation,[27] breathing exercises,[28] stretching, and pre-speech silent concentration.[29] The National Communication Association sells audiocassettes of muscle relaxation exercises for people to use to decrease apprehension. Later in this chapter there is a discussion of *Systematic Desensitization*, a process for reducing speaking anxiety that involves specific techniques for relaxing the body to eliminate physiological manifestations of apprehension.

In the song "I Whistle a Happy Tune" from *The King and I*, the character Anna suggests that others follow her advice when they become apprehensive. She comments that she is able to overcome fear by "whistling a happy tune" and acting as if she is unafraid.

> *"The result of this deception is very strange to tell,*
> *For when I fool the people I fear, I fool myself as well."*

Rodgers and Hammerstein were not communication scholars, but several researchers who are offer the same basic advice. Beebe and Beebe suggest that when sensing tension, speakers should give themselves a mental pep talk. Zarefsky, as well as Brydon and Scott, comment that during the presentation speakers should act confidently even when they feel apprehensive.[30] Essentially, the argument is that attempting to portray confidence will facilitate self-deception and result in a decrease in apprehension.

Some speakers experience "dry mouth" before a talk. It is a nervous reaction that does not reflect thirst, and therefore consuming large amounts of water will not reduce the sensation. Walters suggests the following to reduce the sensation of dry mouth:

- Carefully bite the side of your tongue with your back teeth.
- Press the top of your tongue into the top of your mouth until you salivate.
- Bite lightly on the inside of your cheek.[31]

## Use Your Nervous Energy

Your nervous energy can be channeled into something positive. Speakers can use tension to invigorate their voice, emphasize key words, and reflect enthusiasm for the subject. The late actor Carroll O'Connor commented that a "professional actor has a kind of tension. The amateur is thrown by it, but the professional needs it."[32] Professional speakers may not *need* the anxiety, but can employ the tension to improve their focus and delivery. Like an actor who is energized yet nervous for opening night, the speaker can use the anxiety to enhance the quality of performance.

## Become More Familiar with Making Presentations

Speakers can reduce apprehension simply by making the speaking context less alien to them. Writing in *Business Communication Quarterly*, executive speech coach Stephen Boyd reports that he recommends that each of his clients "take advantage of every opportunity to practice in public, whether volunteering to give departmental reports or opinions in meetings, and always being available to speak."[33] Apprehensive speakers do not become excited about volunteering for additional speaking assignments, but forcing yourself into presentation situations will eventually be rewarding.

Studies have suggested that speech anxiety is reduced by taking a basic speaking class that compels participants to deliver and evaluate presentations.[34] This method for reducing apprehension is sometimes called Rhetoritherapy and/or Skills therapy. Rhetoritherapy proponents argue that learning how to construct a presentation and practice creating and delivering it will reduce anxiety. Skills therapy proponents argue that people become apprehensive because they lack delivery skills.[35] Both Rhetoritherapy and Skills therapy involves instruction in a workshop-like environment. The class you are presently taking likely involves what is covered in Rhetoritherapy and Skills therapy workshops.

The rationale for both Rhetoritherapy and Skills therapy is that knowledge and practice will reduce anxiety. Hattie Hill's recommendation to apprehensive speakers contains less academic terminology but is directed to the same point. Hill, an internationally known speaker and the author of *Smart Women, Smart Choices*, suggests the following: "Keep falling on your face. When the fall doesn't hurt anymore you're there."[36]

## Use Rational Emotive Techniques and/or Cognitive Restructuring

Both *Rational Emotive Therapy* and Cognitive Restructuring are based on the same principle: People who are apprehensive have irrational notions, and these irrational thoughts create speech anxiety.

For example, someone with high speech anxiety might think, "Audience members will see me as nervous and think I am incompetent." This is an irrational thought since, as we have seen, most audience members do not detect apprehension. In addition, most audience members are very supportive of speakers—and certainly are supportive of speakers who are responsible and respectful of the audience. Nevertheless, the irrational thought generates anxiety. Both Rational Emotive Therapy and Cognitive Restructuring seek to alter the notions that generate the anxiety.

Rational Emotive Therapy involves challenging the irrational thoughts that are driving the apprehension. A trainer will ask workshop participants to identify why they feel apprehensive. Each notion identified is discussed and replaced with a realistic and rational belief. Ayres and Hopf suggest that trainers explain Rational Emotive Therapy involves the ABCs. The A stands for the antecedent creating the apprehension, which is typically that a person is required to deliver a presentation. The C stands for the consequence, typically the thought that the consequence of making the presentation will be negative and create anxiety. The B stands for the belief system that creates the consequence.[37] For example, the belief system might include notions that "people will hate me," "people will think I speak poorly," and "people will think I don't know what I am talking about." By challenging the irrational beliefs and substituting a more realistic set of beliefs, Rational Emotive therapists contend that the consequence of the altered belief system will be a reduction in apprehension. Of course, if a person desires to believe that "everyone in the audience will hate me," Rational Emotive Therapy has little chance of success.

*Cognitive Restructuring* is very similar. However, in addition to challenging a person's irrational thoughts, cognitive restructuring involves substituting (i.e., restructuring the thoughts) so that instead of holding the irrational notion, the speaker develops a coping notion to replace it. For example, a speaker who fears addressing a large group and thinks, "Oh, this will be impossible. With all these people it is inevitable that I will look like a fool" can restructure their view, and instead can think, "I have an opportunity here to influence many individuals. It is not often that someone gets this chance, and I want to take advantage of the opportunity."

## Use Systematic Desensitization

Systematic desensitization has proved to be a highly effective technique for reducing speech anxiety. The rationale behind systematic desensitization is that speakers cannot concurrently be apprehensive and relaxed. Therefore, if individuals can associate physical relaxation with concerns they have about the speaking situation, they will be relaxed when they consider, and when they deliver, their presentations.

Systematic desensitization involves six training sessions. The first of these begins with an explanation of the rationale behind the process. Therefore, participants know before they begin why the process is likely to work. Subsequently in this first session, participants go through a series of exercises intended to relax each part of their body. A trainer plays some soothing music and instructs students to follow a procedure. A portion of the relaxation instructions appears below.

> *Tightly clench your left fist. Hold these muscles in the tense position five to seven seconds. Study that tension. Note how strained the muscles feel. Now relax the muscles completely. Notice how pleasant it feels to release that tension. (Wait ten seconds.) Tightly clench your right fist. Hold these muscles in the tense position five to seven seconds. Study that tension. Note how strained the muscles feel. Now relax the muscles completely. Notice how pleasant it feels to release that tension. (Wait ten seconds.) Flex your biceps muscles by bringing your hands toward your shoulders. Hold that position five to seven seconds. Study that tension. Note how strained the muscles feel. Now relax the muscles completely. Notice how pleasant it feels to release that tension...*[38]

In the next four sessions, the trainer begins by conducting the same relaxation exercises. After the exercises have been completed, the trainer asks the participants to maintain their levels of relaxation for ten seconds while contemplating several communication scenarios that escalate in terms of likely degrees of apprehension. For example, the first scenario during sessions two through five would be "Imagine you are alone in your room and you are reading about speeches." The final scenario in session five is "Imagine that you are defending your actions before an ethics committee. You have been accused of unethical conduct. Your accuser is present and you may be expelled should you fail to defend yourself convincingly."[39]

During the systematic desensitization, respondents are asked to indicate if they are unable to maintain their level of relaxation while contemplating the stressful situation. If someone indicates an inability to remain relaxed, then participants return to the relaxation exercises and repeat the process of associating the relaxation sensation with what could be a stressful situation. Proponents of systematic desensitization argue that it is rare for individuals not to be able to maintain levels of relaxation eventually, even when contemplating very stressful speaking situations.

The sixth and final session of the training involves having participants deliver a presentation to the other members of the group.

The principle behind systematic desensitization is that one cannot be anxious and concurrently relaxed. Therefore, associating relaxation with stressful situations will have a transforming effect on the erstwhile apprehensive individual.

## Stand Up & Deliver

On pages 60–66, several methods for reducing anxiety have been suggested. Prepare a three-minute presentation that you will deliver to classmates in this course.

- Identify a speaking experience you have had that caused you to be anxious.
- Which of the various methods presented would be most helpful to you when you prepare to make similar presentations in the future?
- Which of the methods will be least effective?
- *Did you employ any of the methods when preparing for this brief presentation?*

## SUMMARY

- There are several types of communication apprehension:
  - Traitlike
  - Context
  - Audience
  - State or situational
- *Speech anxiety* refers to communication apprehension in presentation situations.
  - It can be audience based.
  - It can involve state CA.
  - It does not mean that the speaker is a traitlike apprehensive.
- There are methods for reducing speech anxiety. These include the following:
  - Recognizing the normalcy of presentation anxiety
  - Acknowledging that audience members do not always discern high apprehension levels even when speakers are very apprehensive
  - Preparing thoroughly
  - Using visualization techniques
  - Rhetoritherapy and Skills training
  - Addressing physical manifestations of apprehension
  - Rational Emotive Therapy, and Cognitive Restructuring
  - Systematic desensitization

## Public Speaking and Other Coronary Threats

*Max Isaacson, a Vice President for the Macmillan Oil company delivered* Public Speaking and Other Coronary Threats *on February 1, 1980. It was delivered in Des Moines, Iowa, to people who had attended a workshop on speech making. As you read through the speech please consider the following questions.*

1. *Does the speaker establish credibility in the introduction to the talk?*
2. *Are the quotes from Webster, Freud, and Carnegie employed effectively?*
3. *Does the pianist analogy make the speaker's point? What is that point?*
4. *Is the presentation persuasive in the way you assume it was intended to be?*

In my job and at other functions, quite often I'm called on to speak and my wife says that I get up so often that I'm living proof of the old adage that hot air always rises. But I have something a little more substantial than hot air to talk about today.

I'm glad you are here because that tells me you've had the dedication and the interest in this important speechcraft course. I can tell you from personal experience that the ability to express oneself well in public is certainly valuable in my business and in every walk of life that I know of.

In addition to my interest in public speaking, I'm happy to be here for another reason. Since I'm on the staff of an oil company, I'm happy to be invited *anywhere* where there is a cordial reception...that's a pleasant accomplishment.

Speaking of accomplishments, your chairman asked me to speak on "Accomplishments Through Speechcraft." A more appropriate title might be: "PUBLIC SPEAKING AND OTHER CORONARY THREATS!" because in public speaking, many are called but few want to get up. You know and I know that it can be scary indeed to get up to address a group. But listen to these statements:

Daniel Webster said:

> *"If all my possessions were taken from me with one exception, I would choose to keep the power of speech, for by it I would soon regain all the rest [of my possessions]."*

Sigmund Freud observed:

> *"Words call forth emotions and are universally the means by which we influence our fellow creatures...by words, one of us can give to another the greatest happiness or bring about utter despair."*

The eminent Dale Carnegie said:

> *"Every activity of our lives is communication of a sort, but it is through speech that man asserts his distinctiveness...that he best expresses his own individuality, his essence."*

Someone else has observed, and I certainly agree, that "self-confidence has *always* been the first secret of success." Of the known phobias—and there is a long list of them—the fear of public speaking consistently ranks at the top in public surveys. It's even more feared than death. But why should intelligent people fear public speaking?

Most of us have at least average intelligence and when we look around us—at co-workers, bosses, politicians—we know that our level of knowledge is as great or greater than theirs, but the thing that so often separates us is our *inability* to feel confident when expressing ourselves...we fear to speak up.

It's true that we make ourselves vulnerable when we speak up...vulnerable to criticism. It's usually easier and more comfortable to stay out of the spotlight and to languish in the comfort of the non-speaker's role, to avoid the risk of feeling inferior.

But I've always been fond of quoting Eleanor Roosevelt on the subject of self-confidence and it was she who said: "No one can make *you* feel inferior without *your* consent." Think about that for a moment. "No one can make you feel inferior without your consent." Isn't that a remarkable statement?

And here are some remarkable figures to prove that man is his own worst enemy. MORE PERSONS KILL THEMSELVES EACH YEAR THAN MURDER OTHERS. There are 25,000 suicides annually in the U.S. and 18,000 homicides. Suicide is the severest form of self-hatred. But a milder form of self-hatred is the inferiority complex many of us secretly harbor.

One of my kids recently told me a riddle. He said, "Dad, do you know what the largest room in the world is?" "The largest room...?" I replied that I did not. He answered, "THE ROOM FOR IMPROVEMENT!" That's why I believe in speechcraft, because it's a valuable means for improvement. It offers what most of us need to become better public speakers.

Isn't it incredible that there is so little emphasis throughout our educational and business training on this needed skill of oral communication? I've found that in high school, college, military service, graduate school and in business, any emphasis on oral communication HAS BEEN CONSPICUOUS BY ITS ABSENCE. And yet, you and I communicate orally more than in any other way when dealing with people.

Sometime ago I attended a conference whose main speaker was a nationally-known management expert and he said that we are not in the oil business, the insurance business, the government service business, the manufacturing business...rather WE ARE IN THE PEOPLE BUSINESS! It behooves us to do whatever we can to improve our communications among people in all walks of life in order to improve human relations.

Where will you go from here? What will you do with the valuable experience you've gained at these speechcraft sessions? Unfortunately, most persons stop their training after the formal speechcraft course has ended. They apparently are satisfied with their progress or don't want to make the effort to continue. But can you imagine a pianist stopping after 10 lessons and saying, "I've arrived—and I'm now accomplished!"? Public speaking takes on-going practice so I would encourage you to stick with it through regular Toastmaster training.

I'm convinced you'll do better on the job, in your community organizations and in your house of worship. One of my biggest thrills was that of becoming a certified lay speaker in the United Methodist Church—just one of the many ways that experience in public speaking can be applied for personal fulfillment and self-realization.

Let me close with a thought that I've shared with graduating high school seniors and other groups concerning the value of self-improvement. It goes like this:

God said, "Build a better world,"  
And I said, "How?"  
The world is such a cold, dark place and so complicated now;  
And I so young and useless, there's nothing I can do,  
But God in all his wisdom said, "Just build a better you."

**Source:** Isaacson, Max D. "Public Speaking and Other Coronary Threats: The Value of Self Improvement," *Vital Speeches of the Day*, February 1, 1980, 46: 351(2).

## Review Questions

1. What is meant by traitlike, situation, context, and audience communication apprehension?
2. What is the difference between communication apprehension and speech anxiety?

3. Why is it normal for most people to be anxious when they make presentations? Cite three reasons.
4. What types of preparatory activities can reduce speaking anxiety?
5. How can visualization and cognitive restructuring reduce speaking anxiety?
6. What is meant by systematic desensitization?

## InfoTrac Question

**Use InfoTrac to find the fall 2003 *Communication Quarterly* article that deals with speaker anxiety levels and audience perceptions of these levels. What is the main point of the article? Is it consistent with the assumptions you had about speaking anxiety prior to reading this chapter and taking this class?**

---

[1] Noonan P. *Simply Speaking: How to Communicate Your Ideas with Style, Substance and Clarity.* (New York: HarperCollins, 1998), 190.

[2] Henry Ford lived from 1863 until the 1940s. He was an industrialist who was instrumental in the development of the automobile industry. The popularity of this particular quote is evidenced by typing it on a Web search engine and noticing how many people identify it as their favorite or one of their favorites.

[3] Song lyric from the Doors's "Break on Through," *The Best of the Doors,* Elektra/Asylum 1985.

[4] Several articles and authors make this claim. See Joe Ayres and Tim Hopf, *Coping with Speech Anxiety* (Norwood, NJ: Ablex Publishing, 1993), xi.

[5] Deirdre Fanning, "The Public Equivalent of a Root Canal," *The New York Times,* 2 December 1990, Business section.

[6] David Gallin, letter to the editor, *The New York Times,* 16 December 1990, sec. 3.

[7] Lucas is one of many authors who refer to the prevalence of speech anxiety. In *Never Be Nervous Again,* Dorothy Sarnoff on pages 2–4 describes the anxieties of public figures such as Fidel Castro, Willard Scott, and Sir Laurence Olivier. Dorothy Sarnoff, *Never Be Nervous Again* (New York: Crown Publishers, 1987), 2–3. The Lucas reference appears in Stephen E. Lucas, *The Art of Public Speaking,* 7th ed. (Boston: McGraw Hill, 2001), 9.

[8] The Isaacson speech was published in *Vital Speeches of the Day,* March 15, 1980, 351–352. Isaacson is one of several people who have made the claim about public speaking being more feared than death. His reference to that appears on page 352 of the *Vital Speeches* version of the speech text. *The Saturday Evening Post* reprinted the speech in the July/August 1980 issue. It appears on page 46.

[9] As indicated, comedian Jerry Seinfeld is credited with making this statement. The comment was actually made in slightly different form in the opening segment of a *Seinfeld* episode ("The Pilot," Part 1 of a two-part episode). The complete statement made in that episode was "According to most studies, people's number-one fear is public speaking. Number two is death. *Death* is number two! Now, this means to the average person, if you have to go to a funeral, you're better off in the casket than doing the eulogy."

[10] Richmond writes about occupational, educational, and social effects of communication apprehension, which manifests itself in quietness. She reports that such communication avoidance behavior can affect occupational choice, job satisfaction, job retention, and career advancement. See Virginia Richmond, "Quietness in Contemporary Society: Conclusions and Generalizations of the Research" in, ed. John A. Daly, James McCroskey, Joe Ayres, Tim Hopf, and Debbie Ayres, *Avoiding Communication: Apprehension, Shyness, Reticience and Communication* (Beverly Hills: Hampton Press, 1997), 265–267.

[11] James McCroskey. "Oral Communication Apprehension: A Summary of Recent Theory and Research," *Human Communication Research* 4 (1977): 78.

[12] Joe Ayres and Tim Hopf, *Coping With Speech Anxiety* (Norwood, NJ: Ablex Publishing, 1993), 4.

[13] Virginia Richmond and James McCroskey, *Communication: Apprehension, Avoidance, and Effectiveness* (Scottsdale, Arizona: Gorsuch Scarisbrick, 1992), 41 and 44. The chapter that includes these pages is indicative of the pervasive problem of speaking apprehension. It is entitled "Scared Speechless: The Fear of Communication."

[14] Mark Sanborn quoted in Lilly Walters, *Secrets of Successful Speakers* (New York: McGraw Hill, 1993), 43.

[15] The factors listed in this section come from James McCroskey, "The Communication Apprehension Perspective," in *Avoiding Communication: Shyness, Reticence and Communication Apprehension,* ed J.A. Daly and J.C. McCroskey, (Sage, 1984), 13–38. See also Michael Beatty, "Situational and Predispositional Correlates of Public Speaking

Anxiety," *Communication Education* 37 (January 1988): 28. McCroskey's full list of factors includes the items mentioned in the text: novelty, conspicuousness, prior history, subordinate status, and dissimilarity, as well as formality, unfamiliarity, degree of attention from others, and degree of evaluation. These other factors have been eliminated from the text section, because they can be seen as facets of the categories that *are* listed and discussed in the text.

[16] Dennis Beaver, "Got Stage Fright? It's a Common Feeling, but One That Can Be Turned into Confidence More Easily Than You Realize," *ABA Banking Journal* 90. no. 2 (February 1998): 96. Also see Ritch Sorenson, Grace DeBord, and Ida Ramirez, *Business and Management Communication* (Upper Saddle River, New Jersey: Prentice Hall, 2001), 224; Steven Beebe, and Susan Beebe, *Public Speaking An Audience Centered Approach, 4th ed* (ABLongman), 21. Also Judith McManus, *How to Write and Deliver an Effective Speech* (Macmillan, 1998), 2.

[17] David Zarefsky, *Public Speaking Strategies for Success*, 3rd ed. (New York: Allyn and Bacon), 23.

[18] Many other authors have identified preparation as a key ingredient in reducing anxiety. For example, Teri Gamble and Michael Gamble, *Public Speaking in the Age of Diversity* (New York: Allyn and Bacon, 1998), 31; Hamilton Gregory, *Public Speaking for Colleges and Careers*, 7th ed. (Boston: McGraw Hill, 2005), 32. In Cheryl Rae Krannich, *101 Secrets of Highly Effective Speakers 2nd ed.,* the author heads a section on speech anxiety with the words "solid preparation is your best defense." (Manassas Park, VA: Impact Publications, 2002).

[19] Lilly Walters, *Secrets of Successful Speakers How You Can Motivate Captivate and Persuade* (New York: McGraw Hill, 1993), 32. Walters claims that the other 25 percent of the solution comprises 15 percent deep breathing and 10 percent mental preparation.

[20] Ibid, 34.

[21] Joseph Tuman and Douglas Fraley, *The St. Martin's Guide to Public Speaking*, (Bedford/Boston: St. Martin's, 2003), 23. Also see Steven R. Brydon and Michael Scott, *Between One and Many*, 2nd ed. (Mayfield Publishing, 1997), 68.

[22] Op. cit. Brydon and Scott 70.

[23] Op. cit. Zarefsky 21. Also Richard Letteri *A Handbook of Public Speaking* (New York: Allyn and Bacon, 2003), 220.

[24] Op. cit. Ayres and Hopf discuss visualization's benefits and approaches on pages 31–47.

[25] Thomas Faranda quoted in op cit. Walters 39.

[26] Moi Ali et al, *Successful Manager's Handbook* (New York: DK Publishing, 2002), 275.

[27] Op. cit. Brydon and Scott 77.

[28] Op. cit. Beebe and Beebe 23.

[29] Op. cit. Sarnoff 72–76.

[30] Op. cit. Beebe and Beebe 23. Op. cit. Zarefsky 21, Op. cit. Brydon and Scott 74.

[31] Op. cit. Walters 42.

[32] Cited in Robert Edward Burns, "Combating Speech Anxiety," *Public Relations Journal* 47, no. 3 (1991): 28.

[33] Stephen Boyd, "Executive Speech Coaching: an On Site, Individualized, Abbreviated Course in Public Speaking," *Business Communication Quarterly*, 58. no. 3 (1995): 59.

[34] Lynne Kelly, Robert L. Duran and John Stewart, "Rhetoritherapy Revisited: A Test of Its Effectiveness as a Treatment for Communication Problems," *Communication Education* 39, no. 3 (1990): 207–226. See also Ayres and Hopf section on Skills Training in *Coping with Speech Anxiety.* Ayres and Hopf make a distinction between delivery training that reduces apprehension, which they call Skills Training, and Rhetoritherapy. The distinction is that Rhetoritherapy reduces anxiety because people who understand how to structure a message will be less anxious, whereas Skills Training reduces anxiety because training in delivery helps people be less anxious when they are required to make a presentation. Op. cit. Ayres and Hopf 69–101. See also Peggy Yuhas Byers and Carolyn Secord Weber, "The Timing of Speech Anxiety Reductions: Treatments in the Public Speaking Classroom," *Southern Communication Journal Volume* 60, no. 3 (1995): 246–256; and Rebecca Rubin, Alan Rubin, and Felicia Jordan, "Effects of Instruction on Communication Apprehension and Communication Competence, *Communication Education* 46, no. 2 (1997): 104–114.

[35] Op. cit. Ayres and Hopf 91.

[36] Op. cit. Walters 34.

[37] Op. cit. Ayres and Hopf 16.

[38] Ibid, 53–54.

[39] Ibid, 60–61. In Ayres and Hopf the portion of the sentence about the potential for being expelled does not appear.

**Chapter in a Nutshell** *Speakers must study their receivers in order to prepare for and deliver high-quality presentations.*

# 5 Audience Analysis: Taking a Receiver-Centered Approach

*The Strategic Speakers' first priority should be not to identify what they will say—though Lord knows, the message is important—but to identify the character of the people to whom they will speak.*[1]

-Burton Kaplan

*I've been to so many workshops where the speaker gave a stupid canned speech and didn't bother to find out that our subgroup was made up of veterans with an average of around 18 years of service... It really infuriates us and it has to be apparent that it infuriates us. And the robot just continues, evidently unable to shift gears.*[2]

-Thirty-Year Employee

## Abstract


Communication should be viewed as an audience-centered phenomenon. This means that the message audience members receive determines what has been communicated. In presentation contexts, speakers must acknowledge this and discover all they can about the audience's attitudes and characteristics before creating and delivering a presentation. The phrase *audience analysis* refers to this exploration. In this chapter we review what needs to be discovered and how speakers can go about analyzing their audiences. Specifically, at the end of this chapter you should be able to do the following:

- Explain why audience analysis can affect the quality of presentations
- Identify what needs to be analyzed regarding audience attitudes, orientation, and presentation context
- Describe methods for conducting audience analysis

## "Five"

The former governor of New Jersey, Christine Todd Whitman, was the commencement speaker at the June 2003 graduation ceremony for Northeastern University, held in Boston's Fleet Center. Unlike most schools, Northeastern is a five-year cooperative education institution. This means that students at Northeastern alternate periods of traditional class work with periods of work experience. Although all students need not participate in co-op, the overwhelming majority do. Therefore, nearly all graduates of the school must attend for five years before they can receive their diploma. The co-op experience provides a proud common bond for undergraduates and alumni of the institution.

As Governor Whitman began her address, it became clear that she was attempting to convey her knowledge of the university. She spoke of the tribulations of student life, commenting on how difficult it must be to get up for an 8:00 A.M. class "after a long night at Our House," a local student drinking establishment. She commented on the frenetic pace of student activity and how it might be necessary to grab a hamburger "at Chicken Lou's," a campus eatery, en route to an afternoon lecture.

The governor's attempt at establishing commonality probably did not have the desired effect. The assembled graduates would know that the governor was unlikely to be familiar with the downscale Our House tavern. As improbable as it would be for her to frequent Our House, the idea that she would opt to dine at Chicken Lou's was preposterous. Lou's is a notorious dive, and the governor seemed hardly the sort to be found leaning across Lou's littered counter shouting over the din for a steak and cheese.

It seemed probable that the governor had a canned speech and had inserted the names of local establishments that had been sleuthed out by assistants. Although this was transparent and would not significantly elevate audience perceptions of the speaker, it was a relatively harmless ploy. However, as the governor continued to speak, it became apparent that she did not know something very central about the audience.

In the course of her ten-minute talk, the governor repeatedly referred to the four years students had spent at the university. Whitman referred to the four years of exams, the four-year "sprint" toward graduation, the four years it took to complete academic goals.

The first time she said "four years," a number of attendees shouted, "Five" to make the correction. The second and third time, more and more students yelled, "Five" when the governor said "four." The last time Whitman said "four," a bellowing chorus of "Five" rocked the Fleet Center. The governor was clearly nonplussed, and attempted to rally by saying, "or five, or six . . .," not understanding the meaning behind the correction, ad-libbing as if she thought the shouting was because a preponderance of attending graduates had not managed to complete their degrees on time.

The bottom line was that Governor Whitman did not know her audience. She made only one brief mention of co-op during her talk, and the reference sounded much like the Chicken Lou's and Our House inclusions—an insertion in a canned speech intended to suggest a familiarity that did not exist. At the luncheon that followed the ceremony, several attendees commented that the student speaker was far more effective than the governor.

- Did Whitman have an obligation to refer to the nature of the university?
- Did the shouting students respond improperly to the governor's error?
- Is there anything inappropriate with Whitman intimating familiarity with Our House if it was unlikely that she was familiar with them?
- Can the overall effectiveness of a presentation be undermined by a flaw like the one described in this incident?

## INTRODUCTION

*Presentations are for the audience not for the speaker. The message embodied in the speech can be enhanced or destroyed by the inclusion or lack of audience analysis.*[3]

Lilly Waters

In Barron's *Dictionary of Business Terms*, an effective presentation is described as one that is "usually *planned, organized and tailored to a specific audience* to help facilitate the behavior change desired by the presenter."[4] [emphasis added]. This definition captures the essence and importance of assuming a receiver-centered approach to speaking.

If you were to attend a training session at your job, you would hope that the trainer would relay information to you in a way that would allow you to access it. The training information would do little good if it was presented in a language you didn't understand, or with an emphasis on matters that were irrelevant, or if it was presented in any other way that seemed to disrespect your needs and character. For the trainer to be effective, she or he would have to make an attempt to understand you. *Audience analysis* is the phrase used to describe the act of discovering all you can about the audience with whom you will be interacting.

Although audience analysis may seem like a natural preliminary behavior for speakers, many presentations do not reflect such preparation. Some speakers actually attempt to analyze their receivers *while* they are speaking, as opposed to analyzing the audience before the talk. A speaker explaining the advantages of direct marketing might ask a group, How many of you are familiar with the concept of direct marketing? How many of you have experience working in retail?

There are two problems with taking this approach. The first is that it presupposes that audience participants will be forthcoming and candid with their responses. Even if they were to be so candid, the speaker would have to adapt immediately to the responses. This is difficult to do even for those with subject matter expertise and years of speaking experience.

The second problem with this approach is more fundamentally inappropriate. Audiences expect professional speakers to have done their homework. When speakers ask questions about the audience's background, they are telling the audience that they did not do what they could and should have done. Would the former New Jersey governor depicted in the beginning of the chapter have benefited by asking early on, "Is this a four- or five-year school?" If she had received a candid response, she could have changed the wording in the presentation, but she would not have altered the perception she had created of someone who was not adequately prepared. Of course, there are times when speakers are thrust into situations and can not be expected to do a thorough audience analysis. However, in many situations speakers know, well ahead of time, that they will be speaking to a particular group.

Audience analysis is essential. Otherwise well-intentioned and well-prepared speakers have failed because they did not seek to discover the attitudes and demographic characteristics of their audiences.

## Ramifications of Poor Audience Analysis

There are several potential repercussions of not taking the time to analyze your audience.

**You may bore the audience.** By not recognizing attendees' intelligence levels you may put to sleep listeners who think the information you are dispensing is not new or necessary.

**You may anger the audience.** In almost all contexts, but particularly business contexts, listeners do not want to have their time wasted. If they are called to listen to a presentation that is irrelevant to them, they may become angered that their time has been stolen. People who have been working in direct marketing for years, who are hoping to hear about innovative ways to do direct marketing on the Web, do not want to hear a verbose elementary explanation of how direct marketing differs from other forms of marketing.

Even if time is not an issue, audience members may feel anger at being disrespected. They may think the speaker was not concerned enough about them to discover who the audience was beforehand.

**You may reduce your chances of success in future speaking situations.** After having misread or not read an audience on one occasion, it may be difficult to regain the respect of the audience when you return. Earning their attention may become an unnecessarily burdensome task.

**You may not be fulfilling your organizational responsibility.** If we assume that there was a reason for making the presentation in the first place, by not reading your audience ahead of time, you may have diminished your capacity to realize the purported goal of the talk. Essentially, you will not have done your job, because it may be difficult or impossible for your receivers to get the message you need to convey.

Of course, the opposite of all these scenarios is refreshingly positive. By having prior knowledge of the audience you can deliver a message that may

**energize the group,**
**create rapport with them,**
**increase the chances for future presentations to be successful,**
**establish yourself as a valuable member of the organization.**

# Elements of Audience Analysis—A Checklist

Audience analysis involves conducting research, prior to delivery, in order to discover the following.

## Audience Perspectives and Knowledge

For example, if you were describing your department's annual accomplishments, you would need to know how much audience members knew about your group and what their attitude was toward your department's role in the organization.

## Audience Demographics

For example, if you were discussing a proposal for early retirement, you would need to know the average age of the attending audience members.

## The Presentation Context

For example, if you intended to deliver a PowerPoint® presentation, you would need to be familiar with the room where you would be speaking. The presentation may require a portable projector and/or screen if the room does not have such facilities installed.

On the following pages, each of the areas identified above are explained in detail and divided into subcategories. The categories and the subdivisions provide a checklist for conducting audience analysis.

**Audience Analysis Checklist**

**Category 1: Audience Perspectives and Knowledge**

- **Subject Knowledge**
  - **Breadth and Depth of Knowledge**
  - **Attitudes toward Subject**
  - **Misconceptions about Subject**
  - **What Audience Does Not Know about Subject**
  - **Technological Background**
  - **Familiarity with Vocabulary, Acronyms, and Initialisms**
- **Audience Motivations and Expectations**
  - **"Prisoners" or Willing Attendees**
  - **Needs and Perceptions of Relevance**
  - **What Audience Wants to Hear**
  - **Audience Expectations**
- **Audience Familiarity with Speaker and Department**
  - **Knowledge of Speaker/Speaker's Department/Unit**
  - **Commonalities between Speaker and Audience**

**Audience Analysis Checklist (Continued)**

Category 2: Audience Demographics
- Age
- Education Level
- Group Affiliations
- Gender
- Ethnicity and Culture
- Income

Category 3: The Presentation Context
- Physical Setting
  - Room Size, Seating Configuration
  - Podium, Screen, and Power Locations
  - Windows and External Noise
  - Equipment
- Time
  - Time of Day, Speaking Sequence
  - Allotted Time
  - Historical Chronology

# Category 1: Audience Perspectives and Knowledge

## Subject Knowledge

Speakers need to discover what the receivers know about the subject to be discussed. Specifically, they need to determine the following:

### Breadth and Depth of Knowledge

The amount of background information necessary for a talk will be a function of how much the audience already knows about the subject. If you are describing a new product to veteran salespersons, you do not need to explain the nature of the company, your organization's selling protocol, or the other products in your line. They will already know that information.

### Attitudes Toward the Subject

If you are a trainer explaining a new benefits policy to affected employees, you would be wise to discover what attitudes the employees may have about the new policy. Simply describing the policy may not be sufficient if the attendees first need to be placated. The group may never like the new procedure, but a smart speaker would be wise to discover the perspective the audience may have on the subject to craft the message appropriately, given those attitudes.

### Misconceptions the Audience may Have about the Subject

Before the audience departs, speakers need to clear up any confusion they have about the message. Speakers cannot rely on question-and-answer sessions to address these concerns because not all audience members will raise the questions that they have during that time. Identifying misconceptions audience members may have allows the speaker to confront and refute the misconceptions in the course of the presentation.

## What Don't They Know That Will Make the Subject Engaging

An audience of veteran employees listening to a state-of-the-organization talk may be ignorant of the state of the organization but may be content to remain uninformed. Your analysis of the group may unearth this apathy, but you may also discover that there is something they don't know that can be made particularly intriguing to them. By being aware of this piece of information you can make the talk relevant to a group that would otherwise be uninterested and passive.

## Technological Background

An issue in contemporary organizations relates to familiarity with technology. Many presentations deal with the launch of some new equipment or software that the organization plans to use. Explaining this new technology often involves training employees whose understanding of technology varies significantly. This is a challenge for speakers, and in some cases the challenge cannot be met. However, it will never be met without an attempt to discover the audience members' background before considering message content.

## Familiarity with Vocabulary, Acronyms, and Initialisms[5]

Phillip Tompkins in *Organizational Communication Imperatives* describes a meeting with a Marshall Space Flight Center engineer who was identifying several problems related to presentation quality at the center. At one point the engineer made the following comment:

> *The briefers use alphabet soup; acronyms like ICN and ICD and so on. I don't believe half the guys hearing a briefing understand it. Even von Braun [the director and brilliant engineer Dr. Wernher von Braun] doesn't understand some of this stuff.*[6]

It is easy for receivers to become confused when they are deluged with esoteric terms and *alphabet soup*. Apparently, the use of acronyms and initialisms made digesting information difficult even for the very knowledgeable engineers who worked at the Marshall Space Flight Center.

We have all read documents that seem to be saturated with initials that are difficult to remember even if we once were familiar with the reference. Using acronyms and initialisms might seem to be an intelligent form of shorthand, but it often disables the receivers. You may have experienced this when reading a document. An author might refer to the National Communication Association (NCA) in an early paragraph. Subsequently, the initials NCA are used throughout. Some readers may recall the reference, but in a lengthy document with many initialisms and acronyms, it can be difficult to remember what they represent.

Most fields have their own terminology, and only those in that field or those familiar with it can understand the jargon. It is prudent and responsible for speakers to gauge audience awareness of jargon. Using terms like *server* or *cookie* or *platform* may seem perfectly reasonable to you, but if your audience members know only that the words relate to computing and not precisely what they mean, your presentation objective may not be achieved. You may have heard people comment that they need to "dumb down" their lecture to the audience. This is a pejorative way of describing the process of assessing your audience and applying your assessments to the talk. In contemporary business, the expression *dumb down* does not always imply disrespect. However, it is wise to remember that people who do not know what you know are not dummies. They are simply likely to have other areas of expertise.

## Ethical Probe

### Simplifying Language

Do speakers have a moral obligation to simplify language for audience members who are not as knowledgeable as the speakers may be?

Assume that a presentation about a new product is being crafted by a team of engineers who worked on the product. Assume that the audience will include an internal group that has been compelled to attend the session by management. These people are not particularly interested or excited about the new product, yet they are required to attend. They do not have the technical knowledge or vocabulary of the engineers. The speakers know these people will be among the audience members.

Do the speakers have a moral obligation to use terminology that this group of audience members can understand?

## Audience Motivations and Expectations

*Don't try selling alarm clocks to people without jobs.*[7]

In addition to analyzing the audience's subject knowledge, speakers need to become familiar with the audience's motivation and expectations.

### Reasons for Attendance: "Prisoners" or Willing Attendees

Trainers sometimes refer to audience members as *prisoners*. They do so because occasionally people attend presentations only because they are compelled to do so. For example, an employee who is labeled a difficult person may be required to attend an interpersonal communication workshop. An employee who does not understand the new marketing strategy, but is under the illusion that he does, may be compelled to listen to a second rendition of a talk about the plan.

It requires more energy to motivate a prisoner than a willing attendee. Therefore, it is essential for the speaker to know why the audience is attending. Recently, a consultant was asked to conduct a workshop for executives on improving presentation skills. The person who hired her told her the attendees often considered this a skill that they already possessed and were insulted to be told to attend this mandatory session. This was important news to the consultant. Although she presented the same information she typically does in such workshops, she was careful to acknowledge the participants' experience in making presentations and not to suggest that the program was in any way a remedial session.

### Audience Needs and Perceptions of Relevance

A speaker should discover what receivers are listening for. Salespeople may be attending a session because they want to hear how the new product stacks up against the competition. Incoming students on the first day of class are typically less interested in hearing about course objectives and more interested in knowing about grading criteria.

If department members are listening to an organizational initiative, the budget administrators will focus on the financial ramifications of the plan; the department head may concentrate on the staffing implications; employees will focus on how the proposal will affect opportunities for promotion. Therefore, it is wise to discover what roles the audience members have in the organization.

Similarly it is important to discover what particular obstacles the listeners need to overcome. For example, a talk that emphasizes the ease of implementing a new procedure for charting incoming calls may be simple enough. However, if you are addressing managers who supervise technophobes, the simplicity of the new procedure may seem to them more complicated than simple. The attendees may need to hear more about how they can address training issues pertaining to the new protocol than about the new protocol itself.

As authors Teri and Michael Gamble comment, most people tune into the WIIFM network, where WIIFM stands for What's In It For Me.[7] Speakers need to be aware of what is in it for the audience members to highlight the relevant aspects of the content.

### *What the Audience Wants to Hear*

Speakers who conduct audience analysis often fall into the trap of discovering what the audience wants to hear and then telling them precisely that. This is a myopic strategy, because the speaker may not be able to fulfill what is implicitly or explicitly promised and may omit meaningful, if troubling, information. However, knowing what someone would like to hear may help in the crafting of a message.

Assume that a group of salespeople has been clamoring for a sales quota reduction. They attend a session at which a senior vice president will be speaking about a new sales plan. Further assume that the plan will not reduce the quota, but may make it easier for salespeople to meet it. Being aware of what the salespersons would like to hear allows the vice president to address the issue and emphasize how the proposal can indirectly reduce the pressure (assuming this claim is credible) without dishonestly placating them. She would have to be aware of what the salespeople want to hear to highlight the pressure-reducing dimension of the proposal.

### *Audience Expectations*

A group that is brought into an assembly hall to listen to the CEO may have heard that the talk will center on layoffs. If that is not the case, the speaker would be wise to disabuse the audience of this notion at the beginning of the talk. Otherwise the audience will wait from the outset to hear what they expect to hear and miss everything else the speaker is saying. If it is the case that the speaker will talk about layoffs, then the speaker still must be aware of this expectation, because it will affect how the message is framed.

## Audience Familiarity with Speaker and Department

In addition to determining what the audience knows about the subject, you should seek to discover what the audience knows about you. Their perceptions may or may not be accurate, but they are important nonetheless.

Similarly, it is wise to discover what the listeners might know about the department or organization that you represent. Perhaps the audience doesn't know you personally, but thinks highly of your employer. This information can make your job as a speaker easier and may change your approach to the talk.

However, it is possible that your division within a company has earned—or simply has—a reputation for being weak and inconsequential. This knowledge also will be helpful. Regardless of the merit of the perception, your comments may be dismissed as the musings of an irrelevant player if you choose to ignore the negative opinion when you prepare to speak to a group outside your department.

## Reverse the Perspective

### Commonalities between Speaker and Audience

Kenneth Burke wrote about the importance of speakers establishing commonality with audiences. He used the words *identification* and *consubstantiality* to refer to the extent to which a speaker can establish this commonality. To be successful, he said, speakers need to identify with the audience members and become consubstantial, i.e., "of the same substance" as the receivers.

Do you consider the idea of identification valuable for speakers?

Do you consider any of the following speaker behaviors effective in terms of establishing commonality? Explain why you think the way you do.

- Speakers using the same slang their audience uses. For example, instructors using words that are likely not part of their vocabulary, but part of student jargon.
- Speakers claiming that their experience is similar to yours. For example, an employer who says during orientation, "I know what it is like to work from the ground up. Twenty years ago, I started just where you are starting today, listening to a speech from a manager named Sharon Oberman."
- Speakers claiming to have a common economic background with the receivers. For example, a college recruiter who says, "I am sure you are concerned with tuition costs at our school. Believe me I can commiserate. I am still paying back my loans, but I tell you it was the best investment I ever made."
- Speakers claiming to identify with the audience's ostensible sense of enthusiasm. For example, a salesperson speaking to potential consumers at a convention who says, "I know that you are as thrilled as I am to be here in exciting Las Vegas for this wonderful conference."

## Category 2: Audience Demographics

The word *demographics* literally means "writing about people." It comes from the root *demos* meaning "people" and *graph,* referring to something written. You have probably completed surveys with questions that related to your race, gender, and age. These questions allow researchers to break down results by demographic group. A study can report how men react as opposed to women or how seniors at universities respond compared with sophomores.

In presentation settings it is important to know the demographics of your audience so you can adapt a message appropriately. It is essential, however, to be careful not to stereotype an audience in terms of demographic categories. This point is made in more detail in the sections that follow.

### Age

College students probably know what the word *phat* means. Readers in their sixties are unlikely to be familiar with this slang term. One would be wise not to assume that *to chill* or *chilling* is a concept familiar to octogenarians. The age of the audience should affect a speaker's word choice.

Age should also affect a speaker's selection of references. An allusion to Indigo Girls may be meaningful to college students in the new millennium, but it has little significance to many people in their sixties. George, Paul, John, and Ringo are names that require no surname for some audiences. When baby boomers heard the two words *George died* on December 1, 2001, they knew precisely which George was being referred to. The Day of Infamy, Uncle Miltie, Ike, the Warren Commission, Kent State, the Miracle on Ice, *The Challenger* disaster, and Napster will each be more or less familiar to audiences depending on the age of the listeners. Referring to events and people that are unfamiliar to your audience can erode the sense of commonality that you may have established or wish to establish with the group.

Finally, knowledge of audience age allows the speaker to be aware of listener sensitivities. Discussing changes to the Social Security system, however reasonable they may be, can be hazardous to speakers addressing senior citizens.

## Education Level: Vocabulary, Common Experience, and Expertise

The fact that someone went to college does not mean they are any more intelligent than someone who did not. However, knowing the audience members' education level may provide valuable information for speakers. It may, for example, reveal attitudes toward education and learning. A speaker talking about the value of higher education to those who did not attend college needs to be sensitive to the possibility that audience members may feel unjustly snubbed because of their educational choices or the circumstances forced upon them.

## Group Affiliations

Knowing what groups audience members affiliate with can provide speakers with additional valuable information.

People who affiliate with the National Rifle Association are likely to be supportive of any presentation that endorses individual freedoms. Greenpeace members will probably be averse to recommendations that the government eliminate national recreation areas. Republicans will probably be delighted to hear talks that extol the virtues of their candidates and criticize Democratic nominees.

Knowing who your audience is in terms of group affiliation can facilitate the delivery of a high-quality message or, in the absence of that knowledge, make the presentation nothing short of disastrous.

An important part of your preparation as a speaker is to find out what kinds of causes, interests, or groups your audience members support.

## Gender

Much has been made in the last twenty years about men's and women's communication patterns. Deborah Tannen's best-selling book *You Just Don't Understand* explained what she claimed were the differences between how men and women communicate. For example, she suggests that "women speak and hear a language of connection and intimacy while men speak and hear a language of status and independence."[9] John Gray's *Men Are from Mars, Women Are from Venus* was similarly popular and heralded by many as an illuminative guide to how men and women differ. Throughout the

United States, departments of communication studies offer courses called Communication and Gender that attempt to explain how gender affects communication.

When preparing for your talk you would be wise to consider the gender composition of the audience. However, you would also be very wise to be careful about how you decide to react to that composition.

A problem with any kind of generalization is that while the generalization may or may not represent normative behavior for that population, it could not and does not represent actual behavior for any one individual within that population. This point is relevant to gender issues in presentations.

It may or may not be true that more women than men "speak and hear a language of connection and intimacy," but to assume that all women and men will behave as the norm is to deny individuals their individuality. Speakers who attribute purported normative behavior to individual audience members are likely to deliver a bruising insult to those who differ from the norm and who desire to be considered, as everyone desires to be considered, as a unique individual. Such an insult, regardless of whether it was maliciously uttered, can be debilitating to a speaker.

Consider the following example. Men typically score higher on standardized math tests than women. Regardless of what you may read anywhere, this phenomenon does not mean that women are inherently poor at math and men are good at math. To draw that conclusion for any reason is to insult and bruise the millions of women who excel in math.

I have heard more than one speaker in a business context discuss a statistical analysis and comment, "You ladies may not be able to follow this, but bear with me for a moment."

It is important to acknowledge the gender composition of the audience and also important not to attribute generalized claims to all members of the group. Tannen's and Gray's writing may be intriguing, but may be less than valuable as a resource for understanding communication. (Both books have met with criticism from communication scholars. For example, Daena Goldsmith and Patricia Fulfs criticized Tannen's book in their article " 'You Just Don't Have the Evidence': An Analysis of Claim and Evidence in Deborah Tannen's *You Just Don't Understand.*" Gray's book was critiqued in Julia Wood's "A Critical Response to John Gray's Mars and Venus Portrayals of Men and Women," in *Southern Communication Journal*).[10]

In three decades of college teaching and conducting workshops for professionals, I have heard dozens of presentations that have transformed presenters from benign workshop participants, coworkers, and classmates into perceived monsters because of insensitivity to gender-related sensitivities.

- A male speaker discussing the managerial style of a doll manufacturing entrepreneur remarked that he was sure "the girls in the audience were familiar with the company."
- A woman speaking to a group of scholars referred to issues women face in the workforce by emphasizing their desire to be home for their husbands when they come home at the end of "a long day." This infuriated female listeners who put in the same long days and did not see their familial role as the homebody greeter.
- A male evening MBA student was speaking to other women and men who were also evening MBA students. All students worked as full-time midlevel managers during the day. The speaker's talk dealt with adjusting to the rigors of business travel. One section described how to pack for business trips and included a demonstration. While demonstrating, the speaker realized that all the items he was folding and packing were his own and, therefore, men's apparel. To compensate for this and in a disastrous attempt to be inclusive he remarked that although the presentation seemed to be centered on the men in the audience, the fact was that women needed to know how to pack their husbands' suitcases. This one statement transformed the young manager from colleague to degenerate in a matter of seconds.

## Ethnicity and Culture

The workforce in the twenty-first century is far more diverse than it was even twenty years ago. Organizations are expanding internationally. Because of the ease of international travel and the always increasing capabilities of communication technologies, our planet has become more and more like the global village that theorist Marshall McLuhan envisioned nearly forty years ago.[11]

A result is that speakers who in the past typically spoke to homogeneous populations are now addressing groups that are ethnically diverse. Becoming aware of the ethnicities represented in the audience is important for at least three reasons.

**Ethnocentrism**: Ethnocentrism refers to the belief that your ethnic perspective is superior to others'. Obviously, explicitly or implicitly suggesting cultural superiority is likely to disturb audience members—regardless of which group they belong to. Speakers have to be vigilant to ensure that remarks do not reflect ethnocentric perspectives.

**Language**: Audience members from other countries are likely to speak a different primary language. Therefore, terms you use in your talk may, in fact, be foreign to them. Also a rapid speaking rate may be a problem for people who commonly speak and listen to another language.

**References:** References to occasions such as Thanksgiving or events such as the Super Bowl may not be universally understood by members of the audience. These allusions may appear harmless, but a speaker who assumes familiarity can unwittingly fortify barriers between groups.

## Income

How much money people earn need not indicate how they think, but it would be wise for speakers to think about their audience members' socioeconomic levels. To pitch a luxury car to people who are barely able to afford a mortgage will not only result in an unsuccessful pitch, but may be perceived as insulting.

# Category 3: Presentation Context

The third area for audience analysis relates to the setting for the talk.

## Physical Setting

### Room Size, Seating Configuration

Speakers would be wise to discover the capacity for the presentation room, as well as the number of people expected to attend. A room that seats two hundred will seem very empty if only fifty persons attend. Audience members often populate the seats in the rear of an empty auditorium, leaving a sea of vacant rows between the speaker and the first group of listeners. Pleas to have people move down are typically met with some uninspired adherents still leaving a vast space between the speaker and audience members. One can avoid this problem by blocking off back rows and side sections of the auditorium to compel persons to sit closer to the speaker. Of course, such a tack can work only if you are aware ahead of time of room size and expected attendance.

Audience analysis also involves knowing and noting, prior to arrival, how the room will be configured. Addressing a group that is seated 270 degrees around the podium is different from addressing an audience that completely surrounds the speaker or one that is seated directly in front of the lectern.

Depending on what the speaker will be doing with the group, it may be valuable to find out if the chairs in the room are stationary or moveable. If the presentation involves participation that includes writing, a speaker needs to find out if the listeners will have desks or tables.

Finally, speakers would be wise to inquire about the chances of last-minute changes to the room. Is it common in a particular organization for a group with high priority to appropriate the site where you are scheduled to speak? If so, can you identify the alternative sites and be sufficiently flexible to present in these other places as well?

### Podium, Screen, and Power Locations

The location of the podium in relation to the room is significant. Novice speakers may assume that the podium will be in the middle of the room. This is not always the case. The podium may be far from where your computer and mouse need to be, and this apparently minor change can be enough to unnerve an apprehensive presenter.

Before the presentation, a speaker should locate the electrical outlets in the room. If power needs to be available for a demonstration or visual support, the speaker should not have to search for the outlet or an extension cord during the talk. For the same reasons, speakers should locate the control panel for the screen and lights in the room. It may seem basic and unnecessary, but it is wise to practice working the switches to be sure the screen can be moved easily or lighting can be adjusted.

### Windows and External Noise

In urban venues, the location of the room and particularly the windows can affect the presentation. If the presentation will be given adjacent to a train line, or a road with heavy traffic, the acoustics in the room will be affected. If for no other reason than to avoid being startled by an additional variable, you should become aware of the window locations and the chances of external noise becoming a factor.

### Equipment

Slight variations in equipment can be disconcerting to a beginning speaker or even someone with experience. A carefully planned PowerPoint® presentation may require a drive that is unavailable on the company's machine. For this reason a speaker should identify the specific piece of equipment that will be used during the course of the talk. Also, it is wise to have a backup plan. In case the PowerPoint® presentation can not be employed, you might bring a set of slides on transparencies to use with an overhead projector.

## Time

### Time of Day; Speaking Sequence

Time is an issue that can affect the presentation. Any instructor or student knows that classes at 8:00 A.M. have a different energy level than those that meet at noon. An early morning presentation is likely to require more time spent on engaging the audience. A speaker should also consider time in terms of the day's schedule. Will you be the last speaker before lunch or the first speaker after lunch? Will you be the person holding up the assembled from attending the free buffet and cocktails offered during the evening reception?

If there will be several speakers, find out when in the sequence you will be speaking. A presenter speaking third in a group of four may find audience members fatigued. It may even be helpful to identify the particular individuals who will speak first and second. Some speakers may be very humorous. Others may have a reputation for exceeding the time limit. If a speaker follows someone who typically is verbose, it might be necessary to ask the moderator to remind all speakers to be mindful of time.

### *Allotted Time*

How long the talk is expected to last is another time factor to consider. If speakers are allotted ten minutes, then planning the presentation to last approximately ten minutes is an important part of the preparation. In some business contexts time restrictions are rigid and those coordinating the program may stop the presentation. More significantly, speaking for longer than the allotted time can reflect inconsideration or lack of preparation. Similarly, speakers want to prepare the talk so that it will not be too short. Even if the presentation contains all the necessary information, it may seem strange to audience members who are not forewarned if the twenty-minute talk they were expecting ends after three. Some listeners may welcome the brevity, but others, rightly or wrongly, might wonder about the extent of preparation.

### *Historical Chronology*

Time is also relevant in terms of chronology of events. Speaking to almost any audience immediately after 9/11 required some reference to the event. For example, an orientation session for new employees held on 9/12 involved a series of speakers, each of whom in their own way prefaced their remarks with some comments about the previous day. Clergy members who had prepared sermons for church or the Jewish high holidays claimed to have scrapped their messages in the wake of 9/11 because recent events required a more relevant talk.

# Obtaining Information

Several methods can be used to obtain information about the audience. They include the following:

Interviews
Focus Groups
Questionnaires
Opinion Surveys
Company Web Sites
Reading Common Publications
Practice Sessions

## Interviews

An easy method for finding out about the audience is to interview the person who contacted the speaker about the presentation. If the head of engineering solicited a talk about marketing policy, the speaker can comfortably interview the head about the nature of the engineers who will be attending. Interviews with others who have spoken to the same population can also be valuable. Finally, it can be helpful to meet informally with persons who will be attending the presentation to inquire about the attitudes and demographics of the rest of the group.

## Focus Groups

A more involved type of interview is called a focus group. Instead of meeting one-on-one informally with others, in a focus group speakers ask five to ten people who may have information about the audience to convene. The speakers proceed to ask questions of this

Please use the following to indicate how you feel about the statements found below the scale.

1 Strongly Agree
2 Agree
3 Neither Agree nor disagree
4 Disagree
5 Strongly Disagree

- The government should not restrict an individual's right to assume health risks.
- Cigarette smoking increases the chances for lung cancer.
- Businesses have the obligation to stockholders to maximize profits.
- Confectioners should be compelled to warn consumers of problems related to obesity.
- Businesses have the right to determine their own policies regarding smoking in their establishments.

Please answer the following questions yes or no.

- Do you presently smoke cigarettes on a regular basis?
  - Yes
  - No

- Do you know any person who has become ill because of cigarette smoking?
  - Yes
  - No

- Do you, or does anyone in your family, own stock or work in the tobacco industry?
  - Yes
  - No

Thank you for your participation in this survey.

**Figure 5-1** Distributing sample surveys before you speak can offer revealing information about your audience.

group. If speakers ask intelligent questions and allow all those in the group to participate, the focus group can assist in identifying characteristics of the audience.

## Questionnaires

It may be possible to distribute surveys to audience members before you speak. Often this is not feasible, but when it is, one can discover information about the audience pertinent to your talk by employing these questionnaires. Figure 5-1 is a sample of such a survey.

## Opinion Surveys

There are Web sites that publish results of surveys administered on a myriad of topics. Visit **http://www.icpsr.umich.edu** or **http://www.gallup.com/poll/index.asp** or **http://www.norc.uchicago.edu** and you may be surprised at the range and depth of information that pollsters are able to glean about audience perspectives.

## Company Web Sites

Whenever I am invited to speak to a group, I interview the person who hired me then go to the group's Web site and read all I can about the nature of their organization. Units within organizations often have their own departmental sites. People within these units may even have a site.

## Read What They Read

If you were going to speak to the International Association of Business Communicators, you would be wise to read through a few issues of *Communication World*, the publication of that organization. If you were to speak to a group of technical writers who consume a trade magazine religiously, then peruse that magazine before you speak to this audience.

## Conduct a Dry Run

A dress rehearsal can also be helpful. If speakers have an opportunity to gather friends to hear the presentation, they may be able to identify problems before they surface in the actual talk. In the same way a writer will have several readers review a manuscript before sending it to print, a preview listening audience can identify some gaps in the talk that reflect a lack of awareness of audience composition.

# CONCLUSION

Audience analysis is an essential preparatory step for speakers. Consider this short analogy. Imagine that you are seated at your desk working on a paper. You find that you need to look up a word. You know that your paperback dictionary is on your roommate's bed. Still looking at the computer screen you reach one hand up and say to your roommate, "Do me a favor and throw me the dictionary."

You would likely expect your roommate to toss the dictionary so that you could easily catch it.

What if he threw it so quickly that you could not possibly grab it?

What if he threw it to your bed instead of your desk?

What if instead of the paperback, he picked up the hardcover dictionary from the floor and heaved it at you?

You would likely be perplexed if not annoyed by the behavior. You would likely ask why he had thrown the book that way.

If your roommate responded by saying that he happens to be adept at throwing dictionaries quickly, or that you *should* have been on the bed, or that you really should not rely on paperback dictionaries, you would probably not find these explanations satisfactory.

Speakers are metaphorically passing dictionaries to roommates. Speakers are, of course, sending messages, not tossing books. However, the principal objective is the same. In the same way that the roommate who tosses the dictionary should attempt to direct it so that you can receive it, speakers must send their messages so that audience members can receive them. To meet this principal objective speakers have to know who the receivers are, where they are, and what their attitudes may be toward whatever they are conveying.

As Gamble and Gamble comment, "Effective speakers speak to audiences . . . Ineffective Speakers speak to hear themselves."

## Stand Up & Deliver

Assume that you have made the "short list" of candidates for a job that you very much desire. You know that you will be asked to deliver a brief 3–5 minute presentation that describes your qualifications for the position.

What would you want to know about the people who will be at your interview?

- Prepare a three-minute presentation that identifies the top five audience characteristics you would want to identify before preparing for the job presentation.
  - Explain why these are relevant.
  - Are any of the five audience characteristics you identified applicable to the audience analysis you need to conduct when you speak to your classmates in this course?
  - If the answer to the previous question is yes, did you consider these characteristics when you prepared the talk to classmates about the audience analysis you would need to conduct for the job?

## Summary

- Audience analysis is a crucial preliminary step for any presentation.
- Audience analysis involves the following:
  - Exploring receiver perspectives and knowledge in terms of audience
    - Subject knowledge
    - Expectations
    - Familiarity with the speakers
  - Identifying audience demographics. Specifically
    - Age
    - Education and income level
    - Gender and culture
    - Group affiliations
  - Analyzing the physical setting for the talk
  - Becoming familiar with time restraints and other temporal issues pertaining to the presentation
- Speakers can study the audience in the following ways:
  - Conducting
    - Focus groups
    - Interviews
    - Surveys
  - Visiting related Web sites
  - Reviewing publications that these specific audiences typically read

## SAMPLE PRESENTATION FOR ANALYSIS

### Women and Minorities in Business

*Edie Fraser, president of the Women's Business Network, delivered* Women and Minorities in Business *on February 7, 2002. The presentation was made at the Second Annual Multicultural Awards Ceremony and Forum in Fairfield, Connecticut. As you read through this presentation please consider the following questions.*

1. *Would you consider Ms. Fraser's remarks inspirational? Please explain.*
2. *Is the miles/journey metaphor an effective use of language?*
3. *Would this speech be effective regardless of the gender and racial composition of the audience? Explain. Would the speaker need to change the talk if she was addressing a group of predominantly white male CEOs? Explain why she would or would not.*

First congratulations to Div2000 for being the premier place for recognizing entrepreneurial leadership and supporting women and minority-owned businesses. What an honor it is to be here today to recognize the accomplishments of so many on the vanguard of change. We salute those in business and government who are supporting minority and women-owned firms. These awards are all richly deserved. And to think that we are only a few miles into a journey of epic proportions! Our work will have even greater impact in years to come.

Women and minorities comprise the backbone of the economy. We are the demographics of the New America. Minorities are the majority in California and soon will be in other states. Think about it, the term "minorities" may no longer have any meaning - except if you are talking about Caucasians. White people will increasingly be come the minority. Embrace change.

Women and minorities have greater market share than ever. We are a dynamic workforce and an entrepreneurial talent base of astounding proportions. And the situation will continue to improve as more women and minorities enter the ranks of business. White males, according to the Bureau of Labor Statistics, will make up only 38% of the workforce by 2005. By 2008, women and people of color will account for about 70% of all new workers. This is only six short years away!...

...Many corporations that support women and minorities are with us here today. To AT&T; Lockheed Martin; SBC; Boeing; Microsoft; IBM; Verizon; Ford Motor; Fed Ex; and GE, congratulations for being the top ten most progressive companies in our global economy. Congratulations to all 50 corporations and 20 government departments and agencies honored here. You are embracing diversity as crucial to our entrepreneurial strength.

We are grateful and thank you. Keep raising the bar on what you can do in this crucial area.

We honor the government for championing multicultural business opportunities. Looking at the Div 50 for 2001, chosen by over 100,000 women and minority-owned businesses, the Department of Defense is working hard to reach out to multicultural and women-owned businesses. We call on our government to work harder.

Our time is now. This past Tuesday Defense Secretary Donald Rumsfeld asked Congress to boost our defense budget to $379 billion in light of the terrorist threat. This is the biggest increase since the Reagan administration. I know minority and women-owned firms in this sector are ready to answer the call of our country's defense.

The national security call reached Lurita Doan, president and CEO of New Technology Management. Her company's work in the security and technology business is vital to not only our economy, but also our security as well. She is single-handedly showing women as worthy recipients of these contracts, having received several hundred million dollars from several government agencies since 9/11. She and others in her industry have the competency to meet this increasing demand. I call on women to go for these opportunities.

...We urge all the government agencies to reach their goal of awarding 5% of contracts to women and an additional percentage to minority-owned business. But we must face up to the fact that the government average for contracts to women is less than 3% across-the-board. Some agencies, such as the Department of the Interior, are exceeding this goal. Others are creating truly innovative plans to reach out to specific minorities. For example, the Department of Transportation is targeting women-owned Native American firms. This has contributed to a staggering annual rate of growth for Native American firms in the past five years, 37%. Their sales growth averages 55% annually.

My friend Patricia Parker is CEO of Native American Management Services, one of these targeted firms. Pat has utilized her own experiences as a formal federal project officer in the government. She is a shining example of the need to use minority businesses to bridge the gap between government and sometimes overlooked constituencies. She is a vital conduit between our civic leaders and those of Native American and Alaskan tribal lands...

...We must never take for granted the fact that we have these opportunities to educate ourselves, to work for equality, and to create value in our business endeavors. We can't forget there are places in the world where the human spirit is quashed, where learning is suppressed and minds are deliberately kept in submission. Look at the situation in Afghanistan. We must be thankful for the opportunities in our free society.

And at no time has opportunity presented itself with such grand potential. As Helen Keller told us, "One can never consent to creep when one feels an impulse to soar." I am proud to join you in building business environments that reflect the diversity at the core of America's greatness. We are entrepreneurial stars, luminaries of business, and beacons of civic leadership illuminating the path to equality, opportunity, and value for all.

Change for the better is happening. Thanks to those companies and government departments that are providing the contract opportunities. You are our champions.

Thank you for your leadership. Stay the course and raise the bar even higher in years to come. We are counting on you. We are counting on one another.

**Source:** Fraser, Edie. "Women and Minorities in Business: We've Come a Long Way Baby! But we've got Miles to Go," *Vital Speeches of the Day*, March 1, 2002, 68, no. 10: 312(5).

## Review Questions

1. What are three specific benefits of conducting a comprehensive audience analysis?
2. How can not analyzing the audience be disastrous for a speaker? Cite three examples.
3. Identify three types of audience "subject knowledge" that good speakers need to discover before preparing and delivering their talks.
4. Why do speakers need to know about audience motivations and expectations?
5. Identify the three specific audience demographic factors that you consider most significant for people speaking to your class.
6. Identify three audience analysis components that pertain to the presentation setting itself.
7. Assume that you are invited to speak to your department's student club about the issue of increasing entrance requirements for the department. How would you discover what you need to discover about this group?

## InfoTrac Question

Find the May 2001 InfoTrac article entitled "Every Audience Is a Puzzle Waiting to Be Solved." What two points made by the author resonate with you? It appears as if the author is encouraging readers to review the other pieces in this May 2001 edition. Are you intrigued enough by this short article to review the other articles?

---

1 Burton Kaplan, *The Manager's Complete Guide to Speechwriting* (New York: Free Press, 1988), 17.

2 Comment made by a thirty-year employee who annually is required to attend workshops on various subjects that management considers germane to his job. E-mail message to author, August 2003.

3 Comment attributed to John Patrick Dolan, an attorney, in *Secrets of Successful Speakers*, by Lilly Walters (New York: McGraw Hill), 29.

4 Jack P. Friedman, *Dictionary of Business Terms*, 3rd ed. (Hauppauge, New York: Barron's, 2000), 528.

5 The word "acronym" is often used incorrectly to mean any series of initials. An acronym is a word that has been formed because of initials. An initialism is a series of letters often used to abbreviate something. For example, USA is an initialism; NASA and UNICEF are examples of acronyms.

6 Phillip Tompkins, *Organizational Communication Imperatives* (Roxbury Los Angeles: Roxbury Publishing Company, 1993), 60. This statement was made by Jim Shepherd, an assistant to Wernher von Braun at the Marshall Space Flight Center.

7 Op. cit. Walters 13. Attributed to Al Lampkin, an entertainer.

8 Teri Gamble and Michael Gamble, *Public Speaking in the Age of Diversity* (New York: Allyn and Bacon, 1998), 85.

9 Deborah Tannen, *You Just Don't Understand* (New York: Ballantine Books, 1990), 42.

10 Daena Goldsmith and Patricia Fulfs, "'You Just Don't Have the Evidence': An Analysis of Claim and Evidence in Deborah Tannen's *You Just Don't Understand*," *Communication Yearbook* 22 (1999): 1–49. Julia Wood, "A Critical Response to John Gray's Mars and Venus Portrayals of Men and Women" in *Southern Communication Journal*, 67, no. 2 (2002): 201–210.

11 Marshall McLuhan, Quentin Fiore, and Jerome Agel, *The Medium Is the Message: An Inventory of Effects* (New York: Bantam, 1967). Also referenced in Marshall McLuhan and Quentin Fiore, *War and Peace in the Global Village*, (Bantam, 1968).

12 Op. cit. Gamble 1994 ed. 71.

**Chapter in a Nutshell** *It is essential to consider the advantages and disadvantages of speaking styles to determine the best approach for a particular audience and presentation objective.*

# Selecting an Appropriate Speaking Style

*Impromptu talks on the spur of the moment are difficult since the moment often arises without the spur.*[1]

-Benjamin Disraeli

*Once a word is spoken a team of four horses can not retake it.*[2]

-Chinese Proverb


## Abstract

Presenters must consider how best to get their message to a particular audience. To do that, speakers have to consider various speaking options. Should presentations be delivered from memory? From an outline? Should speakers read a script verbatim? Is there anything wrong with simply relying on expertise and just "winging it?"

Selecting an appropriate style requires an examination of presentation objectives, audience traits and expectations, and the speaker's own comfort level. In this chapter different speaking styles are identified and their advantages and disadvantages discussed.

Specifically, when you conclude this chapter you should be able to do the following:

- List and describe four presentation styles
- Evaluate the advantages and disadvantages of using manuscript and extemporaneous options for specific audiences
- Describe the problems associated with manuscript and impromptu business presentations
- Assess your own level of skill and comfort level with each speaking style

PHOTO: © RYAN MCVAY/PHOTODISC/GETTY IMAGES

## Describing Nita

When I received the e-mail message telling me that my colleague's wife had passed away, I was relieved to notice that the campus memorial service would be at a time when I did not have a class. Tony had been a colleague of mine for more than a dozen years, and I wanted to attend the ceremony. Although I had often heard him refer to his wife, and had exchanged greetings with her over the telephone, I'd never met her. She too had worked at the university, but ours is a very large institution with multiple autonomous units. It is not that unusual to receive notices about retirement parties for people who have been at the university for the same twenty-odd years that I've been present, yet who are complete strangers to me. Nita, Tony's wife, was such a stranger.

The university has a room called the sacred space, which is used for events related to spiritual life. The sacred space is also used for memorial ceremonies. When I arrived there for Nita's service, I was surprised to find the room crowded. Several people stood behind and alongside the rows of chairs.

The woman, Adrienne, who delivered the eulogy for Nita, was introduced as a dear friend and coworker. I had seen Adrienne on campus, but knew as little about her as I'd known about Nita. She approached the rostrum, took out a sheaf of papers, and spoke from a prepared manuscript. Within minutes I began to get a rich sense of the woman who had been my colleague's wife. In language that was concurrently simple and descriptive, the speaker conveyed Nita's commitment to family and friendship. When referring to Tony and Nita's children, she comfortably and meaningfully stopped and looked at each sibling in turn while delivering a message to each of them. She paused appropriately to look at Tony when she began to describe Nita's commitment to lifelong partnership and Nita's willing sacrifices to make the union a success. Adrienne integrated humorous anecdotes that reflected the deceased's tenacity when working for political and social causes. She also spent some time discussing Nita's dedication to her organizational home—the university. While Adrienne described Nita's allegiance to the university and commitment to work, I noticed concurring nods and smiles on the faces of several people among the assembled.

Throughout the remarks, I was impressed with how Adrienne had selected words that precisely matched the thoughts that she desired to convey. She had apparently considered when to pause, which words to emphasize, and even when to look at certain audience members. Adrienne skillfully integrated the various portions of her eulogy so that the episodes depicting family, work, and civic contributions formed a portrait of the beautiful human mosaic that was Nita.

When I left the room, I felt that I knew this woman, the wife of my colleague, whom I had never once met.

- What made this presentation a success?
- What approach might have rendered it less successful?
- In organizational contexts are such human-related presentations necessary?
- Is it important for organizations to formally recognize the successes of their members?

## INTRODUCTION

The presentations you have heard in school, at work, in religious sanctuaries, from club leaders, and from politicians have all been delivered in one of four ways. The presentations were either impromptu, memorized, extemporaneous, or manuscript talks. The decision that speakers make about which style to use is significant. The choice can dramatically affect the quality of the presentation regardless of how much speakers know about the subject to be discussed. The appropriate style for a presentation varies, depending on the speaking situation and audience expectations. Speaker comfort levels and ease of preparation should be secondary, not primary, considerations.

## IMPROMPTU PRESENTATIONS

An impromptu talk is delivered without any prior preparation. In the vernacular, an impromptu talk is called *winging it*. The speakers may know a great deal about a subject, but if they do not prepare the message, the resulting talk is called an impromptu presentation. A team of experts on the history of film, who know more about film than anyone, would still be delivering an impromptu talk if they had spent no time preparing for the presentation prior to delivery.

There are times when one must deliver impromptu presentations. If an employee is at a meeting and the boss suddenly requests a briefing on the status of a current project, the ensuing response will be impromptu, because the speaker did not know in advance that a briefing would be requested. Also, during question-and-answer sessions, an audience member may ask a question that a speaker had not anticipated. The response to that question will be, by definition, an impromptu talk.

However, when a speaker has an opportunity to prepare, it would be wise to use the time. As discussed in Chapter 2, presentations differ from other communication contexts because there is typically time to prepare. If speakers relinquish that opportunity, they eliminate a significant advantage.

I know now that in three weeks I will be speaking to a group of administrators on the subject of professional presentations. I am very familiar with the substance of my message and have delivered similar talks dozens of times, but to be effective I will need to prepare. I would be foolish to think that because of what I know about professional presentations I could just go to the setting and wing it. A result of not planning and using an impromptu style could be that instead of my talk being well structured and intelligible, it will become disjointed and incomprehensible—*regardless* of how much I know. Not only may listeners be confused, but my status as a speaker may be unnecessarily tarnished. Next time, the coordinators may select someone else to deliver this talk. People may begin to wonder just how much of an expert I am on the subject.

Impromptu speaking presents a challenge, but it is a challenge one should resist. Mark Twain once quipped, "It usually takes three weeks to prepare a good impromptu speech." Nevertheless, many presenters decide that they will just go into a meeting and wing it. It is a shortsighted decision. As Don Keough, former CEO of Coca Cola, has commented, "If you're going to [speak] well, you have to think a lot about the people who are going to be there and about what you really want to say."[3]

## Extemporaneous Presentations

An extemporaneous presentation is delivered from some note system. The notes can be as detailed as a formal outline presented on PowerPoint® slides, or as brief as a few words listed on an index card. Many, if not most, business presentations are extemporaneously delivered. Even when speakers are following an outline that is memorized, the presentation is defined as extemporaneous.

The idea behind extemporaneous speaking is that the words on the outline will trigger recollections of what the speaker wishes to say. When speakers glance at their notes, they will see the reminder, then speak about the subject indicated by the note.

A manager's presentation on departmental rules may be guided by a simple outline that reads as follows:

- Attendance
- Break times
- Chain of command
- Reward system

The speaker hopes that the word "Attendance" will trigger recollections of what to say about the attendance policy.

Unfortunately, as those readers who have used extemporaneous formats know, the trigger frequently does not function effectively. What emerges from the verbal gun is not always precisely what the speaker wished to utter. This phenomenon is discussed in more detail shortly. As we will see, there are advantages as well as disadvantages to using the extemporaneous approach.

## Manuscript Presentations

A manuscript talk is delivered word for word from a text that is prepared ahead of time. Manuscript presentations should not be read as one would read aloud from a novel, but delivered with rate and volume variation, emphases on appropriate words or phrases, pauses for establishing eye contact, and complementary body motion. The presentation Adrienne delivered, discussed in the opening to this chapter, is an example of a manuscript talk.

Manuscript presentations are either written by the speaker or ghost-written for the speaker by associates. People who work in corporate communications departments often write presentations that will be delivered by organizational executives. Lawrence Ragan Communications in Chicago is a consulting group. Among its various activities, which include publishing journals and newsletters pertaining to managerial communication, the company periodically trains corporate communication specialists on how to construct manuscript presentations for their organizational leaders.

When executives give their state-of-the-company addresses to stockholders, they typically deliver manuscript presentations. Most presidential addresses are manuscript talks. On occasions the text for manuscript presentations is distributed to audience members before the presentation is delivered.

A manuscript talk should not be read as one would read aloud a novel. A manuscript talk is *delivered* with appropriate eye contact, word emphasis, pauses, and complementary body motion.

## Ethical Probe

### Instant Analysis

It was common during the 1960s for newscasters to practice what was referred to as *Instant Analysis*. Immediately after a presidential address, news anchors would broadcast an evaluation of the message that had been completed literally seconds earlier. The anchors could comment instantly after the talk because the text of the address had been circulated to the media well before the televised speech. Therefore, the anchors and their staffs could scrutinize, digest, and dissect the message before the president had uttered a sound. As soon as the speech ended, they would detail their, often critical, assessment.

The practice of Instant Analysis was infuriating to many government officials, particularly those in the governing party.[4] Presidents, vice presidents, and their allies thought that before the public could consume and consider important messages, newscasters served up digested versions replete with contrary analysis.

On March 31, 1968, President Lyndon Johnson had copies of his soon-to-be-televised address distributed to news reporters. That evening, the newscasters were prepared to critique the address, which dealt in large part with the controversial Vietnam War. However, when Johnson finished the text the journalists had received, he continued on and announced—to everyone's surprise—that he would "neither seek nor accept" the nomination for president in 1968. Since everyone expected Johnson to be the Democratic candidate that year, these words from the president were astonishing.

The anchors' prepared, fluid instant analysis was now valueless. They had to revert to impromptu speaking to address the most newsworthy part of the president's address. What followed was a less than fluid bit of instant analysis.

Was this unethical? Should Johnson have informed the journalists that there would be an addition to the original transcript?

## Memorized Presentations

A memorized talk is a manuscript presentation that has been committed to memory. If a speaker has memorized the outline for an extemporaneous presentation and delivers the talk from that cerebral outline, the presentation is not considered memorized. For the format to be so classified, the talk would have to be memorized word for word and delivered word for word.

Some people think they can finesse their apprehension by memorizing the talk. This might work but is unlikely to be effective. Memorized presentations can be disastrous for at least two reasons. The most obvious potential problem is that the speaker might forget what words come next. The second problem is that memorized presentations are often delivered without appropriate vocal enthusiasm and can *sound* memorized and robotic. Beginning speakers often deliver memorized presentations as if gazing in the distance at words they have recorded, while spewing them mechanically without emotion. William Stedman in *A Guide to Public Speaking* effectively captures the plight of the speaker presenting from memory.

> *Few situations are more painful for speaker and audience than that in which the man or woman at the lectern stares with anguished eye at the roomful of uncomfortably squirming individuals who are hoping as strongly as the speaker that the lost words will come back before another second passes. This dreaded and inevitable blacking out occurs because speakers reciting from memory are not really thinking. They are only saying words. They are little more than a living breathing phonograph playing back the bit of sound that was put on the turntable sometime earlier. And because the thinking processes have been bypassed, they are as helpless as a short circuited phonograph when something goes wrong. In a manner of speaking, they too have been short circuited. They can't work their way out of the hold because on a reasoning level, they don't know what they have been talking about. All they can do is to put the mental needle back into the groove and try again.*[5]

### Reverse the Perspective

Which style of presentation is easier to follow?

Below are several types of speaking situations. From the vantage point of an audience member, which of the four styles is the best for each of these contexts? What is the reasoning that supports your decisions? As a listener, what additional tips would you give a speaker who chooses the style you have suggested?

- Sales presentation
- Class lecture
- Political campaign speech
- Training orientation
- Eulogy
- Product orientation (explanation of a company product)
- Project status report
- Sermon
- Motivational speech

There are instances when it is inevitable that a presentation will become a memorized talk. If a speaker delivers the same speech day after day in city after city, eventually the talk will become memorized. In those instances, as is the case when actresses and actors deliver their memorized lines, it is quite possible that the speaker can infuse the appropriate enthusiasm into the talk. However, unless a speaker has months to rehearse, it is risky to deliver the talk in a memorized format.

## Evaluating Extemporaneous and Manuscript Presentations

Manuscript and extemporaneous options are the two better choices for business presentations. As indicated previously, there are times when one may be compelled to deliver an impromptu talk, and in other situations it may be inevitable that a presentation becomes memorized. However, most professional speaking situations require either an extemporaneous or a manuscript format. In this section we will consider the advantages and disadvantages of each approach.

### Advantages of Extemporaneous Speaking

#### Eye Contact

If all other factors are equal, an extemporaneous presentation will allow for more eye contact than a manuscript talk. Extemporaneous presentations require that speakers only periodically glance at their notes. Manuscript presentations compel speakers to spend more time with the script because they are delivering the messages verbatim. Speakers can establish eye contact with manuscript presentations, but they are more likely to be prohibitively burdened by the need to deliver word for word.

There is, however, no guarantee that an extemporaneous talk *will* result in sustained and frequent eye contact. High apprehension levels can make speakers reluctant to look at an audience regardless of the format selected. Similarly, people who have not practiced, or who lack confidence in the integrity of their content, may avoid looking at listeners. Speakers who are simply untrained or indifferent also may not establish appropriate eye contact regardless of the style they use. Extemporaneous presentations have been addressed to floors, windows, screens, clocks, and clenched fists.

However, if all variables are held constant, extemporaneous speaking will afford more opportunities for eye contact than manuscript speaking. That is, if the extent of preparation, training, familiarity with content, and other variables are the same, speakers who use the extemporaneous approach will be able to more easily establish and maintain eye contact with their audiences. (In Chapter 11 we discuss techniques for improving eye contact and several other factors that affect delivery.)

#### Content Flexibility

The speaker has much more freedom in extemporaneous contexts than in manuscript ones. This flexibility allows the speaker to read nonverbal feedback from the audience and adapt to it with relative ease. If audience members appear confused, an extemporaneous speaker can review the point to clarify it. If audience members appear bored, an extemporaneous speaker can insert appropriate anecdotes, purge unnecessary content, and/or reassert that the content is relevant to listeners. Manuscript speakers are essentially wed to the text and cannot respond as easily to audience feedback.

### Informality

Some contexts require a degree of informality. Extemporaneous talks appear more natural than manuscript presentations and are far less rigid. If a speaker wants to establish a relaxed atmosphere, extemporaneous speaking is more likely to facilitate meeting that objective.

### Interactivity

In training and sales situations, the format you select must permit interactivity. Your instructors, for example, could not deliver manuscript talks because the classroom is intended to be an interactive environment. The extemporaneous format is conducive to asking questions, soliciting comments, and meaningful audience participation. Manuscript presentations are not so conducive and implicitly discourage speaker-audience interaction. (As discussed on page 102, discouraging speaker-audience interaction is sometimes desirable.)

### Movement

Extemporaneous formats do not require a speaker to stand behind the lectern. Speakers can move about, walk into the audience, or speak directly to an individual or small cluster of people. For some speakers, the advantage of mobility can be transformed into a disadvantage. Someone pacing predictably or moving about peculiarly can be distracting to audience members, who may focus on the counterproductive motions as opposed to the message. There is no doubt, however, that if speakers need to move about, they are better off using an extemporaneous format as long as they guard against the possibility of distracting motion.

### Perception of Confidence

Much of the success of public presentations is a function of the audience members' perception of the speaker. An excellently delivered extemporaneous talk can suggest to audience members that the speakers really know the material since, apparently, they do not need to have all the words in their messages written down in order to present what they know.[6]

## Advantages of Manuscript Speaking

### Precise Word Choice

Some business presentations are simply too important to risk employing the extemporaneous format. Extemporaneous talks require speakers to select words to match ideas while the pressure is on. Often the right words do not come to the speaker when the pressure is on. A manuscript presentation compels the speaker to consider the correct words beforehand and consequently reduces the chances for embarrassing errors. If journalists are listening to a talk and plan to report on the message to millions of readers, speakers will want to make sure they do not utter an inappropriate word that will find its way into headlines. For this reason, corporate and government speech writers labor over the exact words for every key point.

Melvin Grayson, former vice president for corporate affairs for Nabisco, made the following comments about the problems with extemporaneous presentations and the advantages of the manuscript format.

> *I have a horror of extemporaneous speeches, whether I'm speaker or "speakee." I don't like to listen to them, because they're invariably dull and studded with platitudes, not to mention "ers" and "ahs"...I don't like to give [extemporaneous]*

*speeches because of the fear that while groping for the right phrase, I may deliver the wrong phrase—some remark that will come back to haunt me... As corporate communicators, we sometimes forget—whether we're communicating orally or on paper—the immense significance of each word we use. Yet those words are our weapons: our only weapons... The right words strung together in the right way are what separate a good speech—an effective speech—from one that's a waste of everyone's time. Or worse.* [7]

Recently a job candidate for a managerial position was asked to prepare a short presentation that described his philosophy of management. The speaker delivered an extemporaneous address that emphasized his sense that the best managers were democratic and inclusive. The candidate pointed out that when he had worked as a manager in the late seventies, he had supervised several employees who had less than conventional ideas and lifestyles. The remark about lifestyles caused him to chuckle and digress as he described one such employee who lived in a commune. "He was, you know," the speaker said as he groped for the right word, "a, uh, um, a fruitcake." As soon as he had said *fruitcake* he knew he had used the wrong word. This sense was intensified when one of the arbiters attending the presentation remarked dryly that during the seventies he had been "one of those fruitcakes."

"Oh, I meant no disrespect," said the desperate candidate.

No amount of apologies can reverse the damage of using an inappropriate word. An advantage of using the manuscript format is that the chances of using an inappropriate word are reduced.

## Timing

Some business talks are designated for precise lengths of time. If speakers are allotted fifteen minutes to make the pitch, they do not want to find themselves at minute fourteen having progressed only to the middle of the message. Since the manuscript format allows for total preparation and fewer interruptions, one can time the talk precisely. When customers phone a theater and ask how long a play runs, the box office can reply with an exact—to the minute—response, even though the play has a live audience. Similarly in a manuscript talk one can precisely time the presentation. An extemporaneous presentation, because of adaptations and the greater likelihood of audience involvement, cannot be so precisely timed.

## Avoidance of Speech Fillers

Speakers who have problems with *ums, okays, you knows*, or *ers* can avoid the problem by delivering a manuscript presentation. One will never write *um, er, ah*, and *you know* into the manuscript, and therefore the talk will contain relatively few such fillers.

## Organization: Absence of Digressions and Omissions

Extemporaneous presentations can be flawed because speakers, before they are aware of it, may sail off on subjects that are only peripherally related to the topic. Manuscript talks eliminate this problem because digressions, one assumes, are purged during the editing stage of manuscript construction. Similarly, omissions are not a problem. Often speakers who plan their extemporaneous talks thoroughly are irked when they complete the presentation and realize that they left out a particular piece of information. Speakers are unlikely to omit anything in a manuscript talk, because they are delivering the message verbatim.

### Delivery

Although the case has been made that extemporaneous presentations are easier in terms of eye contact and vocal variation, manuscript speaking allows the speaker the opportunity to carefully plan when to use eye contact, emphasize key words, speed up, or slow down. Therefore, a case can be made that manuscript talks can be more efficient in terms of delivery.

### Ability to Convey an Uninterrupted Message

Manuscript speaking is more linear than extemporaneous talks. Speakers have a chance in a manuscript presentation to make an uninterrupted case. This advantage comes with the inherent disadvantage of not being able to reverse a message that a speaker thought would be effective, but that nonverbal feedback suggests is actually ineffective. Nevertheless, if speakers have identified the audience correctly, the manuscript message gives them the opportunity to speak without interference.

### Formality

In the same way that an extemporaneous talk may be appropriate if the situation requires informality, a manuscript talk may be appropriate if the situation requires formality. A sober discussion of ongoing labor negotiations may necessitate a carefully planned out formal address. An announcement expressing appreciation and sympathy after the death of a head of state, or a rival CEO, may require formality as well as precision.

### Ghostwriting

In business or political contexts, an advantage of a manuscript presentation is that the presenter does not have to actually construct the message. Someone in corporate communication can compose the address. This can save executives time, ensure that multiple people are involved in the constructing of the message, and allow for professionals' advice to be used as counsel.

### Consistency

If a company desires to deliver the same talk to each potential client, a manuscript talk guarantees that the same words will be spoken to each audience. Because communication is an audience-centered phenomenon, what is communicated will vary depending on the quality of delivery, the particular audience, and the presentation context, but the message that is disseminated, at least, will be the same. If organizations are concerned with the legal ramifications of a message, a manuscript talk will ensure that each representative delivering the message will not deviate from what has been approved by the company lawyers.

### Text delivery

Some occasions require that the text of a talk be available to listeners either before, during, or immediately after the talk. This is impossible to do if the presentation is extemporaneous, and simply accomplished when using a manuscript approach.

### Reduction of Apprehension

All things being equal, a very high communication apprehensive will be more comfortable with a manuscript. There are fewer things that can go wrong with the content. However, many, many things can still go wrong with the delivery. For example, a high apprehensive might decide after one fearful look at the audience to read the rest of the message at warp speed and eschew any and all eye contact. Still, all factors considered, a manuscript presentation affords the speaker a greater comfort level.

## Which Option Should a Speaker Select?

In some contexts, a speaker has no choice. One simply cannot deliver a manuscript presentation in a situation that requires interaction. It would be insulting to the audience and counterproductive. Trainers, teachers, and in many situations, salespeople, cannot deliver manuscript presentations because the style discourages the interaction that is essential.

Similarly, speakers simply cannot deliver an extemporaneous talk in situations that require precision. Leaders of nations must use the manuscript format when delivering a warning to a hostile invader. In such situations, all global players must hear a precise message. Heads of companies when speaking to stockholders must deliver a manuscript presentation lest an unintentional utterance cause stock prices to tumble.

To determine which approach to take, speakers need to think about the audience and speech goal. In the contexts that permit a choice, acknowledge the advantages and disadvantages of each option, and then select the option that is best for the audience, the presentation objectives, and your comfort level—in that order. See Table 6-1.

As you consider the advantages and disadvantages of speaking styles for your own presentations, you may find the following to be valuable.

Graduate students who enrolled in a course called Business and Professional Speaking were required to deliver three presentations during a ten-week academic quarter. Each talk was videotaped, and students evaluated their presentations on the basis of other student critiques and their own analysis. The first presentation was required to be manuscript. The second one was extemporaneous. The third and final presentation, which carried the greatest weight for the course grade, could be delivered in any style the speaker chose.

Before the first presentation, students were asked to identify the speaking style they believed was most advantageous. Nearly all answered that the better approach is extemporaneous. When the third round of presentations began—when students could select either style for what amounted to the final exam—nearly all opted for the manuscript format.

This phenomenon has recurred for at least ten sections of the course. The reversal of preference is typically discussed at the end of the quarter. Two student comments recur. Students remark that they are surprised to discover that manuscript presentations can be delivered with appropriate eye contact, vocal variation, and enthusiasm. The second recurring comment pertains to the consequences of the presentations. Students claim that they prefer the manuscript format for the final because the final presentation counts more. They say they feel more secure using the manuscript because more is on the line.

In sum, speakers need to be concerned with the style of delivery. There are advantages and disadvantages to extemporaneous and manuscript approaches, and each individual speaker should assess the situation, their audience, and their own strengths and weaknesses when choosing the most appropriate option.

A former graduate student informed me at the beginning of a class that she absolutely refused to deliver anything other than a manuscript speech. She was adamant that her experience with extemporaneous speaking had been disastrous. As far as I am aware, this former student is still delivering manuscript talks even in the most informal situations. This cannot be helpful with career advancement. Similarly, delivering an extemporaneous talk when the situation necessitates a manuscript presentation cannot enhance one's chances for organizational success.

## Speaking Styles: Comparative Advantages — Table 6-1

| Advantages of Extemporaneous Approaches | Advantages of Manuscript Approaches |
|---|---|
| Flexibility and mobility | Total preparation |
| Informality and interactivity | Precision with word choice |
| Allows for audience adaptation and feedback-induced responses | Easier to time |
| Potential for fluid utilization of visual support | Can be delivered by nonexperts |
| Relatively easy to maintain eye contact | Avoids digressions and omissions |
| Reduces chances of monotonous reading | Avoids use of speech fillers |
| Less time required for construction | Can be available for distribution concurrently |

## Stand Up & Deliver

This exercise requires preparing **two** three-minute presentations—one manuscript and the other extemporaneous. Assume the audience is your class.

Below are two similar statements. With which do you agree?

- Extemporaneous speaking is better than manuscript speaking for the presentations I am required to deliver and those I anticipate being required to deliver.
- Manuscript speaking is better than extemporaneous speaking for the presentations I am required to deliver and those I anticipate being required to deliver.

1. Develop a three-minute *extemporaneous* presentation that explains why you selected one statement and not the other, and
2. Develop a three-minute *manuscript* presentation that explains why you selected one statement and not the other.

## Summary

Speakers can employ one of four speech formats when they deliver presentations.

- Manuscript
- Extemporaneous
- Impromptu
- Memorized

- Impromptu and memorized formats may have to be employed, but are risky and should be avoided.
- Extemporaneous presentations have the following advantages:
    - Eye contact
    - Flexibility—Feedback-induced response
    - Informality
    - Interactivity
    - Movement
    - Perception of confidence
- Manuscript presentations have the following advantages:
    - Precision with word choice
    - Timing
    - Avoidance of speech fillers/omissions and digressions
    - Delivery
    - Uninterrupted speaking
    - Formality
    - Ghostwriting
    - Consistency
    - Text delivery
    - Reduction of apprehension
- Speakers should decide which option to use based on the following:
    - Audience needs
    - Presentation objectives
    - Presentation context
    - Speaker comfort level

## Sample Presentation for Analysis

### The Last Best Hope: Words

The Last Best Hope: Words *was delivered by Melvin Grayson on April 3, 1980 when Mr. Grayson was the Director of Public Relations at Nabisco, Inc. The presentation was delivered in New York City to the Society of Consumer Affairs Professionals in Business. As you read through this excerpt please consider the following questions*

1. *Mr. Grayson argues that presentations should be delivered using a manuscript style of speaking. Do you agree with his argument? Why or why not?*
2. *Does the speaker use words effectively to make his point? What words would you change if you were writing or delivering this presentation?*
3. *If you were a member of the audience would you be insulted by any of the comments made by the speaker? Explain.*

When Woody Wirsig invited me to speak here today, he showed me a printed progam and I saw that the speaker originally scheduled for this luncheon was J. Robert Moskin and the title for his talk was to be "Where World Forces Are Heading."

Well I know Bob Moskin. He was foreign editor of *Look* magazine when I was promotion director there. We have a bond between us—the kind of bond you might have found 50 years ago among former passengers of the Titanic.

I felt bad about having you miss that talk of his. It sounded important. WHERE—WORLD—FORCES—ARE—HEADING—so I tried to come up with a brief summary. I recalled the many conversations about world affairs Bob and I used to have, and I tossed in my own experiences and assessments, so now if anyone in this audience wants to ask, "Where are world forces heading? I have the answer. The answer is—"I don't know."

So much for Bob's talk. The title of *my* talk is "The Last Best Hope." It isn't as awesome as Bob's title, but it has a nice ominous ring to it....

...What I'd like to do today is touch briefly on what I think is wrong with the way we communicate and then offer suggestions on possible remedies.

Perhaps a good way to begin would be to point out, for those who haven't noticed, that I'm reading this speech. I read all my speeches, and counsel my colleagues at Nabisco to do likewise.

I read my speeches because if I didn't I'd have to memorize them or ad lib them and neither alternative is a viable one. If I could memorize speeches I'd have been an actor instead of a writer and avoid all this heavy thinking. And if I were to wing it, the few decent thoughts I have would be washed away on a wave of approximations and irrelevancies.

I have a horror of extemporaneous speeches, whether I'm speaker or speakee. I don't like to listen to them because they're invariably dull and studded with platitudes not to mention "ers" and "ahs"...

...I don't like to give ad lib speeches because of the fear that while groping for the right phrase I may deliver the wrong phrase—some remark that will come back to haunt me.

History abounds with examples of what might be called foot in mouth disease, brought on by off the cuff speaking. Among recent ones were George Romney's brainwashing confession, Jimmy Carter's "lusting in his heart" comment, Ed Muskie's tearful defense of his wife, Spiro Agnew's "fat Jap" episode and Richard Nixon's five years with a tape recorder.

But the most cogent reason for reading speeches—and this is the crux of all this—is that only by reading them can we be sure of using the right words, the words we've had a chance to select and orchestrate and polish to perfection. Or at least what we fondly hope is perfection.

According to the Oxford English dictionary there are more than a half million words in our language and no two of them mean precisely the same thing. The right words strung together in the right way are what separate a good speech—an effective speech—from one that's a waste of everyone's time. Or worse.

As corporate communicators we sometimes forget, whether we're communicating orally or on paper, the immense significance of each word we use. Yet those words are our weapons—our only weapons...

...Even the smallest word of all—the indefinite article "a"—can play a key part in conveying information. After Neil Armstrong landed on the moon and uttered the statement he must have rehearsed for weeks—"That's one small step for a man. One giant leap for mankind"—he was horrified to hear it misquoted by everybody from the man in the street to network newscasters. People kept saying, "That's one small step for man, one giant leap for mankind. Americans with no ear for the language and no regard of an astronaut's feelings had left out the "a" and converted a decently turned phrase into semantic garbage...

...Yet as important as words are, we use—and misuse—them as though they're of no real concern. We do this even when we're dealing with issues that can produce profits or losses for our companies amounting to many millions of dollars.

Part of the problem is laziness. We just don't want to work that hard. Part is ignorance. We just don't know that much....

...Most Americans not only lack the inspired prose that moved mankind in the past—prose that changed the world, but are deficient in the fundamentals of the language. We can't spell or punctuate or find the right words or put them together in a cohesive manner. And when I say "we" I include those of us involved in the highest echelons of industrial communications.

Two weeks ago, a friend of mine got this letter from one of the nation's biggest banks.

"Dear Sir: Our records indicate that you have recently used your new Visa charge card. We certainly hope you will continue to enjoy the convenient use of your credit card. If you have not used your credit card, call me immediately."

My friend became so preoccupied trying to figure out what they were trying to tell him that for the next three days, he had no time to use his new credit card...

...All of us in this room are affected. It's our job to explain by means of the English language, our companies' policies to the public, and to convey also in English, the public mood to our management. Are we doing the job? I'd like to think so, but I have to wonder whenever I see an opinion poll showing that 50 or 60 or 70 per cent of all Americans regard Big Business as the enemy and that many of them favor government takeovers of key industries.

We sometimes complain that management doesn't give us the tools we need. But there's a reason for that. We're as derelict in presenting our case to management as we are in presenting management's case to the public. We don't use the right words, and as a consequence we fail to persuade....

**Source:** Grayson, Melvin J. "The Last Best Hope, Words," *Vital Speeches of the Day*, July 15, 1981, 47: 585.

## Review Questions

1. What situations require extemporaneous speaking?
2. What situations require manuscript speaking?
3. When would a businessperson be compelled to deliver an impromptu talk?
4. What are two disadvantages of using the memorized style?
5. What are three advantages of the extemporaneous format?
6. What are three advantages of the manuscript format?

## InfoTrac Question

Use InfoTrac to find the article entitled "Make an Impact with Style." What recommendations does the author make? Find a second InfoTrac article published September 15, 2003, pertaining to the speech patterns of Howard Dean. What is the relevance of this short piece to this chapter?

---

[1] Benjamin Disraeli served as prime minister of England in 1868 and from 1874 to 1880. He also served in the House of Commons. As a politician, he—like all politicians—was required to deliver impromptu presentations on occasion.

[2] Identified as a Chinese proverb in the *Columbia World of Quotations* (New York: Columbia UP, 1996), CD-ROM.

[3] Don Keough quoted in Sandy Linver, *Speak and Get Results* (New York: Fireside, 1994), 13.

[4] See Spiro Theodore Agnew, "Television News Coverage" in *American Rhetoric From Roosevelt to Reagan*, Halford Ross Ryan. (Prospect Heights, Illnois: Waveland Press, 1987), 212–219. "Television News Coverage," delivered on November 13, 1969, is one of a series of presentations Vice President Agnew delivered on the overall topic of the "irresponsible" news media. The reference to the effects of Johnson's disclosure on March 31, 1968, appears on pages 212–213.

[5] William Stedman, *A Guide to Public Speaking* (Englewood Cliffs, NJ: Prentice Hall, 1971), 107.

[6] See the discussion in Albert J. Vasile, *Speak with Confidence*. Boston, 9th ed. (New York: Allyn and Bacon, 2004), 198. Also, see Raymond Zeuschner, *Communicating Today: The Essentials* (Boston: 2003 Allyn and Bacon, 2003), 230. Zueschner comments that "in virtually every situation, audiences prefer extemporaneous speeches, and they rate the speakers who give such speeches very highly." I would qualify this statement by adding the modifier *quality* before the word *extemporaneous*. MBA students and undergraduates regularly comment that they consider speakers who deliver extemporaneously more credible and more knowledgeable than those who speak from a manuscript, as long as the extemporaneous speaker delivers the message effectively. A poorly delivered extemporaneous presentation is not typically rated highly.

[7] Melvin Grayson, "The Last Best Hope: Words," *Vital Speeches of the Day* 47, (July 15, 1981): 585.

**Chapter in a Nutshell** *Presentations require organization. Following a basic method for structuring the message increases the probability of presentation success.*

# Structuring the Message

*Good words by the third time will even bore the dogs.*[1]

-Chinese Proverbs

*[President Lincoln had the] ability to express his convictions so clearly, and with such force that millions of his countrymen made them their own.*[2]

*-Paul Angle*


## Abstract

Often presentations are poorly organized. You have probably listened to many that were difficult to understand simply because there did not appear to be a logical order to what was being said. Businesspeople often comment that presentations they hear include multiple digressions, lack meaningful transitions, and have no discernible objective. One of the easiest things speakers can do to enhance performance is structure their talks intelligently. This chapter discusses how to organize presentations to increase the chances for success. Specifically, at the conclusion of the chapter you should be able to do the following:

- Identify the three essential parts of any presentation
- List what must be present in the introduction to a business talk
- Explain the concept of speaker ethos
- List techniques for hooking or engaging the audience
- Discuss the advantages and disadvantages of several patterns for organizing presentation content
- Explain approaches for concluding presentations

## "Do you ever wonder where your money goes?"

Fifteen graduate students were in the fourth week of a professional speaking course they had enrolled in voluntarily. The assignment for the evening was to prepare a presentation on a work-related theme. The third speaker began her talk by asking her classmates a simple question: "Do you ever wonder where your money goes?"

She, as well as the others scheduled, had a difficult task. The course met from 5:30 p.m. to 7:30 p.m. on Mondays. Listening to talks for two hours can be trying under any circumstance, but it is even more demanding when one is fatigued and hungry. In addition, the presentation topics were not inherently interesting to the listeners. Although each talk would have a professional theme, none of the subjects was likely to be directly related to the listeners' particular jobs. The third speaker followed presentations pertaining to pesticide regulations and the tribulations of franchising a tuxedo-rental business.

Immediately after her initial inquiry, the speaker told the group that she was a banker and had worked in various capacities in her seven years of banking experience. She commented that as an undergraduate she had not given much thought to what happened when she cashed a check. However, once she became a banker, she realized that the life of a check involves a complicated and intriguing odyssey. Once you write a check, she explained, more players have "their hands on your money" than listeners may have realized.

She had hooked the audience. The speaker then took the assembled students through "a day in the life of a check." Using a premade chart, she described each stage of the journey and then discussed common misconceptions related to the handling of "your money." She finished by recapping the salient points of her talk and then said she hoped she had both captured and explained "your interest."

The pun aside, the speaker had in fact captured the interest of the audience. She was peppered with questions during the question-and-answer period, which suggested that she had created an intrigued audience. The written student evaluations were atypically effusive with complimentary remarks. "This clears things up" and "Surprisingly interesting" were recurring comments.

By intelligently structuring her talk, the speaker had engaged, informed, and captivated a very difficult audience.

- The speaker employed a question to engage the audience. What other methods could she have used to intrigue audience members?
- When you have listened to multiple presentations in the same class, what makes one presentation stand out over another?
- What made this presentation successful?

## INTRODUCTION: LEAVING PORT

> "*[H]e who runs his ship ashore while leaving port is certainly the least efficient of pilots.*"[3]
>
> Quintilian

An old maxim about presentations is that a speaker has three obligations when addressing an audience:

- Tell them what you'll tell them
- Tell them
- Tell them what you've told them

In essence, this maxim describes how to structure a business presentation. The speakers describe the agenda in the *introduction* to the talk. Speakers proceed to do what they said they would do in the *body* of the talk. The presentation ends with a recapitulation of the key points in the *conclusion*.

In the next section the scope of each of these structural components is discussed. It may be valuable to keep in mind how many times you have heard presentations that were poorly structured and consequently difficult to understand because they seemed directionless. Following a basic format is a relatively easy way to improve your efficiency as a speaker. Compared with many disorganized speakers, those who present their messages in a structured manner stand out as effective as well as responsible.

The introduction to your talk should include three elements:

I. The presentation objective/s
II. A persuasive hook
III. A verbal or nonverbal reference to your ethos

### I. The Objective

The first words out of a speaker's mouth need not be a statement of objective, but sometime during the course of the introduction, the speaker must clearly articulate the goal. In the introduction to a talk, the speakers are, fundamentally, establishing an agreement with the audience. Implicitly or explicitly, the speakers are promising that listeners can expect to hear about certain subjects. At the conclusion of the talk the audience can evaluate the speakers on the basis of whether the speakers did what they said would be done.

In business contexts, the more specific presenters can be when articulating the objective, the better they will fare. One could say, "The goal of my talk is to describe the status of our project." However, speakers would be more helpful to both themselves and their audiences if they were to detail the facets of the description. For example, "There are four objectives of today's presentation. They are to describe the project status in terms of: what has already been completed; what will be accomplished in the next two months; when we anticipate the final project being finished; and how the completed project will be consistent with what was originally conceived."

There are at least two advantages to being so specific. One is that specificity clearly frames the talk for the audience. Listeners will know precisely what to expect and can be ready to receive each separate part of the presentation. In addition, by clearly articulating each objective when they construct and deliver the message, speakers' presentation goals become more definite within their own minds.

## II. The Hook

Some people attend business presentations because they are hungry for the information they expect to hear at the session. However, this is frequently not the case. Audience members may come to a session because they are obliged to. You may have occasionally attended presentations because a colleague, friend, or family member dragged you there. People go to talks for various reasons even when they are inherently disinterested or even uninterested in the topic. Speakers, therefore, must persuade the audience to pay attention to their message and "hook" or engage them so they will be attentive.

There are a number of methods that can be used to persuade the audience to focus on the talk.

### Establishing Need

An efficient way to hook the audience is to explain why the message will be valuable to them and how the it will affect them.

You probably have observed attention levels spike in your classes when an instructor comments that a particular topic will be on an exam. Similarly, if speakers in business contexts can describe how the message content will directly affect the listeners—and can do so credibly—they are likely to engage the audience. For example,

> *Today, as you are aware, John and I will be updating you on the status of our drive to secure grants for the organization. What we are doing in Development may seem irrelevant to you, but the money we obtain from this campaign is earmarked for in-house improvements. How much we accrue via contributions and gifts will affect you directly, because you will receive a portion of these funds. Therefore, any help we can get from you regarding the initiatives described today will actually be beneficial to you as well as to us.*

### Asking Questions

Speakers often attempt to engage the audience by posing a question. These questions may be asked to stimulate discussion and thereby involve the audience. Some introductory questions are not posed to encourage participation, but rather to intrigue the audience and create a foundation for the rest of the talk. The successful presentation described in the beginning of this chapter began with such an inquiry.

Using questions to hook the audience can be risky. Participants may not respond to the inquiry or may not respond as speakers anticipate they will. If no one reacts to a question intended to stimulate discussion, a beginning speaker may become apprehensive. Similarly, if audience members respond to questions in unanticipated ways, novice speakers can be thrown off course.

There are ways to deal with either scenario. If no person responds to a question, a speaker can rephrase it and see if the new version stimulates a response. If repetitions are not successful, pausing for a few seconds often yields a responsive comment. If pausing does not work, the speaker can simply ask a particular audience member to respond to the inquiry. The ease with which one can react to the nonresponsive audience depends on individual speaker experience and equanimity.

The situation is somewhat different when respondents react to questions with unanticipated comments. Assume that the goal is not only to involve the audience but to construct a platform upon which the talk will be launched. For example, if a team of speakers intends to discuss and peddle an air purifier, they may think it is wise to begin by asking, "How many of you would like to breathe clean as opposed to toxic air?" A reasonable person would assume that all listeners prefer clean air. However, not all listeners will necessarily respond as expected. One could ask a group of twenty, "How many of you are breathing?" and not witness a uniform response. If the next planned statement was "Since everyone wants to breathe clean air—" beginning speakers may become flustered by the implausible reaction to the inquiry. The prepared speaker anticipates unlikely responses to queries and is prepared to react to possible, if unlikely, comments.

A way to avoid this scenario entirely and still use a question to engage the audience is to ask and answer the question yourself. For example,

*If I were to ask how many of you would prefer to breathe clean as opposed to toxic air, I'm sure your response would reflect a unanimous and overwhelming desire to be free of toxins. Therefore, what I have to talk with you about today should be of interest. All of us are inhaling toxins daily, but our company is marketing a product that will make it possible for you to filter the toxins from the air that you are regularly ingesting.*

### Using a Startling Statement

An unusual statistic or astonishing comment can engage receivers. For example,

*Fifty percent of those in the workplace are functionally illiterate. It is essential that we examine the communication skills of our employees and make sure they are adequately trained.*

The claim that 50 percent of the workplace is illiterate may be astounding enough to hook receivers. The caveats with using this approach relate to being sure that the claim is accurate and also that the claim is related to the rest of the talk. A speaker may engage the audience by claiming that 50 percent of the workforce is illiterate, but if the object of the talk is to discuss something peripheral to illiteracy, the long-term effect of using the ploy will be to disengage the audience and erode speaker credibility.

### Using Quotations

*Financial guru Peter Lynch made millions for his clients as he masterfully managed Fidelity's Magellan Fund. Lynch knew something about the value of risk. 'There was no success' he commented, 'when there was no risk.' I'm here to speak to you today about taking an educated risk—one that will not threaten our jobs or health or even salary, but one that deviates from the status quo, and will yield success.*

A quotation from a respected source can engage an audience. A speaker who is considering this approach should also consider this following related point: The power of the quotation depends on the source of the quote as well as the relevance of the message. The source must be credible. Using a quote from someone with a tarnished reputation may reduce the respect audience members have for the speaker.

## Graphics

An attractive graphic, map, or architect's rendering may be intriguing to the audience. If a speaker intends to discuss plans for new construction, a picture of the plan can encourage attention from an otherwise indifferent audience. (See Figure 7-1.)

## Vocal Enthusiasm

Speakers can be engaging simply because they sound as if they will be interesting to listen to. This becomes evident when audience members are watching a series of speakers and an energetic presenter follows someone who has spoken less enthusiastically. Regardless of whom you follow, how you sound can make an audience want to listen, or not listen.

## References

Speakers may have success referring to the occasion, location, or previous speakers.

> *For example, "Moments ago you heard Jane speak about the necessity of keeping our facility accessible to those with disabilities. What I have to say relates to Jane's perspective, because I will be discussing a state-of-the-art accessible parking facility."*

## Challenge

Consider challenging the group. *For example, "I am speaking to encourage everyone here who doesn't like to settle for second best to consider this proposal. We want to be in the vanguard, and this proposal will put us front and center in the public eye."*

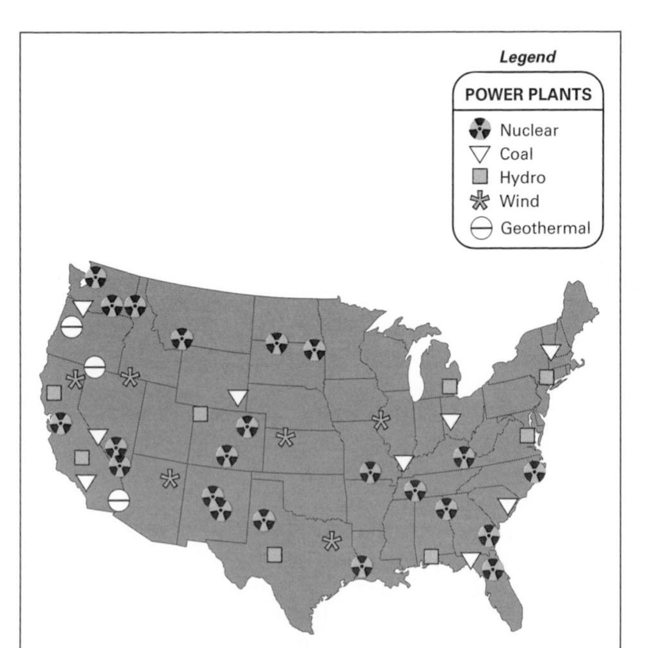


**Figure 7-1** An attractive graphic, map, or architect's rendering may be intriguing to the audience.

## Using Humor

In some situations, an anecdote or joke can be refreshing and engage the audience. However, including humor or stories can be very risky. There are three things to consider regarding the use of humor.

The first is that the story or joke must be appropriate to the situation. Some presentation contexts are somber, and the use of even very funny jokes—that would in other venues be considered hilarious—are inappropriate.

Second, the humor must be somehow connected to the topic at hand. The theme of the anecdote should relate to why you are addressing the group.

Third, speakers intending to use humor as a method for engaging an audience should test the story to make sure it is funny to others besides themselves. Speakers do not want to begin a talk with a tale that they expect will be met with guffaws and instead see perplexed faces when they deliver the punch line.

## Ethical Probe

### The Expense of Humor

Is there anything unethical about using humor that audience members will consider funny if the nature of the joke is disparaging to a particular group of persons not present in the audience?

For example, assume a speaker opposes same-sex marriage. Assume that this speaker is attempting to persuade an audience of college students that same-sex marriage should remain illegal. Further assume that the speaker predicts that the vast majority of students are heterosexual and likely not to be sensitive to issues that homosexuals face. Is it unethical to begin the presentation by telling a joke that one would not relay in an audience with a large gay population? For this exercise do not consider the practical implications of telling the joke—for example, students may react negatively and the speaker may not be as persuasive. Consider the question from an ethical perspective. If the speaker *will* likely satisfy the goal of engaging the audience with the joke, is there anything unethical about using it?

# III. Speaker Ethos

*Ethos* refers to the status that receivers attribute to a speaker. As we discussed in Chapter 3, ethos is a crucial presentation variable. It has been referred to as a "dominant factor in rhetorical communication."[4] We know that audience members are more likely to listen to, and be influenced by, speakers with high ethos.[5] Establishing speaker ethos is an important aspect of presentation introductions.

There are three types of ethos: initial, intermediate, and terminal ethos.

## Initial Ethos

**Initial ethos** refers to the status attributed to speakers before they utter a word. Initial ethos is a function of several factors.

**Reputation.** What the receivers know about the speaker affects the speaker's initial ethos. Someone who is introduced as an expert, or who has earned an untarnished reputation, will be attributed higher ethos than a virtual unknown.

**Dress and physical attractiveness.** People judge others by what they wear and how they look. Several studies reported by McCroskey support the assumption that physical appearance affects a speaker's initial ethos.[6] This may be unfortunate, but it is nonetheless the case. One cannot always be certain whether professional attire is essential for a business talk, but how one is dressed does affect the perceptions of audience members.[7] Damon Runyan, the novelist who inspired the Broadway musical *Guys and Dolls*, commented, "It may be that the race is not always to the swift, nor the battle to the strong—but that is the way to bet."[8] It is quite possible that some environments will consider formal attire as inappropriate reflecting an undesirable stuffiness, but unless the audience analysis has drawn this conclusion, dressing professionally and conservatively in business contexts is the way to bet.[9]

**Posture.** Nonverbal behaviors that typically reflect discomfort or disinterest are likely to have a negative effect on initial ethos. Speakers who lean over the lectern awaiting a signal to begin are not elevating their initial ethos.

**Apparent preparation.** Speakers may increase initial ethos by appearing to be prepared. You may have noticed speakers who are awaiting a signal to begin their talks. Some seem orderly and ready. Others seem confused and disorganized. If speakers appear prepared, their initial ethos is likely to be higher than that of those who appear scattered. Other related factors reflecting preparation include the quality of handouts distributed, folders and other materials placed at audience members' desks, and the quality of graphics projected before the presentation begins. All of these can affect a speaker's initial ethos.

## Intermediate (Derived) Ethos

*The audience sizes you up quickly, from several factors; your depth of knowledge, the experiences you speak from, the love you have for your area of expertise.*[10]

**Intermediate** or **derived ethos** refers to audience perceptions of the speaker during the course of the presentation. It is essentially the speaker's personal stock price that fluctuates during the talk. Intermediate ethos is based on the following factors.

**Content of the message.** If a speaker makes a comment that is factually inaccurate, intermediate ethos is likely to decrease. Similarly, if the content makes sense or if word choice is particularly appropriate, intermediate ethos is likely to increase. It is for this reason that even subject matter experts on a particular topic should not deliver impromptu presentations. The perception of their expertise may be undermined by gaffes that could be construed as a reflection of ignorance.

**Quality of delivery.** *How* speakers say what they say affects the perceptions audience members have of them. A smooth delivery increases intermediate ethos. Disorganized, poorly worded messages pervaded with speech fillers decrease intermediate ethos. Mispronouncing common words affects intermediate ethos, as does the level of vocal enthusiasm.

**Ability of the speaker to establish rapport with the audience.** In August 2003, then presidential aspirant Senator John Kerry spoke at a forum sponsored by the Sheet Metal Workers International Association. Kerry was able to increase his ethos when he told the audience, "[President Bush] is so quick to give speeches about the heroes of New York City. Well, I look forward to reminding him that every single one of those heroes that went up those stairs and gave their lives so that someone else might live was a member of organized labor." [11]

Speakers can enhance their ethos by establishing rapport with their audience and can erode ethos by being unable to establish such rapport. If a group is sensitive to comments about organized labor, it is wise to be aware of those attitudes and speak to their concerns.

Speakers need to analyze the audience in terms of its demographics and psychographics to plan the presentation. In Chapter 5 particularly, but throughout the book, the importance of studying the audience is emphasized. This analysis will not only help speakers tailor the message, but also—as it relates to this section—help elevate intermediate ethos.

## Terminal Ethos

The final type of ethos is called **terminal ethos**. This refers to the perception attributed to a speaker at the conclusion of the talk. Terminal ethos is especially important to anyone who will be returning to speak to the same audience. Terminal ethos will directly affect the speaker's initial ethos in subsequent presentations.

In the introduction to the presentation, speakers should do what they can—in terms of delivery and message content—to enhance the likelihood of being attributed high ethos. Appropriate dress, content accuracy, high-quality delivery, attractive visuals, understanding the audience—all of these factors affect your ethos and contribute to an introduction that will engage rather than disengage your audience.

### Reverse the Perspective

In the preceding pages several points have been made about the introduction to a presentation.

From your vantage point as an audience member either in school, community, or business situations, which of the following affect your initial reaction to speakers and their messages?

- Handouts distributed beforehand
- Graphics displayed on the screen before the presentation begins
- Materials placed at my seat before I arrive
- Clear explanation of presentation goals
- Explanation of why the talk is important to me
- Fluid delivery
- Vocal energy
- What the speakers say about their personal experiences
- Attempts to get the audience involved
- Physical appearance of speakers in terms of attire, attractiveness, and posture
- Sense of humor

## Body of the Presentation

In the body of a business presentation, speakers simply do what they have set out to do. In the introduction, speakers describe what they intend to discuss. In the body of the talk the speaker fulfills the promise.

One can employ a number of methods to structure the body of a presentation. Below is a description of four such approaches: topical, chronological, spatial, and advantages/disadvantages. As you will see, two recurring examples are used to illustrate each approach.

### Topical Format

The topical approach is an easy and effective way to organize presentation content. It involves dividing the talk into subtopics and addressing each subtopic in turn.

For example, a presentation discussing automobile sales trends in the United States might describe production costs, sales history, current economic conditions, influence from global competitors, and percentage increases by quarter.

A presentation about a new computing product could be organized as follows:

- Product applications
- Competitor products
- Cost to consumer
- Financial benefits of launching new product

## Chronological

If the talk involves discussing the evolution of an organization or product, the chronological approach will be effective. The speaker simply structures the presentation in chronological order.

For example, a presentation on automobile sales trends might begin with a discussion of sales from the first year, and proceed to describe profits in each of the last five ten-year periods.

Using the chronological approach, a presentation about a computing product could be organized as follows:

- Conception of product
- Market research
- Production of prototype
- Preliminary sampling
- Initial reviews
- Timeline for launch
- Evaluation period
- Stages of evaluation

## Spatial Approach

The spatial approach separates sections on the basis of the physical qualities of the subject. A spatial pattern used to describe the sales trends might first describe the Northeast, then sales in the Mid-Atlantic states, and then profits in other regions of the country.

The spatial approach as applied to the computer product could be structured as follows:

- Keyboard function
- Tower design
- Monitor specifications

## Advantages/Disadvantages

As the label suggests, this approach organizes content on the basis of the positive and negative aspects of the message.

The advantages/disadvantages approach for the presentation on automobile sales would include the encouraging news about the current sales picture and then identify the problems.

A presentation on a new computing product could be structured as follows:

- **Increased functionality** +
- Additional training needs –
- **Competitive differential** +
- Strain on overworked sales force –
- **Income opportunity** +
- Financial risks in present economy –

Various organizational patterns may be effective for any one presentation topic.

Consider using the topical approach as the default organizational pattern. In professional presentations topical approaches are nearly always appropriate. Table 7-1 summarizes the discussion of organizational patterns.

## Types of Organizational Patterns — *Table 7-1*

| Type of Pattern | Description | Example of Outline (using computer product as example) |
|---|---|---|
| Topical | Easy and effective. Approach involves dividing the talk into subtopics and addressing each topic in turn. | • Product applications<br>• Need for applications<br>• Competitor products<br>• Cost to consumer<br>• Financial benefits of launching new product |
| Chronological | Discusses the subject in terms of its evolution. | • Conception of product<br>• Market research<br>• Production of prototype<br>• Preliminary sampling<br>• Initial reviews<br>• Timeline for launch<br>• Evaluation period<br>• Stages of evaluation |
| Spatial | Divides the topic physically in terms of properties or space. | • Keyboard function<br>• Tower design<br>• Monitor specifications |
| Advantages/ Disadvantages | Describes the subject in terms of assets and problems. | Advantages:<br>• Increased functionality<br>• Competitive differential<br>• Income opportunity<br>Disadvantages:<br>• Additional training needs<br>• Strain on overworked sales force<br>• Financial risks in present economy |

## Transitioning Within the Presentation

An often overlooked issue pertains to the need for transitional statements that link sections in the body of the talk. When speakers do not consider the need for these transitions, segments of a talk can appear unrelated, and the presentation as a whole may seem disjointed. Those who do not think about transitioning *before* they speak often use transitional phrases *when* they speak that are repetitive or inappropriate. For example, one may say, "And another thing" several times during the talk to move from one topic to another. After many repetitions, hearing "And another thing" can become irritating to listeners.

It is not difficult to create transitional statements. It is just a matter of dedicating some preparatory time to the process. Speakers should consider how a previous section is related to a subsequent one and construct a statement that links the two. Below are some examples of basic yet effective transitions.

*On the basis of the extensive market research just discussed, we developed a prototype for the product that will meet the market's needs. Let me discuss the specific nature of that product.*

*As indicated, the costs to the consumer are reasonable and competitive. What makes this product so attractive is that despite this reasonable pricing, the prospects of profitability for our company are simply outstanding. Here are some figures pertaining to the expected profit margin for this new product.*

*Moving on to the Middle Atlantic states we can see that the sales record there is just as strong as it is in the Northeast. We find in Maryland, for example...*

The problem of inadequate transitioning can become particularly glaring when presentations are made in teams. Team presentations and transitions within team presentations are discussed in detail in Chapter 9.

## The Conclusion to the Presentation

The conclusion to the talk is crucial. At the end of a presentation speakers should provide a sense of closure for the audience. Too many important messages end with speakers scanning notes and then looking up to say, "Well, that's about it. Do you have any questions?"

"That's about it" is not an appropriate way to conclude a talk. When speakers say this, it seems as if they have not planned well enough to realize that they have arrived at the end. This apparent lack of preparation is likely to affect the speaker's terminal ethos.

Below are four methods that can be used to effectively conclude presentations. Combinations of these approaches can work as well.

### Summary

A summary of the main points of a business presentation is essential. It is a good idea to complement this recap with visual support. (See Figure 7-2.)

*During the course of our presentation, we have discussed the attributes of our new product, how it compares with competitive products, and why it is in our best interests to invest in its development. We'll be pleased to take any questions you may have at this time.*

## Challenge

The challenge method can also be effective. When this approach is used, one completes the talk by urging the audience to consider the merit of the proposal.

For example:

*We may want to continue to market what we have successfully been marketing. However, there is a risk in maintaining the status quo. Our company has been in the vanguard since its inception, and we want to ensure that we will be—and will be perceived to be—on the cutting edge of any new technology. I urge you to consider this new product, consider where we want to be in the marketplace, and acknowledge the value of staying ahead of the curve.*

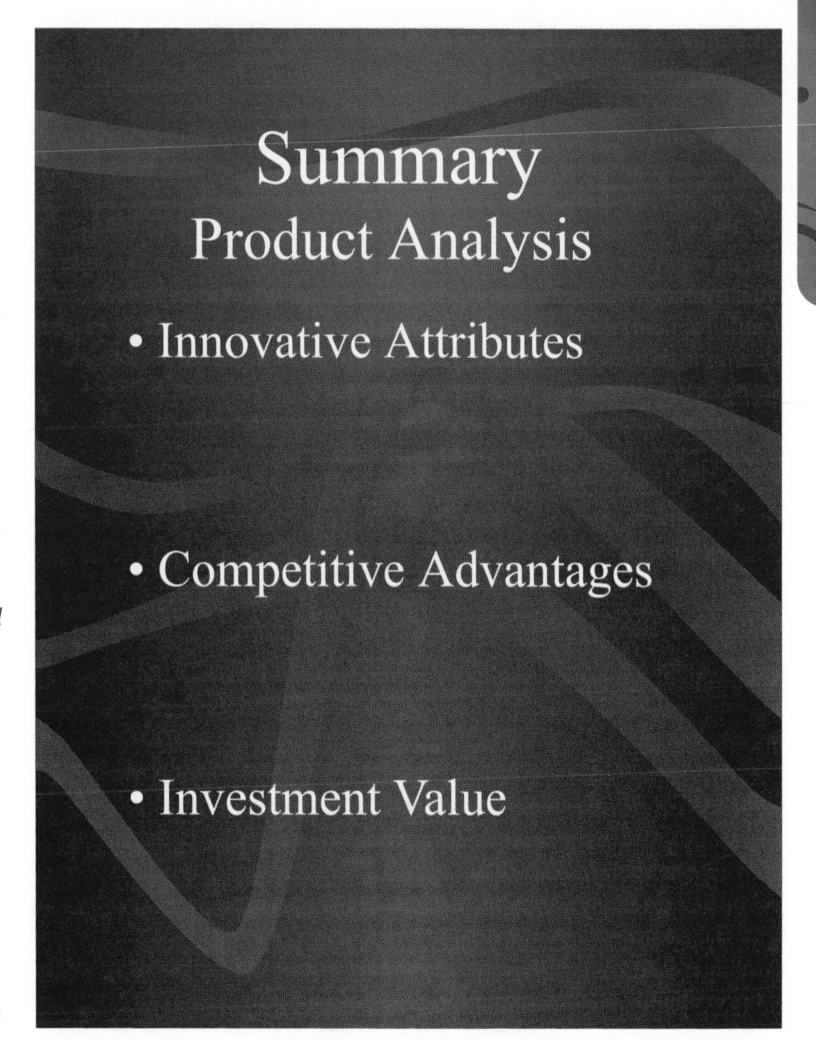


**Figure 7-2** A visual summarizing the main points of the presentation is important in a business presentation.

## Probing Question

Speakers may wish to end their talks by giving the audience a question to ponder. The speaker assumes that the answer to the question will be such that the audience's silent response will seal the case that the speaker is making.

For example:

*All of you present did not get to this professional level because of your reluctance to take risks. You have achieved what you have because you are aware that when we don't grow, inevitably we atrophy. I ask you, 'Would you have advanced as you have without making intelligent decisions that fueled your professional growth?' And similarly, 'Would we continue to advance and prosper as a company without making intelligent decisions and taking intelligent risks with what we market to our customers?'*

## Quotation

A quotation that captures the essence of the message can be another effective way of concluding the presentation. As mentioned earlier, it is important to select a quotation from a source who will be perceived as reputable.

For example:

*Grace Murray Hopper revolutionized the computing industry when she developed COBOL and the compiler as far back as 1952. A pioneer in the military as well as in computing, Hopper suggested what she thought it took to be a winner when she said, "A ship in port is safe, but that is not what ships are built for." We too must be careful not to simply be safe and stay in port. We should do what winning professional women and men must do, and that is take reasonable risks.*

**Stand Up & Deliver**

Construct a three-minute talk *with an appropriate introduction, body, and conclusion* that explains your response to the following questions:

- Of the introduction, body, and conclusion to a talk, which is the most significant component for determining presentation success?
- Of the introduction, body, and conclusion to this talk, which section is the strongest? To which section did you devote the most preparatory time?

In conclusion, it is important to emphasize a point that was made in the beginning of this chapter. It is an unfortunate reality that many people who are otherwise intelligent and capable do not consider how to organize their presentations. Speakers are likely to stand out as responsible and efficient if they structure their messages intelligently and include a clear and compelling introduction, a presentation body that fulfills stated objectives, and a meaningful conclusion.

## Summary

- A presentation should include an introduction, body, and conclusion.
- The introduction should do the following:
  - Engage the receivers
  - Articulate the presentation objectives
  - Establish speakers as credible
- The body should fulfill the objectives articulated in the introduction. Organizational patterns include the following approaches:
  - Topical
  - Spatial
  - Chronological
  - Advantages/Disadvantages
- Transitions should be employed to link related sections of the presentation.
- The conclusion of a business presentation must summarize the key components of the talk. In addition, speakers may find it helpful to end presentations with these:
  - Probing questions
  - Challenges
  - Appropriate quotations

## SAMPLE PRESENTATION FOR ANALYSIS

### Restoring Momentum to the Business Ethics Movement

*Alan Yuspeh, senior vice president of Ethics, Compliance, and Corporate Responsibility at the Health Care Compliance Association, presented* "Restoring Momentum to the Business Ethics Movement" *at the Business Ethics 2000 Conference, sponsored by the Conference Board, on May 10, 2000, in New York City.*

*As you read through this excerpt, please consider the following questions:*

1. *Is it necessary or wise to make the request found in the first paragraph?*
2. *In the second paragraph the speaker lists the specific objectives of the talk. Is this an effective method of introducing the presentation?*
3. *Has the speaker established a rapport with the audience in paragraph 3?*
4. *Is the attempt at humor in the last paragraph effective?*
5. *Would this introduction increase or decrease your motivation for listening to this presentation?*

I ask your forgiveness for reading the text of these remarks, but I hope that you will find enough interest in the points I am going to make to understand my desire for precision of expression.

There are three core propositions that I wish to share with you today for your consideration. First, the business ethics movement in this country lacks the vitality that it should have and sadly appears to have actually lost momentum. Second, American business as a whole serves its constituencies less effectively than it should because business ethics is not receiving the high level of attention it deserves in all too many organizations. And third, there are specific workable actions that could be taken by many companies that would create a greater attention to ethical business practices.

Before I elaborate on these points, I should clearly recognize that simply by virtue of your being here, your organization might well be in the forefront of fostering high business ethics. The observations that I will make in these remarks are summary observations. Of course, they do not apply to every large business organization in this country, but they do apply, I believe, to all too many. I fully recognize that to some extent I may sound like the clergyman who spends each Sabbath lamenting that so many are yet again absent from worship. When we hear such sermons, we often think, Why is he speaking to us? After all, we're here. I am raising these issues with you because I believe that by virtue of your being here, you care about the issues. We should try to achieve some agreement on what business ethics challenges exist and how to solve them by those who care about the subject. I assure you that these comments are not intended to be critical of anyone in the room. I seek only to encourage a discussion about important issues of concern to all of us.

Please permit me to make two other preliminary points. I am truly speaking today about business ethics. By that, I do not mean efforts intended solely to ensure compliance with laws or regulations. And I do not mean efforts that usually fall within the domain of corporate social responsibility, such as corporate philanthropy, community service, or similar initiatives. I mean the day-to-day conduct of large business organizations and whether those organizations emphasize the recognition of business decisions that raise ethical issues and the proper resolution of those issues....

...The other preliminary point I would make is that I think we have had some upward spikes in concerns about business ethics in the last 15 years....

...But if we look at all of these spikes up in this time frame, I am concerned that they look like the 52-week high for a stock that's been falling. I'm not certain whether we're at the 52-week low, but the energy of most of these favorable indicators seems to be either diminishing or stagnant. Though the Business Enterprise Awards, for example, seem to me to have focused attention on companies doing important work, it never truly became the Academy Awards of business, even though the leaders of this effort did all reasonably possible to make it that. The awards were made for five years, from 1991 to 1995, and have not been made since. President Clinton has created a similar award administered by the Conference Board called the Ron Brown Award for Corporate Citizenship. My impression is that we are not likely to find that award ceremony in prime time any time soon. In fact, I wonder how many in the room are aware of the award. It certainly, in my view, has much less visibility than the Malcolm Baldridge Award for Quality, which may carry some interesting message about the relative importance of quality versus ethics.

**Source:** Yuspeh, Alan R. "Restoring Momentum to the Business Ethics Movement," *Vital Speeches of the Day*, July 1, 2000, 66, no. 18: 553.

## Review Questions

1. What are three requirements for presentation introductions?
2. How can speakers improve initial ethos? Intermediate ethos?
3. What are three methods that can be used to engage an audience? What are the caveats associated with each method?
4. Identify three organizational patterns that may be used to structure presentations. What are the major advantages and disadvantages of each?
5. What are three methods that may be used to conclude a presentation?

## InfoTrac Question

Find the October 2004 InfoTrac article entitled "Giving technical presentations to non-technical audiences; Part 6: Building a strong body and summary." What tips do the Reimolds suggest for organizing the body of a presentation? What do they say about the importance of the summary to the business presentation? Find the InfoTrac article entitled "Crafting a Powerhouse Introduction." What factors do the authors claim make for powerhouse introductions?

---

[1] Identified as a Chinese proverb in *Columbia World of Quotations* (New York: Columbia University Press, 1996), CD-ROM.

[2] Paul Angle, in *World Book Encyclopedia* 12 (Chicago: World Book Inc., 1984), 275.

[3] This translation of the Quintilian section in *The Education of the Orator* appears in Eugene White, *Basic Public Speaking* (New York: Macmillan, 1984), 174. In the original Quintilian, the statement is found in Book IV, Chapter 1, section 61. The complete excerpt might be seen as offensively graphic when viewed from a contemporary perspective. However, it does reflect Quintilian's tendency to employ similes and metaphor effectively. The complete excerpt reads as follows: "A faulty exordium [introduction] is like a face seamed with scars; and he who runs his ship ashore while leaving port is certainly the least efficient of pilots."

[4] James McCroskey, *An Introduction to Rhetorical Communication*, 8th ed. (Boston: Allyn and Bacon, 2001), 83. McCroskey actually subtitles the chapter on ethos with those quoted words.

[5] Michael Osborn and Suzanne Osborn, *Public Speaking*, 3rd ed. (Boston: Houghton Mifflin, 1997), 16.

[6] See op. cit. McCroskey 89–90.

[7] See, for example, Dan O'Hair, Rob Stewart, and Hannah Rubinstein, *A Speaker's Guidebook* (Boston, Bedford/St. Martin's, 2001), 276.

[8] Damon Runyan's characters were often gamblers. Several of the songs from *Guys and Dolls*—for example, "Luck Be a Lady Tonight" and "Good Old Reliable Nathan"—deal with betting and bettors.

[9] Several writers make this point. As it pertains to the effects of dress in the classroom, see for example, David Roach, "Effects of Graduate Assistant Teaching Attire on Student Learning, Misbehaviors and Ratings of Instruction," *Communication Quarterly* 45 no. 3 (Summer 1997): 125–141.

[10] Tom Leech quoted in Lilly Walters, *Secrets of Successful Speakers* (New York: McGraw Hill, 1993), 50. Leech is the author of *How to Prepare, Stage and Deliver Winning Presentations* and a full-time speaking consultant.

[11] Senator Kerry's comments were quoted in Glen Johnson, "Democrats Recognize a Good Line: Candidates Recycle Campaign Material." *The Boston Globe*, August 17, 2003, A1.

Chapter in a Nutshell

*Visual aids must be used effectively or they will be counterproductive.*

# 8 Visual Support for Your Presentation

*Visual Aids not used properly could be called Visual Hindrances.*[1]

-James McCroskey

*The sad truth is AV ruins more messages than it helps.*[2]

-Joan Detz


## Abstract

A visual aid should be just that: a visual complement that helps improve the presentation. Occasionally, business speakers mistake esthetic appeal or sophisticated graphics for productive visual aids. Effective speakers intelligently employ various types of visual aids and intelligently avoid common problems that speakers have when using them. This chapter examines the advantages and concerns related to the use of visual support for presentations. Specifically, by the end of the chapter you should be able to do the following:

- Describe how visual support can help a business presentation
- List methods that can be used to provide such support
- Identify common problems related to the construction and utilization of visual support
- Identify guidelines for overcoming these common problems

Visual Support is helpful in a business presentation but when it is used incorrectly content and main points may be missed by the audience.

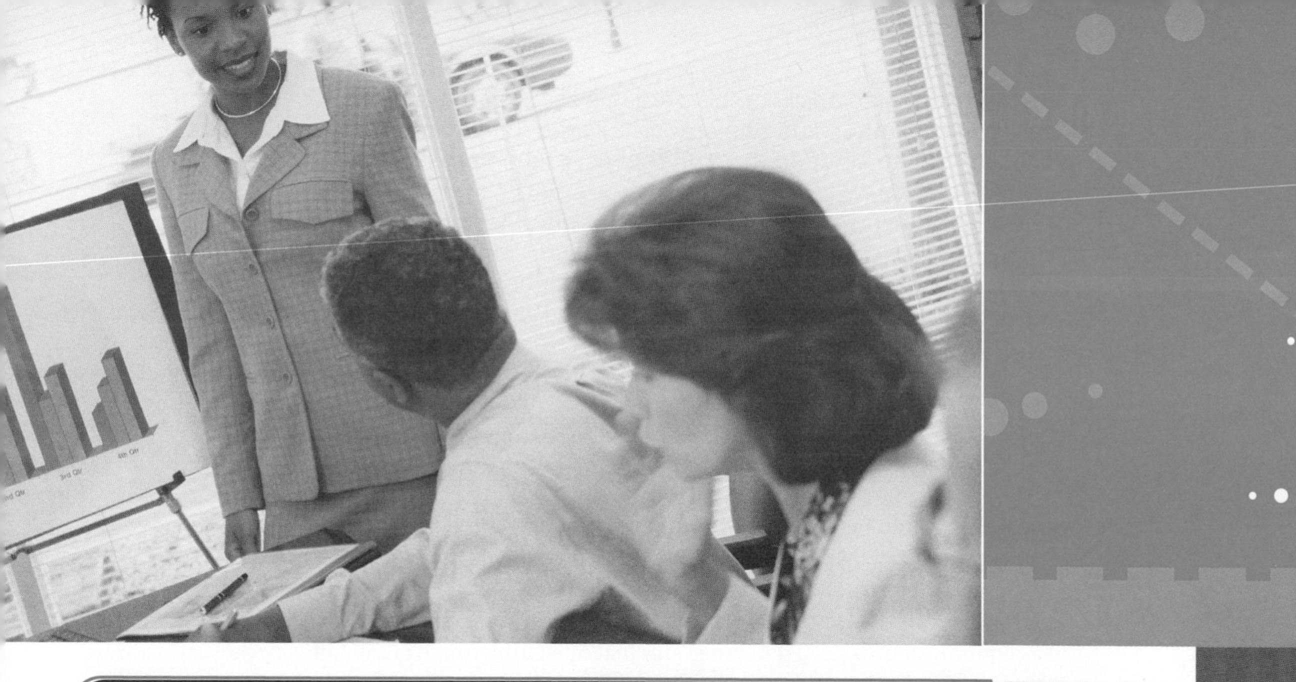

# Visual Literacy

Doug Weyand and Angela Patel were two excellent graduate students who had prepared a presentation on the subject of workplace illiteracy. Both were full-time managers during the day and were matriculating in an evening MBA program to advance in their careers.

They had enrolled in a course called Managerial Communication. One assignment involved studying an issue germane to organizational communication and then delivering an oral presentation to the class based on the research.

The students had prepared diligently for the presentation. They had thoroughly researched the subject and had been startled to discover the extent of the problem. In a way they were excited about what they had unearthed. Like people with missionary fervor, they wanted to spread the word about the pervasive illiteracy that affects all levels of organizations. In addition, they wanted to explain how some organizations had effectively employed interventions to address the problem. Most significantly, they desired to persuade the listeners, who were all midlevel managers, that one could not assume that subordinates, peers, or even superiors were, in fact, literate. The evidence, the students claimed, proved otherwise.

Doug and Angela made these points clearly and dramatically in the introduction to their talk. They engaged the audience with startling statistics about the extent of illiteracy. They described an organization that had lost great sums of money because of illiteracy. Doug and Angela detailed how they would take the listeners through the talk and challenged the audience to pay attention to something that the speakers claimed would be very important to their careers as business administrators.

And then Doug and Angela punched up their first PowerPoint® slide. The word *illiteracy* was spelled incorrectly in the title of their presentation.

Responding to snickers, the students scoured the screen, noticed the error, stared at each other, and panicked. They tried to laugh it off, but appeared to be deflated as they plodded through the rest of their presentation.

- Would this error, inevitably, destroy an otherwise flawless presentation by the students?
- Do you recall situations when visual support backfired in a similar manner?
- Is there a way Doug and Angela could have recovered once they became aware of the spelling error?

## INTRODUCTION

Visual aids should help speakers communicate messages to their audiences. If visuals detract from the message, they cannot be *aids*, regardless of the label attributed to them.

Visuals can provide complementary support for a message, reflect professional preparation, and serve to increase speaker ethos. However, speakers must be, or become, aware of the common hazards related to visual aids that often undermine presentations. Speakers must be committed to utilizing aids in a way that ensures that they are valuable to the speaker and to the audience.

## VALUES OF VISUAL SUPPORT

Although there are occasions when the merit of a potential aid is overwhelmed by other factors, visuals can help speakers convey their messages to audiences. There are several good reasons to use visual support when delivering presentations.

**Visual support can increase audience understanding.** The use of a picture, computer-generated graphic, map, or chart can clarify information for an audience. If speakers are explaining the increase in real estate values over the last twenty years, a chart or graph might powerfully illustrate the rise in prices in a way that words alone can not.

In addition, visual support can reinforce what is being said. A graphic that reads *"Fifty thousand workers can not read this sentence"* will emphasize the problems you wish to address about workplace illiteracy.

**Visual support can increase audience attention.** In Chapter 7, we discussed the importance of engaging the audience. An attractive visual can entice receivers to pay attention to your talk. (See Figure 8-1.)

**Visual support can increase audience retention.** Visual images tend to stay with us for a relatively long period of time. Because speakers wish for audiences to remember what has been said, visual complements can facilitate meeting this objective.

**Figure 8-1** Visual support can reinforce what speakers are saying and increase audience attention.

**Visual support may reduce speaker apprehension.** In Chapter 4 we discussed how preparation can reduce communication apprehension in presentation contexts. Graphics require preparation. The act of creating effective visual aids may reduce anxiety because it compels speakers to prepare ahead of time. In addition, speakers may think that some of the attention will be deflected from them when audience members view the slides or other visual support.

**Visual support can improve presentation organization.** Often graphics are used to outline the agenda for a talk. The act of creating these slides may help speakers consider how they will move through the content of their message. While they are speaking, the slide can help them stay on the road map outlined on the visual. (See Figure 8-2.)

**Visual support can help audience members follow the talk.** In addition to assisting the speaker, a visual outline can help the listeners literally see where the talk is going.

**Visual support can increase speaker ethos.** Visuals that reflect preparation can enhance the status audience members attribute to the speaker. In many business contexts visual support is expected, so the absence of visual aids could in and of itself reduce speaker ethos.

**Session Topics**

- Speaking Styles
- Structuring the Message
- Responding to Questions during Q/A
- Speaking Exercises

**Figure 8-2** Displaying an agenda can help the audience—and a speaker—stay on track.

## Ethical Probe

### Misleading Visual Complements

Assume that an organization is attempting to attract high-quality employees and has hired you to provide visual support for a presentation that will be made at a job fair. Further, assume that the organization is in an unattractive urban location, but is within a mile of a lake and green area. Finally, assume that you would be able to take an aerial photograph of the facility and make it seem as if the physical plant is within steps of the lake and park.

- Would you be unethical if you took such a photo and provided it to the people who had hired you?
- Would it be their responsibility to decide if there was anything unethical about using the photo?
- Would it be unethical for them to use the photo?

## TYPES OF VISUAL SUPPORT

There are several different methods for visually complementing a message.

### Handouts

Speakers may wish to supply an outline of the presentation to the assembled group or a copy of a report that will be summarized during the presentation. In professional contexts handouts are often expected. Coordinators of some conferences, for example, request that speakers prepare a take-away handout. Not bringing one, in these circumstances, is tantamount to being unprepared and tarnishes the presenter's ethos. As we will see, there are problems associated with employing handouts during presentations, but nevertheless they can be helpful and in some situations are, essentially, mandatory.

### Flip Charts

Premade flip charts can be used in the same way computer-generated graphics are employed to identify the agenda for a presentation. The speakers refer to the items on the flip charts as they proceed through the presentation. Flip charts can also be used to record audience comments in the same way a chalkboard is utilized.

### PowerPoint®-Type Graphics

Almost all college students are familiar with PowerPoint®. Businesspeople use it extensively, and your instructors may employ it with their lectures. With PowerPoint®, computer-generated words and images are projected onto a screen. Some PowerPoint® presentations include supplementary sound effects. As we discussed in Chapter 1, PowerPoint® is sometimes used inappropriately and, like all visual aids, should not be viewed as the presentation itself, but as a complementary tool. We examine problems related to PowerPoint® later in this chapter.

### Overhead Projectors

At one point the overhead was the standard method for projecting graphics in a professional presentation. Programs such as Harvard Graphics were used to help create attractive text that could be printed directly onto transparency film. The film would be placed on the overhead, and with the turn of a switch the text would be projected onto a screen.

Currently, overhead projectors are dated and can seem unsophisticated to those familiar with PowerPoint® equipment. (See Figure 8-3.) A business professional recently informed me that as soon as she sees an overhead projector, she loses respect for the speaker. Her argument is that with PowerPoint® relatively accessible, the use of overheads seems archaic and reflects someone being out of touch. Not all business professionals feel this way, but PowerPoint®—when the equipment does not fail the speaker—does provide for more polished-looking graphic support. Overhead projectors are, however, less likely to malfunction or otherwise become dysfunctional.

### Models

A speaker may wish to discuss an object but cannot transport the object into the speaking hall. For example, a salesperson may desire to describe an automobile but cannot lug the vehicle into a conference room. A model of the car may be employed instead.

**Figure 8-3** With the widespread use of PowerPoint®, the use of overhead projectors can seem dated and unsophisticated.

## Maps, Charts, Graphs, and Photographs

A presentation describing the regions of a national hardware company may be accompanied by a map of the country divided into the various regions. How successful one region is compared with another can be supported by using a bar chart. (See Figure 8-4.) The historic increase in franchises may be graphically portrayed. A photograph can be displayed to show the audience the newest building in beautiful Bozeman, Montana.

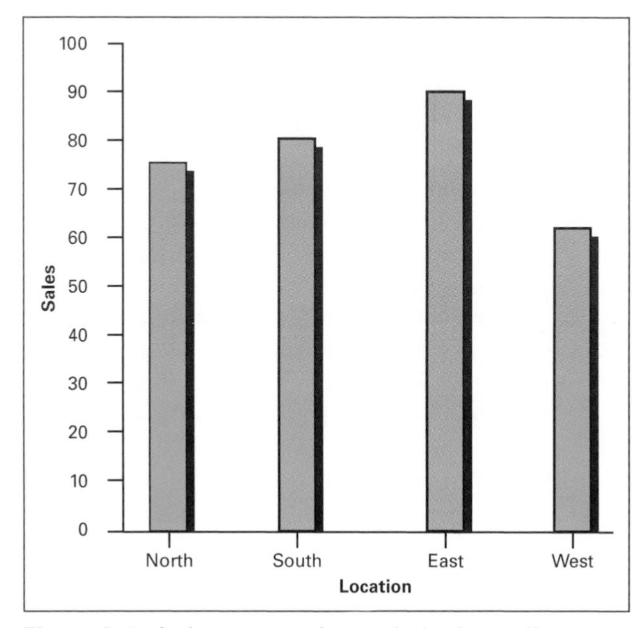


**Figure 8-4** A chart or graph may help the audience to "see" the information in a familiar format.

## People

People can serve as visual complements as well. Describing a new spring fashion line is made easier by having models wear the garments. Explaining a self-defense technique can be aided by assistants who follow the speaker's directions. Describing the transformational effects of cosmetics can be facilitated by applying them to someone.

### Reverse the Perspective

Which methods are most helpful?

Speakers employ visual support to engage audience interest, clarify information, and reinforce points.

From the vantage point of your experience as a listener, which of the methods for visual support listed below are most useful toward meeting these speaker objectives? Explain why you feel the way you do.

a. Handouts
b. Flip charts
c. Chalkboard
d. PowerPoint®-type presentations
e. Overhead projector
f. Models
g. Photographs
h. Maps
i. Charts
j. Other people

# Recurring Problems with Visual Support

The potential for visual aids to actually be helpful does not guarantee that they will be helpful. If not used effectively, visuals have a counterproductive effect.

It is important for speakers to guard against becoming intoxicated by the technology, gimmickry, or even esthetic value of visual support. Many business speakers appear to believe that as long as they have a PowerPoint® presentation, they must have a good presentation. Consultant Lois Kelly has commented that the "best thing that can happen to corporate America is that there is a ban on PowerPoint®."[3] This suggestion may be a bit drastic, but it is important to consider the following common problems associated with using visual support.

### *Speakers tend to address a screen or aid and not look at the audience.*

Establishing eye contact is important. Often speakers who project graphics and images or who use maps, charts, and photos spend more time looking at the screen than at the audience. This may be because the inanimate graphic is less threatening than the people in the room. It may also be because the presenters are as impressed with their creations as the audience members are. Whatever the reasons, speakers should avoid this common and counterproductive tendency.

### The graphic is too small for readers in all sections of the audience.

It may surprise readers, but speakers frequently begin a sentence with the words *As you can see* and then hold up a photo or graphic that could not conceivably be discerned by audience members. This behavior reflects incomplete preparation and is likely to erode speaker ethos. On the contrary, being prepared with adequately sized photographs, maps, and charts is likely to elevate speaker ethos.

### There is too much text written on a slide and speakers appear to simply be reading what appears on the slide.

If a speaker is reading everything that appears on a slide, audience members will begin to wonder why there is an oral component to the presentation. If everything written is uttered, and nothing is uttered beyond what is written, the speaker might have simply printed copies of the slides and distributed them to all those in attendance.

Similarly, if too much appears on a slide then the value of the graphic is limited, since the audience members will be unable to read it all while concurrently listening to the speakers.

### The slides have too many bells and whistles. The effects are not effective.

The object of an aid is to assist the speaker, not eliminate the need for a speaker or deflect attention from the speaker. If audience members focus on the spectacle, they will not be attentive to the message the speaker wishes to convey. In addition, certain graphic displays lose their appeal during the course of a talk. If each piece of text on each slide flies up from the bottom and is introduced by a screeching car sound, the gimmick will be engaging for a short time only, and become as disconcerting as any rhythmic sound after awhile.

### The visuals contain a spelling or grammatical error.

Any such error will erode the ethos of the speakers. Krapels and Davis in the June 2003 issue of *Business Communication Quarterly* report that human resources representatives have commented that one grammatical error on a resume can automatically eliminate a candidate from job consideration.[4] In the same way, one spelling error on a visual aid can affect audience perceptions of speaker qualifications. (See Figure 8-5.)

### Items are passed around.

Engaging the audience is a difficult challenge. When speakers pass around objects, they are actually encouraging listeners to disengage. Speakers are implicitly telling audience members that when the item gets to them, they should cease paying attention to the speaker, and focus on the object. In addition, passing objects around is problematic because the logistics of the procedure can be disconcerting. There may be movement as one member gets up or otherwise moves to pass along the object. There may be people who do not notice that the object is being passed to them, and curious others may attempt to get to the stalled visual. This motion can be disconcerting to the speaker and other audience members as well.

### Handouts can be distracting.

Similarly, handouts—even those distributed before the talk—can be distracting. Audience members may be leafing through the handouts instead of being attentive to the speakers. If the handouts are too detailed and the speakers are saying precisely what is on the handouts, the audience members may lose attention, assuming (correctly) that they can read the material subsequently. Handouts that the speaker refers to should have page numbers. Speakers do not want to remark, "As you can see in your handout" without identifying the location of the referred to section.

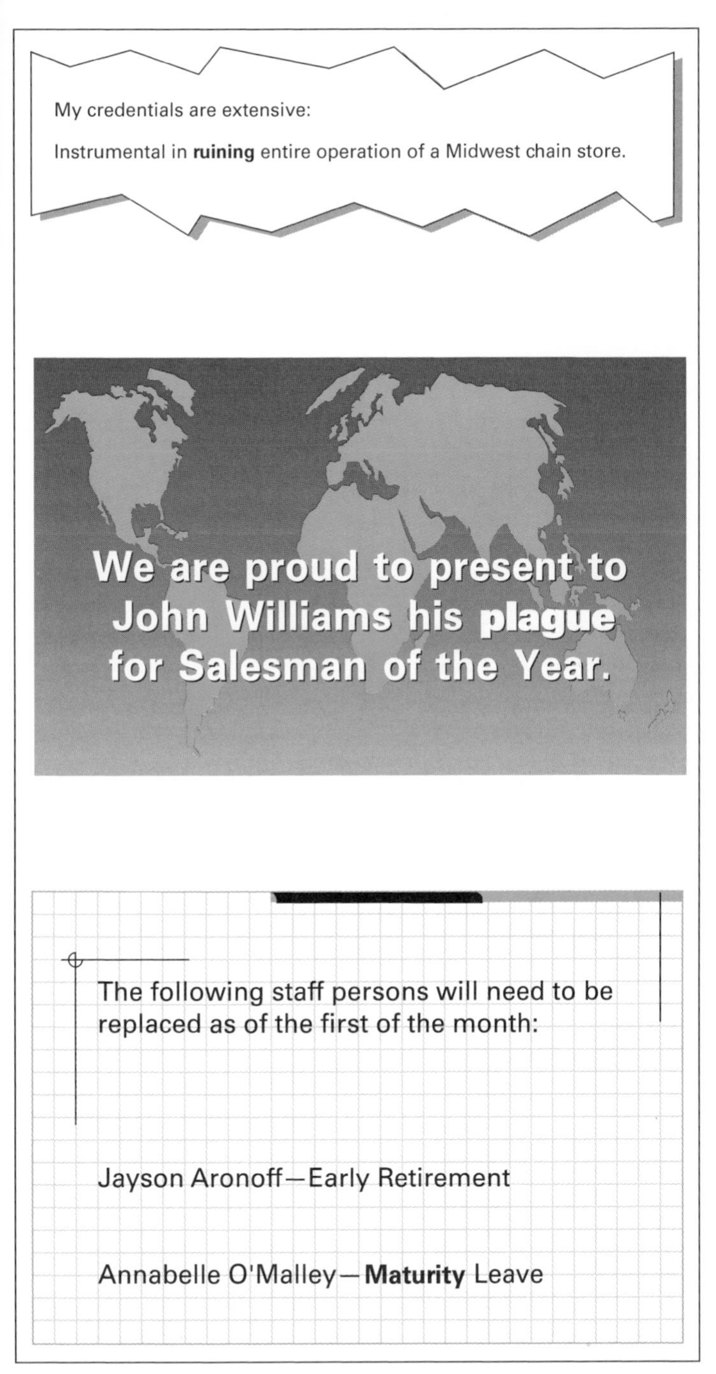


**Figure 8-5** A spelling or grammatical error can undermine a speaker's credibility.[5]

### *Chalkboard/flip chart writing can be indecipherable, inaccurate, and embarrassing.*

Apprehensive speakers may not be able to endure the added responsibility of writing clearly while speaking. Handwritten comments may be incomprehensible. Very intelligent speakers have spelled very simple words incorrectly when using flip charts and chalkboards as visual aids. A six-figure executive leading a seminar on grant writing headed his flip chart with the scrawled words Grant Writing *Tenants* instead of *Tenets.*

### *Tehnical problems erode speaker ethos and confidence.*

Murphy's Law (if anything can go wrong, it will) applies to the use of visual aids. Equipment may not function as it did when the speaker rehearsed. The speaker may need an extension cord. The power outlets may not accommodate the connectors without an adapter. The equipment provided, although only slightly different from the type that was used in rehearsal, may have a feature that makes it valueless to the speaker. As we discussed in Chapter 5, some of these problems can be reduced by comprehensive audience analysis. However, some problems will surface despite excellent preparation.

### *The room is configured in a way that precludes good sight lines.*

Speakers may have prepared the talk with PowerPoint® supplements and secured a room that permits projection. However, some sections of the audience may have an obstructed view of the screen. Audience members will not always follow a request to move up or around so that they can get a better view of the images.

### *Apprehension levels become evident.*

As we discussed in Chapter 4, almost everyone has some degree of speaking apprehension; however, the extent of the anxiety is not always discernible. When visuals are employed, speaker anxiety may become more obvious. Manually describing how a product operates may be more difficult when your hand is shaking. Holding a pen next to a line on an overhead slide may reveal apprehension if the projected pen is moving about uncontrollably on the screen. Presenters may not be able to anticipate or experience this shakiness during rehearsal.

One of the more frightening episodes I observed as an instructor occurred when an undergraduate described his lucrative part-time job shucking clams in Boston's Faneuil Hall tourist area. The young man brought clams in ice and a very sharp knife to the classroom to demonstrate how simple it was to do what he did for part-time work. The man, who claimed to shuck hundreds of clams on a weekend afternoon, could not control his trembling hands when he began to demonstrate the shucking procedure. The speaker certainly commanded the audience's attention, but most observers were less interested in the procedure and more concerned that the trembling speaker would sever a thumb in the process of the demonstration.

### Assistants can upstage the speaker.

A recurring problem when humans are used for visual support is that these assistants can deflect attention and even, wittingly or otherwise, sabotage the presentation. Speakers demonstrating the qualities of a cosmetic product may use an assistant to demonstrate the ease of application. If the assistant contorts her face dramatically while the presenter is applying the product, the value of the assistant as a model has been significantly reduced.

An organization's director of security called a meeting of all employees to describe self-defense procedures. He asked an expert to assist him with the presentation and told the audience that the expert, Cheryl, would demonstrate the procedures as they were being described. At one point during the presentation, when the director had explained with certainty, a "next step" in self-defense, Cheryl turned to him and exclaimed, "No, Mark. That's not the way it's done. Let me show you." The director responded with, "Um, Cheryl, I believe it can be performed in the manner I described." What happened subsequently was a dialogue between the exasperated and embarrassed director of security and the expert assistant. This problem could have been avoided with a rehearsal, but it is indicative of the kinds of problems that can occur when an assistant is used for visual support.

### Valuable displays are left up after they have been used.

An attractive map becomes distracting if it is available for viewing before the speaker is ready to refer to it. Similarly, if speakers have already alluded to a graphic and will no longer be using it, the visual should be removed so that it does not distract the audience from the ongoing presentation.

## Stand Up & Deliver

Assume that you have been asked to explain how any one of the visuals described in this chapter can aid AND detract from a presentation.

- Construct a three-minute presentation that describes how the visual aid you identified can aid and detract from a presentation.
- Employ three visual aids in the course of making the presentation.

## SUGGESTIONS FOR USING VISUALS EFFECTIVELY

The problems identified on the previous pages may seem insurmountable. However, although they occur with discouraging frequency, they can be addressed. Visual aids can be beneficial to your talk. Consider the following recommendations:

- **Use premade graphics.**
  Speakers are under enough pressure during a presentation. By creating maps, charts, outlines, and graphs ahead of time, speakers reduce problems related to misspellings, incomprehensible writing, and sloppy drawings.
- **Follow these guidelines for slide preparation:**
  - Make sure the font is large enough for all to see.
  - Proofread each slide. Have others proofread the slides.
  - Keep them simple. Do not overwhelm the audience with too much text, or too many distracting images.
  - Be able to answer this question: How will using this slide help my presentation?
- **Ensure that assistants are well coached prior to the presentation.**
  Asking for volunteers is very risky. Assistants have to know how to participate, when to participate, and where they must be standing/seated to be helpful.
- **Practice with the visual aid.**
  Practicing without the visual aid has limited value. Speakers cannot predict the problems that can surface unless they have attempted to integrate the aids into the presentation during rehearsal. Consider the following during rehearsal:
  - Time issues: Time the presentation with the use of the visual aid. What takes seconds to pretend to do can take minutes to actually complete. A simple process such as loading the PowerPoint® program or placing a slide on an overhead projector may take longer than anticipated.
  - Power: Ensure that outlets exist where they will be needed.
  - Equipment: Speakers should be completely familiar with the computers, projectors, and control panels that will be used during the presentation.
  - Location: Consider sight lines to screens, placement of lectern, and tables.
  - Eye contact: While using any equipment, speakers should be able to maintain frequent and sustained contact with the audience. Speakers should practice avoiding looking at the screen or other inanimate objects while delivering the message.
  - Coordination: If assistants will be controlling the PowerPoint® display while others address the audience, practice should include coordinating the presentation with the operation of the computer or any other equipment.
  - Pressure: It is difficult to simulate pressure. However, it is wise to conduct a dress rehearsal that is nearly as real as the actual experience will be. Under pressure simple maneuvers can become complex.

    Four MBA students, two men and two women, delivered a talk on proper business attire. At one point the women read directions that men followed for tying neckties and bow ties. Under pressure, neither men—both of whom subsequently claimed that they could perform this act in their sleep—was able to tie the tie. For the duration of the talk—on the subject of appropriate business attire—the two male students addressed the audience with comically short and unkempt ties around their necks.

- **During the talk:**
  - Be vigilant about looking at the audience and not the screen.
  - Replace pointers and markers when not using them. Speakers who are nervous can fiddle with their pens, and this can be distracting to the audience.
  - Remove visual complements when not employing them so that they are not distracting to the audience.
  - Refer to graphics or relevant sections of handouts when speaking. Sometimes slides appear at the appropriate time, but there is no reference to them. The aid cannot be an aid if the audience members see no correlation between what is being said and what they are seeing.
  - Refrain from passing objects around the room.

Visual aids can be valuable and should be used to supplement a business presentation. The key to successful utilization is to acknowledge the potential problems and take steps to reduce the chances that the visual aid will become a visual hindrance.

## Summary

- There are several reasons to use visual aids. They can serve the following functions:
  - Help audience members understand and remember messages
  - Engage the audience
  - Improve the organizational flow of the message
  - Increase speaker ethos
- Visual supplements include the following:
  - Flip charts
  - Computer-generated graphics
  - Human assistants
  - Maps, charts, photos, graphs
  - Handouts
- Many factors render using visual aids problematic.
- These potential problems can be reduced with the following:
  - Preparation
  - Rehearsal
  - Vigilance

## Sample Presentation for Analysis

### Executive Eloquence

*Judith Humphrey, founder and president of the Humphrey Group, delivered the presentation* Executive Eloquence *to the Board of Trade of Metropolitan Toronto on November 25, 1997, in Toronto. As you read through this excerpt from the speech, please consider the following questions:*

1. *Ms. Humphrey asserts that "leadership is not conferred by title. It is achieved every time an executive moves an audience." Explain why you agree or disagree.*

2. *Ms. Humphrey takes a strong stand regarding the use of visual support. Explain why you agree or disagree with her comments.*
3. *The speaker asks and answers the question "Can everybody 'be inspiring?'" Do you agree with her answer? Explain.*
4. *Could visual complements have enhanced the presentation? Explain.*

Every day in corporate board rooms this scene is repeated over and over again. An executive walks to the front of the room, turns on the overhead projector, and begins a narration that bores both speaker and audience.

The same scene is repeated in external conferences, although perhaps with more panache. Speakers with impressive titles walk to the podium on a much larger stage, the lights flash, visuals come to life on the big screen, and the speaker begins a narration that bores both speaker and audience.

As the head of a firm that provides speech coaching to executives, I have worked with hundreds of business leaders who know that something is not right with this scene. In a situation that should be one of their best leadership opportunities, they feel uneasy and frustrated by their lack of impact...

...What goes wrong? Why do executives often speak too long, say too little, and lose their audience? I've found that it's not lack of motivation. Nor is it lack of ability. The truth is that great speaking is an art that must be developed through learning and practice.

Indeed, today executives need to be more inspirational than ever. They must deliver ideas and beliefs that excite the minds and hearts of their audiences. Leadership is not conferred by title. It is achieved every time an executive moves an audience. In today's competitive world, customers, employees, management, boards and shareholders must be turned into believers...

...Visual aids are the bane of corporate presentations. They're uninspiring, and too often dull, cluttered and difficult to decipher. More significantly, they upstage the speaker and make that individual appear to be less of a leader. My advice? Use visuals only when they are absolutely necessary.

Think of yourself as the best visual. Have your audience focus on you—your energy, your conviction, your inspirational qualities. Don't confine yourself to the sidelines. Be the focus of the audience's attention.

I once heard about a presenter who wanted to impress his audience with the best, most colourfull state-of-the-art, glitzy visuals. At the end of the talk, a number of people came up to ask for a business card—not his, but the individual who had created the graphics!

I've worked with enough executives to know that some corporate cultures insist on visuals—at least in presentations. If you must use them, avoid word slides. You want your audience listening to you, not reading while you're talking. Project a simple corporate logo if you need an image. Some material—an organization chart, a network diagram—can be presented visually. But if you do, keep your visual simple. No one should have to study or decipher an image to determine what you're showing...

...there is no greater goal for a leader than to inspire an audience—whether that audience is a CEO, a room of shareholders, a group of customers, or employees.

The question is, can everybody be inspiring? The answer: if they believe they can, and work at it, they can. Consider the great speakers of history. They applied themselves to crafting their remarks. Winston Churchill fainted out of fear at one of his first public speeches. But he got better. In fact he became one of the world's greatest statesmen, because he had a mission. And executives have a similar mission in their companies.

John Caldwell, president and CEO of CAE Inc., once told me: "The reality is, you've got to set a direction for your company, and then you've got to help people get on that bandwagon."

This ability to move the hearts and minds of employees, customers, and other stakeholders is the primary role of senior executives. To achieve this goal takes concentration, desire, and hard work. But when you achieve this leadership, it's worth it.

Source: Humphrey, Judith. "Executive Eloquence: A Seven-fold Path to Inspirational Leadership," *Vital Speeches of the Day*, May 15, 1998, 64, no. 15: 468 (4).

## REVIEW QUESTIONS

1. What are three reasons for using visual complements when making business presentations?
2. What are the advantages of distributing handouts during a presentation? Using flip charts? Employing PowerPoint®?
3. Identify three potential problems that can make the use of visual aids a visual hindrance.
4. Why is it necessary to practice with the visual aid when doing dry runs of presentations?
5. What are the potential problems with using volunteers or assistants to help demonstrate aspects of your talk?
6. How might you have employed visual support to enhance any of your previous presentations in this class?

## INFOTRAC QUESTION

Find the InfoTrac article entitled "Before and After: Use more graphics to make numbers and other data come alive." Are the recommendations by Lerner likely to be applicable to presentations other than the type he describes? Also, review the short article entitled "Visual aids should enhance, not take over presentations." Do you agree with the position taken by the author?

---

[1] James McCroskey, *An Introduction to Rhetorical Communication*, 8th ed. (New York: Allyn and Bacon, 2001), 185.

[2] J. Detz, *It's Not What You Say, It's How You Say It* (New York: St. Martin's Press, 2000), 42.

[3] Kelly is quoted in Alan Zaremba, *Organizational Communication: Foundations for Business and Collaboration* (Mason, OH: Thomson South-Western, 2006), 209.

[4] Roberta H. Krapels and Barbara Davis, "Designation of 'Communication Skills' in Position Listings," *Business Communication Quarterly* 66, no. 2 (June 2003): 92–93.

[5] Examples adapted from W. Clark Ford, "Tricks of the Trade—A Forty Year Collection" (paper presented at Association for Business Communication regional meeting, New Orleans, March 2003).

Chapter in a Nutshell

*Many factors can make group interaction difficult. Teams must overcome these obstacles to prepare for, and deliver, effective presentations.*

# Teams and Team Presentations

*Tell me what a committee of 25 is going to do. Give me a break. I don't know a committee of five that can get anything done.*[1]

-Jeffrey Wigand

*A meeting is a cul de sac where ideas are lured and quietly strangled.*[2]

-Sir Barnett Cocks


## Abstract

Often presentations in business contexts are delivered by groups of people associated with a project. These presentations need to be made seamlessly. However, sometimes team presentations appear disjointed and audience members are left thinking that they have heard several individual talks as opposed to one cohesive presentation. High-quality team presentations require efficient interaction well before the time of the talk. They also require several rehearsals before the presentation date. This chapter discusses problems with team presentations and provides suggestions for overcoming them. Specifically, at the conclusion of the talk you should be able to do the following:

- Identify and define types of group presentations
- Discuss common problems that surface during team projects
- Describe methods that can be used to overcome these problems
- List requirements for effective team presentations
- Describe a process that can be used to improve the quality of team presentations

## Generation

John Arena is a vice president and creative director for *Generation*, a full-service advertising agency. Whenever Generation is invited to compete for a client's business, Arena assembles a pitch team to prepare and deliver a "capabilities presentation" to the potential client. Several agencies like Generation will be making such a pitch. If Generation's presentation is successful, Arena and his team will be invited back for a subsequent round in the competition. The pitch team usually includes another vice president, and representatives from the Creative, Accounts Services, and Media divisions within Generation. Almost always the president serves on the team as well.

"We have several meetings to prepare and rehearse the team presentation," says Arena. "It is imperative that we convince the client that we know them, their market, and their customers. We want them to know that we have a distinctive approach, that we have been successful in the past, and that we anticipate being successful with them. If we didn't feel we would be a good match for a particular client, we would not consider competing for their business.

"The team presentation is crucial and has to be very tight. The time limits are finite and each person on the team must adhere to his or her segment's restrictions or we will not get our message out. Everyone on the team participates in the presentation. No one warms a seat. We have to know what each of us individually is going to say and what everyone else is going to say."

The capabilities presentations vary depending on the individual client, but each one typically includes an introductory statement from the president, a comment about the distinctive nature of Generation, a review of successful case studies, a demonstration of past creative work, and remarks from the Media representative about efficient advertisement placement.

Generation has an excellent success rate. Many agencies are brought in for capability presentations, but only a small percentage is invited back for second rounds. Generation makes the second round at least one out of every two times they make a presentation.

"It is a lot of work," Arena says. "Our agency is busy and the people that I select for the pitch team are not doing crossword puzzles waiting for me to identify them. They are all involved with other projects in their various stages. There is high energy in the meetings and high stakes with the presentations.

We call ourselves Generation because we generate change for customers. We have been very successful at doing that. However, if it wasn't for the team interaction and subsequent presentations, we would not have the opportunities to prove that we can generate such change."

- When you have worked with teams preparing for presentations, have your groups been as prepared as Generation's teams seem to be? What problems have your groups encountered that Generation seems to avoid?
- Why do you think Generation has been able to avoid the problems you have identified?

## Introduction

If your experience is typical, you have been in courses that required groups to research a subject and then present their findings to the other students in the class. Team presentations are also not uncommon in organizational contexts. Instead of a lone representative describing a fund-raising campaign, the whole group that worked on the idea will participate in the description. As was the case with Generation, instead of the artistic director of an advertising company explaining a proposal to a client, all elements of the project team participate in the presentation.

Although many of the same principles of individual presentations are applicable to group presentations, there are some significant differences. These differences pertain to the group interaction that precedes the talk as well as the presentation of the message.

## Types of Group Presentations

Group presentations can be classified into three categories: panel discussions, symposia, and team presentations.

### Panel Discussions

In panel discussions, a group of individuals discusses a subject and is concurrently observed by an audience. These persons, one assumes, are knowledgeable about the subject they are discussing. Each person may begin with a prepared statement, but most subsequent comments are impromptu and are reactions to what others have said. Often panel discussions have moderators. These moderators are required to keep the conversation moving, ensure that all participants have an opportunity to speak, disentangle contentious participants who may be making it difficult for audience members to hear *any* comments, and—if within the ground rules of the discussion—solicit comments and questions for the assembled. A panel discussion has been described as a group conversation, with an audience.[3] It is not a formal team presentation even though a team of individuals may be participating.

### Symposia

Assume that six successful college coaches have been asked to speak at the annual NCAA convention. Each one has been asked to prepare a talk entitled "What's wrong with college athletics today?" The men and women who make up this group enter a ballroom that is occupied by five hundred coaches. A moderator introduces the six coaches, and then each in turn delivers a speech on the subject. Subsequently, the moderator solicits questions from the audience. These questions are directed to Coach Jones or Smith, or any of the coaches who have spoken.

This scenario describes a symposium. Your university, no doubt, hosts student and faculty symposia. Successful alumni may be invited to speak on, for example, "Co-Curricular Activities and Professional Advancement." Assuming that this is a symposium and not a panel discussion, each alumnus would be asked to deliver a talk about their experience. All talks would be germane to the symposium theme. Subsequently, speakers would be asked questions from participating audience members.

Symposia are essentially collections of individual presentations. They are not team presentations in the sense that there is no collaborative work performed by the symposium participants to ensure a cohesive, unified message. In fact, symposium directors may deliberately solicit participants who are likely to present opposing perspectives on the same topic.

### Team Presentations

Team presentations reflect collective effort and are, consequently, significantly different from symposia and panel discussions. Assume that the six coaches described above are asked to form a committee. This committee is charged with studying the question "What's wrong with college athletics today?" and is asked to present its conclusions. The requested talk would be called a team presentation. The meaningful distinction between team presentations and other forms of group presentations is the expectation that the speakers will have worked together prior to the event in order to present a cohesive message.

## Problems with Team Presentations

Because team presentations require preliminary meetings, and meetings are often problematic, team projects are often burdened by stress that can be dispiriting, disruptive, and debilitating. A study of organizational communication problems described by managers found that more than one-fourth of the problems identified were related to meetings.[4] A textbook chapter on the subject of meetings is actually entitled "Why Are Meetings so Boring and Unproductive?"[5]

Your experience with meetings may be more positive. However, it is likely that you have experienced corrosive tensions when you have worked on team projects either in school or at work. Humorist Dave Barry has quipped, "If you had to identify, in one word, the reason why the human race has not achieved, and never will achieve, its full potential, that word would be 'meetings.'"[6] This depiction does not have to be your reality. To avoid group-related problems, team participants should examine the underlying causes of meeting tension.

### Primary Meeting Tensions

Primary tension refers to anxiety that surfaces before a project even begins. Team members may experience primary tension for many of the following reasons:

#### *Anticipated Inequity*

If twelve people are on the team, responsible individuals may fear that many of the others will be less than responsible. This can create some anxiety for the diligent people who may worry that they will end up doing more than their share of work.

#### *Past Experience*

Because groups are often problematic, it is likely that team members have had bad experiences previously. These tense memories may be recalled prior to the beginning of a session and create anxiety.

### Preexisting Personality Tensions

In organizations people become aware of colleagues who are easy to work with and others who are contentious. After an initial group project in a class you know with whom you want to work for the second one. Primary tension can surface when team members know the other participants on the team and expect that some will be obnoxious, tyrannical, or verbose.

### High Communication Apprehension

We discussed communication apprehension in Chapter 4. If team members are high communication apprehensives in presentation situations or group contexts, they will likely experience primary meeting tension. They know they will have to speak during the presentation. They also know that during the preparatory group work they will be expected to interact with the other members. A high communication apprehensive does not look forward to either eventuality. Therefore, these participants will experience tension before any preliminary meeting.

### Other Organizational Projects

In organizational and university life we multitask. It is rare for someone to work on committees that eventually deliver team presentations and have that be their only responsibility. If there are other business and school matters on your agenda, and you fear that the team meetings will usurp precious time, you will experience primary tension.

### Personal Matters

We multitask at work, but are always essentially multitasking, because our personal lives are also important. If parents are ill, a spouse or partner is discontent, or children are having issues at school, working on a team presentation that requires a recommendation about office expenditures may seem relatively meaningless. Team members may become anxious before a meeting when they have more significant personal items on their schedules.

### Lack of Interest

In organizational life employees are occasionally assigned committee work that is of little interest to them. When this occurs, people tend to wonder how or why they were "stuck" with the assignment. If team members feel uninterested in the topic and unjustly selected for the work, this sense can create primary tension.

### Significance and Pressure Related to Assignment

Primary tension can surface because a great deal may depend on the quality of the team interaction and presentation. If the team is meeting to make a report that intends to justify its existence, the interest level and commitment may be high, but the pressure intense. This pressure can create preliminary anxiety.

If a course you are taking has a team project that is worth 75 percent of your grade, the pressure to excel in the group can create nearly palpable preliminary tension. This tension may even ignite some other potential sources of anxiety. For example, if participants are concerned that Joe will be part of the committee because Joe tends to be difficult, the primary tension associated with Joe's presence is exacerbated when the group outcome has great significance.

**Stand Up & Deliver**

Several potential sources of preliminary tension have been just described. Prepare a three-minute presentation that addresses the following questions:

1. In your previous experience at school or at work, which two of these sources have surfaced most frequently?
2. If you were compelled to make this presentation with three other randomly assigned classmates in this class, how would you attempt to avoid any of the sources of tension you identified in response to the previous question?

## Secondary Tensions

Secondary tensions surface during the course of meeting with others on your team. These tensions can be categorized into four areas:

- **Procedural**
- **Equity**
- **Affective**
- **Substantive**

### Procedural

These secondary tensions develop when members think the procedure for communicating is flawed.

For example, members of the group may feel that the agenda is weak or may become annoyed because the leader is not adhering to the agenda.

If a presentation needs to be made in three days and you think your group is not progressing quickly enough to meet the deadline, you may well experience procedural conflict. If you feel as if your group is meeting too frequently or not often enough, or wastes too much time during the sessions, you will likely experience procedural conflict.

Any one of these scenarios can create frustrating tension within the group and can reduce the chances for effective interaction.

### Equity

Equity tensions occur when there is a perception of inequality. Typically equity tensions fall into two subcategories. The first occurs when members think they are assuming a disproportionate share of the responsibilities. In this instance, it may seem as if other participants are slackers or "social loafers"—a term used in the literature of group interaction to describe those who are derelict and allow, if not compel, other group members to do their work.[7]

For example, assume that you have been assigned two portions of the presentation that are far more complex than the one portion that has been assigned every other person. If you become anxious or annoyed because of this imbalance, you are experiencing equity tension.

A second type of equity tension occurs when participants want to be involved in the group but are ignored by more powerful or controlling members. In this situation potential contributors feel bruised because what they say is not taken seriously. Members begin to wonder, "Why am I here?" They may also fear that their limited contributions will become apparent to those who are evaluating the presentation.

### Affective

Affective tension surfaces when people in the group begin to dislike one another. This could be a result of residual procedural, equity, or even primary tensions, but when affective tensions occur, group interaction becomes very complicated. Participants find it difficult to "hear" what adversaries are saying, let alone consider the wisdom of any suggestions. The personality tensions may make individuals contrary and the discussions unnecessarily combative. A perceived foe may suggest a way to structure the talk that is brilliant, but a rival may be unable to see through the personal tension to legitimately evaluate the proposal. When affective tension levels are high, discussing the best way to make the presentation becomes secondary to making sure that you get your way or that others persons' ideas are eliminated.

### Substantive

A positive type of tension is called substantive conflict. This refers to conflict that surfaces because of legitimate disagreements about what is being discussed. Most people typically think of conflict as problematic. However, this is not necessarily the case. Kreps identifies three beneficial aspects of conflict. It can

- Promote creativity and therefore facilitate problem solving,
- Promote the sharing of different ideas and therefore increase the amount of relevant information available,
- Serve to test the strength of opposing ideas.[8]

Obviously, substantive conflict is desirable. If your group immediately selected the first idea recommended by a participant, the potential value of examining alternatives or even refining the initial proposal would be eliminated.

#### Your Attitudes towards Team Presentations

Do the statements below describe your attitudes or your behavior when you participate in meetings prior to team presentations?

Directions: Rank each item from 1 to 5 according to the following statements:

1. The statement describes me very accurately.
2. This statement is somewhat accurate.
3. The statement neither describes me well, nor describes me poorly.
4. This statement is mostly inaccurate.
5. This statement does not describe me at all.

____ A. One weak link in a team presentation and the whole talk is weak.

____ B. I'm a high communication apprehensive when making a team presentation, but relatively stress-free when I speak on my own.

____ C. I like doing things in a structured way. Therefore, because teams are typically not as structured as I would like, I prefer to work independently.

____ D. Team presentations work when people know their part and do their part.

____ E. It doesn't bother me when group members come in late to meetings.

____ F. I'm often a pseudo-listener in meetings. That is, I tend to pretend to listen.
____ G. I have sympathy for some people who "loaf" during meetings because I do that myself sometimes.
____ H. I can't respect people who won't come to a meeting prepared.
____ I. I enjoy being a leader in a group.
____ J. In team contexts, people do not pay attention to minorities and women or respect their ideas.
____ K. Side talking during meetings is not such a bad thing. I think people in general should relax and not be so uptight.
____ L. I don't think it is appropriate for people to use profanity in a meeting—even if we all know each other.

How would you want those with whom you interact in groups to respond to these questions?

## Counterproductive Group Tendencies

Group work requires diligence and intervention. Brilhart and Galanes argue that a key ingredient for success within groups is for individuals to be "participant-observers."[9] A participant observer is someone who actively participates in the group but concurrently observes the process of interaction. Observing interaction is necessary because groups tend to default to counterproductive behaviors. These behaviors undermine the chances for quality both in the preliminary discussion period and during the team presentation itself. If team members observe group interaction as well as participate in it, they are more apt to identify and avoid the counterproductive tendencies that are described in the following section.

## Conformity

An assumption when convening in groups is that "two heads are better than one."[10] However, if two or more "heads" actually act as one, the value of collective communication is diminished.

Irving Janis popularized the word **groupthink** in a book about political decision making and a *Psychology Today* article.[11] Largely because of Janis, *groupthink* has crept into the lexicon and is used to describe a common problem with meetings. It refers to the tendency for groups to make decisions without considering alternatives. Janis described it as *a mode of thinking that people engage in when they are deeply involved in a cohesive in-group, when members striving for unanimity override their motivation to realistically appraise alternative courses of action.*[12]

In other words, when groupthink occurs, one member puts forth an idea and others readily agree without considering its advantages and disadvantages. The group might do this because the suggested idea was presented by a powerful member, or because nobody wants to "rock the boat," or because the members have no great individual stake in the decision. When groupthink takes place, few individual thoughts are expressed, just "group think." Because of this counterproductive tendency, team presentations sometimes reflect bland or untenable solutions to organizational problems.

**The Asch Effect**, named after an experiment conducted by Solomon Asch, describes the extent to which team members are likely to conform even when conformity reflects irrational decisions.

Asch's experiment involved graduate students who were asked to compare twelve pairs of cards. Each pair consisted of what was called a "standard line" card and a "comparison line" card. On the standard line card was a single line. On the comparison line card there were three lines of varying lengths. (See Figure 9-1.)

The procedure for each study was the same.

- Seven to nine graduate students were brought into a room.
- The students viewed the first of the twelve pairs of standard line cards and comparison line cards.
- The first student would then say aloud which line from the comparison line card was the same length as the one on the standard line card.
- Then the remaining students would, one by one, announce which line from the comparison line card was the same length as the standard line card.
- When all nine had announced their selection for the first pair, the students would view the second pair and follow the same procedure.
- The study would continue until each set of cards had been viewed, and each of the subjects had orally declared their votes.

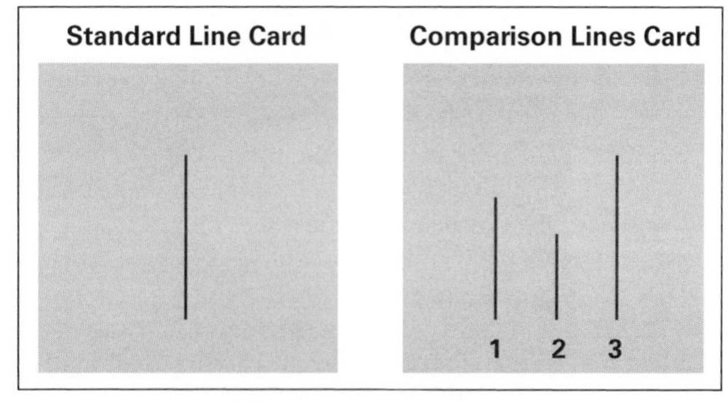


**Figure 9-1** In the Asch experiment there were two cards: the standard line card and the comparison line card.

The correct answer in each case was obvious. For each of the twelve pairs of cards only one line on the comparison card could possibly be construed as the correct match. However, among the seven to nine students involved in the experiment only one was an actual subject. The others were conspirators helping to conduct the experiment. For each of the twelve comparisons, the helpers declared aloud that *another* line—clearly not the correct one—was the one that matched the length of the line on the standard line card. After each of the conspirators said the ***incorrect*** line was the match, the lone actual subject (who was always the last to declare his or her vote) was put in the position of conforming, or disagreeing and identifying the correct and obvious answer.

Four out of five of the (real) subjects yielded to the pressures at least one time out of the twelve. Nearly three of the five subjects yielded to the pressure at least two times out of twelve. As Goldhaber points out, what may be the most stunning feature of this study is that these groups were composed of people who were not familiar with each other.[13] The subjects could not fear that there would be in-house repercussions for bucking the company elite. What might have been the tendency to conform had these people been part of a cohesive group like those who work together to make team presentations? Asch's study has been replicated in countries and cultures beyond North America. Bond and Smith report Asch studies with similar results conducted in Portugal, Kuwait, Brazil, France, Zimbabwe, Fiji, and Ghana.[14]

If team members are willing to succumb to peer pressure when to do so is to agree to an absurd conclusion, how likely are people to succumb to such pressure when the idea, however inappropriate, is not entirely beyond reason? It is apparent that if team members were to succumb to such pressure, teams could endorse untenable suggestions during their presentations.

**Goal lining**, while slightly different from groupthink and the Asch Effect, also can result in conformity. When goal lining occurs, participants see reaching the goal as the lone criterion that determines whether group work has been successful. At first, one might wonder what is wrong with that. Why should the group be concerned with anything other than the goal? The problem with goal lining is that it tends to encourage participants to seek a conclusion without necessarily seeking a *team* conclusion. In the rush to cross the goal line, the group loses the potential value of discussion, creativity, and interaction. If your team sees "getting the presentation done" as the lone goal, you might agree to a procedure that is flawed. For example, assume that someone in your group says, "I'll write up the whole presentation. No problem. Then we'll just divvy it up into sections." This may appear to be a fast way to cross the goal line, but it has potentially disastrous consequences. What if the volunteer is delusional or irresponsible? What if he or she becomes ill? Even if the person is brilliant, dedicated, and healthy, the team presentation will not reflect team input. Each of the other individuals will be risking their individual reputations on the perspectives of one person who, ostensibly, is representing the team.

## Ethical Probe

### Bogus Credit

Assume that seven members within one unit of an organization have been asked to prepare and deliver a presentation that will be delivered to another unit within the same organization. Assume that two of the seven, however, prove to be slackers. Should the group members give the slackers something to say so that it will appear as if they were participants even though they did nothing to contribute to the project?

Consider another variation. Assume that the two persons were not slackers, but that their comments were disregarded every time they made suggestions to the group. Should the two persons participate in the presentation, suggesting that they were involved in the group decisions, even though they were never really allowed to participate?

Finally, consider this third scenario. Assume that the two persons did participate and were angrily opposed to the suggestions developed by the majority. Should these two participate in presenting the opinions of the majority of the team even though they passionately disagree with the team perspective?

## Poorly Conceived Procedure

An agenda is a list of topics to be addressed at a meeting session. Mosvick and Nelson asked 1,600 managers why meetings failed. Of the top six items cited as obstacles, five related to either a poor agenda, no agenda, or not following an agenda.[15]

If teams want to get from a starting point to a destination, they need to follow a well-considered course. Otherwise they will spend hours communicating aimlessly and become terribly frustrated when, despite the hours spent, they did not get where they wanted to go. There is little value in creating an intelligent agenda if groups have no intention of adhering to it.

## Hidden Agendas

Teams can also be undermined because of a related problem. Hidden agendas are, as the name implies, personal objectives that are concealed from the group. For example, a group could be discussing the best method of delivering the presentation. One member of the group may wish to avoid speaking for any significant duration. She or he may suggest that only a few people in the group speak for extended periods of time. This suggestion surfaces not because of the alleged agenda—to make the presentation work best—but because of a hidden agenda—to avoid having to speak.

## Competition versus Cooperation

A spirit of cooperation, as opposed to a spirit of competition, facilitates effective communication in groups. What often happens, however, is that participants tend to become ego-involved and competitive. Differences of opinion are good for groups, but as we have discussed previously, fighting for your opinion simply because it is yours can create affective conflict. As discussions develop in meetings, individuals may become more and more attached to their perspectives and be reluctant to consider opposing points of view.

# INTERVENTIONS

An intervention is a tool or technique used to alter behavior that would likely not be altered otherwise. As it relates to meetings, interventions are techniques that can be used to make these sessions productive and satisfying.

## Types of Interventions

### Buzz Groups

Some teams are large. You may have a dozen people working on the same project. The larger the group, the easier it is for individual members to hide or be ignored. Buzz groups can increase participation and, at the same time, decrease the potential for problems related to equity conflict.

Buzz groups are small subdivisions of the entire team. A group of twelve people discussing the merits of a recommended PowerPoint® format would be separated into six buzz groups composed of two members. Each group of two would discuss the same issue. After a period of time the six buzz groups would reconvene as a group of twelve. Each buzz group would then present to the larger body its perspective on whatever issue was being discussed. Buzz groups do not involve breaking up team responsibilities. Buzz groups make it difficult for shy people to hide and loafers to loaf. Buzz groups also reduce the chances of overbearing people precluding the participation of others.

### Brainstorming

*Brainstorming* is an often misunderstood term. When groups brainstorm, they are not engaged in an open discussion about the merits of a group proposal. Brainstorming involves identifying and recording any and all ideas that pertain to the item being discussed. An essential feature of brainstorming is that at no point during the intervention is anyone permitted to criticize a "brainstormed" idea that another has offered. Assume your group is charged with identifying the criteria for selecting a new company vice president who will "effectively and courageously lead" the organization. Further assume that your group decides it needs to clarify what is meant by the phrase *effectively and courageously lead*. Your group might decide to employ brainstorming. If it did, members would literally call out their conceptions of what it means to be a courageous and effective leader. A group member would record each contribution and create a list of the brainstormed ideas. No suggestion would be evaluated until everyone had exhausted their notions of what it means to be a courageous leader. Even if a member were to suggest an outlandish interpretation for effectiveness, no other member could criticize it. Subsequently, the brainstormed ideas would be discussed and evaluated.[16]

### Problem Census

Problem census involves analyzing the problem before you begin to discuss it. This approach requires that all members of the group offer their sense of the nature of the problem. As is the case with brainstorming, no notion can be dismissed as unreasonable.

For example, a team charged to prepare a presentation on the state of organizational ethics could employ problem census. If it did, one member might suggest that the problem involves defining organizational ethics. Another person might comment that the problem involves an analysis of how other organizations deal with ethical issues. A third person could offer that the problem requires exploring the effectiveness of the company's current code of ethics. After all members had identified their idea of what the task entails, the group would specify its objectives. By conducting the census, a group can determine the dimensions of the project.

### Risk Technique

To avoid issues that surface relating to conformity, meeting members might consider using risk technique. This approach requires each participant to identify risks to any solution. Let us assume that you have completed your research and are planning for your team presentation. You have on paper, but not in stone, what you want to say and how you intend to say it. Risk technique would be used to force participants to find flaws in what has been agreed upon. The idea is to identify any aspects of your solution that can be problematic and need to be addressed.

It works as a polling procedure. Each member of the group plays the devil's advocate and identifies a risk associated with implementing the solution already agreed upon. These lists of risks are recorded. Subsequently the group reviews the list of risks and reevaluates the proposal. Most of the time the reevaluation does not result in the elimination of the proposal, but in the fine-tuning of the resolution so that it addresses the concerns suggested by the risks.

It can be difficult for people to assume the role of devil's advocate, particularly if moments earlier they presented the logic behind, and supported the plan that's being considered. Yet for risk technique to work, each person, regardless of how involved she or he may have been in the composition of the plan, must play the devil's advocate and assume a posture of someone who identifies proposed flaws. That way, the potential for groupthink and Asch Effect conformity is reduced.

## Effective Leadership

One ingredient for group success not yet addressed relates to team coordination and leadership. A leader can transform even the most enthusiastic and potentially capable participant into a disgruntled, embittered, and even sabotaging influence. A leader can also facilitate the creation of an outstanding plan and presentation that would never have developed without dedicated and diplomatic coordination.

Leaders have several responsibilities. A review of them will indicate how influential leaders can be in ameliorating or creating primary and secondary conflict. A leader must do the following:

- **Plan for the meeting.** Define the meeting objectives. Solicit agenda topics, prepare, and distribute an agenda.
- **Get the meeting started.** Group participants often begin haphazardly with members arriving late. A leader has the responsibility to ensure that not too much time is wasted at the beginning of a session.

- **Keep the discussion on track and on time.** Meetings are notorious for lengthy digressions. Discussion that might begin with an analysis of the best place to rehearse the presentation may result in complaints about facilities and an anecdote about the time when Jan could not figure out how the lights worked in an ancient and poorly accoutered conference room. It is up to the leader to keep the discussion on topic. Meeting topics should have time limits. Lengthy digressions result in jamming the last few items on the agenda into an inappropriate time space. A leader is responsible for making sure the group stays on time as well as on track.

  Because of different input and tangential commenting, it is wise for leaders to periodically summarize what has been discussed. After completing one area on an agenda, a summary statement by the leader can provide closure for that area and allow the group to seamlessly segue to the next topic.
- **Solicit comments from some and curtail others.** Effective meetings require input from all participants. Often quiet members need prodding to voice their opinions. Leaders, to the extent that they can, should ensure that reserved participants contribute to the discussion.

  The other side of the problem is related to curtailing a participant who is making it difficult for others to contribute. Some people do not realize that they are monopolizing the conversation. Others are aware but are content to continue. A leader has the uncomfortable task of intervening when a group member is dominating. Otherwise, potentially valuable comments from other members will go unheard, and it may be difficult to complete the meeting's agenda.
- **Employ interventions.** A leader should consider and use approaches designed to improve team interaction.
- **Conclude the meeting.** At the end of the session a leader should summarize the progress of the meeting, indicate what remains to be done, and announce, if the information is available, when the next meeting will take place.
- **Plan for the next session.** Between meetings the leader has the job of planning for the next session. This includes sending out the minutes of the preceding session to committee members, taking care of the logistics for the next meeting, and soliciting additional agenda topics for the next session.

## Examining Leadership Styles

There are three basic leadership styles. **Authoritarian** or **autocratic** leaders are, as the label suggests, dictatorial and nondemocratic. **Laissez-faire** leaders are the opposite of authoritarians. They believe that the best way to lead a group is by keeping their hands off. A laissez-faire leader believes that a group can run itself and that, therefore, to guide it is to wield power that is not only unnecessary but counterproductive. A **democratic** leader is different from both a laissez-faire and an authoritarian. The democratic leader seeks the input and advice from group members. She or he may eventually make the decisions for the group, but those decisions are not made without considering the concerns of other members.

For example, an authoritarian leader would determine the sequence of speakers in the team presentation. A laissez-faire leader would allow the speaker sequence to be determined by the group. A democratic leader would ask for discussion and input about the sequence. She or he might decide to vote if there was a dispute, or make the decision based on the input of the participants.

## De Facto Leadership

A few additional labels are used to describe leadership types in groups. A **de facto** leader is someone who, essentially, is the leader despite the fact that there is a **designated** or **nominal** other leader. Someone may have been designated as the leader but acts as a leader nominally, i.e., in name only. When that is the case, someone else may begin to assume the natural leadership responsibilities. That person is, in reality, or de facto, the leader. Occasionally, an autocratic leader may incur the wrath of a group such that another member becomes the de facto leader. In these instances the de facto leader emerges because the other group members are not attending to the directives of the designated autocratic leader.

Leadership is important for most groups. If it were not, there would be no such phenomenon as a de facto leader. The democratic leadership style is likely to be the most effective. Some low-performance groups may require an authoritarian leader, and for some highly responsible groups, anything other than a laissez-faire leader would be inappropriate. However, your team presentation requires someone who is willing to assume the responsibility of leader.

### Reverse the Perspective

Most people say they would prefer a democratic leader when they are working in groups. In your experience is this always the case? From the vantage point of a group participant, have you ever been in a situation when you needed an autocratic leader or a laissez-faire leader?

- Should athletic coaches, for example, be democratic leaders?
- Should play directors be democratic leaders?
- Should your manager at your last job have been autocratic?
- Should those who coordinate team presentations in classes be democratic leaders?
- Should people such as John Arena, who coordinate team presentations in organizations, be democratic leaders?

## Characteristics of High-Quality Team Presentations

Before delivery, groups should be able to make the following claims about their impending team presentations:

- The introduction to the talk is clear, descriptive, inclusive, and engaging.
- The presentation content comprehensively addresses the team's assignment.
- Each person in the group knows what others in the group will be saying.
- Transitional statements have been considered and created that link one section of the presentation to another.
- The conclusion will summarize the entirety of the presentation and not simply the last segment of the talk.

The following discussion addresses each item on this bulleted list.

## The introduction to the talk is clear, descriptive, inclusive, and engaging.

Team presentations should not be perceived as loose composites of peripherally related speeches. They should be seen as a cohesive whole. The introduction to the team presentation must identify the broad team objective as well as describe how all the pieces that will be discussed mesh with one another. As is the case with the introduction to any presentation, the introduction must seek to engage the listeners and explain what is in it for them to be attentive audience participants.

## The content comprehensively addresses the team's assignment.

When the team views all the pieces of the presentation, all members should think that the message responds comprehensively to the group charge. Any presentation, regardless of whether it is an individual or team effort, must accomplish its mission.

## Each person in the group knows what all others in the group will be saying.

It is shortsighted to assume that if everyone takes care of their own individual area, the group will be successful. Familiarity with all parts of the presentation will ensure the following:

### *There will be no undesired content repetition.*

Awareness of all segments ensures that those speaking third or fourth will not be startled to hear information that they intended to say uttered by previous speakers.

### *There will be no unexpected contradictory statements.*

Similarly, awareness will preclude the possibility that a point made early will be the antithesis of something to be claimed later on.

### *There will be no surprising omissions.*

The presentation will not conclude with one member saying to another, "I thought you were going to handle that information."

### *Members may make intelligent references to other persons' segments.*

If people know what others will be saying, it becomes easier to prepare meaningful transitions and comments alluding to other portions of the talk.

### *There will be no sections that are clearly superficial when juxtaposed with others of significant depth.*

The presentation should be cohesive and consistent. If some segments are relatively detailed and others seem inappropriately thin, the presentation will lack the consistency desired.

### *Individual members and the group as a whole will adhere to time limits.*

Awareness of each person's segment allows the group to gauge how much time the presentation as a whole will take.

### *It will be relatively easy to answer questions during question-and-answer sessions.*

Knowing what others will say will help the moderator, and all group members, know who is best suited to respond to particular questions.

For all of these reasons, it is wise to make sure all group members know what all others will be saying during the team presentation.

### Transitional statements have been created.

Transitional statements are not difficult to create, but they need to be considered before the time of the presentation. The handoff need not be elaborate, but it has to be meaningful. For example, "The product that I have described will meet a very real consumer need for the reasons I've just identified. However, as we all know, the product cannot sell itself without professional marketing and advertising. Pat will now discuss how we intend to market this innovative product."

### The conclusion will summarize the entirety of the presentation.

Every presentation requires a synthetic recapitulation of main points. In team presentations the group has to prepare such a conclusion and make sure the summary includes all aspects of the talk and not just the segment presented by the final speaker.

## Getting There: A Step-by-Step Process

The final section in this chapter describes a process that teams can use to facilitate attaining the desired outcomes while avoiding common problems. As is the case with most procedures, the steps to this process are easy to enumerate. The key to success is the work necessary to complete each step.

### Step 1 Collectively Discuss the Subject

Before the presentation your team will have to meet. Eventually the team will determine the message that you will relay during the presentation.

One technique for facilitating discussion is called the General Procedural Model (GPM).[17] The procedure uses several of the interventions discussed previously in this chapter and involves a number of phases. Below is a modification of GPM applied to the challenges of team presentations.

- Use the *problem census* procedure to identify and clarify the problem or problems. For example, assume that the group's mission is to make recommendations about an organization's code of ethics. The problem census might identify the following dimensions to your problem:
  - We need to define organizational ethics.
  - We need to identify other organizations' codes of ethics.
  - We need to explore how these other codes are enforced.
  - We need to identify our objectives for our code of ethics.
  - We need to identify components to such a code.
  - We need to explain how to communicate the implementation of the code.

- Employ *brainstorming* appropriately. As has been discussed, brainstorming involves identifying, recording, but not evaluating possible solutions to problems. In this phase of GPM, members would brainstorm ideas about each of the facets identified as problems in the previous phase.
- Use the buzz group technique with any group larger than three to evaluate the merit of the various brainstormed ideas.
- Identify the best combination of recommendations from the evaluated list of brainstormed suggestions. At the successful completion of this stage you will have addressed each of the topics identified in the problem census.

At this stage your group would have used the preceding steps to *define organizational ethics, identify other organizations' codes, list what should be the objectives of your organization's code, specify the components of a code your group is recommending,* and *decide on the best way to communicate that code.*

The group should then employ risk technique to fine-tune these solutions. When you have completed the risk technique, your group has determined the content of the team presentation and needs to plan the delivery of this content.

## Step 2 Divide Speaking Responsibilities; Prepare Individual Outlines

At this point your team has already discussed the problem and decided on solutions. You need to decide who is going to talk about what segment of the message. Then, each person is responsible for preparing a detailed outline of their segment of the talk and making copies (or otherwise distributing copies) to the team members.

## Step 3 Review Outlines

Each group member is responsible for reviewing the other members' outlines. This review is necessary to ensure familiarity with all components of the message to be presented. It ensures that there will be no omissions or repetitions. It ensures that the same level of depth exists in each segment.

## Step 4 Discuss Sequence of Speakers and Transitions

What will be the sequence of speakers? How will each person "hand off" to the next person so that segments of the presentation will seem related and seamless?

## Step 5 Identify Message Style

Will the group be presenting extemporaneously or using the manuscript format? Consistency is recommended because it increases the perception of a collective effort.

## Step 6 Plan the Introduction and the Conclusion

As indicated previously, the introduction to the presentation must be clear, descriptive, inclusive, and engaging. The conclusion must reflect the entirety of the presentation, not just the last person's segment.

## Step 7 Practice Individually

All persons need to rehearse their individual segment of the talk. Knowing what you know, and knowing the sequence of what you intend to say, does not necessarily translate into a high-quality presentation. This is particularly the case with extemporaneous talks. Team members need to practice their parts.

## Step 8 Practice the Team Presentation

As a group, the team needs to rehearse the presentation. This should be a "dress" rehearsal. That is, it should include all visuals, and if possible, practice should be in the actual room where you will be presenting. You may not need to actually "dress" as you would for the talk, but your group will want to discuss how you expect people to be attired if you want a similar level of formality.

The rehearsal should include a simulation of the q-and-a session if that will be part of the presentation. We discuss q-and-a sessions in depth in Chapter 12. However, team presentations have unique questions. Your group needs to practice. You should designate a moderator for the questions, i.e., someone who will direct questions that are not specifically directed. You must determine ahead of time how many people should piggyback onto an initial response. If everyone weighs in on one issue, it will limit the number of questions, increase chances for contradictions, and discourage audience members who are uninterested in a particular query. The best way to sense the problem is to experience the phenomenon during a dress rehearsal.

See Chapter 12, "Question-and-Answer Sessions," for more specific information about responding to questions in team presentations.

## Step 9 Evaluation

It is wise to conduct a self-evaluation of your team's interactions. This is recommended so that during your discussions you can rectify any problems. Also, an evaluation of the team and its presentation after the work has been completed can be helpful when you are next assigned a team project.

# SUMMARY

- Team presentations prevail in organizational contexts.
- There are three types of group presentations:
  - Panel discussions
  - Symposia
  - Team presentations
- Teamwork requires meetings. Meetings are often troublesome because of
  - Primary and secondary tensions
  - Counterproductive group tendencies

- Problems in meetings can be overcome with interventions such as the following:
    - Buzz groups
    - Problem census
    - Risk technique
    - Brainstorming
- An excellent team presentation is characterized by the following:
    - Familiarity with subject
    - Segments that are presented seamlessly with appropriate transitions
    - An introduction that explains the theme and the components of the talk
    - A conclusion that reiterates the theme
- A step-by-step procedure can be followed to realize these ends

## Sample Presentation for Analysis

### The Sleepless Executive

*J. Brian Ferguson, chairman and chief executive officer of the Eastman Chemical Company delivered the speech* "The Sleepless Executive" *on November 2, 2003, at the Executive MBA commencement of The Fuqua School of Business at Duke University in Durham, North Carolina. As you read through this excerpt, please consider the following questions:*

1. *Does asking for "a show of hands," as the speaker does in the first paragraph of this excerpt, engage an audience?*
2. *The speaker identifies four things that keep him up at night. How effectively does he segue from the third to the fourth?*
3. *If you were a member of the EMBA class, would you be impressed by the speaker's presentation? Please explain.*
4. *What different challenges would be faced if this had been delivered by a team as opposed to a single individual?*

...Now, I want to shift gears just a moment and ask the graduates themselves a question. How many of you—and I want a show of hands here—how many of you had to work into the night at least a couple of times to finish your studies?

That's what I thought. If there was someone here who didn't raise your hand, by the way, come see me afterwards...I want to know the secret to your success.

OK, here's another question. How many of you had at least one sleepless night worrying about your work? Looks like everybody again.

No surprises there, I guess. What may surprise you, though, is that those sleepless nights are good training.

Why? Because if you're serious about your work...if you want to see your company and your career succeed...if you care about the people you work with...you'll probably have more sleepless nights in your future.

Sorry to be the spoiler here but that's just the way it is.

There's too much competition—globally and domestically—for business to fall into any comfortable pattern today. The work of your company doesn't stop when the clock says five p.m.

Just when you're thinking of going home, there's someone on the other side of the planet thinking about taking your customers. Our world is changing and changing times cause long workdays.

I've gotten used to this idea. So have my fellow CEOs around the country and the world.

The things that keep us awake, though, might surprise you. Some are predictable. But others may not be.

So as you prepare to leave here as new MBA grads—full of strategy and tactics—I thought it might be appropriate to give you a bit of insight into a few things that keep CEOs awake, and why that matters to you.

This isn't a lecture, of course, so you don't have to take notes. But be aware: there will be a test when you get back to work.

So what's first on the list of things that keeps CEOs awake? Wal-Mart.

Now in fairness, I should say it's not just Wal-Mart that keeps us awake. It's Wal-Mart and all the mega-marketers like them. K-Mart and Target in the U.S. Carrefour in Europe...

This isn't any one company's fault, by the way. If Wal-Mart wasn't there, somebody else would be and the pressures would be the same.

But just because it was inevitable doesn't make it any less of a change agent for the economy. Markets move at high speeds. As many of you know, though, companies and people often don't respond as quickly.

This leads me to the second item on my list: nostalgia also keeps me awake.

I'm originally from Texas but I've lived in many places around the world. And I've found that many people, but Americans and Europeans in particular, are nostalgic.

When it comes to running companies, that can be a problem. In fact, it can be a huge problem.

A significant part of my job on a daily basis is trying to shake people loose from their nostalgic look at the world. Many employees just want things to be the way they were 15 or 20 years ago.

My work is to make them understand that we are in a new business environment. That the business strategies we had just 10 years ago aren't good enough for today. That trying to run a company by relying on what succeeded yesterday is like trying to drive a car by staring in the rearview mirror. Sooner or later you're going to end up in the ditch.

...China is the third item on my list of things that keep me awake.

China has probably been responsible for selling more Sominex to business leaders in the U.S. than all of the other countries in the world combined...

...Don't misinterpret this as a knock at our Asian competitors, by the way. The reason they're so successful is because they have good technology, great efficiencies and a strong work ethic. Their commitment to education, in particular, is creating a big windfall for them.

And this brings me to the fourth—and last—item on my list. As the CEO of a company headquartered in the United States—with a sizable part of my employees and intellectual property located here—this last item is probably the biggest issue of all.

As the ultimate consumer of our education system let me put it as simply as I can. If the United States wants to compete long term with the rest of the world, we must revisit... revise...and reaffirm our commitment to education...we are simply not producing enough high school graduates with the right skills for today's work environment. Modern businesses need workers with high-level computer skills. We need employees capable of overseeing sophisticated production systems. We have little use for unskilled labor.

The U.S. Department of Labor recently estimated that by the end of this decade, we'll face a shortage of 12 million qualified workers in this country.

Does this keep me awake at night? Absolutely.

**Source:** Ferguson, Brian. "The Sleepless Executive," *Vital Speeches of the Day,* December 1, 2003, 70, no.4.

## Review Questions

1. How does a team presentation differ from a symposium? How does it differ from a panel discussion?
2. What is meant by primary and secondary tension? How can these affect the nature of team presentations?
3. How can conformity undermine the quality of a team presentation?
4. Identify five desired outcomes of effective team presentations?
5. Evaluate your last team presentation in terms of the five desired outcomes identified in response to the previous question.
6. What do you consider to be the three most significant of the nine steps discussed on pages 155–157.

## InfoTrac Question

Use InfoTrac to find the Oitzinger and Kallgren article in the Spring 2004 issue of *College Teaching.* What recommendations do the authors make that are relevant to this chapter both in terms of preparation for, and delivery of, team presentations?

---

[1] Jeffrey Wigand quoted in *The Boston Globe*, July 5, 2003. Wigand was referring to a twenty-five-person panel that was formed to study a proposed smoking ban in Charleston, South Carolina. Jeffrey Wigand was the tobacco company " insider" depicted in the movie called *The Insider*.

[2] Although this quote is occasionally attributed to columnist George Will and at other times simply attributed to "anonymous," the statement most likely was made by Sir Barnett Cocks, a clerk in Britain's House of Commons who lived from 1907 to 1989.

[3] Stephen E. Lucas, *The Art of Public Speaking*, 8th ed. (Boston: McGraw Hill, 2004), 496.

[4] For several years, I conducted a quarterly study that involved asking evening MBA students who concurrently were full-time employees to describe communication breakdowns they had experienced on the job. In one three-quarter period 27 percent of the problems were meeting related. In one particular quarter 55 percent of the problems dealt with communication in meetings. A discussion of meetings based on this study is found in my article "Meetings: Why We Need Them, Why We Hate Them, How to Fix Them" in the *Journal of Employee Communication Management* (May/June 2001): 23–29.

[5] Sue DeWine, "Why Are Meetings So Boring and Unproductive?," *The Consultant's Craft: Improving Organizational Communication* (Boston: Bedford/St. Martin's, 2001), 206.

[6] Dave Barry, "Twenty Five Things I Have Learned in Fifty Years" in *Dave Barry Turns Fifty* (New York: Crown, 1998), 183.

[7] Social loafing as a term was first used in an article by B. K. Latane and S. Harkins entitled "Many Hands Make Light the Work: The Causes and Consequences of Social Loafing," *Journal of Personality and Social Psychology* 37 (1979): 822–832. Also see Beatrice Schultz, "Improving Group Communication Performance: An Overview of Diagnosis and Intervention" in *The Handbook of Group Communication Theory and Research*, ed Lawrence R. Frey (Thousand Oaks, CA: Sage, 1999), 388–389.

[8] Gary Kreps, *Organizational Communication* 2d ed. (New York: Longman, 1990), 191–192.

[9] John Brilhart and Gloria Galanes, *Effective Group Discussion*, 9th ed. (Boston: McGraw Hill, 1998), 16–17.

[10] The technical term for this phenomenon is *nonsummativity.* This means that the result of a group interaction will be unequal to the sum of its parts. The hope is that the interaction of all will result in a discussion that is positively nonsummative. However, because of the primary and secondary tensions discussed in this section, it is not impossible that the result could be negatively nonsummative. When a result is negatively nonsummative "two heads" are not "better than one" but less qualitatively productive than one.

[11] Irving L. Janis, *Groupthink: Psychological Studies of Policy Decisions and Fiascoes* (Houghton Mifflin, 1982). The article was entitled simply "Groupthink," *Psychology Today* 5, no. 6 (November 1971): 43–46, 74–76.

[12] Irving L. Janis, *Groupthink: Psychological Studies of Policy Decisions and Fiascoes*, 9.

[13] Gerald Goldhaber, *Organizational Communication*, 6th ed. (Madison, WI: Wm C. Brown/Benchmark, 1993), 249.

[14] Rod Bond and Peter Smith, "Culture and Conformity: A Meta Analysis of Studies Using Asch's (1952b, 1956) Line Judgment Task," *Psychological Bulletin* (January 1996): 112.

[15] Roger Mosvick and Robert Nelson, *We've Got to Start Meeting Like This: A Guide to Successful Meeting Management* (Indianapolis: Park Avenue, 1996), 31. The sixth item ranked number two on the list of why meetings fail related to meetings being "Inconclusive: No results, decisions, assignments or follow up."

[16] Brilhart and Galanes suggest that the group take a break after creating the brainstormed list before evaluation. Further, the authors' comment that it might be wise to wait for a separate session for the evaluative discussion or have another group of people examine the brainstormed ideas. John Brilhart and Gloria Galanes, *Effective Group Discussion*, 9th ed. (Boston: McGraw Hill), 302.

[17] John Brilhart and Gloria Galanes, *Effective Group Discussion*, 238.

Chapter in a Nutshell

*Successful persuasion requires evaluating the available arguments that may be used to meet identified persuasive goals.*

# Persuasive Messages

*More than once I have heard good people come out second best to demagogues because they have depended on their righteous indignation and neglected to do their homework.*[1]

-Norman Thomas

*The best way to win an argument is to start out by being right.*[2]

-Lord Hailsham (Quinton Hogg)

## Abstract

Most presentations in organizational contexts are inherently persuasive. Salespersons must persuade potential clients of the comparative value of a company's product. Departments within an organization must sell their ideas to other units to obtain necessary buy-in. Even simple project status reports include persuasive elements designed to convince listeners that the projects are worth continuing. This chapter defines persuasion and describes types of persuasive arguments. Specifically, at the end of this chapter you should be able to do the following:

- Describe what is meant by persuasion
- List four common persuasive objectives
- Identify types of arguments that can be used when trying to persuade
- Use Monroe's Motivated Sequence when preparing presentations
- Discuss ethical issues for persuasive speaking in professional contexts

PHOTO: © JOWDY PHOTOGRAPHY FOR TOASTMASTER'S INTERNATIONAL

## Corax and Tisias, and Cathcart

Corax and Tisias were two Greek scholars who lived in the fifth century B.C. Tisias had been a pupil of Corax, and the two men are associated with some of the earliest writings and thinking about rhetoric and persuasion. In addition, Corax and Tisias coached citizens on the art of speaking so these citizens could be effective rhetors (speakers) in the courts. Robert Cathcart is a contemporary scholar and author of the book *Post Communication: Rhetorical Analysis and Evaluation.*[3] Cathcart has defined rhetoric as a "communicator's intentional use of language and other symbols to influence or persuade selected receivers to act, believe, or feel the way the communicator desires in problematic situations."[4]

According to legend, Corax at one point sued Tisias because Tisias had failed to pay him for his lessons. Because of the suit, these two brilliant orators found *themselve*s in a court of law attempting to "persuade selected receivers to act, believe, or feel the way the communicator desires in a problematic situation."

Tisias made two arguments to the adjudicators. He said that if he was able to persuade the judges that he was correct, then of course he need not pay Corax for the lessons. Second, he argued that if he was *unable* to convince the judges that he was correct, then he *still* should not have to pay Corax. He reasoned that if he, Tisias, was unable to persuade the adjudicators, then he owed Corax no compensation for what had been, apparently, ineffective lessons.

Corax had an opportunity to respond, and he too made two arguments. First, he claimed that if he was able to persuade the judges, then he, of course, should receive payment from Tisias. Second, he reasoned that if the judges determined that Tisias did not owe Corax *any* compensation, that would mean that, in essence, Corax actually *deserved* compensation. He argued that if the judges were persuaded to support Tisias, Tisias's arguments must have been persuasive. If Tisias's arguments were persuasive, this would prove that Corax deserved payment, because Corax had taught Tisias how to create arguments.

- According to Cathcart's definition, who has the stronger case, Corax or Tisias? That is, which argument is likely to persuade the "selected receivers to act, believe, or feel the way the communicator desires in this problematic situation"?
- What factors typically affect a person's ability to "persuade selected receivers"?
- What must any speaker do to prepare for a presentation that has persuasive elements?

## INTRODUCTION

Every day you, and almost everyone you know, engage in persuasive communication. You may attempt to persuade

- An instructor to grant an extension on a paper
- A supervisor to increase your salary
- A restaurant manager to get more attractive shifts
- A friend to let you borrow a car
- An older sibling to obtain a loan
- A younger sibling to get a job instead of requesting a loan
- A classmate to go to a movie
- Roommates to get them to vacuum the living room for once

An examination of any individual's daily interactions would reveal that nearly all communications involve some degree of persuasion. Similarly, presentations in organizational contexts nearly always contain some element of persuasion.

- A report on a department's activities implicitly if not explicitly includes an attempt to persuade listeners that the department is busy, effective, and in need of continued financial support.
- A demonstration of a product's functionality is intended to be persuasive. Presenters are explaining why the product is innovative, valuable, and more effective than the competition or previous versions.
- Presentations of credentials for a vacant position implicitly attempt to persuade the receivers that the aspiring candidate is the best applicant for the job.
- All sales talks, though disguised as informative, are essentially persuasive.

The effects of successful persuasion may be dramatic. Organizational sales can increase. Innovative changes may transform and energize a company. Personal status and wealth can soar.

The repercussions of ineffective persuasion can also affect organizational and personal progress. Any salesperson who draws salary against commission knows the feeling of not meeting a quota. Most employees know the frustration of not being able to convince supervisors of a plan that the employee sees as beneficial to all.

Roger Boisjoly no doubt still wishes he had been successful at persuading the engineers at the Marshall Space Flight Center not to launch the space shuttle *Challenger* on January 28, 1986. Boisjoly worked for a company called Morton Thiokol. Thiokol was an outside contractor for the Marshall Space Flight Center that had been hired to manufacture parts for the *Challenger*. One such part was something that has been referred to as the O-rings. Roger Boisjoly knew that these O-rings needed to be resilient to function and that they would lose resiliency in cold weather. The forecast for the day of the launch was for temperatures too low to guarantee the necessary resiliency. During a teleconference on January 27, 1986, Boisjoly made his pitch and tried to persuade Marshall representatives not to launch. He was unsuccessful.

Sixty seconds after takeoff the *Challenger* exploded. Seven astronauts lost their lives. The terrible deaths of these astronauts became even more horrific when it was discovered that they did not die instantly. The chamber where they were housed likely remained intact until it was shattered, along with its occupants, when it crashed into the ocean. In addition to the loss of human life, the health and growth of the Marshall Space Flight Center and NASA was stymied for many years after the explosion.[5]

The ability—or failure—to persuade within organizations does not always have such dramatic and catastrophic effects. Yet it is wise to examine how to persuade others in organizational contexts and elsewhere. As Aristotle argued 2,500 years ago, speakers are obligated to attempt to be effective with their persuasion.

> *It is absurd to hold that persons should be ashamed of being unable to defend themselves with their limbs, but not of being unable to defend themselves with speech and reason, when the use of rational speech is more distinctive of a human being than the use of limbs.*[6]

## Defining Persuasion

Which of the following are examples of persuasion?

- *"I have several state-of-the-art laptops, loaded with software, that are worth fifteen hundred dollars apiece. I will sell you five for seven thousand dollars. This represents a savings of five hundred dollars."*
- *"I have been in the computer business since its inception. I actually knew Gates when he was starting out. Trust me on this. These machines are better than any others, and you can take my word as an expert on that. Also, I will sell them to you for far less than what they are worth. I know exactly what they are worth and what the competition is selling them for. Seven thousand dollars for five. Don't miss this unusual opportunity for what is—let me assure you—a very good deal for a fine product."*
- *"Many people think all laptops are essentially the same. Tell me, do you want to use an inferior product that will regularly malfunction? More significant, do you want to carry around a no-name brand—a second-tier product—that will, inevitably, make you and your organization appear to be second tier? I will sell you these five machines for seven thousand dollars, and you can feel and be perceived as a major player and a high-quality professional."*
- *"We have done business in the past and I have done you many favors. Do you remember what happened last year when we came through for you when you needed that machine within twenty-four hours? Do you remember that? Also, friend, between the two of us, the economy has been terrible for the past quarter, and this has dramatically affected my income. You know that my kids are both in college at the same time, and that expense, friend, can be devastating. If you were to purchase these five laptops for this seven grand asking price, you would be getting a good deal on a fantastic product and also doing me a favor that I think—and I think you will agree—I deserve. I know you could go across the street, but in this instance, we are talking the same quality, and besides—really—you owe me."*

- *"If you do not purchase these laptops, there could be grave consequences. We can make it difficult for you to obtain necessary materials. We know people who will play ball with us. We can make many things difficult for you. Think about it. The asking price is fair. Why should you have to experience any trouble? Do business with us and everyone will be happy."*

## Persuasion and Being Persuasive

Some of the above examples are more persuasive than others. However, except for the last case, *all* of them are examples of persuasion. Persuasion is defined as *any attempt* to be persuasive that guarantees the receiver a genuine perception of choice. When the speaker attempts to influence others to think or behave in the way the speaker wants, the speaker is persuading—even if the speaker is ultimately not persuasive.

It is not, however, persuasion to threaten customers if they do not purchase a product from you. That is coercion. A thief who puts a gun to your head may be effective in stealing your wallet, but we would not define that as persuasion. The thief will have effectively coerced you into giving over your funds, but you did not actually have an option. In each of the first four examples above, the receiver could elect to purchase the laptops or not purchase them. The receiver is in the position to consider the merit of the arguments and choose accordingly. Some of the arguments are stronger than others, but each is an attempt to persuade.

The challenge for speakers is to be persuasive with their persuasion. That challenge is met by identifying specific objectives and, as Aristotle argued, evaluating and appropriately using all "the available means of persuasion."[7]

### Reverse the Perspective

From your perspective as a listener:

- Which of the four examples of persuasion described on pages 165–166 would have been persuasive to you? Why?
- In each instance, how did the speaker attempt to persuade the listener?
- Assuming that the laptops are good products and worth the price asked, are any of the examples of persuasion unethical?
- How might you have attempted to sell the product differently?

# Persuasive Objectives

The initial step for any speaker who attempts to persuade receivers is to identify the specific objectives of the message. Such objectives can be categorized in one of the following four ways. A speaker may wish to:

- Influence others to consider changing an attitude or behavior
- Change behavior or attitudes
- Actuate, i.e., persuade readers to do something or act
- Reaffirm existing behavior or attitudes

## Influence Others to Consider Changing an Attitude or Behavior

In certain situations, the persuasive objective may simply be to move receivers so that they subsequently may be in a position to act. In these situations, the objective is not to change an attitude or motivate the audience to alter behavior, but rather to have receivers consider a perspective that previously had been categorically rejected.

For example, some professional athletes or actors may have made decisions never to endorse any product that they do not already use. An advertiser may nevertheless wish to persuade these performers to endorse a product. However, identifying this as an initial goal would be foolish, because the performers have adamantly rejected the idea. Therefore, an advertiser may decide to try to weaken the commitment to the position, and not necessarily change the attitude.

Consider a second example. You may think it is in your organization's best interests to curb its tradition of rapid expansion. However, the people you need to convince are those who initiated the policy and consider their ambition to be a badge of honor. Your persuasive goal may be to dilute the intensity of their convictions and consequently influence them to consider changing their attitude toward expansion.

## Change Behavior or Attitudes

In many instances influencing audiences to consider changing an attitude is not sufficient. There may be an urgency that compels the speaker to achieve immediate results. Also, it may be that "changing the attitude" is a reasonable objective given the situation and there is no need for any intermediate step.

Assume that surveys indicate that the general population considers furriers to be unethical individuals who prey on innocent animals. Advocates for furriers may wish to change this attitude, not necessarily to increase sales of fur products, but to make their everyday work less combative. Instead of fighting off activists who are energized by public sympathy, the furriers would like to pursue their life's work in relative tranquility. The furriers' advocates will need to change the general population's attitude about the profession to re-create an image that will be conducive to a less turbulent existence.

Lawyers may wish to dispel the notions that are promulgated by the legion of lawyer jokes depicting attorneys as unscrupulous guns for hire. These attitudes, lawyers may feel, discourage individuals from trusting attorneys, consequently requiring tremendous initial energy to disabuse potential clients of prejudices. Associations of and for lawyers might desire to change the prevailing attitude about the profession so that attorneys can avoid the need to prove their goodwill each time they meet with new clients.

## Actuate

Some persuasion is unsuccessful even if attitudes have been changed. A Democratic politician may seek support from people who typically vote for Republicans. If a group of receivers has, for decades, maintained that Democrats should not be elected, a Democrat may be able to influence the voters to reconsider, and may even succeed at actually changing the attitude. However, unless the Democrats can get the voters to pull the appropriate lever on Election Day, the politicians' persuasion will be unsuccessful.

Consider a second example. A university may have a policy that compels instructors to automatically expel students who have been found guilty of plagiarism. A student advocate may need to convince a faculty assembly that determines policy that this rule is inappropriate when applied universally. If the advocate cannot change attitudes either about the gravity of the offense or the universal application of the expulsion rule, then students will continue to be expelled automatically for plagiarizing. However, even if the attitude is changed, the persuasion will be unsuccessful unless the assembly is moved to act, and as a result, rewrites the policy.

### Reaffirm Existing Behavior or Attitudes

One goal of persuasion is to stimulate dormant attitudes. Company CEO Johnson may agree with HR Director Patel that it is necessary to build an exercise facility for employees. Patel may not need to persuade Johnson to consider the notion or change the attitude. However, Johnson may not be dwelling on the matter. Patel's goal may be to reenergize Johnson's existing belief and thereby ignite embers. The result of the reaffirmation may be the construction of the exercise facility.

## Tools of Persuasion

Persuasive arguments can be classified into the four general areas that are described in the pages that follow. As we discussed in Chapter 5, the foundation for any successful presentation requires the speaker to be familiar with audience members. This foundation is especially vital when considering persuasive presentations. Studying the audience will allow speakers to select which combination of the following methods is the best for their persuasive objective.

### Arguments of Ethos

Arguments of ethos are based on the credibility and authority of the source. As discussed in previous chapters, ethos is defined as the status audience members attribute to the speaker. It is important to emphasize that individuals do not have ethos; ethos is attributed to them. An argument of ethos attempts to persuade receivers not because of the inherent logic within the claim, but because of the person who is making the claim. Below are a number of examples.

> *"I started with this company when I was twenty-three. For thirty years I have witnessed the remarkable growth of our enterprise. And for all of these thirty years, as many of you know, I have been adamantly opposed to expansion, but now I know what we must do for the best interests of our organization. We must accept the challenge of creating a satellite office in Madrid. Trust me. I come to this conclusion reluctantly, but I know it is the right way to proceed."*

> *"You may wonder why I am such a proponent of a conservative three-square-meals-a-day diet. I have successfully completed five triathlons. If it weren't for a nourishing breakfast, a nutritious small lunch, and a sensible dinner I could not have maintained the level of energy necessary to achieve during these grueling events. I have never failed to finish a triathlon, and I almost never miss any one of my three squares. Therefore, I encourage you to take care of your diet, because at the same time you will be taking care of your strength."*

> *"For seven years after high school I worked dead-end jobs. When I finally attended and then graduated from college, a new world opened up to me. I now earn a six-figure income! Do not forsake your chances for success. Life is not a dress rehearsal. Complete your education by going to college."*

Who you are is often perceived as more important than the logical or emotional effect of any other arguments you might employ. For example, depending on the strength of the speaker's ethos, the following message will be viewed as either supportive, encouraging and persuasive, or insincere and meaningless:

*"As many of you are aware, I've been with the company for many years. I can assure you that although budgets are presently lean, our next-quarter forecast is optimistic. Therefore budget and salary increases are right around the corner."*

The following factors will affect speaker ethos in a persuasive presentation:

- **Perceived competence**. Does the speaker appear to be knowledgeable, prepared, and professional?
- **Trustworthiness**. Is the speaker someone who can be depended on? Has this person been honest in the past?
- **Charisma**. Is the speaker physically attractive? Does she or he have power within the organization? Is the speaker able to charm and mesmerize an audience?
- **Dynamism.** Does the speaker appear genuinely enthused about the subject?
- **Reputation.** Has this person earned respect from the listeners for successful work?
- **Attire.** Is the speaker's dress appropriate for the occasion? Does it enhance the speaker's physical gifts and therefore contribute to speaker charisma?
- **Posture.** Are posture and other nonverbal behaviors complementary or at least consistent with the message?
- **Intermediate or derived ethos: quality of content.** Is the "what" or the content of the presentation logical and substantive?
- **Intermediate or derived ethos: quality of delivery.** Is the presentation delivered in a manner that reflects preparation? Are vocal qualities engaging?
- **Intermediate or derived ethos: ability to establish rapport with an audience.** Does the content of the talk reflect an understanding of the audience and a desire to establish rapport with the audience?

## Logical Arguments

A logical argument is based on the integrity of the content within the claim. Essentially, a logical argument appears to make sense and appears able to withstand intelligent scrutiny. The following are examples of such arguments:

*"Surveys have indicated that students enjoy having freedom when they select courses. If we increase the number of required courses within the major, students will have less freedom. We must respect student needs and desires. Therefore, we should not increase requirements that will decrease student opportunity to take electives."*

*"For four years our local municipality has been governed by Mayor Smith. In that time the value of home properties here have gone up, three new schools have been built, and several organizations have decided to headquarter here, thereby driving up the tax base. People from various neighboring communities now speak highly about our town, and for good reason. Mayor Smith's leadership has resulted in changes that have altered perceptions of our community. Vote for Smith in November."*

*"We must again diversify our product line. As you know, ten years ago four of our competitors decided not to diversify when we elected to do so. Three of these four are no longer in existence. The fourth has seen its stock price plummet to a record low. We are now faced with the same decision we confronted a decade ago. We must make the intelligent choice now as we did then and diversify."*

Not all "logical arguments" are in reality logical. The history of advertising, for example, is replete with cases of persuasive campaigns that used "logical" arguments that, under scrutiny, were found to be flawed.

For example, a toothpaste company attempted to persuade consumers by claiming that those who used its brand would endure relatively few dental problems. In the televised commercials a young child would run toward a parent while waving what appeared to be a report. The child would gleefully shout, "Mommy, Mommy. Our group had 23 percent fewer cavities."

The object was to have viewers believe that a test demonstrated the preventive value of the product. It is, of course, logical to use toothpaste that will result in a decrease in cavities. However, when the persuasive argument was analyzed, it appeared that the test compared a group of children who used the product regularly with another group of children who were not compelled to follow a regimen of dental hygiene. Therefore, although the intent was to have receivers believe that logic supported the claim, the argument was not logical. Obviously if a group of people brushed regularly with any brand, they would have fewer cavities than another group who may only sporadically use a toothbrush.

Nevertheless, this type of persuasive argument is classified as logical because it is an appeal to logic. The goal is for the receiver to think that there is logic behind the claim.

### Ethical Probe

**Do advertisers have ethical responsibilities?**

- Did the toothpaste company violate any ethical obligations when it attempted to persuade consumers in the way described?
- Do advertisers have any ethical obligations when they attempt to persuade customers?
  - If you believe they do, what are these ethical obligations?
  - If you believe they do not, why do you feel as you do?
- Can you identify examples of so-called logical arguments that were not logical and were, in your opinion, unethical?

## Emotional Arguments

The overwhelming evidence suggests that on August 4, 1892, Elizabeth Borden, a thirty-three-year-old woman from an affluent family, used an ax to kill her stepmother and father. Her lawyer attempted to refute the case against her in his comprehensive summation to the jury, but likely had his most profound effect with this final point he made to the jurors. "To find her guilty you must believe she is a fiend. Gentlemen: Does she look it?"[8]

Some arguments are persuasive not because they are necessarily logical, but because they affect the receivers' emotions. The twelve jurors took less than an hour to acquit Lizzie Borden, the preponderance of evidence notwithstanding. Apparently, she did not look like a fiend.

Persuasive messages based on emotion involve fear, pity, guilt, and intimations of pleasure. Below are some examples.

### Pity

*"John has worked very very hard on this program. I know he was here all weekend and has spent several late nights at the facility. I cannot compel you to attend this*

*session, but I just want you to know that I think it is the right thing to do. No one who has spent this amount of time on a thankless project should be humiliated by an embarrassing turnout."*

## Guilt

*"Every single person in this room has enjoyed the comforts and convenience of the company cafeteria. And every single person in this room has enjoyed the cleanliness that greets everyone each time we arrive here. We all know who is responsible for the way this place looks. Angie is responsible. To ask you all to chip in what amounts to the cost of a couple of drinks to buy Ang a decent holiday gift is the least we can do for someone who has done so much for us."*

## Happiness

*"Five years ago I started in this business just as you are starting today. Hard work will bring financial rewards, but there is much more than the money. In time all of you who are industrious will feel the satisfaction—the joy—that comes from accepting a challenge and meeting that challenge. The pleasure of owning a beautiful home, of vacationing to exotic places, of pleasing your spouses, of making your parents and children proud—all this awaits those of you who are sitting out there today. There are many smiles on the horizon for each and every one of you. Hard work equals success, and success begets well-deserved pleasure."*

## Fear

*"You might not need to check your brakes every ten thousand miles. Most brakes and pads can last twenty or thirty thousand miles. Of course, the repercussions of failing brakes are serious, as we all know. I can show you some photos of people who have been scarred for life because they did not have adequate brakes on their vehicles. You can do what you want, and probably you will have no problem. But who knows. You might want to play it safe and check the brakes every ten thousand miles just for your own peace of mind...and safety."*

## Responsibility

*"It is possible and even likely that most people do not need extra life insurance. However, how do you want your spouse and children to live if something horrific should happen to you? They will survive, as I am sure they are survivors, but there are important questions to consider nevertheless. What will be the quality of their lives? How can you act responsibly to ensure that they will be happy in case of tragedy?"*

Baird argues that emotional and logical arguments could be and should be complementary. He argues that "When the intellectual qualities dominate with relative absence of the affective appeals, the oration fails just as it does when emotion sweeps aside reason."[9] The most cursory review of persuasive advertising campaigns would indicate that emotional strategies are used quite frequently, often complementing logical arguments. A tobacco company may suggest that its brand has less nicotine than competitors and also that smoking the brand will make it seem like "springtime." A detergent will be shown to not only eliminate dirt from soiled apparel, but also render the person who does the cleaning a valuable life partner. A tire product will not only increase miles to the gallon, but also transform the drivers into responsible parents and environmentally conscious citizens. Similarly, a businessperson can advocate for antipollution measures because it will protect the organization from federal scrutiny as well as allow the executives to feel like considerate community players. Building a new health facility for employees will result in fewer days lost to illness and also make the organization and its members feel better about themselves.

## Arguments Employing Reservations

Any persuasive effort has an opposing side. The arguments that support the opposing side are called reservations. For example, a persuasive case in support of capital punishment would have the following reservations:

- Capital punishment could result in an innocent person being executed.
- Evidence suggests that capital punishment does not deter crime.
- People who cannot afford high-quality representation are more likely to be convicted than those who can afford representation.
- It is "cruel and unusual" punishment.

If speakers suspect that receivers have reservations about the persuasive argument, they must address the reservations to be effective. The following are persuasive arguments that employ reservations:

> *"Some of you may feel that we must increase the number of requirements in the major to ensure that all students are properly prepared for their careers. However, increasing the number of electives does not preclude the possibility that students can select what would be the required courses on their own volition. Moreover, because all students have distinctive goals, it is impossible to identify those courses that should be required for all students for them to be ready for the work world. Students should be permitted to select the curriculum that meets their individual needs and career aspirations."*

> *"Adversaries claim that Mayor Smith has not supported unionization. Although it is true that Smith has been against the unionization of some city employees, she has been a stalwart supporter of the police and firefighter unions. In fact, some of you may not be aware that Smith was a member of the police union when she was on the force. Her position regarding the teacher's union is based on her feeling that we cannot hurt our youngsters by allowing teachers to go on strike. But make no mistake about it, Smith is a strong proponent of education."*

> *"I can understand the concern of those who think that diversifying the line will require tremendous initial costs in equipment, machinery, and even personnel. This is so, but in the long run these costs will translate into profits. Any enterprise must invest in its future. These expenditures are the seeds that will enable us to grow prosperously."*

When preparing for a presentation, speakers should identify all the reservations to the argument. Protagoras, a Greek scholar who is sometimes referred to as the "father of debate," claimed that to be effective, individuals had to be able to argue both sides of the argument. Preparing to argue both sides of an argument will help you identify reservations. Speakers should deal with each reservation in one of three ways.

### Refute the reservation outright if the counterargument is refutable.

If the reservation can be refuted, then refute the reservation.[10] Speakers do not want receivers to contemplate the merit of counterarguments if these reservations can be effectively contradicted. If Mayor Smith is indeed a supporter of unions and was a union member herself, then the reservation that she categorically opposes unionization can be, and should be, countered. If there is no evidence that increasing the number of student requirements within a major prepares students for distinctive career opportunities, then that reservation can and should be contradicted.

### Downplay the significance of the reservation.

Some reservations cannot be refuted. If diversifying the product line will increase expenses, then refuting that reservation will only damage speaker ethos. The speaker must address the reservation, however, and can do so by offsetting its legitimacy with an argument that will downplay its significance. In the example about diversification above, the speaker attempts to downplay the significance of the reservation by claiming that the expenses will eventually result in profits.

A proponent of capital punishment cannot refute the reservation that such punishment may result in the execution of an innocent person. However, the proponent can attempt to counter the reservation by mitigating its significance. In this instance, mitigating the significance is extraordinarily difficult. However, it should be attempted.

> *"There is nothing more precious than human life, and it cannot be disputed that there may be instances when capital punishment will result in the loss of innocent life. However, I am advocating capital punishment only in instances when the murderer has confessed to the crime and the evidence is incontrovertible. Even then, I know, an innocent person may be executed. But when considering the loss of innocent life let us also not forget the legion of innocent people who are slain daily by gutless killers. These victims also represent innocent lives. Thousands of them. Thousands of innocent lives lost because of the whims of incorrigible monsters. These monsters may think twice about their behavior if they know that they too might be taken from this world because of their cowardly inhumanity."*

### Ignore the reservation.

The last resort in dealing with reservations is to ignore them. It *is* a *last* resort. The only reason to ignore a reservation is if it is truly insignificant and if one's best guess is that very few, if any, receivers will have thought of it. If it is insignificant, the persuader is not avoiding his or her ethical obligations by omitting it. If no receiver will think of it, then bringing it up will make your presentation less concise than it needs to be.

Assume that you have been asked to deliver a presentation on any two of the following issues.

- Cigarette smoking should be prohibited in all of our business offices.
- United Way solicitations should not be permitted at work.
- Random drug testing is necessary within contemporary organizations.
- E-mail should be used solely for work-related communications.

(continues)

- Racial minorities and women should be represented within any organization. Aggressive recruitment should be implemented to ensure this representation.
  - Develop a three-minute presentation that includes at least one argument based on ethos, emotion, and logic for the two topics you selected. Address the appropriate reservations.
  - List a reservation for each of the other topics that you did not select.
  - How would you address each of the reservations you identified?

## The Motivated Sequence

Alan Monroe suggested an approach to persuasion that is endorsed by nearly every writer who discusses the topic.[11] Monroe called his approach the Motivated Sequence, and it is often referred to in books as Monroe's Motivated Sequence. It consists of the following five steps:

- **Attention**
- **Need**
- **Satisfaction**
- **Visualization**
- **Action**

### Attention

*"Are you tired of salaries that do not reflect your capabilities and contributions? Do you wish at the end of the day that once, just once, you would be overpaid like so many executives who apparently are paid a million dollars for each of the groveling sycophants who do their bidding? Wouldn't it be nice if once, just once, you got what you deserved?"*

### Need

*"Well, that would be nice. The fact is, however, that in nonunion shops like this one, that will never happen. Throughout the country, if not the world, employees in nonunion facilities are treated like second-class citizens."*

### Satisfaction

*"This could change and there is no reason why it should not. If a union were started here,* last *year would be* the last year *of an abusive administration."*

## Visualization

*"In several local businesses much like this one, unions have been formed. Just like those in these other factories, you too could have better working conditions. You too could force the managing millionaires to meet the monetary mandate of the masses. You too could have what you deserve."*

## Action

*"It is one thing to bellyache about the current situation. It is quite another to do something about it. On March 4 you can do something about it. As you well know, there is a vote in two weeks. Do not be bullied into doing the bidding of the fat cats. If you are tired of being executed by the executives, vote* Yes *for the union. March forth on March 4th."*

# Ethical Issues

Ethical issues pertaining to presentations are discussed in detail in Chapter 3. However, a chapter dealing with persuasion requires some comment about ethical decisions.

Persuasive speakers are faced with choices. Certainly it can be easier to make a sale by misleading receivers. Politicians can gain support or be elected by distorting an opponent's record. Managers can motivate employees to work harder by misrepresenting reality. Despite these possible benefits from unethical persuasion, is it ever appropriate to persuade unethically?

Once, after I had negotiated a deal for a new car, the salesperson attempted to sell me undercoating for the vehicle. Just that morning I had read about the standard preparation for each car like the one I had purchased. I had learned that these automobiles were routinely undercoated in the factory. When I mentioned this to the salesperson, he smiled, shrugged, and said, "Well, you can't blame me for trying."

As argued in Chapter 3 there are at least two reasons why all speakers should be honest when they attempt to persuade others. The first is that people who establish reputations for honesty have less difficulty persuading subsequently than those who have earned a reputation for being dishonest. I have purchased three vehicles since the episode described above and have never returned to that dealership. I could and did "blame him for trying" to sell me an unnecessary service.

More significantly, we should make ethical choices when we persuade because that is what we expect and desire from others when we are receivers. None of us is omniscient. We respect people who are honest, expect to be treated honestly, and are bruised when we are deceived. We therefore have the obligation to make ethical choices when we speak to our receivers.

Dishonest communication behavior may be normative. How normal do you want to be?

# Summary

- Persuasion is an implicit dimension of most business presentations
- Persuasion is a type of communication that attempts to influence receivers while allowing receivers a perception of choice

- Persuasive presentations attempt to
  - Influence receivers to consider a position
  - Change an attitude
  - Take specific actions
  - Reaffirm an existing position
- Persuasive arguments are based on
  - Logic
  - Emotion
  - Ethos
  - Reservation
- Alan Monroe's Motivated Sequence is endorsed by many as a simple method for organizing persuasive messages. It includes the following stages:
  - Attention
  - Need
  - Satisfaction
  - Visualization
  - Action
- Ethical considerations are important to consider when preparing persuasive messages

## Sample Presentation for Analysis

### In Defense of Rhetoric

*Speechwriter Andrew B. Wilson delivered* "In Defense of Rhetoric" *to the Chicago Speechwriter's Forum in Chicago on August 5, 2003. As you read through this excerpt, please consider the following questions:*

1. *Does the introductory anecdote about Judge Sweat serve the speaker's intended purpose? What is the purpose?*
2. *Why do people speak disparagingly of rhetoric?*
3. *Do you consider rhetoric more problematic than valuable? Explain.*
4. *Did the speaker's rhetoric result in a persuasive defense of rhetoric? Explain.*

Dear fellow speechwriters. Dear storytellers and searchers for meaning in turbulent times. Long ago, when prohibition was a hot issue in the state of Mississippi, Judge Noah S. Sweat Jr. gave a speech that took a "stand" on whiskey. It won instant recognition as one of the classics of oratory.

I'm sure some of you know the speech very well. With great drollery, Judge Sweat came down hard on both sides of the issue of whether he was for or against whiskey.

"If when you say whiskey," he began, "you mean the devil's brew, the poison scourge..." and here he put together a string of colorful metaphors lambasting the evils of excessive consumption. If that is what you mean, he declared, he was against it. However, he countered, "if when you say whiskey, you mean the oil of conversation, the philosophic wine..." and this time he was equally brilliant and extravagant in employing rhetoric to extol the benefits of moderate consumption in the company of friends. If that is what you mean, the judge said, he was for it. "This is my stand," he concluded. "I will not retreat from it. I will not compromise."

Inspired by this fearless feat of fence straddling, I propose to tackle a topic that is no less controversial (and intoxicating) than whiskey. I speak of rhetoric itself. Plato condemned it. Aristotle, his pupil, spoke in its defense. The debate over rhetoric has raged back and forth ever since.

Taking a cue from Judge Sweat, I will tell you how I feel about rhetoric.

If, when you say rhetoric, you mean windy effusions and empty promises...or the crafty logic that makes the lesser argument appear the better; if you mean thoughts that are low but words that are sweet and pleasing to the ear...the honeyed whispers of the seducer...and the unctuous urgings of the snake-oil salesman; if you mean the overblown and flowery speech that puts an expectant audience to sleep...or the use of words to evade the need for action; still more, if you mean the lowest form of oratory...bigoted and incendiary speech that...dethrones reason...incites men to violence...and sets tribe against tribe, race against race, and religion against religion; then, certainly, I am against it.

But...if, when you say rhetoric, you mean the well turned phrase and the well constructed speech; the after-dinner toast that creates merriment and cheer at the close of an evening...or the witty and heartfelt eulogy that undoes death...making a loved one seem vividly alive and present; if you mean the ability to render complex issues in clear and simple language...to breathe poetry into policy...and create a sense of urgency; if you mean the gentle art of charming an audience and sending ripples of laughter through a crowded ballroom; still more, if you mean the highest form of oratory...powerful and passionate language that elevates the heart and frees the mind, that unites good people behind a just cause, that lights the fire of liberty...and inspires us to overcome insurmountable odds and fight against wickedness and injustice; well, then, certainly, I am for it.

At this point in his speech, Judge Sweat rested his case, without really taking sides. But I am not finished, and I do not intend to remain impartial.

Rhetoric is no longer admired. It is no longer studied. It has sunk to the bottom of the barrel, linguistically speaking—as a word that is now used almost exclusively in a pejorative sense. I believe that rhetoric deserves a fuller defense—both from an historical and a present-day perspective...

...I will go back to the whole issue of whether rhetoric is a good thing or a bad thing? Clearly, it is both.

It is condemned—loudly and often—for a variety of ills. But is it applauded for the good it does? No, hardly ever. That is a terrible injustice. It is also folly.

**Source:** Wilson, Andrew. "In Defense of Rhetoric," *Vital Speeches of the Day*, September 15, 2003, 69, no. 23.

## Review Questions

1. Define persuasion.
2. How can status reports presented during meetings be perceived as requiring persuasion? How can demonstrations of a product's capabilities be seen as requiring persuasion?
3. What does the word *actuate* mean? How is it applicable to persuasive communication?
4. What is meant by an argument of ethos?
5. Why are logical arguments not always logical?
6. How do salespeople employ arguments of emotion? Arguments of reservation?

## InfoTrac Question

John Graham has written at least two articles found on InfoTrac pertaining to persuasion and business presentations. In a 2004 article he lists twelve guidelines for making persuasive presentations. Which, if any, of these twelve guidelines seem significant to you as you consider how to deliver persuasive presentations?

---

[1] Norman Thomas was born in the late 1800s and was active in the American political arena during the first half of the twentieth century and until his death in 1968. While described at times as an American socialist (and as a six-time presidential nominee of the Socialist party), Thomas vigorously opposed Communism and was active in the American Civil Liberties Union. This quote not only reflects his disdain for demagoguery, but also his sense of the importance of effective advocacy.

[2] Lord Hailsham (Quinton Hogg) was born in 1907 and died in 2001. He served in both the House of Lords and the House of Commons in the British Parliament.

[3] Robert Cathcart, *Post Communication: Rhetorical Analysis and Evaluation* (Indianapolis: Bobbs-Merrill, 1981).

[4] Ibid., 2.

[5] The effects of the disaster on the health of the Marshall Space Flight Center is documented in Phillip Tompkins's book *Organizational Communication Imperatives* (Los Angeles: Roxbury Publishing Company, 1993).

[6] Aristotle, from *The Rhetoric and the Poetics of Aristotle,* trans. W. Rhys Roberts, Modern Library ed. (New York: Random House, 1954), 23.

[7] Ibid., 24.

[8] The complete text of George Dexter Robinson's summation can be found at **http://www.lizzieandrewborden.com/CrimeLibrary/ClosingRobinson.htm**.

[9] A. Craig Baird, *Brittannica Micropaedia,* 15th ed., s.v. "Oratory."

[10] See James McCroskey, *An Introduction to Rhetorical Communication,* 8th ed. (New York: Allyn and Bacon, 2001), 124–125. Also in Richard Perloff, *The Dynamics of Persuasion* (Hillsdale, New Jersey: Erlbaum, 1993), 167. Perloff argues that two-sided messages are better than one-sided messages for several reasons. One is that two-sided messages respect the audience's intelligence. Second, the authors write, "a two sided message allows the persuader to develop counterarguments."

[11] Alan Monroe discusses the Motivated Sequence in *Principles of Speech* (Chicago: Scott Foresman, 1951), 200–203. As indicated in this chapter, it came to be called Monroe's Motivated Sequence. Monroe's Motivated Sequence is still discussed in many texts, including the 15th edition of Monroe's book, published in 2003. The title has changed slightly on a number of occasions over the years. Alan Monroe is deceased, but his name remains listed as one of the authors of this popular textbook.

**Chapter in a Nutshell** *Factors pertaining to delivery are very important and may be more significant than the actual content of the presentation.*

# 11 Verbal and Nonverbal Aspects of Delivery

*There is only one thing worse than saying the wrong thing and that is saying the right thing the wrong way.*[1]

-W. S. Pfeiffer

*Ford's halting manner of speaking contributed to the general impression that he was not smart, that he was unsure of himself.* [2]

-Larry Speakes

## Abstract

"It's not what you say; it's how you say it."

We have all heard that expression. A presentation delivered with vocal variation is far better than one delivered in a monotone. Speakers who cannot or do not find descriptive words for their messages are less effective than those who strive to select appropriate language for their presentations. This chapter examines the "how you say it" component of professional speaking. When you complete this chapter, you should be able to do the folllowing:

- Explain the difference between verbal and nonverbal communication
- Identify specific nonverbal behaviors that can affect the quality of professional presentations
- Discuss issues related to word choice and presentation delivery
- Suggest methods for addressing common problems that affect the quality of speech delivery

# Dr. Um

Ed Jackson was the loyal lieutenant. For seven years he had been Sharon's assistant at the huge city library. On the first Monday of every month when the entire staff met for Sharon's thirty-minute address, Sharon—invariably—remarked that if it were not for Ed's hard work on the research, or Ed's hard work on the grant, or Ed's hard work on the handouts, she would not be prepared to speak to the group that day. Each month after such acknowledgments, Jackson received a sincere ovation from the sixty librarians and staff members who worked at the facility.

Jackson was more than an efficient deputy. He had completed his doctorate in information science, but more significantly, he was a personable and compassionate man. It was to Jackson, not to Sharon, that employees came with their concerns, gripes, and requests. Employees asked Jackson to make the case to Sharon, to intervene for them, to do them a favor. Jackson was no pushover. He was capable of saying no when he had to, but he was also capable of rejecting a request in a way that made hearing "no" almost acceptable. When the staff applauded Jackson at Sharon's monthly meetings, it was out of appreciation for more than the graphics he had composed or the grant he had secured. Ed Jackson was held in very high esteem.

So, when Sharon accepted a new position heading another city's library system there would have been a revolution had Jackson not been selected as her replacement. At the first monthly meeting after his appointment, he was introduced to standing cheers. When the assembled stopped applauding, the erstwhile assistant took out some papers and began to articulate his five-year forecast for the library under his leadership.

What followed was an agonizing twenty-five minutes. Ed Jackson was a different person standing in front of the group than he had been when seated behind his desk. He seemed prepared with the content, but the delivery of the message was distracting. He stood with one hand in a pocket and leaned to his right at an unnatural angle. He spoke slowly, rocked his head indiscriminately in a pattern that resembled a figure eight, and could not seem to utter a single sentence without inserting several very long *ums*. "It has been, um, a pleasure to work, um, with Sharon as her assistant. I, um, wish her, as I am, um, sure you do, a wonderful, exciting time in, um, Milwaukee. I have, um, thought, um, quite a bit about how I, um, might make some changes at our, um, wonderful library."

By the third sentence the *ums* were excruciating.

Ed Jackson, this intelligent, responsible, and heretofore respected man, was transformed in a twenty-five minute period into someone who would need to be endured once a month. As much as the audience wanted Ed to do well, the staff sessions came to be dreaded. In time, the monthly presentations were noted in appointment books throughout the library with two words: "Dr. Um."

- Is it likely that a person as respected as Ed could lose prestige because of a speaking problem? Why or why not?
- Is the opposite true? Can people who are not bright or industrious gain esteem because of how they deliver—even vapid—messages? Why or why not?

## INTRODUCTION

### Silence, Words, and the Perception of Meaning

Abraham Lincoln once commented, "[It's] better to remain silent and be thought a fool than to speak out and remove all doubt."[3]

Lincoln's remark was probably intended to discourage people from speaking thoughtlessly. In some instances, his advice is most wise. However, it is important to understand that being silent does not preclude the perception of meaning. Silence may not definitively convey intelligence or ignorance, but it may well convey something to a particular receiver. A study published in the *Journal of Nonverbal Behavior,* for example, examined how audience members reacted to speakers' silences and *ums* during a presentation. The researcher determined that the frequency of the silences and *ums* affected audience perceptions of speaker preparation.[4] Similarly, body motion, dress, posture, and other nonverbal factors may affect what audience members think about a speaker and what they take away from a message. These determinations can be a function of individual audience members' experiences as well as their cultural backgrounds.

In addition, word choice can influence attitudes about a presentation regardless of audience familiarity with the words selected. A person who tells you that a meal was "simply divine" is likely to create a different impression from another who consumes the same fare and says the food is "really great." In both cases the receiver will know that the speaker enjoyed the meal, but different messages about the speaker and the food are likely to be conveyed on the basis of the words selected to describe it.

In this chapter we discuss how both nonverbal behaviors and the words we use—the verbal dimension—affect the quality of the messages we deliver to our audiences.

## UNDERSTANDING NONVERBAL COMMUNICATION

*"We can not withdraw our cards from the game. Were we as silent and as mute as stones, our very passivity would be an act."*

—*John Paul Sartre*

When we speak to our audiences, we relay information nonverbally through our voice, body motion, and eye contact. In fact, *most* of what receivers perceive as meaningful is based on nonverbal messages. According to researcher Albert Mehrabian, 93 percent of what we communicate is a function of nonverbal messages and only 7 percent is determined by the verbal components of our message. Although some researchers quibble with Mehrabian's percentages, the fact is that much of what receivers perceive is based on nonverbal messages.[5]

This creates problems for speakers. Nonverbal messages are often relayed inadvertently. They can complement the words that are used, but can also contradict the words that are spoken, or convey other messages entirely. Receivers actually tend to trust nonverbal messages more than verbal ones.[6] If a speaker hesitantly approaches the lectern, stands with a drooping posture, and sighs wearily before uttering a sound, receivers are unlikely to believe the subsequent statement "I am very happy to be here." If an alleged theater expert discusses the famous Tennessee Williams character Blanche Dubois, but mispronounces her last name, a receiver might "hear" that the speaker is actually not much of an expert at all.

As the above examples suggest, nonverbal messages can tarnish a presenter's ethos. However, nonverbal messages can also help elevate speaker status and make speakers appear to be more focused, energetic, and prepared. If a lack of concern for nonverbal behavior can have negative effects, acknowledging the nonverbal factors that affect delivery can also have a positive effect on audience perceptions of the speaker and the presentation.

## Misconceptions about Nonverbal Messages

Nonverbal communication has been a popular topic of conversation for at least the past twenty-five years.[7] Unfortunately, a result of this popularity has been that several misconceptions about nonverbal messages have been promulgated.

During a presentation skills seminar, an insurance executive delivered a talk on new products his organization intended to launch during the upcoming fiscal year. I noticed that during the talk he periodically, robotically, and arbitrarily thrust his arm into the air. The message he had delivered was interesting, but the receivers in the group could not get beyond the motions that punctuated the message. At the conclusion of the talk, several participants commented—diplomatically—that they had "noticed" the gestures. The speaker responded, "I'm glad you picked up on that. I wanted to put some body language into the speech for effect."

There are several incorrect notions about nonverbal messages that should be dispelled before examining how nonverbal behavior can affect delivery. One of these misconceptions is that it is wise to indiscriminately "put some body language into a speech for effect." Arbitrary motion is likely to appear to be arbitrary and peculiar to those witnessing the behavior. It is true that the absence of any motion is also distracting. Nevertheless, body motions should not be forced into a presentation to meet some quota.

### Nonverbal Messages and Meaning

A second misconception is that nonverbal messages typically have concrete meanings. They do not. As Grice and Skinner succinctly write, "Few if any nonverbal signals have universal meaning."[8] Nevertheless, occasionally one can spot an *expert* who claims otherwise. Below is a list of several claims made in a popular magazine:

- Open hands and an unbuttoned coat indicate openness in a person.
- Suspicion is indicated by crossed arms, glancing sideways, touching or rubbing the nose or eyes, buttoning the coat, and drawing away.

- Cooperation is shown with open hands, sitting on the edge of the chair, unbuttoning the coat, tilting the head, and hand-to-face gestures.
- Body movements that indicate reflection include peering over one's glasses, taking one's glasses off or cleaning them, pipe-smoking gestures, biting on the end of one's glasses, and putting one's hand on the bridge of the nose.[9]

Open hands might indicate cooperation to some people. To others it might indicate something else, if it indicates anything at all. Speakers are not indisputably conveying a sense of cooperation when they sit on the edge of their chair. Perhaps some might glean that from the choice of perch, but various meanings or no meaning might be attributed to that action. Arrive late to a talk and one receiver may think you are irresponsible, another may believe you are a very busy and important executive, and a third will be too busy contemplating an upcoming vacation to notice.

Neither the speaker nor the receivers should assume that nonverbal messages typically have discrete meanings. Manusov and Billingsley underscore this point when they write, "...when we view another's [nonverbal] behavior we may be inclined to judge that it is a direct reflection of some aspect of the other's character, mood, feeling, or belief. We may feel that we really have access to what is really going on inside the other's mind or heart. But we are also likely to be wrong." [10]

There are specific nonverbal actions that have one-to-one relationships between the action and a unit of meaning. They are called emblems and are usually contextual. For example, if someone were to ask how many years I've owned my car, I could put up five fingers. In that context, the gesture means something specific. If someone asks you if you have experience in accounting and you nod your head up and down, that movement means something specific.

However, most nonverbal messages do not mean something specific. They indisputably can be and often are meaningful, but what they mean can vary. Students must be aware of how certain nonverbal behaviors might be interpreted, but cannot assume that certain gestures and behaviors will be interpreted or even noticed by all observers. Therefore, readers should reject counsel that declares that open hands *will* mean *x*, and sitting on a chair *will* mean *y*—as quickly as arbitrarily "throwing body motion into a speech" is discarded.

## Nonverbal Messages and Body Language

Another misconception is that nonverbal behavior is a synonym for body language. *Body language* is a term that was popularized in Julius Fast's 1970 book of that title. Our bodies, in terms of posture, movement, gestures, and physical appearance, may indeed convey (various) meanings to receivers. However, there are other nonverbal factors that are similarly meaningful.

For example, time is a nonverbal factor that affects presentations. Individuals who speak longer than audience members anticipate or who arrive late to their talks may be relaying unintended messages to receivers. Vocal characteristics also create *non*verbal messages. The word *verbal* means "of, relating to, or consisting of words." The word *verbalize* simply means to put something into words. Many people say they want to meet and discuss something verbally, meaning they desire to have a face-to-face oral interaction. A verbal message, however, can be relayed either in writing or orally. Therefore, mispronouncing the name *Dubois* is an error pertaining to the *non*verbal category of vocalics because the problem does not pertain to the word *Dubois* but the nonverbal vocalic factor of how the word is spoken.

Even the quality of paper used for handouts is a nonverbal factor that can affect how audiences perceive speakers. Physical distance between the speaker and the audience may also affect a presentation and be perceived by audience members as meaningful.

Obviously, nonverbal behavior includes several areas that do not pertain specifically to the professed language of the body.

## Nonverbal Factors Affecting Presentation

*"What you do speaks so loud that I cannot hear what you say."* [11]

Nonverbal messages that affect the quality of presentations can be placed into several categories. Below is a list and then a description of each of these categories.

- Paralanguage
- Eye contact
- Body motion (kinesics)
- Physical appearance
- Time
- Space and distance

### Paralanguage

*Herbert Hoover, who carefully crafted a speech as an engineer might construct a bridge, succeeded only in boring audiences with his droning voice.*[12]

Paralanguage (sometimes referred to as vocalics) refers to how we say what we say. Rate, pronunciation, voice inflection, and other vocal characteristics may affect how audience members perceive speakers and their messages. There are several paralingual factors that affect delivery.

#### Rate and Volume

One's performance during presentations is affected by the speed of delivery and a speaker's ability to project. As we have emphasized throughout the text, the goal of any presentation is to have audience members receive the message. Audience members will be unable to digest a message that is uttered too rapidly. You may find it difficult to take notes when an instructor is racing through a lecture. Similarly, it is difficult to take mental notes when words are spoken too quickly.

In large rooms particularly, it is important to make sure your volume is loud enough for all those assembled. It is not especially helpful to ask if everyone can hear you. Some who cannot may indicate their difficulty. Others may be too shy to comment. Still others may be content *not* to be able to hear what you have to say.

**Common Problems with Rate and Volume**

- The speaker talks too rapidly.
- The speaker talks more rapidly during the actual presentation than during rehearsals for the talk.
- The speaker's voice is not audible to all receivers.
- The speaker's voice drops in volume at the end of sentences or at the end of the talk.

### Suggestions

- Audiotape rehearsals and actual presentations to become aware of speed issues and volume variations.
- Practice delivery in the room where the presentation will be delivered and have friends sit in the rear of the space. Have friends raise their hands when you are not audible.
- If speed problems persist after awareness, practice speaking at what seems to be an exaggerated, slow pace.

## Pitch, Inflection, and Emphasis

*Pitch* refers to the tone of your voice. Listening to a person speak using a consistent tone can be boring. We typically refer to such a consistent speaking voice or speaker as *monotone* (literally, "one tone"). As often as not, when we complain about a person who speaks in a monotone, we really mean that she or he is not varying the rate, volume, or pitch of the voice, and both the sounds and rhythm have become predictable.

*Inflection* refers to pitch and volume variation within a sentence. Understanding the meaning and effects of inflection may be easier if you consider a dictionary definition of the term. *Inflection* is defined as the "act or result of curving or bending."[13] When we speak, our voices tend to "curve and bend," sometimes in ways that are disconcerting. For example, a common problem for speakers is that they raise their voices at the end of declarative sentences as if the sentences are questions. You may have even asked people for their name and heard responses like "Pat Wilson" sound like "Pat Wilson?" This can be confusing to listeners attending to any one sentence and very annoying if habitual throughout a talk. Another common problem with inflection occurs when a sentence is uttered in a "singsong" pattern. For example, "I am here to speak to you about benefits" should not arbitrarily ascend at "here" and "to you" and then descend on "benefits." Over the course of even a short presentation, this inflection pattern will, very literally, drive an audience to distraction. A third common problem related to pitch and inflection occurs when speakers, often very innocently, use a tone that sounds condescending or patronizing to listeners.

The words speakers emphasize within a sentence and at any time during a talk can affect how successful they are when they deliver a presentation. When speakers desire to highlight a point, they should emphasize the salient words, phrase, or sentence that makes that point. Sometimes it is wise to emphasize words simply to maintain audience attention. Readers will note that newscasters stress words that are not necessarily the most significant words in their message. Of course, it is important not to emphasize words indiscriminately when such emphasis will distort meaning. Someone who declares that "**Union** activity will be fine with me" is saying something quite different from someone who says, "Union activity will be fine with **me**." In the former instance the emphasis suggests that other activity may not be fine with the speaker. In the second case the implication is that there are others who would not welcome union activity.

### Common Problems with Pitch, Inflection, Emphasis

- The speaker's voice does not contain variation in pitch and/or inflection. The voice is a monotone.
- The speaker raises the voice at the end of sentences, making statements sound like questions.
- The inflection becomes rhythmic and predictable.
- Inappropriate emphasis changes the meaning of the message.

## Emphasis and Variable Meaning

Leo Rosten in *The Joys of Yiddish* demonstrates how emphasizing different words in sentences can create very different meanings. In response to a request to purchase two tickets for a friend's concert a person might remark, "Two tickets for her concert I should buy?" Rosten explains how by emphasizing different words, the response can have several meanings.

Placing Rosten's example within the context of the university, imagine being contacted by a classmate who suggests that you should buy two tickets for his girlfriend's lecture. Assume that you respond by saying, "Two tickets for her lecture I should purchase?" As Rosten points out, seven different meanings are likely, depending on which of the words in the rejoinder are emphasized.

***Two** tickets for her lecture I should purchase?*
It would not enter my mind to consider buying one, and you want me buy two?

*Two **tickets** for her lecture I should purchase?*
Someone is actually printing tickets for your girlfriend's presentation?

*Two tickets for **her** lecture I should purchase?*
After the way she has treated me over the past semester, I should go to her talk?

*Two tickets for her **lecture** I should purchase?*
Don't you think it is somewhat pretentious to call her presentation a lecture?

*Two tickets for her lecture **I** should purchase?*
Why have you selected me as a potential customer?

*Two tickets for her lecture I **should** purchase?*
Is your inquiry an implicit instruction on morality or obligation?

*Two tickets for her lecture I should **purchase**?*
You are *selling* tickets to her lectures? If you were giving them away, I would be unlikely to attend. [14]

### Suggestions

- Audiotape your talk and listen for vocal variation.
- Ask friends to listen to your talk and comment on vocal variation.
- Plan to emphasize certain words when you speak.

## Articulation, Pronunciation, and Enunciation

These three related, but different, vocal factors can strengthen or weaken the quality of a presentation.

*Articulation* refers to distinctly uttering the words you are saying. For example, some people do not say *arctic* correctly and say *artic* instead. Many people say *goin'* instead of *going*, *dint* instead of *didn't*, or even *revelant* instead of *relevant*. One can advance the argument that poor articulation does not affect communication because the audience will "know what you mean." This may be true. The audience members will likely know what you mean. However, when you say *artic* for *arctic*, they may (a) know you are speaking about latitude and (b) assume that you are uneducated and not allow you any latitude for the incorrect articulation. If you conclude your sales pitch with "I would like you to go 'wit' our company," some customers may prefer to go wit' a competitor because they may sense that you are not sufficiently professional.

*Pronunciation* refers to the correct way to emphasize syllables within a word. The correct pronunciation of the word *syllable* is (SYLL-a-bil) not (sill-AB-el). Incorrect pronunciation can damage speaker ethos, because the audience may think it reflects a lack of preparation or intelligence.

At a funeral a clergyman consistently mispronounced the name of the deceased. This understandably infuriated the family, who had arranged for the eulogy and had provided the correct pronunciation specifically to avoid such embarrassment. Similarly, speaker ethos can be damaged if words are mispronounced, because it may seem that the speakers did not write the speech or that they are using words that they do not really know. If you are arguing in support of a smoke-free workplace, you will want to pronounce *carcinogen* and *carcinogenic* correctly. If you tell your managers that they must be *fiscally* responsible, you will be ridiculed if you add an additional syllable between the first and second in *fiscally*.

Finally, incorrect pronunciation can affect the meaning of words. Emphasizing the wrong syllable of the word *desert, confidant,* or *present*, for example, changes the meaning of the words.

*Enunciation*, like pronunciation and articulation, can help your talk be successful or be a less than positive influence. Enunciation refers to distinctly uttering consecutive words. In formal speaking situations, one should say, "What do you think? What are you going to do? You can forget about it" as opposed to "Whaddayathink" or "Whatchagonnado" or "Fuhgeddaboutit." Those who default to the latter options are not enunciating clearly, and, if they desire to be successful in most business arenas, may have to forget about it.

### Common Problems with Articulation, Pronunciation, and Enunciation

- The speaker does not say the final *g* sound in *going*, *swimming*, and similar words.
- The phrase *going to* is not enunciated clearly and becomes *gonna*.
- Mispronounced words damage speaker ethos.

### Suggestions

- For enunciation and articulation problems, listen to a tape of your talk with people who hail from a different part of the country.
- If unsure of how to pronounce a word, check any standard dictionary. How the word should be spoken appears in parentheses immediately following the entry.
- Review a list of commonly mispronounced words. (See Table 11-1.) Identify any words that you regularly mispronounce.

## Common Problem Words — Table 11-1

Check your dictionary to see which of these you pronounce correctly.

| | |
|---|---|
| Affluent | Posthumous |
| Applicable | Preventive |
| Apricot | Pulitzer |
| Athlete | Re |
| Caste | Recognize |
| Clique | Respite |
| Corps | Schism |
| Data | Sieve |
| Draw | Spontaneity |
| Formidable | Strength |
| Mischievous | Temperature |
| Niche | Vegan |
| Paradigm, Paradigmatic | |

### Accent

People occasionally refer to a speaker's *foreign accent*. This is a common phrase, but is actually a redundant expression. In this context, an accent is defined as any tone or inflection that is different from those used by you or those in your geographic area.[15] The expression *foreign accent* is therefore redundant, because any accent, by this definition, would be foreign to you. We all have an accent to certain others.

There are two issues related to speaker accent that are important to consider.

The first is that listeners can understand persons with accents, but may have to work harder to do so. Since our world is not likely to become less diverse, it behooves listeners to become accustomed to working industriously in order to get through the communication noise associated with accents.

The second issue is related to the first. Those who speak with an accent must realize that some listeners will not be appropriately industrious. When many listeners hear a tone or inflection that is foreign, they give up. This is an unfortunate reality and may reflect ethnocentric or even xenophobic perspectives. Yet, it may be wise for speakers to be particularly careful when articulating, enunciating, and pronouncing words.

### Speech Fillers

*Ums* and *ers* plague many speakers and the receivers who are compelled to endure them. When the speech fillers are pervasive, the common audience response is to marvel at their frequency and not focus on the speaker's intended message.

The first step in addressing problems with speech fillers is becoming aware of how often you employ them. This can be done by taping a message and counting the regularity of the interjections. Another method involves asking friends to listen to the talk. Have them raise their hands each time you say *er* or *um*. Initially, you will sense the upcoming negative reinforcement, which may cause you to deliver practice talks in a halting fashion, hesitating each time you feel an *um* coming on. However, continued sensitivity and diligence will result in a relatively smooth delivery.

### Reverse the Perspective

Several vocal factors were discussed in the previous pages. Which three create the most disconcerting and distracting problems for you as a listener?

- Accent
- Articulation
- Emphasis
- Enunciation
- Inflection
- Pitch
- Pronunciation
- Rate and volume
- Speech fillers

What recommendations would you make to colleagues who were creating these problems for you as a listener?

## Eye Contact

Speakers need to establish eye contact with the audience. Even if speakers do not actually make eye contact with the listeners, it is important that receivers have the impression that the speakers are maintaining eye contact.[16] The best way to leave that impression is to actually have frequent and sustained contact with the audience.

Avoiding eye contact can be a function of apprehension. Speakers may be reluctant to observe what they fear will be negative nonverbal reactions and, consequently, may avoid looking at the audience. You probably have had the experience of not wanting to, or being unable to, look into the eyes of another when you are speaking to them. Similarly, apprehensive presenters avoid eye contact when they are uncomfortable.

There are three common problems related to eye contact during presentations. The first was just discussed: speakers will avoid eye contact and speak to inanimate objects to avoid the audience.

The second is that speakers attempt to finesse their apprehension by gazing in the direction of the listeners, but still avoid any meaningful eye contact.

The third problem is that speakers, having been coached to establish eye contact, glance very briefly at members of the audience. These glances are not sufficiently sustained to be meaningful. You may have seen individuals lifting their heads abruptly throughout a talk and then snapping their heads down. There is no real bond made when one does this. It appears as if the speaker intends to meet some quota of appropriate instances of eye contacts.

Speakers who are unaware of their counterproductive habits can become aware by simply watching a videotape of their behavior when speaking to an audience.

A second method for improving eye contact involves observing others speak and identifying those behaviors that are counterproductive. Speakers who are aware of others' annoying tendencies are more likely to avoid the behaviors themselves.

Third, there is no substitute for training yourself to establish eye contact with audience members for meaningful durations. Initially, the behavior might be and appear to be robotic. However, with greater experience speaking in front of groups, it will become more natural to maintain these bonds. Of course, if a reason for your inability to establish eye contact is because of your insecurity and unfamiliarity with the content of your message, the best cure is sufficient preparation.

### Common Problems with Eye Contact

- Directing eye contact away from the audience and to inanimate objects
- Gazing at the audience as a whole and not at individuals
- Very rapid "eye contacts" that are not sustained long enough to be meaningful

### Suggestions

- Watch a videotape of your talk.
- Observe others' counterproductive tendencies.
- Practice establishing eye contact.
- Become confident in content so that lack of confidence does not fuel the avoidance behavior.

## Body Motion

Follow this simple rule as it relates to body motion when you speak. Your movements should be consistent with, and not a distraction from, your message.

*Kinesics* is the term used to describe nonverbal behavior involving body motion. Hand gestures, pacing in front of the audience, even facial expressions—because they require movement—all fall under the category of kinesics.

The following brief anecdote illustrates how kinesic behavior can undermine a speaker's well-conceived message.

A student speaker who very carefully prepared each of his presentations delivered an emotionally heart-rending talk about innocents who have been incarcerated. However, it was difficult to believe that he was serious, because one of his peculiar mannerisms was to smile periodically and indiscriminately during his talk. These smiles would often follow a sad story about some victim of the judicial system. Student evaluators asked him afterward if he really meant what he said.

There are several other problems that recur pertaining to kinesics. All are related to motion that is distracting as opposed to complementary or supportive.

One problem occurs when speakers arbitrarily but rhythmically move or shake their legs during the course of talks. Similarly, hand gestures that are unrelated to the message being uttered can result in listeners becoming attentive to the odd motions instead of the content of the talk.

Another chronic problem arises when speakers assume a posture that appears uncomfortable or peculiar. Speakers, for example, may place their hands in front of their stomach, or on their hips, for long stretches during a talk. Although that gesture does not mean anything universal, it may be distracting, since it appears so unnatural.

A third recurring problem is that speakers will develop a rhythmic pacing in front of the room. Movement behind the lectern is not necessarily detrimental. An absence of motion can actually seem peculiar and be distracting. However, predictable pacing can make a listener dwell on the persistence and regularity of the motion as opposed to the message being relayed.

The first step toward improving any of these tendencies requires becoming aware of the behavior. Using videotape to record your presentations typically is an excellent vehicle. Speakers can witness motions that are counterproductive and become sensitive to the behavior.

### Common Problems with Body Motion

- Audience members dwell on the extraneous motion, specifically
  - rhythmic pacing and unrelated gesturing
  - abnormal and uncomfortable-looking postures; for example, hands folded in front of chest

- Facial expressions contradict nature of message; for example,
  - a humorous message presented by a frowning speaker
  - a sad message presented by a speaker who appears to be suppressing laughter

### Suggestions

- Watch videotapes of your presentations.
- Identify behaviors that distract you and therefore are likely to distract audience members.
- Refrain from bringing pens or unnecessary objects to the front of the room.

## Physical Appearance

### Clothing/Artifacts

Artifacts are those things made by humans. Archaeologists typically look for artifacts, hoping to find some clues about the nature of earlier civilizations. In the analysis of non-verbal messages, *artifacts* refer to things made by humans that convey meanings to receivers. Dress and jewelry are two common factors that fall into this category.

For better and mostly for worse, people are often evaluated on the basis of clothes, jewelry, eyeglasses, and color coordination. The expression "clothes make the wo/man" may not be true, but receivers dwell on how someone is attired. An old salesperson's wheeze is that one should always polish the back of one's shoes, because that is the last thing a buyer sees. Salespeople, apparently, assume that even the shine of one's shoes can be a factor affecting impressions and persuasion. Whether one wishes it were otherwise or not, the fact that dress affects audience perceptions is incontrovertible.[17]

### Common Problems Related to Artifacts

- Speakers do not realize the significance of attire on audience perceptions, or they believe audience members should not and therefore will not allow dress to affect their perceptions of the presentation.

- Speakers are not familiar with the audience, audience expectations, or the occasion. Chapter 5 discusses the importance of audience analysis. People may be aware of the importance of dress, but be unaware of a particular audience's expectations regarding dress. This might result in someone appearing overly formal in an informal environment.

### Suggestions

- Attempt to recall incidents when someone's clothing affected how you perceived that individual.
- Study your audience and the speaking venue before you decide what to wear for your presentation.

## Stand Up & Deliver

How would these types of attire affect listeners' reactions to this speaker?

Assume that a guest lecturer who is applying for a job at your university has been invited to make a presentation to your class. Further assume that the speaker is considering the three types of attire indicated by the photos.

Prepare a three-minute presentation that addresses each of the following questions:

- Would the selection of clothes affect the reaction to the message?
- If your answer is yes, why would the reaction be different and how would it be different?
- If your answer is no, why do you think that dress would not be a factor?
- Why have you dressed for this presentation the way that you have?

## Time

### Chronemic Factors

> *There is only one thing more blunderful than saying nothing and that is taking a long time to do it.*[18]

> *I am convinced that someday there will be a president who announces his program in less than twenty minutes. I don't care if he is a Republican or a Democrat. I'm going to support him.*[19]

*Chronemics* refers to time and how time affects presentations. It can affect audience perceptions of speaker consideration, responsibility, and preparation.

A commencement speaker addressing graduates of the Culinary Institute of America was told specifically to speak for ten to fifteen minutes. Nevertheless he droned on for twenty-five minutes about a product called the Shelf Recovery Fryolater and was oblivious to the nonverbal feedback from the assembled audience that fairly screamed, "Please end." You may also have attended presentations that might have had merit, had your singular recollection of the experience not been its duration. Similarly, speakers who are asked to speak for thirty minutes may seem unprepared or irresponsible if they abruptly conclude in five.

#### Common Problems with Time

- The speaker has not considered that time might be an issue for receivers.
- The speaker has not timed the talk during rehearsals.
- Equipment issues usurp significant portions of allotted time. (See Chapter 8 for issues related to using equipment.) A malfunction may force a speaker to jam a forty-minute talk into twenty-five minutes.
- Early sections of a talk consume more time than expected. Similarly, you may be presenting as a team, and those speaking early on exceed their time allotments. (See Chapter 9.)
- An audience arrives later than you expect. You may be there, ready, and prepared for your twenty-minute pitch. If the audience is delayed, you may have to cram your talk into a shorter period.
- The time of the talk is not conducive to attentiveness. The presentation is delivered after six others have pitched a similar product.

#### Suggestions

- Try to remember when you were frustrated as an audience member by a lengthier-than-expected talk.
- Rehearse and time sections of your talk.
- Ask your hosts to schedule you at a time when you will be least likely to be affected by time issues.
- Practice with the equipment you intend to use during your talk.
- Identify sections that you can most easily purge if your time is cut short.

## Space and Distance

### Proxemics

*Proxemics* refers to the study of space and how it affects communication. Receivers might find it awkward when speakers stand close to one portion of the room and apparently

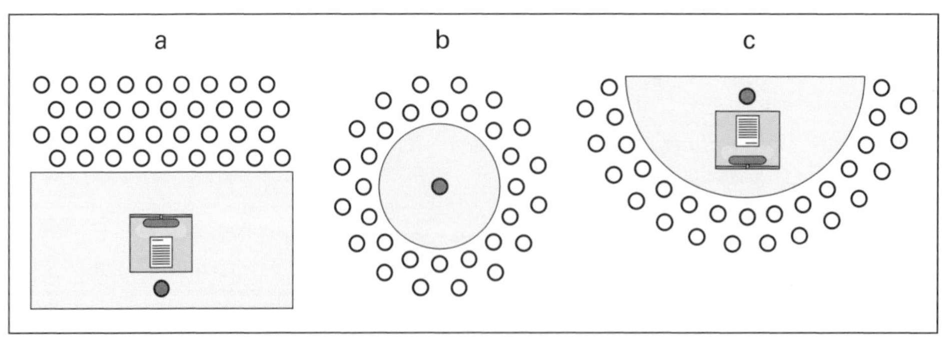


**Figure 11-1** The space between speaker and receiver affects receipt of communication.

desire to stand away from another section. Occasionally speakers will stand in front of the first row of an audience, and this placement makes it difficult for those listeners who are essentially behind the speaker.

The space between speaker and listener should seem appropriate to the receivers, and be conducive to hearing and seeing the speaker. (See Figure 11-1.)

## Olfactics/Haptics

Smell (olfactics) and touch (haptics) are unlikely to affect most presentation settings. They can, but rarely do. Some authors suggest that presenters arrive early and greet each audience member with a handshake. The quality of the handshake could relay some information. Certainly, if a speaker were to hug arriving listeners, that would have an effect. Strong cologne might be discernible to audience members sitting close to a speaker.

# Verbal Dimensions of Delivery

*Words have a magical power. They can enable the orator to sway the audience and dictate its decisions.*[20]

Sigmund Freud

On October 22, 1962, President John F. Kennedy addressed the nation and the world. He intended to announce that the United States would prevent the Soviet Union from continuing to bring missiles to Cuba and store them there. The world would be told that the United States would be establishing a naval blockade to halt the transfer of these missiles.

However, Kennedy never identified the action as a blockade. For days preceding the speech, members of his staff debated the wisdom of using the word *blockade*. It was feared that the word might sound too bellicose and consequently might trigger an unleashing of hostilities. The staff decided to substitute the word *quarantine* for *blockade*. The thinking was that *quarantine* sounded less aggressive.[21]

When speakers deliver their messages, they must select words intelligently. Word choices "direct listeners to view the message in one way rather than another."[22] For this reason, the same military action may be labeled a *massacre* by some world leaders and a *preemptive strike* by others. One group's *terrorist* becomes another group's *freedom fighter*. Choice of language can affect the perception receivers have of both the speaker and the presentation.

# Criteria for Language Selection

## Clarity and Accuracy

*"Clearness is the first virtue of eloquence."*[23]

When choosing the language to employ, speakers, of course, should select words that clearly and accurately reflect their ideas. It is surprising how often individuals seem to be careless when making these selections. The following questions may provide a helpful guideline when considering word choice:

### Does the word mean what you think it means?

The words you select to use must mean what you think they mean, and match the thought you wish to express. Speakers who say *antidote* when they mean *anecdote* are using a word that does not match the thought they wish to express. More significantly, when speakers substitute *antidote* for *anecdote*, their credibility suffers (assuming that audience members are familiar with the distinction).

If you say *transgress* when you mean *digress*, an audience familiar with the words will know you have transgressed. If you employ *dilemma* as a synonym for *problem*, you will inform those in the know that you are not.

Manuscript speakers have more of an opportunity to check and be certain that the words they use do, in fact, match the ideas they wish to communicate. Extemporaneous speakers must select words as they are delivering the message. Both manuscript and extemporaneous speakers, however, can be victims of assuming that the words they use are correct when they may not be.

### Is the word selected the best word to match the thought?

Words that are closely aligned in meaning typically have shades of difference. Selecting one word as opposed to another can make your message more clear and accurate. Consider the following four examples:

- When you were first smitten, did you find your lover *nice* or *charming?*
- Can excessive alcoholic consumption have *bad* or *insidious* consequences?
- Are the conditions for the homeless *sad* or *miserable?*
- Did your partner *usurp* control or *take over* control?

### Does the word have a low "level of abstraction"?

Some words have very concrete meanings. If I were to tell you that I need a *pencil*, you would have a clear idea of what I mean. There are different types of pencils, of course, but what you think of when you think of *pencil* is likely very similar to what I think of when I say *pencil*. However, if I were to say that in a democracy citizens are *free*, the word *free* would have a very high level of abstraction. What you mean by *free* and what I mean by *free* can vary greatly. If the object of a talk is to clearly relay information, it may be necessary to either define terms with high levels of abstraction or use terms that have low levels of abstraction.

### Are you aware of the connotations as well as the denotation of the word?

Occasionally speakers will use a word that literally is utilized accurately, but has come to mean something quite different from its denotation. For example, referring to an instructor as a *pedagogue* might seem as if it is perfectly appropriate. The denotative meaning of *pedagogue* is "teacher." However, the word *pedagogue* has come to mean "someone who is rigid and condescending." Speakers, therefore, need to be careful when they employ words they have just learned, in order to make sure that they are not utilizing a word that denotatively is correct, but connotatively is incorrect.

### Are you using a malapropism?

Mrs. Malaprop is a character in a play called *The Rivals* by Richard Sheridan. The word *malapropism* is derived from this character. Throughout the play Mrs. Malaprop unintentionally, but humorously, uses words that are inappropriate but sound akin to an appropriate word. For example, she says of a guest that he is the "very *pineapple* of politeness," meaning *pinnacle*, of course, not *pineapple*.[24] She claims that her "*affluence* over my niece is very small" meaning, of course, *influence* not *affluence*.[25] The television character Archie Bunker also used malapropisms, saying, for example, *groinocologist* instead of *gynecologist*.

Most of us laugh when we hear malapropisms such as *pineapple* for *pinnacle*. Less obvious ones may also be humorous, but can be devastating to speaker credibility. What would you think of a speaker who encouraged you to study nutrition because such activity would be *eatifying*? This error is not simply nor primarily an articulation gaffe. It is one thing to mispronounce *edifying*, but another to think that the word somehow refers to food.

### Are you deliberately creating ambiguity?

As we discussed in Chapter 3, some scholars suggest that communicators intentionally attempt to use language ambiguously to "complicate the sense making apparatus of receivers."[26] Although this has received support, it is not to be recommended. It damages the ethos of speakers in the long run if it becomes common knowledge that they intentionally are ambiguous. If clarity is the first virtue of eloquence as suggested by Cicero, and a good speaker is a good person speaking well, as suggested by Quintilian, then anyone who desires to be an eloquent speaker should avoid deliberate ambiguity.

## Appropriate Language

You may have selected the best word to match your idea. You may know precisely what it means and can use it correctly. However, it still may not be the best word to use in a professional presentation. Consider the following factors pertaining to the suitability of language for the audience:

### Will the receivers understand the word?

If you believe that the word—regardless of how apt it may be—will be unfamiliar to your receivers, then do not use it. Elementary-school students have a smaller vocabulary than your classmates. If you were to talk to first graders about the value of reading, you would need to select different words than those you would select if you were delivering a talk to peers on the same subject.

Similarly, speakers must be very careful not to use jargon, slang, and technical terms that are familiar to those in your groups when speaking to those who are not in your groups.

### Is the word employed simply to show off?

Even if a word is a good word to match an idea, and even if you suspect the audience will be familiar with the word, you may not want to use it in your talk. In addition to getting the gist of the message, the audience may sense that you are an affected snob.

### Does the word fit the occasion?

You may have heard speakers in presentation settings use slang or spew profanities. Many profane words have very low levels of abstraction. Audience members usually know precisely what is meant by the utterance. However, as a rule—despite the low level of abstraction, despite audience familiarity with the word, even despite the fact that it might be the best word to match the precise idea the speaker would like to relay—profanities are typically inappropriate for professional presentations. Listeners who are not confused about the literal meaning of the word may dwell on why the speaker chose to use the profane word or what the usage may say about the speaker.

### Is the word likely to be offensive?

The expression *politically correct* has been used, often disparagingly, to refer to language use that meets a standard for propriety. Columnists dub the utterances of politicians on race and gender issues *politically correct*, intimating that more appropriate language would have been selected had there not been a fear of political repercussions for using the different terms. It is unfortunate that being sensitive to what may offend listeners has become ridiculed in this way. There is sense, both political and common, in being sensitive to our receivers. Some men and women may think there is nothing inappropriate about referring to women as *girls*, but such a reference is offensive to many men and women. Being responsive to what others consider offensive is a responsibility of communicators. regardless of the context.

## Ethical Probe

**Choosing Words Sensitively**

On January 15, 1999, a white mayoral aide used the word *niggardly* when addressing two associates in a meeting about budget cutbacks. The speaker was chastised for using the word, and initially, the mayor requested and accepted the aide's resignation.

*Niggardly* is a rarely used term that means "stingy." The word has nothing to do with racial epithets or persons of color despite the fact that the first two syllables sound like they do.

The position taken by many blacks and whites was that there was nothing wrong with using the word. Black leader Julian Bond thought the mayor's decision to accept the resignation was inappropriate. Bond said speakers should not have to "censor" their language to meet "other persons' lack of understanding." (The aide, David Howard, was later reinstated.)

The position taken by others—both blacks and whites—is that usage of the word was inappropriate and even unethical. The speaker should have realized that *niggardly* is a word that is rarely employed and is not in the common vocabulary of most listeners. Knowing full well the incendiary nature of the word *nigger* the use of niggardly was insensitive and reflected poor judgment.

- What is your position on this matter? Was this unethical?
- Should the speaker have been reprimanded in any way?

### Are the words creating a redundancy?

The individual words in the sentence "We have won seven consecutive games in a row" are not used incorrectly, but they are creating a redundancy. Sometimes these sound humorous and affect how audience members perceive the speaker. Consider the following examples:

- One of the advantages of this product is that you can reuse it over and over again.
- This, unfortunately, will be a drawn-out process that will continue for a long time.

- What will happen is that our competitors will simply duplicate the same thing again.
- The negative attitude of last quarter still lingers.
- The injuries continue to perpetuate on this team, and this makes it difficult to compete.
- This is a brand-new innovation.
- I expect everyone to give us 100 percent effort and perform to their complete capacity.

### Common Problems with Language Selection

- Using the incorrect word. It is very common to hear speakers refer to the need to include some *antidotes* in their talk. Antidotes should not be required.
- Using insensitive language. Slang and profanities can be offensive to various audiences, and speakers should be sensitive to whom they may be offending.
- Using technical language. Speakers do not often acknowledge that jargon familiar to them is likely to be unfamiliar to audience members.
- Using words you did not intend to use in extemporaneous and impromptu speaking. Listening to a tape of your presentation can be humbling when you hear yourself saying something you did not mean to say.

### Suggestions

- When planning your talk refer to a dictionary when you are considering using an unfamiliar word.
- Review a list of commonly misused words.
- Have colleagues listen to your talk specifically to identify words that are inappropriately used.
- Tape a rehearsal of an extemporaneous talk. When playing it back, listen to make sure that you are not, inadvertently, using a word incorrectly.
- Become vigilant when listening to other speeches for usage that is incorrect. By becoming sensitive to others' transgressions you may avoid similar errors.
- If you are delivering a technical talk, ask colleagues in other fields to listen to a rehearsal. Ask them to identify any words they do not know.
- When in doubt, do not use slang expressions.

## Making Presentations More Lively

Most beginning speakers should be encouraged to walk before they run. Some of the advice in this section is in the "run as opposed to walk" category. However, at some point readers may want to employ these techniques when writing and delivering presentations.

**Parallel Wording**

In the famous Gettysburg Address, Lincoln said, "We can not dedicate, We can not consecrate, We can not hallow these grounds." The parallel wording of "We can not" is only one of the many factors that makes the Gettysburg Address memorable.

**Usage of Similes and Metaphors**

When you compare a phenomenon to another, it often clarifies that which you are describing. "Sharon Simpson had a smile that was as bright as the sun." "After the stock market crashes of the early 2000s it seemed to many investors that they were hemorrhaging money." The former example is a simile because it makes the comparison by using the word *as*. The latter example is a metaphor because the comparison is implied.

**Word Reversal**

In his 1961 inaugural address President Kennedy reversed word order to achieve a memorable effect. Kennedy wanted citizens to become more involved as contributors and challenged listeners with the words, "Ask not what your country can do for you. Ask what you can do for your country."

**Alliteration**

Alliteration involves repetitive use of the same sounds to make a message memorable. For example, "The bumbling braggarts have bombarded our beautiful burg with behaviors that are abominable." Vice President Spiro Agnew was known for such alliteration. He criticized the news media by referring to them collectively as the "nattering nabobs of negativity" and by claiming that newscasters' "passionate pursuit of controversy" was limiting the "politics of progress."[27]

**Rhetorical Question**

Vice presidential candidate Richard Nixon used this technique very effectively in his highly successful and highly controversial 1952 Checkers speech. He posed questions to the audience that he knew would be answered in a way that was consistent with his speaking goals. President (then Senator) Nixon was attempting to explain why he had a fund that opponents considered illegitimate. He asked the viewers several rhetorical questions: "Do you think that when I or any other Senator makes a political speech, has it printed, [sic] should charge the printing of that speech and the mailing of that speech to the taxpayers? Do you think, for example, when I or any other Senator makes a trip to his home state to make a purely political speech that the cost of that trip should be charged to the taxpayers? Do you think when a Senator makes political broadcasts or political television broadcasts radio or television, that the expense of those broadcasts should be charged to the taxpayers? Well, I know what your answer is..."[28]

## Summary

- Delivery involves both verbal and nonverbal factors
- Nonverbal issues are those aspects of messages that are communicated without words
- Nonverbal messages
  - Transcend body language
  - Rarely have universal meanings
  - Are decoded in various ways by audience members
- Relevant categories of nonverbal messages include the following:
  - Kinesics—body motion
  - Paralanguage—vocalics
  - Oculesics—eye contact
  - Proxemics—space
  - Artifacts—dress
- Verbal factors pertain to the words selected by speakers

 When selecting words

- Make sure they match your ideas
- Make sure they are appropriate for a given audience

## SAMPLE PRESENTATION FOR ANALYSIS

### Beyond Giving a Speech

*Patricia Ward Brash delivered* "Beyond Giving a Speech" *to members of Women in Communication in Milwaukee on August 18, 1992, when she was the director of communications for the Miller Brewing Company. As you read through this excerpt, please consider the following questions:*

1. *Can the fate of careers, as the author suggests, hinge on the outcome of presentations? If this excerpt is representative, what would be the speaker's fate? (Assume that the delivery is strong.)*
2. *Does the Columbus reference make the case for the importance of audience analysis? Explain why or why not.*
3. *The speaker makes two clear points in the last paragraph of this excerpt. Does the speaker do what she clearly said speakers should do?*

I appreciate this opportunity to share some thoughts with you on the preparation and delivery of presentations. All of us in communications recognize that the further we advance in our profession, the greater our opportunities and requirements for giving presentations. We also recognize that it's wise to get experience: as much...as soon...as often as possible.

In addition, we can all benefit throughout our careers from taking public speaking courses and studying to improve our presentation skills.

Today I would like to focus on three main areas:

- Preparation, including content
- Delivery, and
- Use of visuals

Let's begin with preparation, which includes every aspect of effective presentation skills, such as deciding upon the objective, content development, delivery, and visual support.

It's important to identify our goal before we concentrate on the message, and we should begin by asking ourselves whether our objective is:

- To inform
- To persuade
- To inspire
- To motivate to action, or
- To entertain.

Of course the answer will depend largely upon the composition of the audience. We should tailor every presentation to the audience, to the occasion and to the theme of the meeting. This involves finding out as much as possible about the knowledge level of the audience and their interests. We should get to know them, talk with them, listen to them, and understand their needs. Only after we have carefully studied the audience are we ready to do research on the topic.

A classic example of someone who tailored his message to the audience and the occasion was Christopher Columbus.

Before Columbus met the King and Queen of Spain, navigational experts in both Portugal and Spain had already recommended against backing his rather unusual proposal to reach the Far East by sailing in the opposite direction—westward.

But Columbus understood the art of persuasion, of tailoring the message to the audience, and he knew how to put together an effective presentation. He knew, for example, that the Queen had a fervent desire to win more converts to her religion. So he made frequent references to the teeming masses of the Orient, just waiting to be converted.

Columbus learned that the Queen loved falcons and exotic birds, so he searched carefully through the accounts of Marco Polo's travels to the Orient and marked in the margin all references to those kingdoms where there were falcons and exotic birds.

He knew the King wanted to expand Spain's commercial power, so he made frequent references to gold, spices, and other fabulous riches of the East.

All these points were worked into his presentation, which won the backing that resulted in discovery of the New World.

While few of us are called on to make presentations where the stakes are quite that high, many of us do make presentations where a critical contract, approval of a major marketing program, or the fate of our own careers can hinge on the outcome.

Regardless of the nature of our presentation, we should begin by developing an introduction that gives the audience a clear understanding of what we are going to talk about and how we plan to proceed.

We might want to gain their attention with an unusual remark, story, surprising fact or question.

We might want to tell them about important benefits they will receive—the way Columbus did.

The basic purpose of our introduction is to establish rapport with the audience and "tell them what we're going to tell them."

**Source:** Brash, Patricia Ward. "Beyond Giving a Speech: Becoming a Poised, Polished Presenter," *Vital Speeches of the Day,* November 15, 1992, 59 no. 3: 83(4).

## Review Questions

1. Identify two common misconceptions related to nonverbal messages.
2. How can vocalics, proxemics, chronemics, and kinesics affect the quality of a presentation? (Give one example for each.)
3. What is the difference between enunciation and articulation? How can either affect the ethos of a speaker?
4. What three criteria should be employed when selecting words for a professional presentation?
5. How can parallel wording or alliteration render a presentation particularly memorable?
6. In one of your previous presentations, how could selecting different words to match your ideas have improved its effectiveness?

## INFOTRAC QUESTION

Find the InfoTrac article by Tad Simons in the April 2003 edition of *Presentations*. Are his points meaningful? Do people who use these words during business presentations inevitably hurt the quality of their talk?

---

[1] Burton Kaplan, *The Manager's Compete Guide to Speech Writing* (London: The Free Press, 1988), 47.

[2] Larry Speakes, *Speaking Out* (New York: Avon Books, 1988), 68. Speakes was the press spokesman for Ronald Reagan for much of the Reagan presidency.

[3] The sixteenth president of the United States is the author of many memorable quotes. Interested readers might want to visit **http://home.att.net/~rjnorton/Lincoln78.html** to peruse his insightful remarks.

[4] Nicholas Christenfeld, *Journal of Nonverbal Behavior,* no. 3 (Fall 1995): 171–186. Christenfeld suggests that unbroken speech is preferable to speech interrupted by *ums* and extended pauses. Some of the other findings in this article are counterintuitive, and interested readers might want to review it.

[5] Mehrabian, author of *Silent Messages.* 2nd ed. (Belmont, CA: Thomson Wadsworth, 1981) and other books, originally made the claim in an article entitled "Communication Without Words" in *Psychology Today* 2 no. 4 (1968): 53. Some researchers quibble with the figure Mehrabian uses. Some claim that 65 percent is based on nonverbal messages. Others argue that the percentage is in the 80-percent range. Whatever statistic you believe, clearly nonverbal messages are important factors affecting communication success. See also Dale Leathers, *Successful Nonverbal Communication,* 3rd ed. (New York: Allyn and Bacon, 1997), 5–6.

[6] Dale Leathers, *Successful Nonverbal Communication,* 3rd ed. (New York: Allyn and Bacon, 1997), 6–7. A similar discussion is found in Mark Knapp and Judith Hall's *Nonverbal Communication in Human Interaction,* 5th ed. (Belmont, CA: Thomson-Wadsworth, 2002), 15–16. They conclude that people tend to believe those signals that are harder to fake. Therefore a person with a trembling voice who says, "I am not nervous" tends to have the verbal signals undermined by the more credible nonverbal ones, which are more difficult to fake.

[7] The time "at least twenty-five years" was identified for the following reasons: In 1970 Julius Fast published the popular *Body Language.* Mark Knapp's text *Nonverbal Communication in Human Interaction,* in its sixth edition (now coauthored with Judith Hall) was first published in 1972. The Knapp book was one of the first texts dedicated to this subject, if not the first. Finally, the *Journal of Nonverbal Behavior* was first published in 1979. The publications indicate a time period when it was popular to explore nonverbal messages. A result of this popularity was a good deal of misinformation as well as valuable information.

[8] George Grice and John Skinner, *Mastering Public Speaking* (New York: Allyn and Bacon, 1995), 250.

[9] Cynthia Hamilton and Brian Kleiner, "Communication: Steps to Better Listening," *Personnel Journal* (February 1987): 21.

[10] Valerie Manusov and Julie Billingsley, "Nonverbal Communication in Organizations," in *Organizational Communication: Theory and Behavior,* ed. Peggy Yuhas Byers (New York: Allyn and Bacon, 1997), 66.

[11] Ralph Waldo Emerson, nineteenth-century American essayist and poet.

[12] From *US Presidents as Orators,* ed. Halford Ryan (Westport, CT: Greenwood Press, 1995), xvi.

[13] *Merriam Webster's Collegiate Dictionary,* 10th ed.

[14] Based on the example in Leo Rosten, *The Joys of Yiddish* (New York: McGraw Hill, 1968), xvii–xviii.

[15] See discussion in Rudolph Verderber and Kathleen Verderber in *The Challenge of Effective Speaking* (Belmont, CA: Thomson Wadsworth, 2003), 201–202.

[16] George Grice and John Skinner, *Mastering Public Speaking* (New York: Allyn and Bacon, 1995), 262.

[17] When teaching MBA classes that focus on preparing, delivering, and evaluating business presentations, I have found that some of the harshest critics of unprofessional dress during presentations are the students themselves. Typically the students in these classes are full-time managers and aspire to rise in the ranks of their organizations. For additional support about the importance of dress when making presentations see Notes 6, 7, and 9 in Chapter 5.

[18] Burton Kaplan, *The Manager's Complete Guide to Speech Making* (London: The Free Press, 1988), 7.

[19] Senator Orrin Hatch after President Clinton's seventy-seven-minute State of the Union address in 1999.

[20] Sigmund Freud, quoted in L. Perry Wilbur, *Stand Up, Speak Up, or Shut Up: A Practical Guide to Public Speaking* (New York: Dembner, 1981), 13.

[21] *The Cuban Missile Crisis 1962, A National Archive Documents Reader,* ed. Laurence Chang and Peter Kornblush (New York: The New Press, 1992), 365. See also Elie Abel, *The Missile Crisis* (Philadelphia: Lippincott, 1968), 115.

[22] David Zarefsky, *Public Speaking,* 3rd ed. (Boston: AB Longman, 2002), 261.

[23] Quintilian makes this statement in *The Education of the Orator* in Book II, Chapter 3, Section 8. George Campbell comments similarly when he writes of the "first and most essential" nature of "perspicuity." *The Philosophy of Rhetoric,* ed. Lloyd Bitzer (Corbondale, Illinois: Southern Illinois University Press, 1963), 216. Eugene White writes that "from Cicero and Quintilian to the present, responsible speechmakers have agreed that 'clearness is the first virtue of eloquence.'" *Practical Public Speaking* (New York: Macmillan, 1982), 339.

[24] Richard Sheridan, *The Rivals,* act III, scene III. Oxford University Press ed. (New York: Oxford University Press, 2002). The "pinnacle/pineapple" malapropism is on page 77.

[25] Ibid., act IV, scene II. The "affluence/influence" malapropism is on page 97.

[26] There are several authors who recommend this behavior. The article that introduced the notion of strategic ambiguity was published in *Communication Monographs* in 1984 and authored by Eric Eisenberg. See Chapter 3 for more information on strategic ambiguity. Also see Alan Zaremba, *Organizational Communication: Foundations for Business and Collaboration* (Mason, Ohio: Thomson South-Western, 2006), 85–90.

[27] The "passionate pursuit of controversy" and the "politics of progress" quotes come from a speech written by Patrick Buchanan and delivered on November 13, 1969. "Nattering nabobs of negativism" was in a speech delivered on September 11, 1970, in San Diego. William Safire takes credit for ghostwriting the alliterative "nattering nabobs of negativism."

[28] This speech is variously called "Checkers," "My Side of the Story," "Apologia," and the "Fund speech." It was delivered on September 23, 1952, and published in *Vital Speeches of the Day* on October 15, 1952, 11–15.

Chapter in a Nutshell

*Question-and-answer sessions can enhance the perceptions audience members have of speakers or can undermine an otherwise excellent presentation.*

# 12 Question-and-Answer Sessions

*...we [President Reagan's Press team] would anticipate questions and answers on the subjects that...might come up. Then we would put together a briefing book by the Friday before a press conference for the President to take along to Camp David and study over the weekend. It would have several dozen domestic and foreign topics, with questions and answers on each topic... In press conferences, out of thirty questions and follow-ups we might fail to anticipate one.*[1]

*-Larry Speakes*


## Abstract

Speakers must prepare for question-and-answer sessions as diligently as they prepare for other parts of the presentation. Q-and-a sessions can erode credibility if speakers appear confused by simple inquiries, seem inappropriately defensive, or deliver their responses poorly. The opposite can also be true. Speakers may increase their terminal ethos with admirable responses during q-and-a. This chapter discusses the question-and-answer portion of presentations. Specifically, at the conclusion of this chapter you should be able to do the following:

- Discuss how to prepare for q-and-a sessions
- Describe a procedure for delivering answers to questions
- List common problems in q-and-a sessions
- List common questions pertaining to q-and-a
- Identify methods for addressing these problems and questions

## Eloquent Q-and-A

Bob Whitaker was speaking to an audience of nearly 100 persons on a cold, snowy Monday night in Boston. The turnout was surprising given the wintry conditions, but many had endured the weather because of their very personal interest in the subject of the talk.

Whitaker had written a book entitled *Mad in America: Bad Science, Bad Medicine, and the Enduring Mistreatment of the Mentally Ill.*[2] In it, Whitaker describes how people with mental illnesses have been poorly treated in this country. He argued that the mentally ill in America are far worse off than similarly afflicted people who live in underdeveloped countries. Whitaker cited examples of barbaric treatments that are almost unimaginable. These treatments, he suggested, were conceived and perpetuated less because physicians considered the therapies to be valuable and more because the physicians had economic or ego-related investments in the remedies. Finally, Whitaker took issue with the drug companies. He argued that many claims about the therapeutic value of antidepressant drugs are based on flawed studies.

The perspectives of the book were nothing short of controversial.

The audience was composed primarily of people who were either strongly in favor of what Whitaker had written or strongly opposed. Many listeners had been patients themselves. Others were family members of patients. Some listeners were physicians or studying to be physicians. Only a few in attendance were ambivalent about Whitaker's subject.

The presentation was to be taped by C-Span, a factor that intensified the atmosphere in the auditorium. Sometime later in the month Whitaker's message and the subsequent q-and-a session would be broadcast on the Book Channel.

Whitaker began his presentation by thanking the attendees for coming out on the blustery night to hear what he had to say. He proceeded to calmly and carefully speak about the book that he had written. He read some excerpts, presented his notions about the treatment of the mentally ill, and supported his perspective with various studies cited in the book. At the end he took questions from the audience.

There was no shortage of questions. They came from various places in the auditorium and reflected an assortment of philosophical perspectives. A worker from C-Span brought a microphone over to each questioner to ensure that queries would be audible for the telecast. The microphone also served the purpose of making the questions audible to all in attendance.

Several of the questions were asked by people who said they had suffered periods of terrible depression. In a number of cases the queries were wrought with emotion and were convoluted as well. Several questioners were contentious. These questions were often as much statements of contrary philosophy as they were inquiries.

Whitaker seemed to be familiar not only with his subject and the general nature of his audience, but with many of the individuals among the assembled. Regardless of the nature of the query, he summarized the essence of each question as he began to respond to it. In some cases he referred to the questioner by name and included some additional information about the speaker before responding. Not once did Whitaker back down from his position when confronted with difficult questions; not once did he raise his voice or in any way ridicule the perspective of the questioner. He simply calmly addressed the singular points in the statement or question. Whitaker appeared to have extensive subject knowledge, a sincere concern for the mentally ill, and an unflappable—yet not condescending—demeanor when faced with criticism.

Although the presentation itself had been illuminating, the question-and-answer session sealed the effect. By appearing to be well-informed, respectful, articulate, and unequivocal, Whitaker won over many in the audience, even those who had come to criticize him.

- Have you attended presentations that included argumentative question-and-answer sessions? What were the circumstances that created controversy?
- What took place during the combative incidents?
- How did the speakers react to the hostile questions?
- What made the speakers effective/ineffective in these q-and-a situations?

## Introduction

Question-and-answer sessions are an integral part of a speaker's message. Some authors have even commented that in business contexts the q-and-a segment can be the most important part of the presentation.[3] The question period can indicate how much speakers actually know and how well they have prepared. In effect it becomes the conclusion to the message and determines one's terminal ethos.

The demise of many politicians is rooted in poor answers during q-and-a. In 1988 Governor Michael Dukakis's presidential bid never recovered from his response to Bernard Shaw during a presidential debate.[4] Gerald Ford's inaccurate claim in response to a journalist's inquiry in 1976 stunned television viewers throughout the world.[5] On the contrary, Ronald Reagan and Bill Clinton were adept at responding to questions during q-and-a. Reagan was well briefed regarding potential questions he might face and was prepared with responses. Clinton seemed remarkably familiar with all questions, even those dealing with remote parts of the world or those concerned with relatively insignificant matters.

Few persons become presidents, but most people will find themselves in situations when, after a presentation, they are required to respond to questions. Preparing for these sessions is as important as preparing for any other part of the presentation.

# Responding to Questions Efficiently

## Preparatory Steps

Speakers should take three preliminary steps to prepare for question sessions:

- Anticipate potential questions
- Formulate short extemporaneous speeches in response to anticipated questions
- Practice delivering these responses in a simulated environment

### *Anticipate probable questions.*

The first step for speakers requires predicting questions they might hear during q-and-a. Speakers will, of course, not be able to anticipate all possible inquiries. There is no crystal ball and some inquiries can be peculiar. However, often questions that are asked are very predictable. A careful review of the audience analysis and the presentation content itself will help speakers identify which points within the talk are likely to stimulate questions. Speakers who are having trouble identifying potential questions should ask colleagues to listen to the message and have them list questions they would ask if they were to attend the presentation.

After predicting questions, speakers might wonder if they should include within the presentation the content that would preclude the anticipated questions. In many cases it would be wise to incorporate that content. However, there are reasons why that may not be possible or even recommended.

Time constraints, for example, create limitations on the content that can be included in a talk. Speakers may decide to omit certain points—even if they are relevant—because there is no room in the talk for this information given the time restrictions.

Some anticipated questions may deal with peripheral or irrelevant issues. Speakers may anticipate that these peripheral concerns could arise during q-and-a, but think that such content is not sufficiently central to include in the presentations. For example, a speaker may describe a search for new hires in a department. Individuals may wish to know if this means that Jill, who is on maternity leave, will remain out; if Jack, who is on family leave, will return; or even if the search will attempt to illicitly screen potential hires who might subsequently take family-related leaves. Speakers should be ready to respond to such anticipated questions, but do not necessarily need to incorporate this peripheral content into their prepared message.

There is another reason for omitting content pertaining to anticipated questions. Speakers may wish to address salient points during the q-and-a session and therefore deliberately leave out certain information. For example, if the safety features of a children's toy are extraordinarily competitive, speakers may wait until someone inquires about safety to describe this powerful advantage. Deliberately leaving out content in anticipation of questions is very risky. It is, of course, possible that the desired question will never be asked during q-and-a. However, as we discuss later in this chapter, there is a way to deal with this possibility. It may be advantageous to save a powerful argument for q-and-a.

### *Create extemporaneous responses to anticipated questions.*

After speakers have predicted the questions that may surface, the next preparatory task is to outline responses to the questions that have been anticipated. In Chapter 6, we discussed the disadvantages of impromptu speaking. To avoid these problems, speakers should create an outline of the mini-speeches they will be delivering in response to the anticipated questions.

### *Practice the prepared responses in a simulated q-and-a period.*

In the same way that the presentation has been rehearsed, speakers should rehearse the q-and-a session in a simulated environment. In the simulation, colleagues pretend to be audience members and ask questions, and the speakers practice delivering their planned responses to these questions.

## Reverse the Perspective

This exercise has two parts.

- What questions would audience members typically ask after each of the presentations described below?
  - Instructor on first day of class introducing the course
  - Advertising group explaining ideas for marketing the company's new sports utility vehicle to an in-house audience
  - Tobacco spokespersons explaining the community service activities of their organization to an external audience
  - Bob Whitaker's book presentation
  - Politician endorsing mandatory sentencing for drug-related crimes at a town hall-type of meeting
  - HR representative discussing the implementation of flex time at work
  - Restaurant manager speaking to waitstaff on the need for mandatory (unpaid) meetings for all employees
- Outline a response for the two most difficult questions you identify in part 1.

## DELIVERING RESPONSES TO QUESTIONS

There is more to delivering an answer during q-and-a than simply answering the question. Consider the following procedure for delivering responses during these sessions:

### Step 1: If necessary, repeat the essence of the question.

The first decision a speaker has to make is whether it is necessary to repeat the question that has been asked. Frequently, but not always, it is essential to do so. There are several reasons why it may be necessary to repeat the question.

**Repeating the question will include people who may not have heard it.** In a large room it is quite possible that all audience members will not be able to hear all questions. Even in tiny rooms, questioners may pose their questions inaudibly. Unless listeners can somehow decipher the question by hearing the answer, the response to an inaudible question is meaningless. Some audience members may ask others seated nearby for the question. Others, however, will be content to be excluded. Consequently, question-and-answer sessions that are intended to involve the entire audience can become private dialogues between inquirer and respondent.

After a softly spoken inquiry, some presenters look out into the audience and ask, "Did you all hear that?" Listeners will not necessarily respond candidly to such a question. The speaker has to make a decision. If unsure, speakers should default to repeating the question.

**Repeating the question allows speakers to make sure they heard it correctly.** One reason for repeating the question is to make sure you answer the right one. It is possible that a speaker's sense of a question is different from the questioner's. It may be obvious to everyone but you that you are answering the wrong question. By repeating what you believe is the essence of the inquiry you will answer the wrong question only if the questioner is reluctant to correct you.

**Repeating the question may clarify it for the audience even if the presenter heard it clearly.** If speakers understand the question, but think it was poorly expressed, they might need to repeat it so that they don't lose the audience members who gave up trying to decode an awkwardly stated inquiry.

**Repeating the question buys time.** Speakers should attempt to predict the questions they may receive. However, it is likely that some questions will not have been anticipated. Paraphrasing and repeating the question gives the speaker time to think about the response.

**Repeating the question allows the speaker to change it subtly.** Assume a question is asked that a speaker does not want to address. By changing the question slightly in repetition, a speaker can create a bridge to more comfortable territory. This can be considered an unethical strategy, and it is certainly a risky one. Listeners may lose respect for the speaker because of the deliberate evasion. Persistent questioners might recognize the dodge and ask follow-up questions. However, some speakers will choose to restate questions especially when dealing with a hostile audience. Consider this for example:

"Given your position in support of outsourcing aren't you essentially forcing me out of my job? Aren't you essentially saying, 'Let's cut costs by eliminating benefits to the dedicated employees who made this company what it is today'?"

"The questioner asks me if we intend to outsource all of our operations and then eliminate the workforce. Outsourcing can help us presently, but we have no intention of losing the many employees who have worked for us so conscientiously over these past twenty-five years."

**Do not repeat a question that does not require repetition. Repeat controversial questions carefully.** If a questioner booms an inquiry that is unmistakably clear, then do not repeat the question. Assume a person asks, "*Will you be returning next week when our group meets again?*" Repeating such a question will make speakers seem robotic, as if they were coached to repeat all inquiries regardless of need.

It is also wise to consider how portions of a repetition can be transformed by unethical adversaries. The expression *sound byte* has found its way into contemporary jargon. In the hands of an unethical individual, a careless repetition can be made to sound like an endorsement for an unpopular position. For example, a questioner may ask, "Do you support abortions in the third trimester?" When you repeat the question, you may say, "Do *I support abortions in the third trimester?* Absolutely not." An unscrupulous adversary might excerpt the italicized portions of the repetition and use it against you. To avoid this unlikely, but not-unheard-of scenario, the speaker might repeat questions on controversial issues by avoiding using first-person pronouns in the repetition. For example, "The questioner asks about support for third-trimester abortions." An immoral adversary can, of course—regardless of what is uttered—piece together portions of an opponent's talk to disparage the opponent.

### Step 2: After repeating the question, direct the answer to everyone.

Speakers should direct their responses to the entire audience. The speaker should make eye contact with the questioner when taking the question, when completing the answer, and occasionally during the response. However, speakers should include the entire audience while presenting the answer.

### Step 3: Get confirmation from the questioner and take another question.

After responding, obtain some verbal or nonverbal feedback from the questioners indicating that their inquiries have been addressed. Asking "Have I answered your question?" can seem contrived or simply redundant if speakers say it after each response. Usually, some nonverbal confirmation can assure the speaker that the question has been addressed to the audience member's satisfaction.

### Step 4: Conclude the question-and-answer session. Restate your main point.

There ought to be a designated time for questions and answers. Even the most careful speaker will be unable to hold audience attention for too long. Therefore, after a number of questions have been addressed, the speaker should indicate that one or two more will be taken, and then attempt to end the session after addressing a question comfortably. Of course, if speakers are making a sales presentation and the potential customer has additional questions, there should be no artificial limits precluding potentially deal-making inquiries.

After taking the last question, the speaker should summarize the presentation very briefly. During the q-and-a session, speakers may have been taken hither and yon. Therefore, it is wise to restate the important points of the presentation before departing.

## Ethical Probe

**Is it unethical for speakers to plant easy questions?**

Assume speakers are apprehensive about an upcoming q-and-a session. To reduce the tension associated with the event, the speakers ask friends to sit in the audience. When the q-and-a session begins, the friends raise their hands to be recognized and then pose predetermined questions. Is this unethical?

Is it unethical to do this only for the first few questions to relax the speakers before they take questions from the "real" members of the audience?

## Counterproductive Tendencies

Speakers, even very bright, industrious, and otherwise well-prepared speakers, often behave during q-and-a in ways that undermine their performance. Readers might want to think about these tendencies and be careful to avoid them when delivering answers.

## Saying, "That's a good question" after each or several questions

Sometimes people ask questions that make speakers, very honestly, want to comment that the question is a good one, or that they are glad a particular point was brought up. Speakers who occasionally make these comments will not do irreparable damage to their presentations. However, there are two potential problems with making such remarks.

The first is that some speakers make complimentary comments after *each* inquiry. When this occurs speakers lose credibility because it is unlikely that every single question can or will be "a good question." Even if they all are "good questions" it will sound canned to make similar remarks after every inquiry.

The second problem is that if the congratulatory "That's a good question" is uttered sometimes and not every time, those who were not so stroked may think they have been tacitly insulted. "What was wrong with my question? My question was not a good one?" Although these musings may seem childish and may be childish, they are natural reactions.

For these two reasons, then, it is not a good idea to regularly evaluate the questions you hear.

## Implicitly disparaging questioners

Speakers often preface the repetition of a question with "If I understand you correctly." Sometimes this can be stated harmlessly. However, often the phrase is vocally tinged, creating a message that suggests that the question was poorly constructed. Speakers should be careful when repeating the question so as not to be sharing a laugh with the rest of the audience at the expense of the person who had the courage to make the inquiry.

## Explicitly disparaging questioners

Some audience members may wish to be recognized during q-and-a, but then may speak aimlessly. Speakers occasionally deride a questioner who, without malice, is so unfocused. There is little to be gained by derisive cheap shots. We have all said things that are foolish at times, and no one enjoys having their transgressions highlighted for mass ridicule. "Is there a question in there somewhere?" and "May I look forward to an inquiry sometime in the future?" are comments I have heard from speakers. Such remarks occasionally yield belly laughs from some audience members. However, the questionable short-term gains for the presenter will be transformed into long-term losses. Audience members, even those who may find the quips humorous, are likely to consider the speaker's comments gratuitous.

## Reflexively repeating a question

Having been coached to repeat a question, some speakers blurt back the repetition quickly and meaninglessly. This type of repetition defeats the purpose. When speakers restate the question, they should be framing the answer for the audience. By blurting the question back in the direction of the questioner, speakers are not framing the question for the audience but proving that their short-term memory is sound. Speakers do not want to seem like they are robotically performing a task. As we discussed earlier, speakers should also not repeat *every* question. Questions that are succinct, clear, and audible have been framed already by the questioner.

## Restating the question incorrectly

It is stunning how often this occurs. Listen carefully to other students in your class as they attempt to repeat questions. Unless the questions are very clear, you will notice that several persons have difficulty identifying the essence of many of the questions. This may be because speakers become apprehensive in the speaking setting. It may also be because some questions are poorly expressed.

Nevertheless, a recurring problem for beginning speakers relates to understanding the question. Speakers need to concentrate during the q-and-a session. Many questioners may be unwilling to correct speakers who respond to the wrong question. Some questioners may be reluctant to comment even when speakers request assurance that they have identified the question correctly. Speakers will reduce their terminal ethos if they answer the wrong question, particularly when the question that was posed was not particularly complex.

## Answering the question while looking directly at the questioner

When someone asks a question in an interpersonal context, speakers—very appropriately—look at the questioner when responding. During q-and-a sessions after a presentation, this natural tendency is likely to be counterproductive.

Of course speakers should look at the questioner when listening to the question. However, speakers must remember that q-and-a is a continuation of the talk. Therefore, the speaker's response should be directed to all listeners as well as the questioner. A very common problem for speakers during q-and-a is the tendency to look directly at the questioner for the duration of the response and—visually at least—ignore the rest of the audience.

## Being apparently unprepared for very predictable questions

Many speakers do not spend the requisite time preparing for the q-and-a period. As a result, some questions that are central to the topic can apparently stump speakers and leave them speechless. A bank representative recently gave a presentation to customers about the tax advantages of one of her bank's products. In her talk, she commented that one of the advantages of the product was that interest accrued from it was taxed at only 5 percent. At the end of the presentation a potential customer asked about the 5-percent tax rate. Her inquiry was simple:

*"Why is the 5 percent considered an advantage? All bank interest in this state is taxed at 5 percent?"*

The speaker seemed startled by this question and then uttered, self-effacingly but nonetheless disastrously, *"It is? I didn't know that. I just give the talk the way they tell me to. My husband does my taxes. This isn't my area of specialty."*

Having emphasized the alleged tax savings throughout the talk this comment reflected a lack of preparation, reduced her credibility, and affected how listeners considered other portions of the presentation.

## Becoming defensive

It is easy to become defensive during q-and-a. Speakers may fear that their weaknesses will be exposed by contentious listeners. However, most audience members hope that you do well and do not consider q-and-a an opportunity for attack.[6]

Even when speakers receive a confrontational question, it is best to take the high road. Consider responding with the following type of remark. *"Obviously, we have differing opinions. I hear your point and respect your arguments. However, I believe my recommendations will work. Perhaps we will forever disagree, but I promise to consider your position, and I'll ask, respectfully, for you to do the same."*

### Speaking too long in response to a single question

Quintilian said that "If we devote too much time to the final recapitulation, the conclusion will cease to be an enumeration and will constitute something very much like a second speech."[7] Quintilian was referring to extended conclusions, but the same sentiments apply to long-winded orations in response to particular questions. One does not want the q-and-a session to render the presentation meaningless. Spending too much time on one answer, or with one questioner, or on the entire q-and-a period, will not only make it difficult for you to maintain the attention of the audience, but may also make the main part of your speech a footnote to the q-and-a.

## FAQ ABOUT Q-AND-A

In a chapter about q-and-a it seems fitting to present, and respond to, some frequently asked questions about q-and-a.

What should you do if you don't know the answer to a question?

There is nothing wrong with saying "I don't know" to a question that you don't know the answer to. Nobody, regardless of how intelligent or expert they may be, knows the answers to all questions. Bluffs can be detected as such even by audience members who do not know the correct answer. Those who do know the correct answer may correct you, and even if they do not, your stature in their eyes will plummet like a heavy stone in a pond if you attempt to answer a question by winging it.

Of course, if "I don't know" is the only answer speakers have to all questions, they will be standing on precariously fragile ground. Speakers must be familiar with topics that are clearly central to their subject. A presentation on the need to contribute to The United Way compels the speakers to be familiar with the mission of The United Way.

However, assuming that you have done the requisite homework, saying "I don't know" to questions when you do not know is what you should say.

Can you say, "I'll get back to you later?"

The same advice applies. There is no reason why speakers cannot make such a promise (assuming that they intend to fulfill it). The only problems would occur if speakers answered very basic questions in this manner or if, on a prior occasion, a speaker had made such promises and not "gotten back to" questioners.

How do you answer questions in a team talk?

Team presentations are discussed in Chapter 10, where several recommendations are made regarding preparing for and delivering presentations in teams. One recommendation is for each member of the team to be familiar with what others will be saying. Another recommendation is to rehearse the cohesive presentation as a team beforehand.

That rehearsal should include a simulated q-and-a session. A common problem with team presentations is that when a question is asked, team members glance at each other as if unsure who will respond to that particular inquiry. If all speakers are familiar with each person's area, the team can more easily decide who should take the question. However, to preclude any confusion, one person on the team should be designated as a coordinator. That person should be even more familiar with each component of the talk than anyone else. When a question is asked, the coordinator can direct an undirected question to the appropriate person. For example, "Sam, I think you are the best person to respond to Abdul's question."

The coordinator and team should be wary about too many persons piggybacking on to the same question. Comments by several team members may be contradictory. Even if the various responses are consistent, the team does not want to dwell on any one question interminably. For the same reasons discussed earlier, the q-and-a portion of a team presentation should not dwarf the main part of the talk.

What if someone is persistently contentious or heckles you?

The counsel on querulous questioners is relatively consistent. The speaker is better off taking the high road whenever dealing with someone who is contentious. Identify that you disagree, but respect the position of the other. If you need to, comment that you want to move on to other questioners but are willing to discuss the issue after the presentation, either in person or via e-mail.

Heckler are in a different category. Hecklers are not interested in debate. They are interested in throwing the speaker off. If the heckler is persistent, and cannot be removed, complete the talk, comment that you regret that your message has been obstructed by the listener, and end the talk.[8]

What if someone asks the same question that another person recently posed?

As indicated earlier, there is fool's gold in deriding a questioner in front of others. The comment "I guess you were not paying attention" will make some audience members chuckle at the expense of the questioner. There is no benefit in being so derisive. Assuming that the person's inquiry was innocently repetitive, answer it again, and give the person the respect she or he deserves for being a human who sometimes makes mistakes. Your audience members will respect you for respecting the audience member.

Repetitive questions can be frustrating but it is important to treat each questioner with respect.

What if I receive a loaded question?

A loaded question, as the name suggests, is one that is "loaded" with an implicit statement as well as a question, or is loaded with multiple questions. The classic loaded question that you may have heard is "When did you stop beating your wife?"

Consider a related question that has business implications: "*When are you going to stop harassing employees?*"

The way to answer a loaded question is to unload or unpack it. "*When are you going to stop harassing employees?*" actually contains two parts. The first is the assertion that the organization is harassing employees. The second is the question "When do you intend to stop?" The response to the question should address both components of the loaded question.

For example, a speaker may respond in the following way:

> *"Well, Andy, apparently you believe that there has been harassment of employees. I am genuinely sorry that you feel this way. What constitutes harassment for some may be different from what constitutes harassment for others. However, I can assure you that we do not condone and will not tolerate such behavior. We will look into any and all allegations. If you or any person in attendance here today believes they have been harassed, let me know and I promise you that we will address the situation quickly, firmly, and correctly."*

**Q:** Instead of repeating the question, can I incorporate the question in the answer?

**A:** Yes, but... This is possible, but not as easy as it may seem to be. The speaker must be certain that the question is clearly apparent when phrasing the response. Here is an example:

> Q: *How can we accomplish our sales objectives given the retrenched workforce?*
>
> A: *I agree that it will be difficult to accomplish sales goals given the retrenchments, but I suggest that we can do it. Moreover, even though we may find ourselves working harder, the increased responsibility will translate into increased commissions.*

**Q:** What if I am faced with a "false dilemma"?

**A:** A question that includes a false dilemma implies that a situation has only two alternative solutions, both of which are bad. These questions are considered *false* dilemmas when there are several other solutions in addition to the two identified by the questioner. For example, "*How can we handle today's employees? They are either overly ambitious know-it-alls, or grousing malingerers.*"

As is the case with the loaded question, unpack the false dilemma.

> *"I agree, Leslie, that we have a problem with some employees who are ambitious to a fault and others who seem to excuse themselves from work for minor illnesses. However, we can be aggressive in purging both types from our ranks, because there is another category of employee: those who are diligent and—even if upwardly mobile—respectful to the organization and the administrators who created the foundation for our enterprise."*

**Q:** What if a question has several sub-questions?

**A:** Answer each meaningful sub-question individually. If possible, group like questions together before responding.

**Q:** What if nobody asks any questions?

**A:** Give the audience some time. Count to ten in your head. Repeat that you would be happy to address questions that listeners may have. If still nobody asks a question, bring up one that is typically asked. For example, "I'm surprised that nobody has asked me about...," and then answer the question yourself.

Most often—eventually—someone will ask a question. Once the ice is broken, other questions will follow. If nobody asks a question, it is possible that the speakers were so brilliantly comprehensive that no one has anything to say. Although such a scenario is not impossible, it is unlikely that a great presentation would render an audience speechless. Typically a great presentation intrigues audience members and stimulates questions. If no questions are asked, you may be the last speaker before the cocktail party.

However, give the audience members time to inquire. If they want to, and they have time, they probably will begin to ask questions.

What if I deliberately leave out a point in my speech anticipating a question during q-and-a, and nobody asks me that question?

Earlier in the chapter we discussed the possibility that speakers may deliberately leave out a point that they hope will surface during q-and-a.

Let us assume that speakers have an excellent answer to the question "Is this product environmentally safe compared with our competitors' products?" Let us assume that speakers believe that the answer to this question will guarantee the sale for the company because not only is their product environmentally safe, but there is proof that competitors' products exude toxins. The speakers may desire to leave this point out of their talk and set up a "straw man" during q-and-a. They may think that someone will ask the straw-man question about environmental safety and that the speakers can then knock down the straw man with a compelling response.

However, it is possible that no person will ask the straw-man question.

This is a big risk if the speakers think the argument is powerful. However, experienced speakers can avoid this risk by bringing up the question themselves. For example, "You may be interested in how safe our product is compared with others. Recent studies have just been completed on this subject..."

Speakers who deliberately leave out salient points must be cautious. They must be confident that they will have the equanimity and time, after all questions have been asked and answered, to make the powerful argument they have been waiting to deliver.

## Stand Up & Deliver

Prepare a three-minute presentation that addresses the following items:

- What are the three most significant hazards pertaining to q-and-a sessions?
- Explain how one would avoid these hazards.
- Describe how you prepared for the q-and-a session that will follow this short presentation.

## Summary

- Question-and-answer sessions are the de facto conclusions to presentations
- Often speakers do not take appropriate care to plan these sessions
- Speakers can become successful during q-and-a by
  - Anticipating questions
  - Preparing responses to questions
  - Practicing delivering responses
  - Following a simple procedure when taking questions from audience members
  - Being vigilant about avoiding common problems that speakers confront during q-and-a.

## Sample Presentation for Analysis

### How to Stop Boring Your Audience to Death

*Charles Francis delivered* "How to Stop Boring Your Audience to Death" *on January 16, 1996, when he was the president of Idea Bank Inc. The speech was delivered to the New York Chapter of the International Association of Business Communicators. As you read through this excerpt, please consider the following questions:*

1. *Do most speakers "bore their audience to death"?*
2. *Would this excerpt suggest that this speaker would be boring?*
3. *Are quotations, anecdotes, and humor the panacea that the author suggests?*
4. *Is there merit to the request made by President Bush? Explain.*
5. *What questions would you predict that Mr. Francis might need to respond to during a question-and-answer session following this presentation?*

As professionals who earn your living communicating with people, and helping others to do the same, I know you all grapple daily with that implacable foe—audience boredom.

It's a challenge, no matter what medium you are using—print, video, or human speech. It isn't that people aren't interested. It's just that, from the time we open our eyes in the morning to when we go to bed at night, all of us are assailed by messages of every kind and description. They emanate from the radio, newspaper, television, magazines, the daily mail, billboards—even the screens of our personal computers. I read recently that no less than 70 percent of what one hears is forgotten an hour after hearing it. There is a catchy acronym for this lack of memorability. It's called MYGLO for "My Eyes Glaze Over," a physical phenomenon that takes over the minute you lose the audience's attention.

The famous advertising man David Ogilvy perhaps said it best, "No one ever sold anybody anything by boring them to death."

There are three magic talismans that can greatly increase your ability to hold people's attention. They are known to every professional writer and speaker, but even professionals don't call on their occult powers as often as they should. These three powerful Genies are, simply: quotations, anecdotes, and humor. Let's examine each of them in turn.

For reasons I have never been able to understand, some speakers shy away from using quotations, thinking perhaps that their use will make their remarks sound stilted. President George Bush was on record as telling his speechwriter that I don't want any more quotations from that guy Thucydides. True, the name of that ancient Greek historian is a mouthful for anyone but, if the thought is important enough to express, why not just say "A famous historian once said," etc.?

No one made better use of quotations than that unrivaled communicator Winston Churchill. By his own admission, quotation collections were a filling station to fuel his eloquence. "Quotations," he said, "when engraved upon the memory give you good thoughts."

As someone who has on his library shelves more than 1,000 quotation books of all descriptions, I can assure you that Churchill was right. Browsing through them can be stimulating and thought-provoking even if you end up not using a single quotation. That is because there is not a thought in our heads that has not been worn shiny by someone else's brains. Mark Twain used to maintain that Adam was the only man who could say something with the assurance that he was the first man on earth to say it.

Presidents Jack Kennedy and Ronald Reagan—two of the most gifted speakers of the 20th century—both were fond of quotations and used them with great effectiveness. As a young man running for Congress in his native Boston, Kennedy carried around a loose-leaf notebook containing his favorite quotations. Reagan, who before entering politics was a professional speaker for the General Electric Company, learned to use quotations, anecdotes, and humor with a skill that later on in his presidency earned him the title, "The Great Communicator."

**Source**: Francis, Charles. "How to Stop Boring your Audience to Death: Databases, Anecdotes, and Humor," *Vital Speeches of the Day*, February 15, 1996, 62, no.9: 283(3).

## Review Questions

1. Why do q-and-a sessions affect a speaker's terminal ethos?
2. What three steps can be taken to prepare for q-and-a sessions?
3. Identify three reasons why it may be necessary to repeat a question during q-and-a.
4. What are three counterproductive tendencies of speakers during q-and-a sessions? How can they be avoided?
5. How should a speaker respond to loaded questions? Questions that include false dilemmas?
6. Why should speakers say, "I don't know" when confronted with questions that they do not know the answer to? When can this become a problem?
7. Consider a presentation you have given previously in this class or elsewhere. How would you have prepared for q-and-a on that occasion to ensure the best possible outcome?

## InfoTrac Question

Use InfoTrac to find the article by Teresa Brady pertaining to abrasive questions asked during presentations. What tips does Brady provide to reduce the problems related to these questions? Which of these tips make sense to you?

[1] Larry Speakes, *Speaking Out*, with Robert Pack (New York: Avon, 1988), 292.

[2] Robert Whitaker, *Mad in America: Bad Science, Bad Medicine, and the Enduring Mistreatment of the Mentally Ill* (Cambridge, MA: Perseus Publishing, 2002).

[3] For example, Hamilton Gregory in *Public Speaking for College and Career*, 2nd ed. (New York: McGraw Hill, 1990), 269.

[4] Bernard Shaw said to Governor Dukakis: "Governor, if Kitty Dukakis was raped or murdered, would you favor an irrevocable death penalty for a killer?" Without emotion and without missing a beat Dukakis replied, "No, I don't, Bernard. And I think you know that I've opposed the death penalty my whole life." This comment seemed unfeeling, and Dukakis came off as insensitively arrogant. In Eileen Shields-West, *World Almanac of Presidential Campaigns* (New York: World Almanac, 1992), 242.

[5] Ford indicated with his response that he believed the Eastern European countries were not dominated by the Soviet Union. At the time, in 1976, the Eastern European countries were, and had been, incontrovertibly dominated by the Soviet Union. Max Frankel, the journalist asking the question, gave Ford an opportunity to take back his comment when he said, "Did I understand you to say, sir, that the Russians are not using Eastern Europe as their own sphere of influence in occupying most of the countries there, and making sure with their own troops that it is a Communist zone?" Ford responded by essentially restating his position. Paul Boller, *Presidential Campaigns* (New York: Oxford University Press, 1996), 346.

[6] See, for example, Steven Brydon and Michael Scott, *Between One and Many*, 2nd ed. (Mountain View, CA: Mayfield, 1997), 71. Also, Joseph DeVito, *Elements of Public Speaking*, 7th ed. (New York: Longman, 2000), 35.

[7] Quintilian, *The Education of the Orator*, Book VI, Chapter 1, Section 2, translated by Rev. John Selby Watson (London: George Bell & Sons).

[8] There are various suggestions for dealing with hecklers, all of which revolve around this idea of taking the high road and not engaging in a battle. See, for example, Richard Letteri, *A Handbook of Public Speaking* (New York: Allyn and Bacon, 2002), 224–226.

Chapter in a Nutshell

*Listening is more difficult than it appears to be. Effective criticism of presentations is beneficial to both speakers and listeners.*

# 13 Evaluating Yourself and Others: Your Role as Critical Listener in Presentation Contexts

*He that wrestles with us strengthens our nerves, and sharpens our skill. Our antagonist is our helper.*[1]

-Edmund Burke

*Do not trust to the cheering, for those persons would shout as much if you and I were going to be hanged.*[2]

-Oliver Cromwell


## Abstract

Members of an audience have a responsibility to critically evaluate the presentations they hear. In civic, business, and even social contexts, the careful assessment of messages by audience members can help speakers as well as organizations become more efficient. In addition, the act of identifying strengths and weaknesses in other presentations will help evaluators discover what speaking behaviors they wish to avoid and which behaviors they wish to adopt when they assume the role of presenter. This chapter discusses issues pertaining to evaluating presentations. Specifically, at the conclusion of this chapter you should be able to do the following:

- Discuss problems related to effective listening
- Identify suggestions for improving listening efficiency
- Describe what is meant by critical thinking
- Discuss methods for assessing the quality of critical thinking
- Identify common fallacies used in public presentations
- Describe methods for tactfully communicating feedback to presenters

## The Consultants, the Convocation, and the Court

On a Monday in the spring of 2002, two experienced consultants arrived at a company's headquarters to conduct a presentation skills workshop. The consultants had a deserved reputation for being engaging and affable. The most frequently recurring comments on evaluation sheets from past participants were always "Enjoyable session. Very valuable."

The consultants began this particular workshop and soon afterward started to wonder if they were dealing with humans or inanimate objects. No matter how the speakers attempted to engage the audience, regardless of what "tried and true" humorous anecdote they pulled from their collection, despite any and all attempts to encourage interaction, each member of the group sat in their seat as if they were attending a funeral.

At a break, the consultants approached the session contact and expressed their confusion. "These people are not responding at all," one of them said. "What is going on?"

"Well, I don't think they can really listen to you today," the coordinator said. "Half of the staff was let go on Friday now that the economy has gone south. These are some of the survivors, but I think they are thinking about their colleagues, and may be wondering if the ax will fall on them anytime soon."

In the fall of 2003, all incoming freshmen and transfer students at a large university were invited to a convocation that was to usher in the new academic term. During the ceremony the main speakers were the university provost, the school's president, the president of the student association, and two students introduced as Presidential Scholars who spoke in tandem.

The provost offered welcoming remarks and introduced various people to the new students. The president similarly greeted all and emphasized how difficult it was to be admitted to the institution and how proud those in attendance should feel since they represented the one person out of eight who had been invited to enroll. The president of the student association encouraged students to participate in government and play an active role in their education.

The Presidential Scholars were last and spoke about how they had felt when they were freshmen. In addition to discussing the academic routes they had chosen, they relayed some humorous anecdotes about their experiences.

One of the two students described how excited he had been to attend school, but how he had inadvertently set his alarm clock for P.M. rather than A.M. and missed his first class. A reference to this error surfaced on a number of occasions as the two students exchanged humorous gibes throughout their talk.

Two hours after the session, seventy-six students who had been invited to the convocation completed a survey asking them about what they had listened to and retained from the session.

Nearly 60 percent of the students surveyed said they had not retained one thing because they had decided not to attend the convocation.

Those who had actually attended were asked the following questions:

- To which of the four presentations did you pay the most attention?
- What information that you heard during the convocation was most significant?
- What do you predict that you would be likely to retain?

No students indicated that they had been most attentive to the provost. A few students said they had been most attentive to the university president, and a few others said they listened most attentively to the president of the student association. The overwhelming majority said they had paid the greatest attention to the Presidential Scholars.

Nearly half of the attending respondents reported that the most significant piece of information from all of the talks—and the piece of information they were most likely to retain—was the same: Remember to set your alarm clock to A.M. rather than P.M.

* * *

In May 1965, Collie Leroy Wilkins, a Ku Klux Klan member, was on trial for the drive-by murder of a white civil rights worker named Viola Liuzzo. The evidence against Wilkins seemed substantial. An FBI agent who had infiltrated the Ku Klux Klan by pretending to become a member was actually seated next to Wilkins in the auto when Wilkins pulled the trigger. Another agent named Shanahan testified that the bullet that killed Liuzzo came from Wilkins's gun. Leroy Moton, an African American who was sitting in the automobile next to Liuzzo, testified that he had seen Wilkins pull the trigger.

The all-white jury listened to the final appeal from Wilkins's attorney. The attorney made the following arguments:

- You cannot trust the testimony of anyone who lied when he took an oath to join the Ku Klux Klan.
- You cannot trust the testimony of an African American. Leroy Moton was "under the spell of narcotics."
- Shanahan was "shanty Irish" and could not be trusted because of that and because he was a Catholic.
- Viola Liuzzo was not really "white" because she was a member of the NAACP and was sitting beside a black man in an automobile.

The final appeal to the jury was filled with racial epithets that ridiculed African Americans, Catholics, and Jews. The final statement of the appeal was this: "I urge you as patriotic Americans not to find this young man guilty." Essentially the lawyer was arguing that one should not be found guilty for murdering a civil rights worker.

The trial ended with a hung jury. In a subsequent trial five months later, Wilkins was acquitted. What factors affected the efficiency of the listeners in the: consulting workshop, university convocation, and trial of Collie Leroy Wilkins?

# Introduction

In this class and in your careers you will spend more time listening to presentations than delivering them. Your ability to effectively evaluate messages will be helpful to your classmates during this course and to your colleagues at work once you graduate. In addition, receivers' careful assessments of presentations can help them identify speaker behaviors they would like to adopt and those they would like to avoid. For this reason, students who enroll in presentation workshops often comment that the evaluation component of the course—that is, listening to and critiquing classmates—is nearly as valuable as the presentations they are required to deliver themselves. Effective evaluation of presentations requires efficient listening, careful analysis, and tactful communication of criticisms. Each of these areas is discussed in this chapter.

# Listening Effectively

## The Importance of Listening in the Presentation Context

Most people are aware, at least superficially, of the importance of listening for personal and professional success. However, despite this awareness poor listening has been identified as the most common cause of communication breakdowns.[3] In presentation contexts, efficient listening is critical for several reasons.

Inefficient listening can result in the following:

- **The adoption of counterproductive policies.**
  The inability to listen carefully and evaluate proposals may result in an organization pursuing a plan that is illogical and counterproductive. Often speakers are either explicitly or implicitly requesting that audience members analyze and react to what they hear. Even when such analysis is not apparently desired, responsible citizens of an organization or community are obligated to listen effectively so that they may intelligently critique messages.
- **Victimization.**
  Poor listening may result in receivers being duped by unethical speakers both within and outside the organization. P. T. Barnum is alleged to have quipped, "There's a sucker born every minute." Barnum died in 1891, but he and others of his ilk have sired many loyal descendants. There are many unprincipled individuals who believe there are many "suckers" and are willing to persuade them by any means necessary. Careful listening protects individuals from being victimized by unscrupulous presenters.
- **Misinterpretation of customer feedback.**
  Customers may react to presentations with insightful, or even incisive, comments. Speakers must listen effectively to this feedback to respond to client needs. When we think of listening in presentation contexts, we typically consider the listening skills of audience members. However, speakers become listeners when they consume reactions to their messages. Effective listening allows speakers to understand, digest, and react to what they hear from their audiences.
- **Not understanding specific assignments or organizational policies.**
  Inefficient listening in the classroom can result in confusion about what to do and how to do it to satisfy course requirements. Similarly, employees who attend orientation sessions, for example, and who do not listen effectively may follow inappropriate procedures and consequently perform tasks inadequately. There is, often, a very pragmatic reason for making presentations. Speakers may need to impart information pertaining to logistics, safety, and protocol. Not attending to presentations properly can have embarrassing and even career-threatening effects.

# Listening and Hearing

Listening and hearing are two fundamentally different processes. People hear sounds even when they are not listening. There are three significant distinctions between the two activities.

The first distinction is that listening is an attentive behavior. This means that people are actively, as opposed to passively, involved in the process of listening. If you are sitting on your porch and hear the sounds of a baseball game being played in a nearby park, you are not listening to the sounds unless you begin to attend to those sounds and actively attempt to discern what is going on in the game by listening.

A second difference between hearing and listening is that skill in listening is something that people learn. Hearing for those not impaired is a physical phenomenon that requires no real training. Most people were able to hear sounds as an infant before they had developed many skills. Because listening is a skill, it can be developed or it can atrophy. People can become more or less adept at listening, whereas hearing is a function of one's physical capabilities.

The third difference between hearing and listening is that listening is a sporadic activity. Radios are often turned on in homes for background noise. Periodically, persons who are at home may tune in to what they are continuously hearing on the radio. Similarly, when listening to a lecture, sounds from instructors and students are continuously audible, but most students only sporadically pay attention to these sounds. Responsible students in a classroom will spend more time listening than those less committed, but even the most dedicated students will not stay focused continuously.

## Reverse the Perspective

Throughout the book the *Reverse the Perspective* segments have been designed to help you become more efficient presenters by asking you to adopt the perspective of those in the audience. By thinking about how listeners feel when they are audience members, readers may be able to clearly identify how they would like to behave when speaking.

Since this chapter deals with listening and evaluating, this *Reverse the Perspective* segment asks readers to evaluate the listener from the perspective of the speaker.

When you are a speaker, which of the following makes you believe that a particular audience member is an effective listener?

- Regular note taking
- Sporadic note taking
- Requests for clarification
- Intelligent questions during the presentation
- Intelligent questions after the presentation
- Challenges to the position taken
- Informal discussions after the presentation
- Posture
- Eye contact
- Other nonverbal factors

## Listening and Selectivity

Listening is a selective process. It involves four stages:

- Selective exposure
- Selective attention
- Selective perception
- Selective retention

### Selective Exposure

When you decide to attend class on a given day, you are putting yourself in a position to hear information related to the class. If you were to choose to skip a session or not take a particular class at all, you would be consciously or subconsciously avoiding any potential information that could be presented in that class or course. If the Human Resources department sends a mass e-mail inviting all employees to a presentation on medical benefits, employees can decide to go or skip the lecture. If they go, they have selectively exposed themselves to what might be said at the session. Students invited to a convocation can decide to attend or avoid it. If they go, they have selectively exposed themselves to what the provost, president, and students may say.

### Selective Attention

Once you arrive at a presentation, you can focus your attention on what the speaker has to say. However, you may also attend to other stimuli. You can dwell on the aesthetics of the PowerPoint® slides that accompany the presentation, the presenter's attire, or even the presence of unlikely attendees at the session. You are selectively attending to the various stimuli available.

### Selective Perception

If receivers choose to attend to a spoken message, they can *perceive* various meanings from what is said. The receivers select what to perceive from what they hear.

Speakers often—and counterproductively—choose to perceive what is consistent with what they previously believed, or what they desire to believe. For example, a consultant may address client representatives and say, "Although you are doing some excellent things here, there is much that is problematic. You must address these problems or your company could lose market share." The client group could take away the prefatory message that they are doing some "excellent things" and choose to disregard the information about the organization's potential demise.

The opposite is also true. The client could choose to hear the criticism and disregard the positive comments. A student with low self-esteem may choose to hear that "there could be some improvement" from the instructor's remark: "Your performance is simply outstanding. Of course there could be some improvement, but that is the case with anyone anytime. You are simply an excellent student."

DeWine, James, and Walence conducted a study that yielded findings that are relevant to selective perception. The authors were evaluating a specific testing instrument that is used to assess the quality of communication in organizations.[4] The data from the study indicated that "managers maintain their own form of organizational reality. The administrators select and accept issue analysis and recommendations...according to their own perceptions of organizational reality and what is most appropriate for their organization regardless of the nature of the recommendations."[5] In other words, the author's comment that when managers hear these test results, they tend to accept what is consistent with what they desire and expect, regardless of the actual results and recommendations. This description of how some managers react to assessments depicts what is meant by selective perception.

### Selective Retention

Two weeks after a talk, what do you remember from it? *Selective retention* refers to the fact that listeners select, subconsciously or otherwise, what to recall. Effective listeners choose what is significant. Ineffective listeners may choose to remember a humorous anecdote that was relayed.

A student may have attended a class two semesters ago and not be able to recall anything substantive about it beyond the instructor's tendency to speak about his old Chrysler. You may have attended the same class and be able to recall many applicable portions that will help you when you take the more advanced course. In this scenario, you were a more efficient listener than the other student because you selected, consciously or otherwise, the important things to retain.

## Obstacles to Effective Listening

In addition to the potential problems related to selectivity, there are several other probable barriers to effective listening.

### Physical Distractions

External noise, such as road traffic, side conversations, or sounds emanating from nearby rooms can make effective listening difficult.

### Psychological Noise

Personal and professional matters may preoccupy a listener. It is difficult to listen to a supervisor drone on about the daily drivel even if it contains some nugget of value if the listener is overwhelmed with contemplations regarding a lawsuit or a difficult family member. The two consultants described in this chapter's opening vignette faced preoccupied listeners who were consumed with psychological noise.

### Physiological Problems

Some of us are more fortunate than others. As has been discussed, listening is not the same as hearing, but does require the ability to hear. Hearing deficiencies will be an impediment to effective listening.

### Contrary Perspectives

Receivers who attend a session determined to reject a proposal will be unable to listen effectively to evaluate that proposal. In such instances, the receiver's objective when listening is to identify flawed claims, not to assess the merit of the idea as a whole. Such a contentious orientation will only allow the listener to identify and store faults with an argument. This behavior will consequently preclude efficient listening.

These attitudes may exist because of a personal bias against the speakers. If another student in your class has earned your animosity, it may be very difficult for you to dispassionately assess the quality of his oration. If individuals previously criticized one of your efforts, you might, despite the merit of their criticism, be looking for cracks in their armor when they present.

Contentious perspectives can also exist because of a hidden agenda. A new parking lot may be in the best interest of the organization, but it also may block two members' views of the river. These persons may very selfishly not want to hear the clanking of construction for six months or look at a wall for the rest of their careers when they would otherwise be gazing peacefully at sailboats. They are unable to listen attentively because of a hidden agenda.

## Semantic Distractions

Semantic distractions occur because of the words a speaker selects. If listeners are unfamiliar with a word or believe they *are* familiar with a word that they actually do not know, there will be semantic distractions. Semantic distractions may also occur if a receiver dwells on why a speaker selected a particular word. As indicated in Chapter 11, this can happen when speakers in professional contexts use slang, profanity, or jargon.

## Information Overload

On occasion there is simply too much for a receiver to field. If receivers are attending an orientation session at which seven different officers speak about how their divisions function, receivers are likely to become so flooded with facts that they quit trying to retain it all. You may remember this from your orientation at the university. Within a two-day period you may have heard speeches from dorm directors, health officers, the athletic department, your academic chairperson, and the president of the institution. Too much information can overwhelm even the most responsible listener, making it impossible to listen effectively.

## Differential Time

Conversely, the phenomenon of *differential time* is an enormous obstacle for listeners to overcome. Listening pioneer Ralph Nichols reported that receivers were able to process what they heard much faster than speakers could speak. He claimed that listeners could process many more words than the approximately 125 words a minute a speaker could utter.[6]

The difference between the number of words one can hear and the words one can speak has been called differential time.[7] At first glance the existence of such differential time may not seem to be a problem. However, it can be an immense problem, because most listeners tend to waste differential time.

This may also seem harmless. You may think, "What is the problem with wasting the time, if you have the time to waste?" The problem is that listeners who squander differential time and daydream typically spend more than the differential time away from the speaker. When they return from the reverie, the speaker is on to another subject and the listener may not be able to get the gist of what is being discussed. Listeners who return from inattentiveness and discover that they are lost often do not scramble to discover what has been missed. Instead they return to daydreaming. Therefore the existence of differential time and the tendency not to use it is an obstacle for listeners.

## Feigning Attention

Nichols argues that most receivers are more adept at feigning attention than paying attention.[8] If you were to observe your classmates from the vantage point of the instructor, it would seem as if most listeners are being attentive to the teacher's presentation. Nichols argues that it is likely that many of these people are simply faking it. Audience members have learned how to nod strategically, narrow their eyes to appear to be analyzing complex information, and even have learned how and when to utter sounds to acknowledge a point. Since feigning attention is a skill that many possess—and because faking attention is easier than actually being attentive—many receivers simply assume a posture of listening. Faking attention, of course, militates against effective listening.

## Distractions Based on Pervasive Use of Speech Fillers

Even industrious and responsible listeners can easily become distracted by speakers who pervasively interject meaningless filler words like *ums*, *ers*, and *you knows* during a presentation. We have discussed problems with speech fillers previously in the text, but it is important to note in this section that interjections do create obstacles for listeners.

# Becoming an Effective Listener: Active Listening

*Active listening* is a phrase used to describe the opposite of the common tendencies to passively attend to what is presented. An active listener is aware of potential obstacles to effective listening, works to avoid these obstacles, and becomes a critical consumer of information.

Specifically, active listeners do the following:

## Arrive at a Session Prepared to Work

Many people view presentations as an opportunity to kick back, sip their coffee, and contemplate other matters. Listening is work. What separates an effective listener from an ineffective one is sometimes simply a matter of industry.

## Identify the Speakers' Objectives

Receivers should attempt to learn the purpose of a presentation before it begins. In many situations this is impossible. In your classes, it is likely that you know what another student's presentation will be about only once you get to class. In these instances, be committed to identifying the speech objective as soon as possible once the speakers begin.

In some classes, assigned presentation topics are publicized and students can become familiar with a team's speaking agenda before the presentation. Often in organizations, the objective of a presentation is made public before the presentation date. Your ability to be an effective listener and valuable critic will depend on whether you are aware of what the speaker is trying to do.

## Use Differential Time Wisely

Instead of wasting differential time, active listeners use the moments they have. Three related activities can be helpful to the active listener during differential time. The first is to identify the main points of the message and paraphrase what has been said. The second is to consider the evidence that the speaker is using to support these points. The third is to attempt to predict where the speaker will go next.

For example, assume that you are listening to a club president who is advocating that club members participate in community service activities. An active listener would periodically summarize the points made by the speaker, assess the merit of the arguments pertaining to community service participation, and then attempt to predict the speaker's next argument about the merit of becoming involved with community service.

## Evaluate Persuasive Arguments Critically

Critical thinking has emerged as a staple of many college programs throughout the country. The fuel that has energized this emergence is the sense that all citizens must be able to critically assess what they read and hear.

Ruggiero defines *critical thinking* simply as "the process of evaluating ideas."[9] Gellin is more elaborate and writes that critical thinking is "the ability to evaluate and analyze arguments correctly; correctly deduce conclusions and make inferences from data; use inductive reasoning; and recognize assumptions as described by critical thinking instruments."[10]

Such critical thinking instruments include the following:

- Watson-Glaser Critical Thinking Appraisal
- Cornell Critical Thinking Test
- California Critical Thinking Skills Test
- Critical thinking test of the Collegiate Assessment of Academic Proficiency[11]

To be efficient evaluators when listening to presentations, audience members must be able to think critically. Jurors listening to a lawyer's final statement; consumers attending a salesperson's pitch; employees evaluating a management proposal; supervisors listening to a report from subordinates; citizens listening to political candidates—all must critically evaluate the messages they hear. To do this, listeners must be able to separate the sound logical arguments from the arguments that may seem logical but are actually fallacious.

# Evaluating Fallacious Arguments

The words *specious*, *spurious*, and *bogus* all have similar meanings. They are all adjectives that describe something that is counterfeit—i.e., not the real deal. A specious gem may look real, but under scrutiny is a cheap imitation. A spurious argument is one that contains faulty reasoning. Something that is bogus is simply not true. Perhaps there are so many variations of words meaning "phony" because there is so much that is phony. Critical thinkers have to be able to examine arguments to detect which claims are accurate and which are not.

A fallacious argument is one that contains a fallacy—some flaw of reasoning that undermines and corrupts the claim. The following are several types of flawed arguments that critical thinkers must be able to identify:

Listeners must be able to distinguish between sound, logical arguments and those that may seem logical but are actually fallacious.



## Hasty Generalization

*When the Johnson boy went away to State U, he got himself into the drug scene. When*

*Swinson's daughter went to State, she too got into drugs. Therefore, concerned parents of this community cannot afford to send our children to State because, as these examples make clear, attending State results in drug involvement.*

The so-called hasty generalization fallacy occurs when conclusions are drawn on the basis of a number of incidents that do not sufficiently support the conclusion.

The argument is fallacious because of three related reasons:

- There are not enough examples. Hundreds of students have gone to State U. Only two examples are cited.
- There are likely offsetting examples. Many of the hundreds who went to State did not become involved with drugs. These two people represent a tiny percentage of all who enrolled. This percentage could be less than the average percentage at all universities.
- There could be intervening variables. For example, Johnson and Swinson may have been involved with drugs before they left. Johnson and Swinson may be atypical of most students. Johnson and Swinson may have had siblings who had been involved with drugs.

## Post Hoc Ergo Propter Hoc

*As soon as we decided to increase our entrance standards, we saw the endowment to the university shoot up. Therefore, we must give credit to those who had the courage to make this change in admissions, because if not for them our endowment would not be at its high level.*

*Post hoc ergo propter hoc* literally means "after the fact, therefore because of the fact." In other words, this type of argument suggests that because something occurred after another occurrence, the second phenomenon was caused by the first.

The argument in the example is fallacious for the following reasons:

- There may be no evidence that the admissions change created the effect.
- There may be other causes for the effect. For example, the university may have launched an endowment campaign at the same time that they increased admission standards.
- There may be evidence that this phenomenon is an aberration. For example, perhaps at four other times in the past twenty years the endowment has gone up. In two instances there had been no increase in admission standards. In one instance the admission standards actually dipped.

## Red Herring

*It is absurd to think that our fraternity should be punished for public obscenity. After all, we have the highest grade point average of all fraternities on campus, and in each of the last four years we have had the highest number of brothers on the dean's list of all Greek organizations.*

The red herring argument gets its name from a practice used by farmers to distract hunters. They would drag a red herring through their property, hoping that the smell would discourage fox hunters because the hunters' dogs would be thrown off by the herring's scent.[12] When someone consciously employs a red herring argument, they attempt to persuade by including an unrelated argument that they hope will distract the listeners from examining the central issues of their case.

In the example, the inclusion of information about academic success is a red herring. If done intentionally, the speaker is hopeful that this unrelated fact will distract the listeners from the real issue of whether the brothers behaved obscenely in public. If used unintentionally the speaker is under the illusion that there is a relationship between the unrelated phenomena.

## Non Sequiturs

A related type of fallacy is called the non sequitur. *Non sequitur* literally means "it does not follow." When speakers employ non sequiturs, they attempt to justify a statement on the basis of one that is unrelated. Therefore, the conclusion does not follow from the argument. Here is an example:

> *We should put more money into our campus television station because communication studies departments throughout the country are extraordinarily large.*

These arguments do not follow. The size of communication studies departments is not necessarily related to the amount of money that should be allotted for the television station.

## Ad Hominem

> *John is originally from New Jersey. New Jersey, as you must know, is notorious for its pollution problem. John is in no position to tell us how we should handle our industrial waste problem. Therefore we can dismiss from the get-go any notions he has about dealing with our waste.*

An ad hominem argument is one that is not based on the integrity of the argument, but rather is founded on the characteristics of the person or group supporting the argument. In the example, the merit of John's ideas is unrelated to where he was born, regardless of the pollution record of his home state.

## Misplaced Authority

An individual who is an authority in one area is not necessarily an expert in others. Speakers sometimes invoke the name of an authority to support a position when the authority is misplaced, i.e., not a genuine expert in this area. For example,

> *The need to use federal money to support struggling organizations has been endorsed by such public figures as LeBron James and Meryl Streep.*

LeBron James may be a great basketball player. Meryl Streep is revered as one of the best in her profession. Neither James nor Streep becomes an expert in the areas of fiscal spending because of their skill in other areas.

## Appeal to Tradition

> *For one hundred years our community has permitted the sale of guns to law-abiding citizens. Why we should stop now is a mystery to me.*

The fact that something has always been the case does not mean that it ever was legitimate or that its historic existence was based on intelligent choices. In the example, the argument is fallacious, because no evidence has been provided to suggest that traditionally it was good or wise to sell guns to law-abiding citizens.

## Ad Populum

*Louise has endorsed this plan. So has Mark. So has the always-obstinate Sam. All reasonable people seem to be supporting this initiative, but we need your support also.*

The ad populum argument is also called the bandwagon fallacy. Speakers occasionally attempt to make a case for a proposal because others have endorsed it.

In the example, the ad populum argument is fallacious because it offers no other proof than its popularity. You may remember using these arguments when you were a child and requested permission to do something because "Sharon, Walter, Dick, Joanne, and Shirley" were doing it. Your parents no doubt questioned the fallacy when they said, "If Shirley jumped out of the window, would you do it, too?" Critical listeners, like wise parents reject an argument simply because it is advanced because of its popularity.

## Slippery Slope

The slippery slope argument is based on the assumption that the domino effect is inevitable. Speakers who employ this argument suggest that although one step is innocuous, it will inevitably lead to something corrosive. Here is an example:

*Once we allow students into our program with less than a 2.7 cumulative average, we might as well abandon any restrictions on transfer students. Then we will inevitably be reduced to being the laughingstock of the university. Once that happens, we will be out of a job, because the university will not allow us to continue if we are perceived as an illegitimate academic department.*

The slippery slope assumes that the effects of one action will inevitably result in an avalanche. It is fallacious unless supporting evidence can be provided that justifies the notion that the alleged consequences are likely to occur.

## Straw Man

The straw-man fallacy is a very clever approach to refuting counterarguments. When the straw man is employed, the speakers identify reservations that people have by depicting them incompletely or inaccurately. Then they can easily knock down the "straw man" they have set up. Here is an example:

*My suggestion to promote an early retirement program will work. I know you have heard grumblings from detractors. They have said that the company will expend a significant amount of money with this program. This is so, but consider the amount of money we will save. Consider this chart. By 2006, we will have saved a million dollars in salaries. By 2009, we will have saved more than ten million. Therefore, I think we can see that the detractors' position is short-sighted.*

This argument is fallacious if the detractors' point about money was different from the straw-man argument identified. Let's assume detractors acknowledge that salary expenses will go down, but that too many people will opt for early retirement. Therefore, the detractors' point is that *total expenses* involved with the program—hiring, training, processing early retirement petitions, and so on—will *exceed* the salary savings. If this is actually the position of the detractors, then the speaker in the example has set up a relatively weak and inaccurate straw-man in order to (fallaciously) refer to the position taken by opponents.

## False Dichotomy (sometimes called false dilemma)

In this argument speakers present their solution as the better of two choices. It is a false dichotomy if more than two choices are involved. Here is an example:

> *We have two choices here. We can pay for the damage we did to the room during our party or we can get thrown out of the university. I for one do not want to get tossed out. Therefore, I believe you will agree with me that we are better off to just pay the money, as outrageous as it may be, and remain at the institution.*

This argument is fallacious because there are likely to be more than the two choices that have been presented by the speaker.

## Argument by Inappropriate Analogy

> *Yes, I know that Walter is not the best accountant we have. However, this department is all that Walter has. Asking Walter to move into another department would be like taking a fish out of water.*

This fallacy is a result of a comparison that is not comparable. A speaker attempts to persuade an audience that an actual event is akin to another. In this example, if Walter would truly expire professionally were he to leave the department, then the analogy would be appropriate. However, that is not likely.

An argument by analogy is inappropriate if the situations are not analogous. Specifically, if the differences between the compared items are greater than the similarities, a critical listener would identify this argument as fallacious.

# Communicating Your Evaluations

Any method for communicating assessments to speakers has to meet several criteria.

Primarily, the feedback has to be presented diplomatically so that the speakers can digest the message without feeling as if they are being attacked. Regardless of the accuracy of your assessments, the feedback is valueless if the speakers cannot consume it because the messages are too toxic.

Secondly, the feedback has to be thorough. As has been discussed throughout this text, presentation quality is based on many factors. Whatever critical method is employed has to address all those facets that, when combined, comprise a high-quality presentation.

Third, the feedback has to be honest. It does speakers no good to hear how wonderful their talk was if it was not. In an attempt to appear friendly, cowardly evaluators can tell everyone their talks are splendid. Friendship at times requires constructive criticism.

### Ethical Probe

Two contrary and defensive speakers have just made a collaborative presentation to your group. Your assessment of these individuals is that they are honestly working hard and honestly want to hear how they can improve, but they nevertheless are bristly and react to any criticism, however constructive, as if it were a personal attack. Should you tell these speakers that their presentation needs work if it does, or is it ethical, given their characters, to simply tell them that their talk was "very good"?

## Written Reports

One method for communicating feedback to speakers involves some form of written report or evaluation. Several of these types of documents are displayed in Figures 13-1, 13-2, and 13-3.

The following issues should be considered when completing written evaluations:

- Writing evaluations during a presentation can be distracting to a speaker. It might be good to wait until the speaker is finished before recording your responses.
- The more one can write that describes reactions, the better it is for a speaker. Comments like "Good" or "Weak" or checking a 1, 2, or 3, is not as valuable as explaining why you thought a presentation was good or weak.
- A spoonful of sugar helps the medicine go down. It does the speaker no good if all comments are so sugar-coated that the constructive criticisms are impossible to detect. However, in the absence of paralingual cues, written comments that are critical can appear to be harsher than intended. Therefore, those who complete written evaluation forms should be sensitive to the listener and couch criticism in language that will make it possible to digest.

## Oral Evaluations

Oral evaluations can be used either as a complement to, or in lieu of, written evaluations. Speakers typically desire to hear immediate oral feedback in addition to whatever written feedback they will receive subsequently.[13]

The following has been advocated by Grice and Skinner as a procedure for communicating criticism:

1. Say something positive.
2. Be specific.
3. Be honest but tactful.
4. Personalize your comments.
5. Reinforce the positive.
6. Problem-solve the negative, if you said something critical.
7. Organize your comments before you say them.
8. Provide the speaker with a plan of action (e.g., "Perhaps the next time...").
9. End positively.[14]

A modification of this protocol is illustrated in the following example:

- Introduce positively. Be specific.
  - *"I enjoyed listening to your talk and found many parts interesting."*

- Identify specifically what you liked about the talk.
  - *"The section that explained how we are selling in relation to our competitors included data I had not heard before."*

- Tactfully indicate what might have been improved.
  - *"I did have trouble with the amount of material that appeared on the slides."*

- Offset the criticism.
  - *"The quality of the information was not an issue. Even the quantity was impressive, because it reflected the extent of your preparation, but the information was overwhelming."*

**Speaker**______________________________ **Total Points**

**Grade**

**Topic**_______________________________

**5=excellent 4=good 3=average 2=below average 1=poor**

**Speech to Inform with Presentational Aids Evaluation**

| **Speech Composition** | | | | | |
|---|---|---|---|---|---|
| Dynamic Introduction/Clear Thesis | 5 | 4 | 3 | 2 | 1 |
| Preview Main Ideas | 5 | 4 | 3 | 2 | 1 |
| Use of Signposting | 5 | 4 | 3 | 2 | 1 |
| Smooth Transitions within Body of the Speech | 5 | 4 | 3 | 2 | 1 |
| Effective, Vivid and Clear Use of Language | 5 | 4 | 3 | 2 | 1 |
| Strong Conclusion | 5 | 4 | 3 | 2 | 1 |
| **Vocal Dynamics** | | | | | |
| Volume and Projection | 5 | 4 | 3 | 2 | 1 |
| Use of Expression and Inflection | 5 | 4 | 3 | 2 | 1 |
| Appropriate Rate/Effective Use of Pauses | 5 | 4 | 3 | 2 | 1 |
| Clear Vocal "Signposting" | 5 | 4 | 3 | 2 | 1 |
| Articulation and Intelligibility | 5 | 4 | 3 | 2 | 1 |
| **Body Movement** | | | | | |
| Relaxed Posture/Control of Nerves | 5 | 4 | 3 | 2 | 1 |
| Appropriate Movement & Gestures | 5 | 4 | 3 | 2 | 1 |
| Physical Connection to Visual Aid | 5 | 4 | 3 | 2 | 1 |
| **Delivery Components** | | | | | |
| Rehearsal and Preparation | 5 | 4 | 3 | 2 | 1 |
| Use of Note Cards/Text/Visual | 5 | 4 | 3 | 2 | 1 |
| Eye Contact | 5 | 4 | 3 | 2 | 1 |
| Extemporaneous Style (well-spoken, good flow of ideas, not memorized or read) | 5 | 4 | 3 | 2 | 1 |
| **Informative and Visual Aid Components** | | | | | |
| Incorporation of Visual Aid with text | 5 | 4 | 3 | 2 | 1 |
| Adequacy of Data/Evidence | 5 | 4 | 3 | 2 | 1 |
| Incorporation of "oral" citations | 5 | 4 | 3 | 2 | 1 |
| Appropriateness of Visual Aid for topic | 5 | 4 | 3 | 2 | 1 |
| Overall Effectiveness of Speaker with Visual | 5 | 4 | 3 | 2 | 1 |

**Figure 13-1** This evaluation form allows the listener to evaluate the speaker by circling a rating for each category.

*Source:* Courtesy of Susan Picillo, Northeastern University.

- Problem-solve the negative.
  - *"I think you might have still made a forceful point about our comparative efforts if you had purged the slides comparing us with the companies in Finland, Uruguay, and Lichtenstein."*

- End positively.
  - *"All in all I found this report quite valuable."*

**HCOM544 Professional Communication**
**Persuasive Instructor Evaluation Sheet**

**Name:** **Time:**

**5=excellent** **4=good** **3=average** **2=below average** **1=poor**

**Use of Evidence(1/3)**

- Incorporation/citation of sources
- Making evidence "come alive"
- Appropriate forms of evidence

**Delivery (1/3)**

- Vocal delivery clear and effective
- Gestures and body movements
- Effective eye contact
- Use of note cards

**Use of Audio/Visual Aid (1/3)**

- Ensuring aid is subordinate to point being made
- Clear use of aid to supplement point
- Timing of presenting and removing visual aid
- How action is built into visual aid (pointer, finger, etc.)
- Eye contact while using aid
- Aid is visible/audible to all audience
- Orienting audience to aid
- Appropriate use of aid (characteristics particular to aid)
- Identified source and qualifications (if appropriate)

**Time Management**

**Other Comments (Introduction, Conclusion, Use of 4Ss, Q&A)**

**Grade: (-.5 OT)=**

**Figure 13-2** This evaluation form is more open-ended, allowing the student to write in the ratings and provide comments.

*Source:* Courtesy of Walter Carl, Northeastern University.

## Criticism and Those Criticized

Although the approach on page 234 can be a helpful prescription for providing feedback, one must be careful about sounding robotic while offering criticism. The extent to which one needs to dwell on the positive will be a function of the personalities of those who are listening to the criticism. Some speakers will desire that there be little in the way of sugar-coating. Others require several packets of sweetener.

Most reviewers and critics are sensitive to speakers when they review presentations. Some evaluators are insensitively caustic. It may not take more than one acidic comment to make speakers reluctant to listen to other critiques. However, as speakers, we need to be able to endure criticism even if it is inappropriately expressed. Hundreds of years ago Michel Eyquem de Montaigne made the following observation, which is still relevant in the twenty-first century: "We need very strong ears to hear ourselves judged frankly and because there are few who can endure frank criticism without being stung by it, those who venture to criticize us perform a remarkable act of friendship."[15]

**Foundations of Communication** **Group Presentation Evaluation Form**
**Motivated Sequence Speech**

**Coherency of the presentation (how well each portion relates to the overall whole)**

**Transitions from one segment to the next**

**Interest and creativity value of presentation**

**Feasibility of the solution**

**Recognizable and appropriate organizational structure (i.e., motivated sequence)**

**Time management**

**Managing Q&A/discussion portion**

**Demonstrated teamwork during presentation**

**Figure 13-3** This survey does not incorporate ratings but instead allows the listener to personalize a response.

*Source:* Courtesy of Walter Carl, Northeastern University.

## Stand Up & Deliver

The following types of fallacious arguments have been discussed in this chapter:

1. Hasty generalization
2. Post hoc ergo propter hoc
3. Red herring
4. Non sequitur
5. Ad hominem
6. Misplaced authority
7. Appeal to tradition
8. Ad populum/bandwagon
9. Slippery slope
10. Straw man
11. False dichotomy

(continues)

Prepare a three-minute talk that responds to the following:

- Which three of these fallacies are likely to deceive most listeners?
- In your experience have there been repercussions from being deceived by fallacious arguments?
- Do speakers have an ethical responsibility to eliminate fallacious arguments, or is the burden on the receiver to assess the quality of arguments? Why do you feel as you do?
- Are any of your arguments in support of your answer to the previous question fallacious?

## SUMMARY

- The ability to evaluate presentations has value for those
  - Who desire to improve their own presentations
  - Who need to assess the merit of arguments presented by others
- Evaluation requires effective listening and critical thinking
- Listening is different from hearing
- Ineffective listening is affected by
  - Physical distractions
  - Psychological noise
  - Physiological problems
  - Selective attention
  - Information overload
  - Wasted differential time
- Active listening requires
  - An awareness of potential distractions
  - Work
- Critical thinking involves careful analysis of messages to
  - Identify fallacious arguments
  - Draw meaningful conclusions
- There are several tools that can be used to evaluate speakers
- Critiquing presentations requires tact, courage, and skill
- Listening to criticism can require strength of character

## Sample Presentation for Analysis

### With a Little Help from My Friends

*Dale Johnson delivered* "With a Little Help from My Friends" *to the Automotive Public Relations Council in Detroit on May 12, 1994, when he was chairman and chief executive officer of the SPX Corporation. As you read through this excerpt, please consider the following questions:*

1. *What does the speaker identify as communication obstacles for CEOs? Has the speaker avoided these obstacles?*
2. *Does the Bradley anecdote make the point? What is the point? Do you agree with it?*
3. *Is the "foundation of effective communications" what the speaker identifies it to be in paragraph 6? Assuming it is, has the speaker helped create that foundation in this talk to this particular audience?*
4. *Are there arguments in this excerpt that you would consider fallacious? Explain.*

This morning I want to talk with you about the importance of communications, from the CEO's point of view. Well, I'm willing to guess that everybody in this room believes in the importance of regular communication with our various publics.

And I'm also willing to bet that just about every CEO on this planet would say he or she believes in the importance of regular communication.

But—to paraphrase Freud—what does a CEO want? What does a CEO expect from his or her public relations counsel? More important, what does a CEO need from experts like you?...

...It's as basic as this: People can't communicate unless and until they share certain understandings. If I only speak Greek, and you only speak English, we're going to have a tough time of it!

If I hold one set of cultural assumptions and beliefs and you hold another, we're going to be tripped up by misunderstandings.

The foundation of effective communications is a community of people who hold certain understandings in common. Creating a community requires constant affirmation and reaffirmation of the ties that connect one human being to another.

In a business, that means sharing the vision, sharing an understanding of how the individual person and his or her job fits in with the mission of the organization.

This is particularly obvious in communicating with the people in a corporation. A corporation is simply a social structure that lets many people come together to do something none of them could do on their own; understanding the unifying mission is what holds that corporate community together. Having a mission, and believing in it, is what motivates people to stretch and excel.

Day in and day out, communicators have a responsibility for helping to build that underlying sense of community and shared goals...

...CEOs need you to put that message into terms the media, the public, and all our stakeholders understand. And you don't need to be a prophet to predict you'll encounter resistance here!

Executives tend to be comfortable with their nice, safe, stuffy business language!

Bring a group of business people together in a room, and they chatter on about "boundaryless organizations," "dotted-line responsibilities," "reengineering," "matrix organizations," "multi-disciplinary teams," "bottom-line" this and "top-of-the-line" that.

We need your help to see the error of our ways. Helping executives understand how their words and messages fall on others ears is a real service to mankind...

...It's all too easy for a CEO to become insulated from reality—it's a real occupational hazard. So the public relations professional can perform an immensely valuable service by keeping management attuned to reality as perceived by our publics, and by laying it on the line when there's unpleasant news to be told. An understanding of the public's real opinion is very powerful knowledge.

A professor named Joseph Nolan gave a great example of why this is so important. It seems that Senator Bill Bradley was at a Washington dinner one night, and a waiter came around passing out one pat of butter to each person. Bradley politely asked for two pats of butter.

"Sorry, buddy," said the waiter. "It's one to a customer."

"Well," said Bradley. "I guess you don't know who I am. I'm a senior member of the United States Senate. Before that I was an all-star basketball player with the New York Knicks. Before that I was a Rhodes Scholar."

"I guess you don't know who I am," said the waiter.

"No," said Bradley. "Who are you?"

He looked Bradley in the eye and said, "I'm the guy in charge of the butter!"

That's the way the world really works— no matter how high up the ladder you climb, you'd better keep paying attention to the people in charge of the butter. In the end, they're the ones who deliver the goods.

**Source**: Johnson, Dale. "With a Little Help From My Friends: Ten Ways for Company Communicators to Help a Chief Executive," *Vital Speeches of the Day*, August 15, 1994, 60, no. 21: 66b(4).

## Review Questions

1. Identify and explain three specific reasons why effective listening can affect professional success.
2. What is the distinction between listening and hearing?
3. Describe selective: exposure, attention, perception, and retention.
4. Identify three common problems affecting listening and listeners.
5. What is meant by fallacious reasoning? Describe three common types of fallacious reasoning.
6. Describe a recommended procedure for providing constructive criticism to speakers.

## InfoTrac Question

Suzuki suggests four components for critical listening in a July 20, 2001, article found on InfoTrac. What are these points? Would these help you evaluate the merit of a persuasive presentation? Another InfoTrac article on this subject appears in the fall 2003 edition of *Communication Studies*. In it Stitt,

Simonds, and Hunt discuss methods employed to rate the quality of oral presentations. How applicable is this article to students and teachers who evaluate the quality of oral presentations in a class on professional speaking?

---

[1] Edmund Burke, from *Reflections on the Revolution in France* (New York: Liberal Arts Press, 1995).

[2] Oliver Cromwell was a revolutionary leader who ruled England from 1649 to 1658. Apropos of this quote it was said of Cromwell that "few leaders have inspired more love and reverence, and at the same time more fear and hatred." W. M. Southgate, *WB Encyclopedia,* s.v. "Cromwell."

[3] George Grice and John Skinner, *Mastering Public Speaking,* 2nd ed. (New York: Allyn and Bacon, 1995), 62.

[4] Such tests are called audits, and the authors were examining a particular type called the ICA audit. For more information about audits see Alan Zaremba, *Organizational Communication: Foundations for Business and Collaboration,* 2nd ed. (Mason, Ohio: Thomson-South-Western, 2006), 342–366.

[5] The quote is found in Sue DeWine, *The Consultant's Craft* (Boston: Bedford/St. Martins, 2001), 149. The study was conducted by DeWine, S. James, and W. Walence, and presented in the paper "Validations of Organizational Communication Audit Instruments" at the International Communication Association meetings in Hawaii in May 1985.

[6] The actual number of words a receiver can process is identified variously, depending on the report. In a 1996 publication, listening processing is cited at 500 words a minute and speaking at 125–150 words a minute. Andrew Wolvin and Carolyn Gwynn Coakley, *Listening,* 5th ed. (Madison, WI: Brown and Benchmark, 1996), 232. Ronald Adler and George Rodman cite a processing figure of 600 words a minute in *Understanding Human Communication,* 8th ed. (New York: Oxford University Press, 2003), 119. Ralph Nichols and Leonard Stevens write that readers can process about 1,200 a minute and listeners can process "more than 300 words per minute" in *Are You Listening?* (New York: McGraw Hill, 1957), 78.

[7] Adler and Rodman refer to differential time simply as "spare time" on page 119. Nichols discusses the phenomenon of differential time in various publications, including his co-authored book cited in Note 6 above, pp. 78–79, and in "Listening Is a Ten Part Skill" in *Nation's Business* 45 (July 1957): 60.

[8] Nichols makes this point in several publications, including a book he wrote with Thomas Lewis called *Listening and Speaking* (Dubuque, Iowa: Wm. C. Brown, 1954), 24–25, and on page 58 in the *Nation's Business* article cited above. In that article the reference to faking attention is also on page 58. This notion of faking attention is referred to fifty years later as *pseudolistening* in most contemporary books. See, for example, the discussion in Julia Wood, *Communication Mosaics* (Belmont, CA: Thomson-Wadsworth, 2001), 134. Readers in the first decade of the twenty-first century might find it interesting that an icon of the 1957 *Nation's Business* article appears on the International Listening Association Web site in 2005.

[9] Vincent Ryan Ruggiero, *Beyond Feelings: A Guide to Critical Thinking* 4th ed. (Mountain View, CA: Mayfield, 1995), 16.

[10] Alan Gellin, "The Effect of Undergraduate Student Involvement on Critical Thinking: A Meta-Analysis of the Literature from 1991–2000" (PhD diss., State University of New York at Buffalo, 2003), 14.

[11] Ibid. These examples follow the definition provided by Gellin.

[12] Interested students might enjoy visiting the Web site **http://www.word-detective.com/042601.html** and reading this detailed description of the etymology of the phrase *red herring.*

[13] Oral feedback is not necessarily synonymous with public feedback. Some writers have suggested that public feedback—that is, instructor/trainer public criticism subsequent to a speech—is detrimental. See Neeley Silberman, Jo Sprague, and Douglas Stuart, *Instructor's Manual to Accompany the Speaker's Handbook,* 5th ed. (city followed by colon Harcourt College Publishers, 2000), 8. However, most students desire to hear, very soon after their talk, how their peers and trainers responded to their presentation. This oral feedback should be carefully structured by a facilitator so that the public nature of the discussion is constructive and encouraging.. For a summary of perspectives on oral and written feedback, see Cassandra Book, "Providing Feedback: The Research on Effective Oral and Written Feedback Strategies," *Central States Journal* 35 (1985): 14–23.

[14] Op. cit. Grice and Skinner 415.

[15] Michel Eyquem de Montaigne was a sixteenth-century essayist.

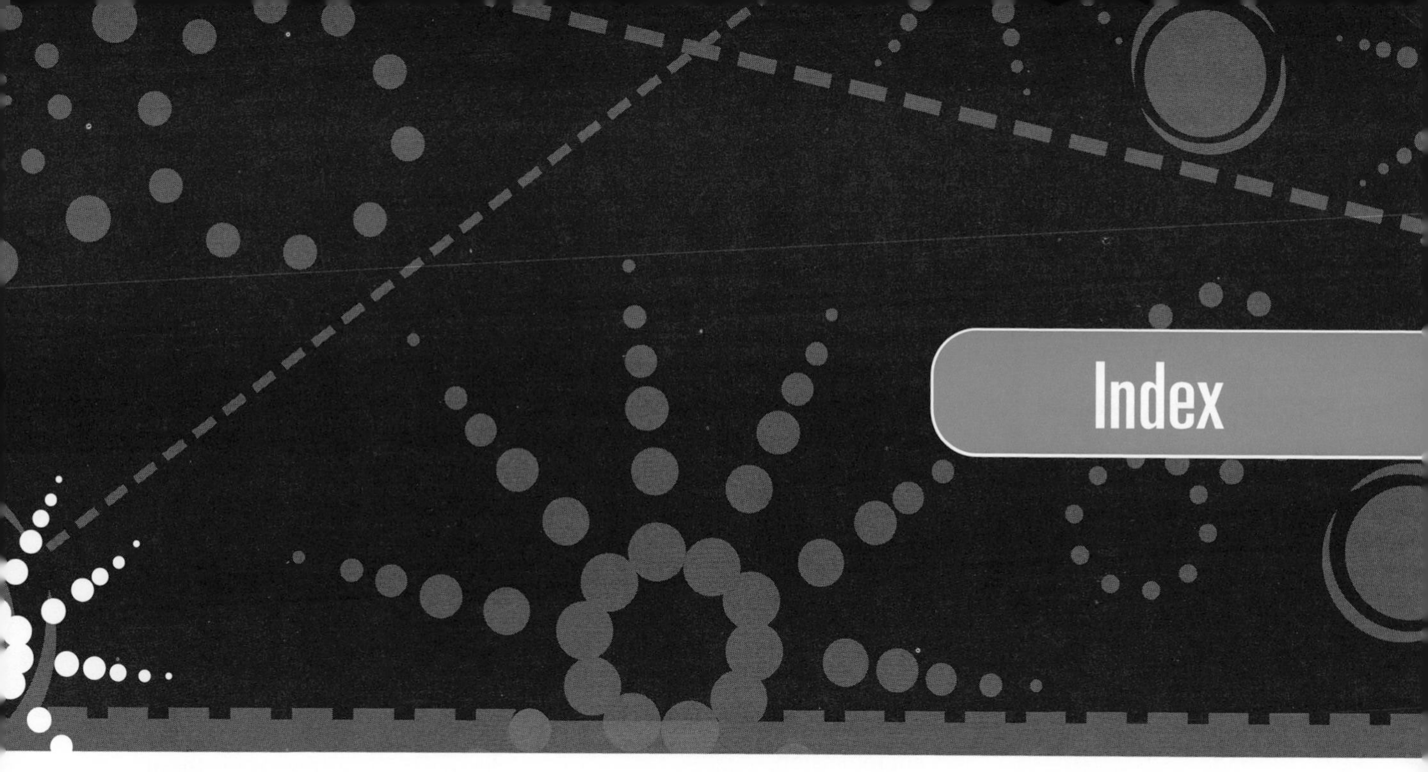


# Index

## B



## C

# D



# E

## F



## G



## H



## I

## T



## U



## V



## W

## Y



## Z